International Political Economy Series

General Editor: Timothy M. Shaw, Professor and Director, Institute of International Relations, The University of the West Indies, Trinidad & Tobago

Titles include:

Glenn Adler and Jonny Steinberg (*editors*)
FROM COMRADES TO CITIZENS
The South African Civics Movement and the Transition to Democracy

Glenn Adler and Eddie Webster (*editors*)
TRADE UNIONS AND DEMOCRATIZATION IN SOUTH AFRICA, 1985–1997

Einar Braathen, Morten Bøås and Gutermund Sæther (*editors*)
ETHNICITY KILLS?
The Politics of War, Peace and Ethnicity in Sub-Saharan Africa

Deborah Bräutigam
CHINESE AID AND AFRICAN DEVELOPMENT
Exporting Green Revolution

Pádraig Carmody
NEOLIBERALISM, CIVIL SOCIETY AND SECURITY IN AFRICA

Gavin Cawthra
SECURING SOUTH AFRICA'S DEMOCRACY
Defence, Development and Security in Transition

Jennifer Clapp
ADJUSTMENT AND AGRICULTURE IN AFRICA
Farmers, the State and the World Bank in Guinea

Neta C. Crawford and Audie Klotz (*editors*)
HOW SANCTIONS WORK
Lessons from South Africa

Staffan Darnolf and Liisa Laakso (*editors*)
TWENTY YEARS OF INDEPENDENCE IN ZIMBABWE
From Liberation to Authoritarianism

Susan Dicklitch
THE ELUSIVE PROMISE OF NGOs IN AFRICA
Lessons from Uganda

Kevin C. Dunn and Timothy M. Shaw (*editors*)
AFRICA'S CHALLENGE TO INTERNATIONAL RELATIONS THEORY

Kenneth Good
THE LIBERAL MODEL AND AFRICA
Elites Against Democracy

Peter Gibbon, Stefano Ponte and Evelyne Lazaro (*editors*)
GLOBAL AGRO-FOOD TRADE AND STANDARDS
Challenges for Africa

International Political Economy Series
Series Standing Order ISBN 978–0–333–71708–0 hardcover
Series Standing Order ISBN 978–0–333–71110–1 paperback
(*outside North America only*)

You can receive future titles in this series as they are published by placing a standing order. Please contact your bookseller or, in case of difficulty, write to us at the address below with your name and address, the title of the series and one of the ISBNs quoted above.

Customer Services Department, Macmillan Distribution Ltd, Houndmills, Basingstoke, Hampshire RG21 6XS, England

Global Agro-Food Trade and Standards

Challenges for Africa

Edited by

Peter Gibbon

Stefano Ponte

and

Evelyne Lazaro

Introduction, conclusion, selection and editorial matters
© Peter Gibbon, Stefano Ponte and Evelyne Lazaro 2010
Individual chapters © contributors 2010

All rights reserved. No reproduction, copy or transmission of this publication may be made without written permission.

No portion of this publication may be reproduced, copied or transmitted save with written permission or in accordance with the provisions of the Copyright, Designs and Patents Act 1988, or under the terms of any licence permitting limited copying issued by the Copyright Licensing Agency, Saffron House, 6-10 Kirby Street, London EC1N 8TS.

Any person who does any unauthorized act in relation to this publication may be liable to criminal prosecution and civil claims for damages.

The authors have asserted their rights to be identified
as the authors of this work in accordance with the Copyright,
Designs and Patents Act 1988.

First published 2010 by
PALGRAVE MACMILLAN

Palgrave Macmillan in the UK is an imprint of Macmillan Publishers Limited, registered in England, company number 785998, of Houndmills, Basingstoke, Hampshire RG21 6XS.

Palgrave Macmillan in the US is a division of St Martin's Press LLC,
175 Fifth Avenue, New York, NY 10010.

Palgrave Macmillan is the global academic imprint of the above companies and has companies and representatives throughout the world.

Palgrave® and Macmillan® are registered trademarks in the United States, the United Kingdom, Europe and other countries.

ISBN-13: 978–0–230–57951–4 hardback

This book is printed on paper suitable for recycling and made from fully managed and sustained forest sources. Logging, pulping and manufacturing processes are expected to conform to the environmental regulations of the country of origin.

A catalogue record for this book is available from the British Library.

Library of Congress Cataloging-in-Publication Data
Global agro-food trade and standards : challenges for Africa / edited by
 Peter Gibbon, Evelyne Lazaro, Stefano Ponte.
   p. cm. — (International political economy series)
 ISBN 978–0–230–57951–4
 1. Farm produce—Standards—Africa. 2. Food industry and
trade—Standards—Africa. 3. Agriculture—Economic aspects—Africa.
 I. Gibbon, Peter. II. Lazaro, Evelyne. III. Ponte, Stefano.
 TX537.G56 2010
 363.19′26096—dc22   2010002687

10 9 8 7 6 5 4 3 2 1
19 18 17 16 15 14 13 12 11 10

Printed and bound in Great Britain by
CPI Antony Rowe, Chippenham and Eastbourne

Contents

List of Tables, Figures and Map	viii
Acknowledgements	xi
Notes on Contributors	xii
List of Acronyms	xvi

1 Agro-Food Standards and Africa: An Introduction 1
Peter Gibbon and Evelyne Lazaro

Governing through standards	1
Trends in agro-food standards	3
Standards, global value chain restructuring and exclusion	10
Interventions aimed at greater inclusivity	14
The contributions to this volume	18

2 Product Carbon Footprint Standards and Schemes 21
Simon Bolwig and Peter Gibbon

Introduction	21
Why carbon footprinting?	23
Methodological issues in product carbon footprinting	24
ISO environmental standards and carbon footprinting	26
Characteristics of product carbon footprinting schemes	28
Consumer perceptions of and reactions to PCF	38
Discussion and conclusion	39

3 Institutional Capacity for Food Safety Conformity in Tanzania 43
Adam Akyoo and Evelyne Lazaro

Introduction	43
The spice sector in Tanzania	45
Standards for spices	45
Local capacity for standards conformity assessment	55
Concluding remarks	66

4 An Analysis of Organic Contract Farming Schemes in East Africa — 70
Peter Gibbon, Adam Akyoo, Simon Bolwig, Sam Jones, Yumiao Lin and Louise Lund Rants

Introduction	70
Contract farming in Africa	71
The economics of organic farming	74
The organic contract farming schemes surveyed	75
Research questions and methods	82
Results	85
Interpretation	94
Conclusion	96
Appendix: analytical strategy	98

5 Challenges and Opportunities of Organic Agriculture in Tanzania — 101
Emmanuel R. Mbiha and Gasper C. Ashimogo

Introduction	101
Background	101
Developments in organic production, processing and marketing in Tanzania	103
Problems, prospects and future outlook of the organic sector	109
Conclusion	111
Appendix	112

6 Sustainability Standards and Agro-Food Exports from East Africa — 120
Evelyne Lazaro, Lone Riisgaard, Fredy Kilima, Jeremiah Makindara and Raymond Mnenwa

Introduction	120
Sustainability standards	121
The standards and their local adoption	123
UTZ CERTIFIED coffee in Tanzania	125
GlobalGAP certified vegetables in Tanzania	127
Social standards in the cut flower industries of Kenya and Tanzania	131
Conclusion	134

7 Localizing Private Social Standards: Standard Initiatives in Kenyan Cut Flowers — 136
Lone Riisgaard

Introduction	136
Private social standards and cut flowers in Kenya	138

	Kenyan social standard initiatives	144
	Conclusion	157
8	**Food Safety Standards and Fishery Livelihoods in East Africa** *Reuben M.J. Kadigi, Ntengua S.Y. Mdoe, Ephraim Senkondo and Zena Mpenda*	162
	Introduction	162
	The development of the Nile perch value chain in East Africa	164
	Livelihood dimensions	169
	Conclusion	182
9	**When the Market Helps: Standards, Ecolabels and Resource Management Systems in East African Export Fisheries** *Stefano Ponte, Reuben M. J. Kadigi and Winnie Mitullah*	184
	Introduction	184
	Meeting food safety standards	185
	Sustainability and fishery management systems	190
	Ecolabelling	195
	Conclusions	200
10	**European Food Safety Regulation and Developing Countries' Regulatory Problems and Possibilities** *Morten Broberg*	205
	Introduction	205
	The EU's food safety regime	205
	Identifying the barriers	206
	Overcoming the barriers	217
	Perspectives for the future	223
	Appendix: Application of the European food safety regime and developing countries *Ekaterina Bang-Andersen*	225
11	**Conclusion** *Stefano Ponte*	232
	The content, coverage and proliferation of standards	232
	The governance of standards, local participation and issues related to conformity	234
	Standards, value chain restructuring and welfare outcomes	239
	Final remarks	242
References		244
Index		265

List of Tables, Figures and Map

Tables

2.1	Selected characteristics of the surveyed product carbon footprinting schemes (as of January 2009)	29
3.1	Tanzania standard physical and chemical requirements for black/white pepper, chillies and capsicum	47
3.2	Limits of micro-organisms in spices (Tanzania national standards)	49
3.3	General microbiological specification – Germany and Netherlands	49
3.4	EU Food Safety Standards for Spices	50
3.5	Summary of legislation on aflatoxins in developed spice-importing countries	52
3.6	Maximum pesticides residues limits in Germany, Netherlands and United Kingdom	53
3.7	Requisite laboratory equipment for Salmonella testing	55
3.8	Summary of physical capacity for food safety testing by institution, 2008	57
3.9	Summary of professional capacity for food safety testing by institution, 2008	58
3.10	IMO and TANCERT fees schedules	64
4.1	First and third generation contract farming in Africa	73
4.2	Organic contract farming schemes surveyed, 2005–09	76
4.3	Descriptive statistics (means)	78
4.4	Profit models for scheme participation	86
4.5	Poisson models for organic farming practices	89
4.6	Regression results for net revenue from certified crop(s)	92
4.7	Regression (FIML) results for yield per tree (log), Kawacom and Esco (2009 survey) schemes	96
5A.1	Tanzania: organic producers, products and area under production	112
6.1	The case studies	121
8.1	Mean value of household assets (Tsh) of participants in the Nile perch export and other fisheries	171
8.2	Mean annual household net income for different groups of actors in the Nile perch and other fishery value chains (Tsh)	177

8.3	Tests of significance for paired comparisons of mean annual household net income from fishing activities	179
8.4	Mean household gross income, operating costs and net income from fishery activities (Tsh)	180
8.5	Estimate of aggregate net income per annum for fishers and boat owners in the Tanzanian part of Lake Victoria	181
9.1	Exports of Nile perch to all destinations (chilled and frozen fillets, gutted and headed) from Lake Victoria (1992–2007; million USD)	187
10.1	Members raising and supporting concerns with the European Community under WTO SPS Committee procedures, 1995–2008	221
10A.1	Evolution of notifications since 1997	226
10A.2	Notifications arising at borders by hazard category 2005–07	227
10A.3	Notifications by origin of the product, classified by world region	228
10A.4	Notifications by region of origin of the product, expressed in terms of US$ billion worth of EU food imports from the region of origin	228
10A.5	Notifications by notifying EU Member State 2002–07	229

Figures

3.1	The supply chain(s) for Tanzanian spices	46
4.1	Distributions of (a) average prices received and (b) proportion of coffee crop processed for certified organic farmers and non-organic farmers	95
8.1	The Nile perch value chain in East Africa before the start of exports	165
8.2	The contemporary Nile perch value chain in East Africa	167
8.3	Mean value of household fishing assets, Nile perch collectors	172
8.4	Mean household land holdings, Lake Victoria fishery participants	172
8.5	Mean value of households' other assets, Lake Victoria fishery participants	173
8.6	Mean household livestock holdings, Lake Victoria fishery participants	173
8.7	Mean household adult labour equivalent level, Lake Victoria fishery participants	174

8.8	Net income portfolio for Nile perch fishers and crew	175
8.9	Net income portfolio for fishers and crews in other fisheries	175
8.10	Net income portfolio for boat owners in Nile perch fishery	176
8.11	Net income portfolio for boat owners in other fisheries	176

Map

1	East Africa	xx

Acknowledgements

This collection is based upon research carried out at the Danish Institute for International Studies and the Department of Agricultural Economics and Agribusiness at Sokoine University of Agriculture, Tanzania, under a common research and capacity building programme on 'Standards and Agro-food Exports' (SAFE). The programme was financed by the Danish Development Research Council (FFU), to whom the editors express their gratitude. We also gratefully acknowledge the permission of the Tanzanian Bureau of Standards to use the material presented in Tables 3.1 and 3.2 and to Charles J. Kithu of Spices Board India to use the material presented in Tables 3.3–3.6.

Notes on Contributors

Adam Akyoo is an assistant lecturer and currently a PhD student at the Department of Agricultural Economics and Agribusiness, Sokoine University of Agriculture. He has been involved in research on agricultural risk management, artisanal mining in Tanzania, international food standards on spices and has also worked as a banker (both development and commercial) during the 1990s. He has research interests in value chain development, agricultural finance and new institutional economics. He has published on issues of food safety standards and agricultural risk management in Tanzania.

Gasper C. Ashimogo was an associate professor in the Department of Agricultural Economics and Agribusiness, Sokoine University of Agriculture before his sudden death on 28 October, 2008. He obtained a PhD in agricultural economics from Humboldt University of Berlin and a Masters degree in agricultural economics from the University of Nairobi, Kenya. He had extensive research experience on agricultural marketing and trade. He also served as a consultant on issues related to rural poverty, agricultural market development and food security.

Ekaterina Bang-Andersen is a Masters student at the University College London. At the time of writing she was an intern at the Danish Institute for International Studies (DIIS).

Simon Bolwig is a senior researcher at the Risø National Laboratory for Sustainable Energy, Danish Technical University. At the time of writing, he was a Project Researcher at DIIS. He researches and publishes on standards and certification programmes relating to climate change, including private 'carbon accounting' standards for consumer products and biofuels, their interplay with regulatory policy and their importance for developing country exports and trade more generally. He has also led work to develop methodologies for integrating poverty and the environment in global value chain analysis.

Morten Broberg is a consulting senior researcher at DIIS and Associate Professor in international development law at the University of Copenhagen. His primary research focuses upon the European Union's relations with developing countries. He is the author of several books and articles, primarily within the field of European Union law.

Peter Gibbon is a senior researcher at DIIS. His current interests include agro-food standards and commodities. He is the co-author of *Trading Down: Africa, Value Chains and the Global Economy* (Temple University Press, 2005) and co-editor of recent special editions of *Development Policy Review* on Africa and the WTO Doha Round (2007) and of *Economy and Society* on the Governance of Global Value Chains (2008).

Sam Jones is a PhD Fellow at the Department of Economics, University of Copenhagen, specializing in Development Economics and with a focus on sub-Saharan Africa. He has published widely, including articles on organic contract farming, as well as contributions to various edited books concerning economic development in Mozambique. At the time of writing, he was employed as a Researcher at DIIS.

Reuben M. J. Kadigi is a lecturer in the Department of Agricultural Economics and Agribusiness, Sokoine University of Agriculture. He holds a PhD in Agricultural Economics from SUA and a MSc in Management of Natural Resources and Sustainable Agriculture (MNRSA) from the Agricultural University of Norway. He has published extensively in the fields of water resources management and governance, valuation of water resources, productivity of water, fisheries, livelihoods and poverty analysis.

Fredy Kilima is a senior Lecturer in the Department of Agricultural Economics and Agribusiness at Sokoine University of Agriculture. He has researched on agricultural marketing, agricultural finance, livelihoods and poverty, and the impact of food safety standards on livelihoods. He has published on agricultural credit, market reforms and price integration in Tanzania.

Evelyne Lazaro is a senior Research Fellow in the Department of Agricultural Economics and Agribusiness of Sokoine University of Agriculture. She holds a MSc in Agricultural Economics from Michigan State University and a PhD in Agricultural Economics from SUA. She is interested in natural resource management in African Agriculture, in knowledge, science and technology for development and sustainability standards.

Yumiao Lin is the CSR Coordinator at the Humanitarian Water and Food Award Association. At the time of writing, she was a student assistant at DIIS. Her interests include Corporate Social Responsibility and sustainable development.

Jeremiah Makindara is a lecturer in the Department of Agricultural Economics and Agribusiness at Sokoine University of Agriculture. His main interests and publications are in agribusiness and entrepreneurship research, strategic management, social capital, gender issues and agro-food standards.

Emmanuel R. Mbiha is an associate professor in the Department of Agricultural Economics and Agribusiness, Sokoine University of Agriculture. He holds a PhD in agricultural economics from Wye College, University of London and a Masters degree in agricultural economics from the University College of Wales, Aberystwyth. He has extensive experience in agricultural policy, agricultural marketing and trade, and publishes in these areas with a special focus on Tanzanian agriculture.

Ntengua S. Y. Mdoe is a professor in the Department of Agricultural Economics and Agribusiness, Sokoine University of Agriculture. He has been involved in research on food security, livestock development, livelihoods and poverty, and the impact of food safety standards on livelihoods. Value chain development, rural development strategies and agricultural policies are among his other areas of interest. He has published on issues of dairy development, food security, rural livelihoods and poverty in Tanzania.

Winnie Mitullah is a researcher and lecturer at the Institute for Development Studies (IDS), University of Nairobi. She holds a PhD in Political Science and Public Administration. She has researched, written and consulted in the development area, with a focus on fisheries, urban housing, urban economy, politics, institutions and governance, and the role of stakeholders in governance.

Raymond Mnenwa is currently a PhD fellow at Sokoine University of Agriculture. His research interests include value chain development, business development, marketing and poverty alleviation. He has published in areas related to small business development, milk marketing and poverty reduction.

Zena Mpenda is a lecturer in the Department of Agricultural Economics and Agribusiness at Sokoine University of Agriculture. She holds an MA in economics from Gaborone University, Botswana. She is currently undertaking a PhD in international trade and food safety standards in agro-food exports for developing countries. She has researched in the fields of agro-processing, marketing, valuation of waste management and value chain development.

Stefano Ponte is a senior researcher at DIIS. He is interested in the changing role of Africa in the global economy and has published extensively on the agro-food sector, governance and upgrading in value chains, sustainability standards and labels, and on new forms of corporate social responsibility.

He is author of *Farmers and Markets in Tanzania* (James Currey, 2002) and co-author of *The Coffee Paradox* (Zed Books, 2005), *Trading Down: Africa, Value Chains and the Global Economy* (Temple University Press, 2005) and *Brand Aid: Celebrities, Consumption and Development* (University of Minnesota Press, 2011).

Louise Lund Rants is a Masters student in International Economics and Development, Faculty of Life Sciences, University of Copenhagen. At the time of writing, she was a student assistant at DIIS. She is interested in economic growth, development and aid.

Lone Riisgaard holds a PhD in International Development Studies from Roskilde University, Denmark. She is currently a Project Researcher at DIIS, where she was also attached during her PhD studies. She has researched and published on sustainability standards, Corporate Social Responsibility and Global Value Chain analysis, with focus on the cut flower value chain originating in Kenya and Tanzania.

Ephraim Senkondo is a professor at the Department of Agricultural Economics and Agribusiness, Sokoine University of Agriculture. His research interests include the economics of rain water harvesting, soil and water, malaria control, aquaculture, risk management, agro-forestry, livelihoods and the impact of food safety standards on livelihoods, with specific focus on Tanzania.

List of Acronyms

AAS	Atomic Absorption Spectrophotometer
ADEME	Agence de l'Environnement et de la Maîtrise de l'Energie
ADI	Acceptable Daily Intake
AEA	Agricultural Employers Association (Kenya)
AEAAZ	Agricultural Ethics Assurance Association of Zimbabwe
ALARA	As Low As Reasonably Achievable level
ASTA	American Spice Trade Association
BMU	Beach Management Unit
BRC	British Retail Consortium
CIES	Consumer Goods Forum
CNI	Change in Net Income
CO_2e	Carbon dioxide equivalent
COLEACP	Comité de Liaison Europe-Afrique- Caraïbes-Pacifique
COT	Committee on Toxicity of Chemicals in Food Consumer Products and the Environment
COTU	Central Organisation of Trade Unions (Kenya)
CSR	Corporate Social Responsibility
DANIDA	Danish International Development Agency
DFID	UK Department for International Development
DRC	Democratic Republic of Congo
EC	European Commission
EFSA	European Food Safety Authority
EIO	Environmental Input-Output
EMRL	Extraneous Maximum Residue Limits
EPA	Economic Partnership Agreement
EPOPA	Export Promotion of Organic Products from Africa
ETI	Ethical Trading Initiative (UK)
EU	European Union
FAO	Food and Agriculture Organization of the United Nations
FDA	(US) Food and Drug Administration
FFP	Fair Flowers Fair Plants
FFV	Fresh Fruit and Vegetables
FIML	Full Information Maximum Likelihood
FLO	Fairtrade Labelling Organization
FLP	Flower Label Program (Germany)
FPEAK	Fresh Produce Exporters Association of Kenya
FSC	Forestry Stewardship Council
GAP	Good Agricultural Practices

GC	Gas Chromatograph
GCLA	Government Chemist Laboratory Agency (Tanzania)
GDP	Gross Domestic Product
GFP	Golden Food Products (Tanzania)
GFSI	Global Food Safety Initiative
GHG	Greenhouse Gases
GHG-P	Greenhouse Gas Protocol
GHP	Good Hygiene Practices
GMP	Good Manufacturing Practices
GSC	Global Service Corps
GTZ	Deutsche Gesellschaft für Technische Zusammenarbeit
GVC	Global Value Chain
GWP	Global Warming Potential
HACCP	Hazard Analysis and Critical Control Points
HEBI	Horticultural Ethical Business Initiative (Kenya)
HPLC	High Performance Liquid Chromatograph
ICC	International Code of Conduct for Cut Flowers
ICS	Internal Control System
IEC	International Electrotechnical Commission
IFS	International Food Standard
ILO	International Labor Organization
IMO	International Marketecology Organization (Switzerland)
IOAS	International Organic Accreditation Services
ISEAL	International Social and Environmental Accreditation and Labelling Alliance
ISO	International Organisation for Standardization
ITC	International Trade Centre
IUF	International Union of Foodworkers
KEBS	Kenya Bureau of Standards
KEWWO	Kenya Women Workers Organisation
KFC	Kenya Flower Council
KHRC	Kenya Human Rights Commission
KIA	Kilimanjaro Airport (Tanzania)
KLM	Royal Dutch Airline
KNCU	Kilimanjaro Native Cooperative Union (Tanzania)
KPAWU	Kenya Plantation and Agricultural Workers' Union
LCA	Life-Cycle Analysis
LDC	Least Developed Country
LOD	Limit of Determination
LVFO	Lake Victoria Fisheries Organisation
MAFSC	Ministry of Agriculture, Food Security, and Cooperatives (Tanzania)
MNE	Multinational Enterprises
MPS	Milieu Programma Sierteelt (Netherlands)

MRL	Maximum Residue Limits
MSC	Marine Stewardship Council
MSc	Master of Science
MSY	Maximum Sustainable Yields
MUWAKIHA	Muungano wa wakulima wa kilimo hai Arumeru (Tanzania)
NFQCL	National Fish Quality Control Laboratory (Tanzania)
NGO	Non-Governmental Organization
NOAEL	No Observed Adverse Effects Level
NOP	National Organic Program (US)
OCFS	Organic Contract Farming Scheme
OECD	Organisation for Economic Cooperation and Development
OLS	Ordinary Least Squares
PA	Process Analysis
PCB	Polychlorinated Biphenyl
PCF	Product Carbon Footprint
PCI	Premier Cashew Industries (Tanzania)
PCL	Product Carbon Labelling
PIP	Programme Initiative Pesticides
PMO	Producer Marketing Organization
PPB	Parts per Billion
PPM	Parts per Million
PSS	Private Social Standard
SAFE	Standards and Agro-Food Exports (Research Programme)
SANAS	South Africa National Accreditation Service
SIDA	Swedish International Development Agency
SPS	Sanitary and Phyto-sanitary
SQF	Safe Quality Food
TA	Technical Assistance
TANCERT	Tanzania Organic Certification Association
TBS	Tanzanian Bureau of Standards
TCB	Tanzania Coffee Board
TFDA	Tanzania Food and Drug Authority
TIRDO	Tanzanian Industrial Research and Development Organisation
TNC	Tesco's Natures Choice
TOAM	Tanzania Organic Agriculture Movement
TPAWU	Plantation and Agricultural Workers Union of Tanzania
TPRI	Tropical Pesticide Research Institute (Tanzania)
UFPEA	Uganda Fish Processors and Exporters Association
UK	United Kingdom
UKAS	United Kingdom Accreditation Service
UNBS	Uganda National Bureau of Standards

UNCTAD	United Nations Conference on Trade and Development
UNDP	United Nations Development Programme
US	United States
USAID	United States Agency for International Development
WBCSD	World Business Council on Sustainable Development
WHO	World Health Organization
WIETA	Wine Industry Ethical Trade Association (South Africa)
WRA	Workers' Rights Alert (Kenya)
WRW	Workers Rights Watch (Kenya)
WRI	World Resources Institute
WTO	World Trade Organisation
WWF	World Wildlife Fund for Nature
WWW	Women Working Worldwide

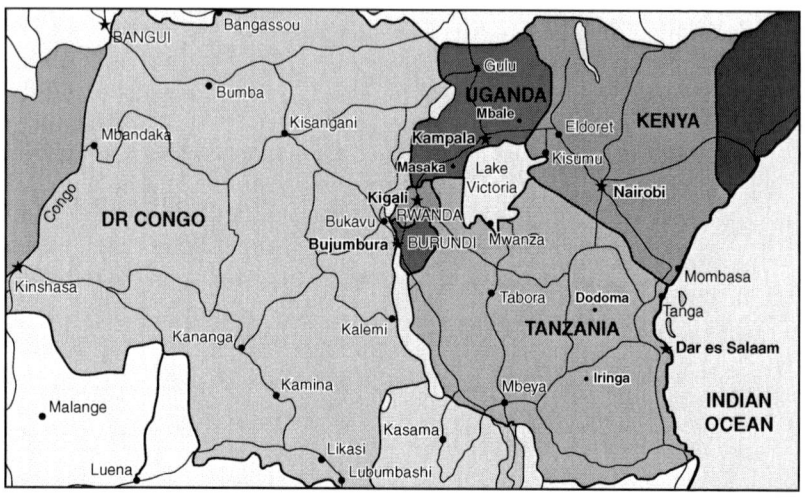

Map 1 East Africa

1
Agro-Food Standards and Africa: An Introduction

Peter Gibbon and Evelyne Lazaro

Governing through standards

Governing through standards – rather than through laws and regulations alone – emerged as a tendency in industrialized countries in the 1980s and 1990s. This occurred against a background of the rise of idealized market paradigms in the public sector, an unfolding of new discourses concerning governmental transparency and accountability and the growing political influence of issue-focused Non Government Organizations (NGOs) (Rose, 1996; Power, 1997; Brunsson, Jacobsson et al., 2000). The tendency spans public administration, cultural life and the economy – albeit in different forms in each context, driven by different constellations of actors and circumstances. As a result, while developments in standards may still occur as a result of changes in regulation, it is more illuminating to see standards as the dominant form taken by early twenty-first century regulation.

In the agro-food sector, in common with the rest of the economy, the circumstances causing this development include the reorganization of production and distribution in global value chains driven by retailers and branded manufacturers or processors, the tendency for competition – especially in retail – to take increasingly oligopolistic forms and massive related investment in brand development and protection. 'Buyer-driven' global value chains expose the weakness of multilateral regulatory regimes and at the same time privilege low-cost steering mechanisms that can secure uniformity of performance across suppliers. On the marketing side, oligopolistic competition involves efforts to win greater brand (including own-brand) share, while on the sourcing side it aims at reducing costs by transferring functions and their costs to suppliers. Thus, suppliers become responsible for securing and visibly demonstrating their conformity to uniform performance requirements (Gibbon and Ponte, 2005). At the same time, heavy investment in brand development has a built-in logic of continuously expanding the range of performative uniformities sought from suppliers, as brands seek to keep ahead of consumers' concerns on all issues from food safety to climate change. Hence buyers invest in establishing standards and methods of verifying conformity to them either individually, in concert with other buyers or via broader coalitions involving NGOs and sometimes government. In this context, competition also migrates to the area of standards.

The rise of idealized market paradigms in the public sector plays out in ways that complement these trends. It provides a new model for regulation in emerging areas of public concern and for reforming existing models in established ones. As a result, according to Brunsson (2000) 'official power evaporates' in its classic hierarchical sense. In emerging areas of public concern such as climate change, pseudo-market systems may be created; in established ones like food safety, authority tends to be fragmented, re-bundled and distributed to new actors. In both cases, business is devolved major new responsibilities but at the same time granted substantial discretion in how these are fulfilled. Rather than occurring through a combination of trust and direct operational inspection, verification of fulfilment increasingly demands documentation of managerial controls (Power, 2003).

While at national level within Europe[1] this tendency has gone furthest in the historically liberal United Kingdom (UK), against the background of a different set of circumstances it is also evident within the European Union (EU) governance system. Here, the establishment of a single market has necessarily entailed legal harmonization. However, given the EU's limited centralized authority, the latter process normally has had to take the form of restating laws in terms of 'essential requirements', often defined only in terms of outcomes. Thus, discretionary fulfilment has again become the rule, alongside forms of conformity verification emphasizing managerial system requirements (Majone, 1996). In both national and EU-level public sector governance, such requirements explicitly or implicitly involve benchmarking the performance and integrity of systems against standards, both managerial and sectoral.

To the extent that these tendencies continue to roll out in time and space, their impacts may prove profound. Two main groups of consequences can be predicted: first, in relation to agro-food standards and, second, for the structure of global value chains. In turn, these may have a number of mainly exclusionary implications for African agro-food sectors, unless countervailing interventions occur. The remainder of this chapter begins by reviewing and reflecting on the available evidence on the extent to which standards are indeed proliferating and changing in significance. It then turns to evidence on the consequences of the developments identified for value chain restructuring and – through this – economic exclusion and welfare. Thirdly, it reviews the record of interventions that have been made with a view to mitigating the consequences of such trends. A final section briefly introduces the contributions of the chapters in the current volume to these discussions by theme, while a summary of their empirical contributions is provided in Chapter 11.

Trends in agro-food standards

Every recent contribution to the literature on agro-food standards notes that agro-food standards are subject to a profound series of changes. The main areas in which this is said to be occurring is in respect of numbers of standards (increasing), standards' content (more demanding), inter-relations between standards (more competitive) and standards' ownership and governance (more diverse). Attention has also been given to the implementation and control of standards, although the conclusions of the literature in this area are less clear-cut.

Numbers of standards

Kern (2008) states 'there are now nearly 400 private standards governing food industry activities in operation in Europe'. It is implied that this represents a dramatic increase. However, it is probably necessary to qualify this impression. As Daviron (2002) observes, in the period before and during the existence of International Commodity Agreements, quality descriptions and grades were always applied to tropical commodities in relation to the *national* standards of producing countries. Hence, for at least half a dozen tropical agro-products there were as many standards as there were recognized producing countries. Furthermore, as is pointed out in Jaffee and Henson (2004), there was historically a greater degree of variation in importing country standards in respect to, for example, safe limits of contaminants in different foodstuffs than there is today. National and international market liberalization of tropical products, and the associated disintegration of nationally based quality control systems, has almost certainly led to a decreasing number of standards being applied to these products. And convergence of food safety requirements, particularly within the EU, may have had similar consequences.

Yet there has been a clear proliferation of other types of standard, all emerging in developed countries. In particular, there are a growing number of private food safety standards going beyond the requirements of developed country governments. There are also growing numbers of 'sustainability' and ethical standards.

Homer (2008) explains the increasing numbers of developed country private food standards in terms of brand protection measures by large-scale retailers, in the face of regular public food safety scares. It is necessary for retailers to protect their brands by developing or amending standards because reactions in the political–legal system to such scares tend to be slow or timid. In other words, retail brands feel the need to signal to consumers that they are more concerned than governments. However, he also points out that such standards are generally not displayed on labels and instead have a business-to-business status. Thus, retailers do not (yet) fully compete against each other in terms of food safety.

The proliferation of 'sustainability' and ethical standards is somewhat harder to explain, since these tend to build on more diffuse and longer-term consumer concerns. Nonetheless, Daviron and Ponte (2005) list five such standards in the coffee sector, Bernstein and Cashore (2007) list seven in the forestry sector and Riisgaard (this volume) mentions no less than 16 in the cut flower sector. A general trend in each case is for the emergence of one or more relatively demanding standard(s) to trigger their challenge by others, either as too permissive or too strict.[2]

Standards content

Whereas during the 1990s a dominant theme in the standards literature was the transition from product to process standards, more recent contributions (for example, Nadvi and Wältring, 2004; Fulponi, 2007) emphasize the blurring of this distinction and the overlap of the resulting hybrid standards with management standards.[3] Both the retention of some focus on the product and the overlap with management issues relate to another tendency commonly identified – that for standards to strive to cover the entire production and distribution chain or cycle for a specific product. A 'whole-chain' focus arises from the reorganization of production and distribution in global value chains with distinctive lead firms, as well as from the increasing prevalence of legal obligations for those at the end of chains to exercise due diligence in relation to product provenance. However, a 'whole-chain' focus also relates to projects of product differentiation through 'high road' standards such as Fairtrade and Forestry Stewardship Council (FSC), where users are secured with premium products on the basis of integral chains of custody (Bernstein and Cashore, 2007; Henson and Humphrey, 2008).

However, according to the literature, the focus of standards is not merely becoming more vertical. Many standards are (also) being extended in a horizontal direction to cover a wider range of substantive issues. For example, GlobalGAP started life as a food safety standard but today incorporates reference to environmental issues and (in its aquaculture rules) to impacts on local communities (Henson and Humphrey, 2008). Most 'sustainability' standards meanwhile have added rules on labour in recent years. Organic standards have also branched out into new areas including climate impacts of produce transport (Gibbon and Bolwig, 2007).

The literature also maintains that standards are becoming more detailed and/or stringent. This is challenged by Gibbon (2008) on the history of EU organic standards, who argues that rather than becoming steadily stricter, some standards pass through a cycle of development. Once formalized, standards become more detailed, reflecting increasing influence over them by technical experts. However, at a given point this trend becomes perceived by non-experts as creating barriers to entry (or trade) and a counter-movement sets in whereby standards are redefined in terms of a small number of principles.

According to this perspective, many agro-food standards would have to be depicted as still in the first phase of this cycle. Relative to GlobalGAP Version 2 (2004), Version 3 (2007) increases or redefines in stricter ways 40 out of a total of 256 'control points'. Likewise, Version 3's Quality Management System Checklist for the GlobalGAP Group Certification option covers 141 control points rather than 94, as in its original version (Cooper and Graffham, 2008; Graffham and Cooper, 2008). Moreover, it is not clear how the 'cycle of development' perspective might apply to standards such as FSC or Marine Stewardship Council (MSC) which were formulated in terms of a small number of principles – and management plans for their materialization – from the outset.

At least in terms of standards whose main focus is food safety, the overall trend appears to be unidirectional towards greater stringency, notwithstanding the fact that the casting of many requirements in a language of management systems may open up for discretion in some areas of implementation. In particular, the range of activities for which Hazard Analysis Critical Control Point (HACCP) systems are required has increased both in public and private standards (to cover processing of food of plant origin, for example), as has the range of hazards for which it is required to carry out testing (for example, pesticide residues, veterinary medicine residues, dioxins and naturally occurring toxins). In private standards such as GlobalGAP, requirements for traceability – almost completely absent from both private and public standards in the early 1990s – extend down to lot or farm site level. Furthermore, where infrastructure requirements are specified in GlobalGAP, these are in exhaustive detail.[4]

Standards competition and harmonization

The literature identifies three different sets of circumstances where the relation between agro-food standards takes on competitive forms. The first of these is when standards emerge in entirely new areas. Under such conditions different groups of 'pioneers' usually will give emphasis to different objectives and activities when they seek to codify a normative set of practices. This occurred most obviously in the organic movement in the 1980s, where a range of pioneer groups in different countries, or even different regions of the same country, wrote standards independently of each other. While competition between standards was not an objective of these activists, it did emerge once these standards became publicly recognized labels.

As the literature points out (cf. Hallström, 2000), where standards emerge today in new areas it is not only, or even mainly, 'pioneer' practitioners who are involved in their competitive development. Standard-setting has been commercialized, in the sense that there is now a distinct category of economic actor that makes a living from it, that is, management consultancies, consultancies with expertise in specific technical areas subject to standardization, consultancies made up of professional 'standards experts' and auditing companies. As Bolwig and Gibbon (this volume) show, eight out of the 13 product carbon labelling (PCL) standards that have emerged since 2007 are owned by consultancies.

On the other hand, three of the remaining PCL standards identified by Bolwig and Gibbon (op. cit.) were developed by brand owners. This relates to the second set of circumstances identified in the literature when standards become characterized by competition, namely when a brand tries to take control of a standard and use it for product differentiation (Henson and Humphrey, 2008). As Homer (2008) notes, the emergence (or predicted emergence) of publicly recognized standards in a given field is normally treated by brand owners as a threat. This is because it reduces their options – especially for pushing down suppliers' prices. On the other hand, annexing such a standard – or pioneering it in the case of one that is likely to emerge – enables a brand to be enhanced. While product carbon labelling standards are perhaps the best example of annexing, there are plenty of others. The British retailer Marks & Spencer has a 'Fair Partner' label annexing Fairtrade standards. The Swiss supermarket Migros has a 'Migros Bio' label annexing organic standards, and so on.

The final set of circumstances where standards competition arises is, as noted earlier, in the wake of broad backing being attained for a demanding social or environmental standard. The emergence of such a standard creates problems for operators (producers or retailers, or both) who have not participated in its development and who feel challenged by its requirements. Since they feel that they would be damaged by doing nothing they devise alternative, low road standards, either with lower entry barriers or where the burden of conformity is shifted to others (O'Rourke, 2006). This is the main source of standards competition in the forestry sector, as well as in the clothing sector. More generally, the emergence of organic standards in the 1980s and 1990s can be considered to have triggered a whole series of lower road environmental alternatives.

Given these trends, it is hardly surprising that agro-food standards harmonization initiatives generally have little traction (Fulponi, 2007). Even where standards are not employed competitively they usually embody too many sunk costs for their owners to be willing to abandon them. Moreover, harmonization is a labour-intensive and time consuming process, for which owners of standards often lack adequate resources. Hence even where there is a relatively high level of goodwill, as in the case of competing organic standards, harmonization projects mostly lead only to new standards claiming to have the status of 'reference norms'. This was the main outcome both of the lengthy process development of the Codex organic standard and more recently of the International Task Force on (organic) Harmonization and Equivalence (2003–08).

Even securing recognition of equivalence between standards has proved difficult in most cases. At present such agreements are rare outside of business-to-business food safety standards (Fulponi, 2007). Here the Global Food Safety Initiative (GFSI), under the aegis of the Consumer Goods Forum (formerly CIES), has succeeded in establishing a quadrilateral agreement whereby British Retail Consortium (BRC), Dutch HACCP, Safe Quality Food (SQF) and International Food Standard (IFS) give mutual recognition to each others' standards. The Consumer Goods Forum is a trade organization made up of 400 major multiple retailers and food manufacturers and the explicit mandate of GFSI was to 'drive cost efficiency in the supply chain and reduce the duplication of audits'.[5]

Ownership and governance

Up to and including the 1990s, most agro-food standards initiatives tended to be owned by producers (organic standards), grass-roots organizations (fair trade) or retailers (private food safety standards). As is widely recognized in the literature, the main development since – dating from the birth of FSC in 1993 – has been the rise of 'multi-stakeholder' standards. These are so far all in the ethical and environmental areas and are owned by NGOs together with either producers and distributors or retailers and branders, or both. Multi-stakeholder initiatives are especially evident in the Anglo-Saxon countries, Switzerland, the Netherlands and the Nordic Countries.

Klooster (2005), Bernstein and Cashore (2007) and Ponte (2008) depict the first generation of such initiatives as following a common 'natural history'. The process starts with NGO campaigns, normally in the form of consumer boycotts exposing bad practices. The boycott phase concludes as a few firms recognize that self-verification in respect of avoiding such practices lacks legitimacy. At the same time NGOs recognize that boycotts entail certain problems, notably resource intensiveness and unintended consequences. In a second phase NGOs reformulate their principles in more operational form; and some firms recognize that a market premium may be earned by publicly adhering to such principles. This second phase ends with an agreement to formulate a standard subject to third party certification. A third phase involves the elaboration of standards governance mechanisms that are commonly perceived, by NGOs and progressive firms, as securing political legitimacy for the standard.

More recently, the literature recognizes that some new multi-stakeholder initiatives by-pass certain of these stages (Ponte, 2008). Moreover, a number of other trends have been identified. These include a widening of 'stakeholders' to include trade unions and local community organizations, the emergence of multi-stakeholder initiatives in developing countries (such as the Horticultural Ethical Business Initiative in Kenya) and the unveiling of 'omnibus' or cross-sectoral multi-stakeholder initiatives, such as the UK Ethical Trading Initiative (ETI). A further development is that governments financially sponsor such initiatives, for example, the UK government in relation to ETI.

One result of the rise of multi-stakeholder initiatives has been for owners of other types of standards to reform their ownership structures. Hence GlobalGAP for example has introduced a category of associate membership, opening up for participation by Rainforest Alliance and the Ghanaian Ministry of Agriculture, amongst others.[6] Moreover, earlier multi-stakeholder initiatives that were established without much developing country participation have undertaken organizational changes aimed at rectifying this situation (Ponte, 2008).

The uniformity of this trend reflects a tendency for standards themselves to be standardized, particularly in respect of governance. Governance of multi-stakeholder standards usually reflects a set of common norms, inherited from the FSC model (Bernstein and Cashore, 2007) and subsequently codified by the International Social and Environmental Accreditation and Labelling Alliance (ISEAL).[7] These include organization of different interested parties in separate 'chambers' – and sometimes sub-chambers – with equal voting rights on a common governing body in order to assure 'decision making by a consensus of interested parties' (ISEAL, 2006). They also include making standards available in the public domain, reviews of standards at least every five years, use of public consultation when revisions to standards are proposed, publication of written responses to contributions to public consultations and provision of 'meaningful opportunities for participation in standards consultations by all parties who will be affected' (ibid.).

The promulgation of norms in relation to social and environmental standardization reflects the increasing degree of institutionalization enjoyed by expert knowledge in this area. Arguably, experts acquire greater autonomy and authority as a result of consensus-based decision-making being assigned explicit priority. Since open horse-trading is frowned on, problematic decisions tend to be referred to parties deemed to be politically neutral. Some more recent multi-stakeholder initiatives even have technical experts sitting together in distinct 'chambers' (Ponte, 2008). O'Rourke (2006) detects a trend for NGOs to become more prominent in multi-stakeholder initiatives over time. This may be the case with some such initiatives: but it is important to note that even where this occurs, it too may be on the basis of claims to special types of expertise such as 'participatory auditing', rather than reflecting the triumph of NGOs' political arguments.

Standards implementation and control

Whether standards or standards-based regulations are implemented 'to the letter' is obviously critical to their status as barriers. The more general literature on 'governing through standards' suggests that implementation in this form is not common. This reflects, amongst other things, the intrinsic complexity of many standards and regulations, limitations in surveillance capacity, intrinsic difficulties in detecting certain types of non-conformity and social and economic pressures on inspectors or auditors. Furthermore, just as standards development is subject to expert colonization, so too is conformity to standards – on both sides of the process. Hence, according to Power (2003), implementation of standards may involve 'elaborate games of compliance', including constructions of consultation by some specialists and representations of corporate performance by others. This important subject is little explored in the agro-food standards literature and, where it has been, contributions do not point in a clear direction.

Implementation and control of standards affects agro-food trade from developing countries through: (1) international assessment and approval or accreditation of national systems of control in exporting countries, including laboratory testing capacity (Golub and Mbaye, 2002; Jaffee and Henson, 2004; Jensen, 2005; Ponte et al., this volume; Akyoo and Lazaro, this volume); (2) food safety-related border controls in developed countries (Jaffee and Henson, 2004; Gibbon, 2006a; Broberg this volume; Bang-Andersen this volume); (3) accreditation and control of private certification and inspection bodies (Gibbon, 2006a); and (4) the working practices of private certification and inspection bodies (Ponte, 2008).

The literature on the first of these issues suggests that, as far as international assessment of national systems of food safety control in exporting countries is concerned, the picture is somewhat uneven. Quite a large number of low income countries have managed to get onto the EU's List 1 of countries subject to reduced levels of control for import of fishery products, as a result of positive assessments of their systems of national control. This achievement has been largely the result of the upgrading efforts of private operators and public authorities in the countries concerned, but it has also reflected EU inspectors' flexible interpretation how many stages in the export chain need to implement HACCP or risk assessment procedures. Certainly in the cases of Senegal and the countries bordering Lake Victoria, the interpretation applied has been consistent with the survival of artisanal participation in fishery chains destined for the EU (Ponte, 2007). On the other hand, Jaffee and Henson (2004) suggest that flexible interpretation by EU authorities is less evident in relation to meat exporting countries (see also Perry et al., 2005; Scoones and Woolmer, 2009).

As regards border controls, the literature reports two apparently unrelated findings. The first is great unevenness between developed countries in exercising border controls (Gibbon, 2006a; Bang-Andersen, this volume), while the second is an overall trend for border controls to be applied more frequently in relation to agro-food imports from developing countries (Jaffee and Henson, 2004; Bang-Andersen, this volume). On accreditation and control of private certification and inspection bodies, Gibbon (2006a) reports that the situation within the EU closely reflects that in respect of border controls, with Northern European countries applying more consistent controls than Southern ones.

The working practices of certification and inspection bodies, particularly in developing countries, is an almost unexplored topic – with Ponte (2008) appearing to be the only study in this area. Ponte observes that certification of the South African hake fishery to MSC standards was also achieved through requirements being interpreted flexibly, against a background where MSC was very interested in increasing its number of certified developing country fisheries. He also notes that the main focus of verification exercises was on documentation of management systems, although certifiers also fudged certain issues within this area.

A general conclusion from the literature in this area is that standards and standards-based regulations are not fully enforced in a consistent way. However, research in the area is insufficient to draw more precise conclusions about implications for African agro-food exports.

Standards, global value chain restructuring and exclusion

Two broad perspectives on the relation between development in standards and developments in value chain structure are found in the literature. The first is that of Reardon and Huang (n.d.) and others, who argue that developments in standards are a major source of value chain restructuring, leading to these chains becoming shorter (as layers of suppliers are dropped) and thinner (as fewer and larger players survive and greater vertical integration becomes the rule).

The other is the position taken in Gibbon and Ponte (2005). Here, value chain restructuring is seen as arising largely independently of developments in standards, primarily as a result of greater economic concentration at the developed country end of chains (increasing buyer power) and financial market pressures towards externalizing an increasing range of functions originally undertaken by buyers. A central aspect of this change is the emergence of a category of 'first tier supplier', across a wide variety of value chains, who provide a full supply chain management service to lead firms. Standards fit into this picture by providing means for lead firms to govern some aspects of product quality at a distance, through first tier suppliers. But it is buyers' escalating demands in terms of more conventional aspects of product specification, volume requirements, continuity of supply and delivery conditions that are the primary reasons for shake-out of second and third tier suppliers. Thus, the greatest degree of shake-out has been experienced in the relatively standards-light chains driven by large discounters such as Wal-Mart.

As Reardon and Huang also cite, with 'demands for suppliers at each link to have a wider range of capacities and to perform them more efficiently' (ibid.) as a ground of value-chain restructuring, there is considerable overlap between these positions. But they differ in emphasis in terms of the types of value chain restructuring focused upon in relation to standards. While those following the Reardon and Huang argument are most concerned with general rationalization of value chains, those closer to the Gibbon and Ponte position are also interested in the differentiation of new standards-specific value chain strands.

Standards-based differentiation of value-chain strands

Traditionally, segregated strands of value chains tended to be established where buyers were interested in securing consistent access to product with some proprietary technical specification. Rondet (1997) and Daviron (2002) describe this occurring for specialty rubber in the early 1990s. Buyers wanted rubber with particular processing behaviour characteristics, which initially proved impossible to translate into a tree variety or husbandry specification. Thus they entered intensive, long-term relations with particular estates aimed both at defining relevant product characteristics and at stabilizing a production procedure 'from the tree to the tyre factory yard' reproducing them. Over time a new product, a standard, a form of certification and a differentiated value chain strand thus emerged.

New value chain strands have similarly emerged in some chains where environmental or ethical norms or new product quality requirements are required by standards, especially where there is (also) a requirement for 'chain of custody' traceability. Examples include production certified to, amongst others, FSC, organic, Rainforest Alliance, UTZ CERTIFIED and Fairtrade standards. These strands are nonetheless less differentiated than those described for rubber, since in each case producers and intermediaries can and do sell product into 'conventional' chain strands.

Differentiation of standards-based strands is often associated with change in chain structure, although this differs from chain to chain. No change occurred in the FSC chains dominated by large furniture retailers, who simply leveraged their equally large developed country suppliers into conformity (Klooster, 2005). However, the specialty rubber chain referred to by Rondet and Daviron shortened and became more exclusive, since the tyre companies involved used only estates as partners. In the case of standards typically applied in the coffee and cocoa sectors, chains have also been rationalized, but mostly not at the expense of smallholders. Although in Africa only estates are currently certified to the Rainforest Alliance standard, UTZ CERTIFIED, Fairtrade and organic standards are applied to smallholder production – in the latter two cases almost exclusively. For each of these standards the main change in chain structure provoked is an elimination of intermediaries between smallholders and international trading companies or processors.

Exclusionary thinning and shortening of chains

Most of the reasoning behind the 'thinning and shortening' argument derives from the economic literature on food safety standards compliance, with its emphasis on the lumpy physical investments required, the economies of scale that apply and the demands for new management capacities that arise (for example, Unnevehr and Jensen, 1999; Antle, 1999; Buzby, 2003). Smaller operators lack the scale and financial and human resources necessary for successful compliance and are thus likely to lose market access.

However, systematically enhanced capacities are not required by all standards in practice, including those applied to African agro-food production. For example, where cooperatives already exist, compliance obstacles to Fairtrade standards are mainly confined to costs of certification. The same applies to organic standards, since their central requirement (non-use of synthetic chemicals) is already met involuntarily by most African smallholders. As regards standards such as Rainforest Alliance, UTZ CERTIFIED, FSC and MSC which may be associated with additional categories of conformity cost, non-conformity is not generally associated with loss of market access in the North. In the case of cocoa and coffee there will not even necessarily be a loss of access to premium export prices. This is because for these crops traditional quality attributes such as low moisture content remain or may even have become more salient in both certified and conventional markets.[8] Attaining this attribute only requires smallholders to invest more labour in post-harvest processing.

If 'exclusion' is taken to refer to loss of export market access for a given product, then it is only in the case of fresh fruit and vegetables (FFV)[9] that there is evidence of generalized smallholder exclusion, at least in the absence of donor intervention. But the evidence in this case is comprehensive, spanning FFV export chains in Cote d'Ivoire (Minot and Ngigi, 2004), Ghana (Danielou and Ravry, 2005), Kenya (see, amongst others, Graffham et al., 2008), Senegal (Maertens et al., 2007; 2008) and Zambia (Graffham and MacGregor, 2008). In Kenya, 79 per cent of the 9,000+ smallholders supplying 11 of the 18 major exporters with peas and beans in 2003 had been eliminated by mid-2006 (Graffham et al., 2008). In Senegal, an 80 per cent fall in the number of smallholders farming green beans for export occurred between 1998 and 2007 (Maertens et al., 2007), while smallholders were totally eliminated from the tomato export chain over the same period (Maertens et al., 2008). In Zambia, 95 per cent of the smallholders involved in the fresh vegetable export chain in 2003 had been eliminated by 2006 (Graffham and MacGregor, 2008).

Where to attribute causality remains an open question. Has exclusion occurred because FFV chains (unlike those for coffee or cocoa) are driven by large supermarkets? Or is it because of the stringency of GlobalGAP rules? Or is it perhaps because of the special properties of FFV (for example, high perishability and vulnerability to pest damage), particularly in African environments?

Gibbon (2003) argued that large supermarkets are the main driver of exclusion, citing evidence from mainland Europe showing that where regulation has preserved a role for independent wholesale markets (such as in France and Spain), more FFV sourcing from Africa is based on smallholder cooperatives. At that time, the mainland EU markets referred to were standards-light ones. Since then, mainland Europe has witnessed a combination of retail market concentration and the application of stricter standards. And, as acknowledged by Gibbon (2003) and subsequently underlined by Sergeant (2008), imports from Africa from all sources make up a much smaller share of total developed country FFV sales through non-supermarket channels than they do through supermarket channels. This is because of the general absence of counter-seasonal FFV from non-supermarket channels.

Results from the Regoverning Markets programme reported by Reardon and Huang (n.d.), comparing levels of exclusion associated with supermarket chains in six developing countries and Poland and Turkey, appear to support the argument that it is in chains where large lumpy investments are required to maintain participation in supermarket chains that most smallholder exclusion occurs. These requirements include irrigation as well as cooling equipment and are neither confined to FFV nor – contrary to the authors' conclusions – necessarily related to escalation in food safety standards. It is also worth recalling Jaffee's (2003) observation that the reduction in smallholder participation in Kenyan horticultural chains between 2000 and 2002 mainly related to adoption of new FFV varieties whose cultivation required artificial lighting.

Welfare effects of exclusion

Existing discussions concerning the welfare effects of inclusion or exclusion are also largely focused upon the FFV sector, although there is a limited related discussion of smallholder costs and benefits of inclusion in chains to which 'sustainability standards' are applied. With a few exceptions, the latter discussion is mainly based on qualitative evidence. Where quantitative methods have been used (Pariente, 2000; Bacon, 2005; Giovannucci and Potts, 2008) the results show that certification to sustainability standards is associated with increases in prices, net incomes and income security, although none of the works cited distinguish benefits of conformity to standards from benefits of participation in the schemes or cooperatives through which certification is generally organized. Nor do they control for biases in selection into such schemes. These problems are also evident with some of the FFV studies which will be discussed, although to a more limited degree.

A theme of many recent contributions on the welfare effects of African smallholder exclusion from FFV export chains is that the consequences of such exclusion have to be set against benefits associated with employment on large FFV export farms, which is assumed to have grown as a result of smallholder displacement (Maertens et al., 2007; 2008; Humphrey, 2008).

This is sometimes linked to arguments that even where smallholders remain in such chains, the benefits they derive are limited.

In respect of net household benefits to smallholders from participation in GlobalGAP-certified FFV production, different studies report wildly inconsistent results.[10] Gogoe (2002) for 10 Ghanaian pineapple smallholders, Graffham and MacGregor (2008) for 25 Zambian fresh vegetable smallholders, Graffham, Karehu and MacGregor (2008) for 102 Kenyan fresh vegetable smallholders and Asfaw et al. (2008) for a Kenyan fresh vegetable smallholder sample of undisclosed size report annual net incomes from farm production below US$750. On the other hand, McCulloch and Ota (2002), based on a somewhat larger sample, and Mwangi (2008) based on a sample of 1020, both report means around US$2000. McCulloch and Ota include the value of own-farm consumption in their figures, whereas most of the first group of studies mentioned do not (although details are sketchy), but this seems unlikely to explain the differences.

Two studies from Kenya and Senegal, respectively, comparing household incomes from smallholder FFV export production with incomes of households with members employed on FFV farms (McCulloch and Ota, 2002; Maertens et al., 2007) at least provide results pointing in the same direction. In the Kenyan study, smallholder household incomes are over three times higher than farm workers' household incomes, while in the Senegal one they are 70 per cent higher. However, both studies also show that households with members employed on large FFV farms have household incomes roughly double those of households dependent on other forms of employment. A similar result on benefits of large farm employment is reported by Maertens et al. (2008), in relation to the Senegalese tomato sector. This study further finds that households with employment on large farms tended to be larger and to have less land than those who did not.

Broadly, it is unsafe to conclude from these studies that smallholder benefits from participation in certified FFV export chains are negligible, or that their elimination is fully compensated for by benefits from employment on large farms. The studies whose methodologies are more fully described suggest that smallholder revenues are both substantial and much higher than those of large farm workers. Any assessment of aggregate welfare outcomes of the different types of participation in certified FFV production would at least need to consider data on smallholder numbers and numbers of persons employed on both large and small FFV farms.

Interventions aimed at greater inclusivity

The literature identifies three types of intervention aimed at improving developing country – and in particular developing country small-scale producer – access to those export markets requiring conformity with new generations of standards: (1) support to national systems of conformity and conformity assessment; (2) design of more smallholder-friendly conformity assessment procedures; and (3) support for upgrading smallholder capacity to conform.

If only because most such interventions are financed through development assistance, and because donors find it easiest to provide assistance on a government-to-government basis, the most common type of intervention until recently has been the first of those listed. This entails support to Ministries or other national institutions designated by the EU system as 'Competent Authorities' for managing food safety, mainly in respect of capacity building and infrastructure. It has also entailed similar support to national standards institutions and national laboratories (aimed further in these cases at supporting their international accreditation and their participation in international standard-setting). In countries with perceived potential for meat exports there has also been support for epidemiological surveillance. The reasoning behind this support is that functioning Competent Authorities are a pre-condition for market access, that participation in international standard-setting will both generate more developing country-friendly standards and spill-over effects in domestic institutions and that international accreditation of conformity assessment bodies will reduce local costs of certification (cf. Jaffee and Henson, 2004).

While the literature discussing such interventions generally confirms that there are benefits from support to Competent Authorities' efforts to develop functioning food safety systems,[11] it is more sceptical in respect of support to standards institutions and laboratories – whether this is in relation to international standard-setting or to improving local conformity assessment capacity. Data on developing country participation in international standard-setting bodies is thin and it may well be that there has been little improvement in its level. On the other hand, there is equally little evidence that more recent standards or standards revisions are more developing country-friendly, except in regard to conformity assessment arrangements, which will be discussed separately in a moment. According to van der Meer (2007), moreover, little or no evidence of local spill-over effects from this participation can be detected.

Van der Meer argues that support to improved developing country conformity assessment capacity is usually also ineffective. This is because 'the most important capacity in a country in successfully managing complex food safety...systems is not necessarily...technical...but rather [that] to make holistic assessments of long-term interests, and periodically a comprehensive strategy and action plan. [But] the reality is far removed from this. [Such] capacity is often absent...[and] countries still have difficulties in articulating their needs' (2007: 289–290).

Van der Meer explains this in terms of overlapping responsibilities and competition between agencies and ministries and lack of external accountability. As a result, donors are mainly presented with uncoordinated shopping lists for training, laboratory equipment, for institutions lacking surveillance or other work programmes or operational budgets that could support them. This in turn means such investments that donors undertake have low impact. The private sector meanwhile makes its own arrangements, either along their own value chains by using foreign buyers as information and testing sources, or by reducing ambitions and exporting only to standards-light markets.

Design of more smallholder-friendly conformity assessment processes appears to have originated in the organic sector in the late 1990s in the guise of 'internal control systems' (ICSs). Such systems were soon after granted recognition in the EU Organic Farming regulation (though exclusively for developing country production). They entail obligatory individual farm registration and checks that each farm's certified sales do not exceed its registered output capacity. But they require annual inspection of all farms only by trained internal inspectors. Certification is based on an evaluation of the records of the internal control system and on external inspection of a sample of scheme members, with the sample size subject to modification in line with certification bodies' assessment of the system's risk level. ICSs thus entail an elaborate internal management system but reduce unit costs of external certification by up to 90 per cent.

Most other sustainability and ethical standards applied in developing countries have developed similar arrangements or are in the process of doing so. For example, FSC launched a 'Small and Low Intensity Managed Forests' initiative in 2001–02, with lower sampling frequencies, streamlined technical requirements and requirements for consultation only with local as opposed to national stakeholders (Klooster, 2005). GlobalGAP developed Option 2 for smallholders in 2005. Group certification in this case allows for collective marketing and some collective infrastructure, including an office, a plant protection materials store, a pesticide disposal pit, a waste disposal pit, a grading shed and charcoal coolers. However, traceability and pesticide residue testing requirements remain targeted at the individual farm level and the Quality Management System requirements are increasingly exacting (see above).

Because of their technically demanding character, implementation of ICS-type models calls for a special type of expertise and as a result a new layer of consultants has emerged in many developing countries, concerned with their design and with providing training to expedite their operation. In the coffee sector there are enough different standards with (varying) ICS-type arrangements to make it worthwhile for some international coffee trading companies (for example, Neumann, Efico) to set up foundations to channel donor funding for provision of specialist consultant advice.

Donor support to such foundations overlaps with direct support to certification on the one hand and to the promotion of farmer institutions whose members can be subjected to certification on the other. Both are extremely widespread. A survey of organically certified exporters in Uganda in 2006 reported that all, without exception, had received support from at least one donor for certification-related purposes and that some had received support from up to seven different donors (Gibbon, 2006b). In this case the average volume of support was not great (see Gibbon et al., this volume). In the case of GlobalGAP certification, on the other hand, the volume of support seems very substantial. Graffham et al. (2008) report that donors contributed on average US$436 per smallholder to the investment costs associated with smallholder compliance in Kenya, plus making a contribution to recurrent costs. Smallholder certification to GlobalGAP in Kenya was supported by DfID, GTZ, USAID, the EU's COLEACP/PIP programme and the World Bank (Humphrey, 2008).

The promotion of farmer groups and similar institutions in order to create a demand 'from below' for certification through ICSs, as well as to reduce buyers' transaction costs more generally – and thus to increase the likelihood of smallholder inclusion – is perhaps the most canvassed of all contemporary interventions in relation to standards. It is a central recommendation of the Regoverning Markets programme (Proctor and Digal, 2008) as well as of the DfID-supported 'Standard Bearers' programme (de Battisti et al., 2008). Though intuitively appealing, in practice it is fraught with problems. Many of these stem from the sorry history of cooperative farmer organization in Africa. In East Africa this started promisingly during the inter-war period as a movement of better-off farmers aimed at by-passing the arbitrary power over markets enjoyed by chiefs appointed by the colonial authorities. However, already by the 1940s the colonial authorities had established departments of government aimed at forming and promoting cooperatives and from this point on cooperatives mainly played the role of regulating markets on the state's behalf. They also became notorious for corruption. As a result, farmers are normally cynical about efforts to organize anything resembling them, and such organizations as do emerge often reproduce the rent-seeking of their predecessors.

None of this appears to have diminished donor enthusiasm for their support. Thus, Ouma (2008) observes in relation to interventions aimed at GlobalGAP certification in Kenya that 'there was a strong focus on farmer groups, regardless of linkages to exporters, track record, the nature of their internal management or their resource endowments'. This probably contributed to the high casualty rate amongst such interventions. Only two of the six donor-supported GlobalGAP group certification arrangements examined by Graffham, Karehu and MacGregor (2008) were running efficiently.

It is worthwhile considering what an alternative policy agenda might look like. This would continue with support for upgrading the capacities of Competent Authorities but complement this with another point of departure. This would be to step back and analyse the practical experiences of those private sector operators, particularly those sourcing from smallholders or artisanal producers, who have successfully negotiated conformity with the new generation of export market standards. It is critical to understand what these operators do that enables successful conformity, what facilitates their conformity most and what hinders it. It seems that many of the resources making this possible are obtained from other actors in their own value chains rather than from other environments. Therefore, it is also critical to determine how support directed along existing value chains can enable conformity to be scaled up and generalized.

The contributions to this volume

This volume aims at deepening and extending the areas of discussion reviewed above, mainly but not only with empirical reference to East Africa. It does so along three thematic lines on: (1) the content, coverage and proliferation of standards; (2) the governance of standards, local participation and issues related to conformity; and (3) value chain restructuring, inclusion or exclusion dynamics and welfare outcomes. The remaining part of this section indicates the thematic contribution of the various chapters of this volume, while Chapter 11 will compile and compare their empirical results.

Trends in the numbers of standards, and in competition between them, are discussed by Bolwig and Gibbon (Chapter 2) in relation to the emergence of product carbon footprinting as a new area of standards proliferation, and by Riisgaard (Chapter 7) in respect of standards dealing with labour issues. Ponte et al. (Chapter 9) also take up the issue of the inter-relation between different standards, but in terms of the capacity of standards in one area (environment) to amplify or mitigate outcomes provoked by successful conformity to standards in another area (food safety).

Trends in the content of standards and standards-based regulation are examined in detail by Broberg (Chapter 10) in relation to the new EU food safety regime as they are by Bolwig and Gibbon (Chapter 2) in respect of product carbon footprinting standards. Both chapters examine the coverage of the new standards, how they attribute responsibility for implementation and how they require implementation to be demonstrated. Broberg (Chapter 10) builds on the analysis of these questions to ask whether claims are justified that the new regime represents an increased burden to developing country exporters.

Issues of governance in standards initiatives are explored particularly by Riisgaard (Chapter 7). Her chapter examines how standards devised in developing countries are managed and implemented in developing ones, in relation to the pre-existing alignments of local political actors and the opportunities represented to these actors through buying into standards. Issues of implementation and control in relation to food safety standards are also addressed, in Bang-Andersen's Appendix to Chapter 10.

On issues of conformity, Akyoo and Lazaro (Chapter 3) contribute a case study on the public standards conformity apparatus in Tanzania. Reflecting the issues raised in earlier sections of this chapter, they pose questions not only about the level of current capacity but also about its distribution, what it is used for and the extent to which it is guided strategically. Gibbon et al. (Chapter 4), and to some extent Lazaro et al. (Chapter 6), examine what institutional features arise to facilitate compliance in Africa, focusing on contract farming in particular. The issue of whether standards are complied with 'to the letter' or not is handled in Chapter 6 on sustainability standards, Chapter 7 on cut flower standard initiatives and Chapter 9 on fish export standards, fishery management and ecolabelling.

Standards-related value chain restructuring in East Africa is examined in detail by Gibbon et al. (Chapter 4) and by Mbiha and Ashimogo (Chapter 5) for chains for organic products, by Lazaro et al. (Chapter 6) for chains to which GlobalGAP, UTZ and different ethical standards have been applied and by Kadigi et al. (Chapter 9) for the Nile Perch export chain. These chapters ask to what extent, in the wake of the application of new generations of standards, participation by small producers has increased, remained the same or been reduced – and for what reasons. In reviewing these issues, these chapters also describe the consequences of donor-driven initiatives to promote inclusiveness.

While Lazaro et al. (Chapter 6) provide a mainly qualitative analysis of welfare outcomes of participation in certain standards-heavy chains, Gibbon et al. (Chapter 4) and Kadigi et al. (Chapter 8) provide detailed quantitative analyses, in both cases comparing outcomes for chain participants with those of non-participants. Gibbon et al. (Chapter 4) present a mainly econometric analysis of effects of participation effects in six different organic contract farming schemes in East Africa, while Kadigi et al. consider effects for several different categories of participants in export and non-export fishery chains emanating from Lake Victoria.

Ponte et al. (Chapter 9) complement the contributions of Broberg (Chapter 10) and Kadigi et al. (Chapter 9) by tracing, first, how the East African Nile Perch sector responded to the challenge of the new EU food safety regime and succeeded in maintaining market access and, second, the environmental consequences of this success. They furthermore link to the issue of donor interventions aimed at improving local capacity for standards conformity by examining the evolving content and scope of the relationship between government and private sectors.

Notes

1. Outside Europe it is perhaps most noticeable in Australia and New Zealand.
2. This process is also evident in respect of ethical standards in, for example, the clothing sector (cf. Fransen and Burgoon, 2008).

3. The International Social and Environmental Accreditation and Labelling Alliance (ISEAL), a body whose aims include setting norms for social and environmental standard-setting, prescribes in its 2006 Code of Good Practice that 'Standards should be expressed in terms of a combination of process, management and performance criteria, rather than...descriptive characteristics' (ISEAL, 2006).
4. Under Option 2 (Group Certification) central plant protection material stores have to be a minimum 1.7 m × 1.2 m × 1.5 m and are required to be constructed with a cement base, brick walls, a bunded entrance, a wooden door with a lock and a ventilated metal roof (Graffham and Cooper, 2008).
5. Source: www.ciesnet.com/2-wwedo/2.2.../2.2.foodsafety.gfsi.asp, date accessed 2 June 2009.
6. In 2008, GlobalGAP also appointed 'in collaboration with DfID and GTZ' an 'Observer for Africa and Smallholder Ambassador', Johannes Kern, www.openpr.com/.../Focus-on-Smallholders-EurepGAP-Appoints-an-Observer-for-Africa.pdf, accessed 26 July 2009.
7. See note 3.
8. In the case of cocoa, price differentiation also applies in relation to bean cleanliness and freedom from mould. Thus, the tendency towards marginalization of traditional quality attributes described by, for example, Fold (2002) is far from comprehensive. There are parallels with cotton, where the salience of traditional quality attributes like freedom from stickiness has recently increased (Fok, 2002).
9. Minten et al. (2007) provide an example of a *processed* vegetable chain in Madagascar where no rationalization has occurred. The scheme described, which incorporates 9000 smallholder green bean farmers exporting to the mainland Europe market, was not GlobalGAP certified. Interestingly, Mwangi (2008) states that in 2006, while there were only 2210 smallholders certified to GlobalGAP for fresh vegetable production, there were 6000 certified to the same standard's processed vegetable rules.
10. In order to make comparisons easier, all income results have been converted to US$ from the currencies they are reported in the original studies, using average conversion rates for the year in which the survey is reported to have occurred.
11. cf. Jensen (2005) on French support to Senegal.

2
Product Carbon Footprint Standards and Schemes

Simon Bolwig and Peter Gibbon

Introduction

Concern over climate change has stimulated interest in estimating the total amount of greenhouse gasses (GHG) produced during the different stages in the 'life-cycle' of goods and services – that is their production, processing, transportation, sale, use and disposal (Brenton et al., 2008; Edwards-Jones et al., 2008; Øresund Food Network, 2008). In this chapter we refer to the outcome of these calculations as product carbon footprints (PCFs), where 'carbon footprint' is the total amount of GHGs produced for a given activity and 'product' is any good or service that is marketed. PCFs are thus distinct from GHG assessments performed at the level of projects, corporations, supply chains, municipalities, nations or individuals.

A PCF like other GHG assessments is expressed in terms of global warming potential (GWP). GWP embraces the impact of different GHGs (CO_2, N_2O, CH_4, O_3, and so on) on global warming and the GWP of all GHGs are expressed in terms of the impact on global warming of the equivalent weight (usually in grams or kilograms) of CO_2–equivalent (CO_2e). This is because the GWP of a given volume of a GHG varies between the different GHGs (for example, the impact of 1 kg of CH_4 on global warming is equivalent to 25 kg of CO_2). After summing up all the GHGs produced at each stage in the life of the product, the PCF can then be expressed as grams or kilograms of CO_2e per unit of product. For example, the carbon footprint of a 330 ml can of Coke that has been purchased, refrigerated, consumed and then recycled by a consumer in the UK is 170 g CO_2e (Coca Cola Great Britain, 2009). We emphasize, however, that very different footprint values for the same product and country can be obtained, depending on the databases and calculation methods used (Kejun et al., 2008; Edwards-Jones et al., 2009).

There are both private and public standards for how to calculate (and reduce) the carbon footprint of products and for how to verify and report PCF information. The development of public PCF standards is at a very early stage. The first with the ambition to cover a wide range of diverse products, PAS 2050, was published in October 2008 by the British Standards Institute, while the International Organization for Standardization (ISO) started work to develop a 'carbon footprint of products' standard (ISO/NP 14067-1/2) in late 2008 (ISO, 2008a). The World Resources Institute (WRI) and the World Business Council on Sustainable Development (WBCSD), authors of the widely used Greenhouse Gas Protocol (hereafter GHG-P) for project and corporate level GHG assessments, started to develop their Product and Supply Chain GHG Accounting and Reporting Standard in September 2008. This new standard, expected to be published in May 2010, will include guidelines on both product life-cycle accounting and calculation and reporting of corporate 'Scope 3' emissions (corporations' indirect emissions, other than those already counted under 'Scope 2' which refers to emissions from generation of bought-in energy) (Greenhouse Gas Protocol, 2009). The eventual ISO and WRI-WBCSD standards are not likely to differ much from the PAS 2050; firstly, because the PAS 2050 builds on earlier GHG assessment standards of ISO and WRI/WBCSD (see below) and, secondly, because PAS 2050 is formally recognized in relation to the ISO/NP 14067-1/2 process and is a major source of input to the WRI/WBCSD work. Finally, in Japan, the Ministry of Economy, Trade and Industry initiated the development of a voluntary PCF scheme in June 2008; a trial project period commenced in April 2009 and will cover 57 different products (Ikezuki, 2009).

Public standards and regulations pertaining to the carbon footprint of transport fuels are also of recent date. The EU Renewable Energy Directive, formally adopted in March 2009, requires transport biofuels to save 35 per cent in GHG emissions relative to fossil fuels, rising to 60 per cent by 2018 (EC, 2009a; Bolwig and Gibbon, 2009b). Similarly, the State of California has adopted a Low Carbon Fuel Standard, which from 2011 will require companies to lower the overall carbon intensity of their various fuels at a rate that will increase every year until 2020, or else buy credits from companies that sell cleaner fuels (CEPA, 2009).

This chapter is primarily concerned with private PCF schemes and standards, which – except in the area of transport fuels – have developed at a faster pace than the public ones. A number of private certification schemes have emerged in the last couple of years that offer retailers and manufacturers methodology and expertise to footprint their products, as well as in some cases procedures for verifying and certifying or labelling PCF assertions. The majority of these schemes are operated by private (for-profit or not-for-profit) consultants, while a few have been developed by manufacturers or retailers. In the absence of any dominant public PCF standards, all these schemes except two, which use the PAS 2050 standard, can be regarded as supplying *de facto* private standards.

In light of these observations, the aim of this chapter is to provide an overview of existing PCF schemes and standards that can help inform the discussion of research priorities, policy options and public investments in this area. The second section briefly discusses the business and environmental rationales of PCF as well as the possible risks and biases. This is followed by a discussion of the life-cycle analysis (LCA) methods and by international (ISO) standards that PCF may draw upon. Based on a global survey of 13 private PCF schemes, we then examine some salient characteristics of PCF as carried out in practice, including the geographical and product coverage; the combination of PCF with other sustainability criteria; the approaches and methods used; the kind of certification offered; and the communication of the PCF information to consumers.[1] This is followed by a section considering how consumers perceive and respond to PCF. A final section concludes.

Why carbon footprinting?

It has been estimated that the consumable goods and appliances that the average consumer in the UK buys and uses account for 20 per cent of his or her total carbon emissions (not counting the energy to run them), of which food and non-alcoholic drinks, at 9 per cent, comprise the largest category (Carbon Trust, 2006).[2] It is therefore worth investigating if and how influencing consumers' purchasing decisions through the provision of information about the global warming impact of different products can contribute to climate change mitigation.

Surveys in several OECD countries suggest that consumers are increasingly interested in information about the climate impact of products, while they also indicate that many other factors besides a low-carbon footprint determine what products end up in the shopping basket and that consumers are generally sceptical about the 'climate-friendliness' of retailers and manufacturers. As this chapter will show, some retailers and manufacturers have responded to these trends in consumer interests and behaviour by calculating, and sometimes displaying, carbon footprints for a small number of products. In most cases these initiatives were not launched with the main purpose of increasing market share of the product itself through improved differentiation, but rather as part of a general effort to demonstrate commitment to climate change mitigation to consumers, and to lawmakers planning to introduce strict regulatory measures (for example in the UK), or as part of broader corporate social responsibility (CSR) policies.

Calculating the carbon footprints of products can also help companies reduce GHG emissions at the levels of the corporation and the supply chain by identifying major emission sources as well as ways to achieve reductions quicker and at lower costs. Indeed, investing in reducing carbon footprints may give positive returns through significant energy-cost savings. Some argue that the core value for companies of PCF lies in these internal 'carbon management' uses rather than in the public display of carbon footprints (carbon labelling).[3]

On the other hand, PCF if adopted at a large scale could have significant cost and (negative) demand effects on producers and exporters in different parts of the world, including in developing countries (Edwards-Jones et al., 2008). Research on the governance of global value chains for food products shows that retailers and other 'lead firms' located near consumers to a large extent define product quality standards and at the same time are able to push the cost of complying with these increasingly demanding standards (along with other performance requirements) down the supply chain to producers (Gibbon and Ponte, 2005). There is also a risk that PCF schemes and standards may involve discriminatory practices that affect competitiveness and trade (Brenton et al., 2008; Kasterine and Vanzetti, 2009). This is particularly clear where special emphasis is placed on transport, for example by using life-cycle analysis only for this part of the product life-cycle. This will of course tend to favour domestic producers over more distant ones (Bolwig, 2008).

Methodological issues in product carbon footprinting

Life-Cycle Analysis or Assessment (LCA) is the basic method used in carbon footprinting. LCA 'studies the environmental aspects and potential impacts throughout a product's life-cycle (that is, cradle to grave) from raw material acquisition through production, use and disposal' (ISO, 2006). Several methodological issues related to LCA stand out in the present context. First, there is no single LCA method that is universally agreed upon and therefore no agreement on PCF calculation methods. Second, different definitions of the boundary of the LCA, in terms of which life-cycle stages, emission sources and GHGs area considered, will produce very different results (Büsser et al., 2008). Sensitivity analysis is therefore of key importance. Third, there is a lack of comprehensive data for LCA, data reliability is questionable and several databases with different data specifications (for example, in terms of reference units) are often needed to perform an LCA. Fourth, carbon footprints are rarely accompanied by detailed methodological accounts (or by the results of sensitivity analyses, if performed at all). They are therefore difficult to assess by third parties or to compare with the footprints of like products. Fifth, relatively few analysts have so far acquired the skills to carry out hybrid methods that combine environmental input-output analysis with LCA, which are the best option for product-level GHG assessments, as discussed below. Sixth, the inherent complexity and lack of exactness of carbon footprint analyses contrasts with the need to communicate the results in a simple, clear and unambiguous way to consumers.

There is a vast literature on LCA methodology which we cannot review here, including a dedicated journal, the *International Journal of Life Cycle Assessment*. The remainder of this section is mainly extracted from Wiedmann and Minx (2007), who discuss the different LCA methodologies for calculating the carbon footprints of products or activities. They observe that the task of carbon footprinting can be approached from two different directions: bottom-up or top-down. Process Analysis (PA) is a bottom-up method, which has been developed to understand the environmental impacts of individual products (or processes) from 'cradle to grave'. The bottom-up nature of PA-LCAs means that they suffer from a system boundary problem so that only on-site, mostly first-order impacts are considered. PA-based LCAs are also not suitable for the assessment of carbon footprints for entities such as households or industrial sectors (ibid.).

Environmental Input-Output (EIO) analysis is a top-down approach and provides an alternative to process-based LCAs (ibid.). Input-output tables are economic accounts representing all activities at the meso (sector) level. In combination with environmental data they can be used to estimate carbon footprints in a comprehensive way, taking into account all higher-order impacts and setting the whole economic system as boundary. But environmental IO analysis is less suitable for assessing micro systems such as individual goods and services, as it assumes homogeneity of prices, outputs and their carbon emissions at the sector level. A big advantage of IO-based approaches, however, is that they require much less time and labour to perform once the model is in place than do bottom-up process-based approaches.

These considerations led Wiedmann and Minx (2007) to propose a hybrid-EIO-LCA approach to the assessment of micro systems, which integrates the PA and IO methodologies. In this approach, on-site, first- and second-order process data on environmental impacts is collected for the product system under study, while higher-order requirements are covered by IO analysis, drawing on generalized tools, such as the Bottomline[3] tool (CenSA, 2009). Yet they also observe that while such hybrid assessments are considered state-of-the art in economic ecological modelling, the literature and models are still new and few are at present able to carry them out in practice. While this situation will improve fast in developed countries, the capacity of most developing countries to carry out hybrid-EIO-LCA is likely to remain limited.

There is scant discussion in the literature about the possible bias against developing countries imparted by using one type of PCF methodology rather than another (see Edwards-Jones et al., 2008). This revolves substantially around the issue of where system boundaries are set. Generally, the more direct and indirect inputs to the PCF that are considered, the fewer biases there should be against developing countries. Excluding, for example, emissions from the manufacture of capital goods used to produce footprinted products, as in PAS 2050, means a bias against labour-intensive industrial production systems could be imparted. This discussion parallels that of the implications of excluding 'other indirect' or Scope 3 emissions from corporate footprints (see next section). Another important issue is the lack of appropriate LCA databases for developing-country conditions, implying high levels of uncertainty and subjectivity in PCF calculations, for example in relation to the use of default values for land use change (Edwards-Jones et al., 2009).

ISO environmental standards and carbon footprinting

Since 1997, ISO has published a number of standards that are relevant to carbon footprinting. This process is ongoing: in 2008 the organization announced that its Technical Committee 207 had begun a work programme on carbon footprinting of products (ISO, 2008b).

The first ISO standards in this area to be issued were the ISO 14040 series dealing with LCA, which describe the procedures that should be followed in conducting LCAs. They were consolidated into two revised standards in 2006, without substantial change. A second standard is ISO 14025 (2000) on 'Environmental labels and Declarations – Type III Environmental Declarations'. This recommends the functional unit approach in communication of LCA results – as opposed to reporting mass or volume, which are considered as insufficient to allow comparison. This group of standards was adopted against a background wherein several approaches to LCA had been developed over the previous two decades. There was a resulting danger that, as the method became more widely used, its results thus would be incommensurate and lack credibility.

ISO 14064 (2006–07) has a somewhat different focus. This group of standards is concerned not with the measurement of the overall environmental impact of the production, consumption and disposal of specific products or services over an unspecified time period, but with corporate and 'project'-level GHG emissions within annual time frames. The immediate background is the emergence of a number of emission 'cap and trade' programmes or schemes, each with similar, though different, approaches to emission measurement and validation.[4] The wider background is the probable adoption of a mandatory scheme in the US and the probable integration of the US and other large emitters into a post-Kyoto Protocol agreement. These developments have the potential to create a huge global market in emission credits[5] and to stimulate a substantial number of new offsetting projects in developing countries, under the Clean Development Mechanism. In this context, these standards aim at facilitating a harmonized system for organization- and project-level carbon accounting.

Although a Working Group that contained experts from 45 countries drew up ISO 14064 over a 4-year period, most of its elements appear to be derived from a single source, the GHG-P, launched in 1997 by WRI and WBCSD and revised in 2000 to include a corporate accounting and reporting protocol. Comparisons of the two standards (McGray, 2003;

Spannangle, 2003) agree that their main differences are that (i) GHG-P, unlike ISO 14064, provides detailed guidance notes and calculation tools, while (ii) ISO 14064, unlike GHG-P, covers verification.

ISO 14064-1 deals with corporate GHG accounting while ISO 14064-2 deals with project accounting. ISO 14064-3 deals with validation and verification of GHG plans and accounts and ISO 14065 deals with the accreditation of bodies that carry out third party validation or verification.[6] In all cases, the standards only lay down a series of managerial steps that shall be followed in planning, executing and monitoring activity. Specific actions to be taken at each step, for example the choice of methodologies for quantifying emissions or how to determine the skills of verifiers, remain at the discretion of the corporation or whatever regulatory authority manages a scheme. In this sense there is a strong resemblance to the ISO 14000 and ISO 9000 series of standards.

The standards have been criticized in some quarters for lack of prescription in what are construed as key areas. For example, with respect to corporate GHG accounting (ISO 14064-1), managers are required to identify the boundaries of the emissions that they will quantify. It is stated, that in doing so, they shall include direct emissions from activities of the corporation and indirect emissions from the generation of electricity consumed by the corporation (Scopes 1 and 2, respectively, in the GHG-P) and that they shall 'consider' the inclusion of other indirect emissions (the GHG-P's Scope 3). The standard's main objective here is to establish transparency in respect of what is being measured, rather than to require that all emissions be considered.[7]

Perhaps the part of ISO 14064 that will prove most relevant to whatever ISO standards are eventually developed for carbon footprinting are the provisions on verification in 14064-3. These state that a verification plan shall be formulated which sets out objectives, a data collection approach, a sampling plan, a schedule for performing tests and a system for maintaining test records and other relevant documents ('Process documentation' and 'Communication and reporting documentation'). In respect of 'objectives', verifiers shall not only consider where to draw system boundaries (see above) but also be transparent as to whether they are requiring 'reasonable' or only 'limited' assurance. Finally, there are a series of requirements concerning the competence and experience of verifiers. 'Competences' are defined in terms of a list of suggested – but not mandatory – skills (rather than specific qualifications), while 'experience' is defined in terms both of relevant work experience and attendance at training events and seminars. Examples of suggested skills include knowledge of legal rules, knowledge of the sector, knowledge of emission quantification, knowledge of monitoring methodologies, knowledge of GHG data auditing and knowledge of risk assessment or verification techniques.

Characteristics of product carbon footprinting schemes

In March 2009, the authors carried out a review of documents and websites, resulting in the identification of 31 schemes worldwide that take either a product or a supply chain approach, or both, to carbon footprinting, as opposed to the more common company and project level GHG assessments. From this list (provided in Bolwig and Gibbon, 2009a) we identified 15 schemes worldwide which have carbon footprinted products (as opposed to supply chains) and that are operational in the sense that at least one such product is being retailed.[8] Of these we surveyed 13 schemes during March–May 2009, while two – Bilan CO_2 (France) and Greenice (Australia) – were excluded due to difficulties in obtaining critical information. Data collection was assisted by a questionnaire, filled in by the scheme operator, by the authors through interviews with scheme staff or by the authors based on a review of website documentation. The cases where website information alone was used were ones where scheme operators failed to respond to the questionnaire. The remainder of this section reports the results of the survey of 13 PCF schemes.

Background and context

Table 2.1 shows selected characteristics of the surveyed PCF schemes (more characteristics are listed in Bolwig and Gibbon, 2009a). All schemes were launched during 2007 or 2008. They were typically developed over 1 to 2 years, which is a short time when considering the many technical problems involved in PCF; most operators were thus still developing their methodologies at the time of the survey. The schemes cover Canada, the EU, New Zealand, Switzerland and the US. With the exception of Landcare Research and the Carbon Label Company, all operate only in their home markets.[9]

Seven schemes are operated by not-for-profit consultancy companies and environmental organizations, and two by for-profit consultants. The remaining four are user-operated (that is the companies themselves assess the products they manufacture or sell) schemes deployed by, respectively, a retailer, a bioethanol importer and producer, and two clothing and footwear manufacturers. External funds contributed to the establishment of at least six schemes, of which three received government support – either to establish the scheme itself (Indice Carbon Casino) or to develop the methodology and expertise on which the scheme builds (Carbon Reduction Label and CarboNZero).

Inclusion of additional sustainability criteria in product assessments

Seven schemes limited their product assessments to GHG emissions, while five included one or more other environmental criteria, for example energy efficiency, chemical use, biodiversity restoration, resource consumption, use

Table 2.1 Selected characteristics of the surveyed product carbon footprinting schemes (as of January 2009)

Scheme	Country	Operator	Operator type*	Year launched	No. of products footprinted	Types of products footprinted	GHG reduction commitments	Verification method
AB Agri GHG Mcdelling	UK	AB Agri	FP consultant	2008	1	Dairy	Yes	Third-party
Approved by Climatop	Switzerland	Climatop	NFP consultant	2008	70	All goods and services	Yes (relative to other products)	Third-party
Carbon Connect	Canada	The Carbon Counted	NFP consultant	2007	22	All goods and services	No	Second-party
Carbon Reduction Label	UK	Carbon Label Company	NFP consultant	2008	2800	All goods and services	Yes	Third-party
Carbonlabels.org	Canada	Conscious Brands	FP consultant	2008	1	All foods	Yes	Second-party
CarboNZero	New Zealand	Landcare Research	NFP consultant (gov. owned)	2008	100	All goods and services	Yes	Third-party
Certified CarbonFree	US	Carbonfund.org	NFP consultant	2007	44	All goods and services	Optional	Second-party
Climate Conscious Label	US	Climate Conservancy	NFP consultant	2008	2	All goods and services	No	Second-party
Footprint Chronicles	US	Patagonia	Manufacturer	2007	14	Clothing and footwear	Yes	Self-verification

Table 2.1 (Continued)

Scheme	Country	Operator	Operator type*	Year launched	No. of products footprinted	Types of products footprinted	GHG reduction commitments	Verification method
Green Index rating	US	Timberland	Manufacturer	2007	8 models	Footwear	Yes (corporate level)	Self-verification
Indice Carbone Casino	France	Casino France	Retailer	2008	33	Own-brand food and drinks	Yes (corporate level)	Self-verification
Stop Climate Change	Germany	AGRA-TEG	NFP consultant	2007	11	All goods and services (mainly food)	Yes	Third-party
Verified Sustainable Ethanol Initiative	Sweden	SEKAB	Importer and producer	2008	1	Ethanol	Yes (relative to fixed baseline)	Second-party

* FP = for-profit, NFP = not-for-profit.
Source: Authors' survey.

of organic production methods, recycling, distance travelled or an indicator for 'total environmental impact'. The latter group were typically proprietary schemes of manufacturers or retailers, for which PCF was part of broader CSR strategies, including corporate-level emission reductions. In one instance, the Verified Sustainable Ethanol Initiative, PCF was combined with a range of environmental and social criteria, with the broader aims of 'shifting the entire Brazilian ethanol industry towards more sustainable production' (against a background of widespread critique of this industry) as well as of 'expedit[ing] the development of international regulations for sustainable biofuels' (SEKAB, 2009). Many of the users of the schemes operated by consultants clearly also applied PCF as part of a broader CSR strategy, but we did not collect detailed information on this aspect. It is clear, however, that for companies such as Casino, Tesco and Patagonia, PCF was a minor part of their climate change activities.

Product type, volume and origin

Six schemes offer PCF for all goods and services, while the rest limit themselves to specific product types (food and drinks, clothes, footwear and biofuel) according to the product specialization of the scheme operator. It was not possible to make a complete inventory of all products certified by the 13 schemes. It is clear that, though agricultural value chains have received the most attention, PCF has by no means been limited to food and drinks, for which GHG LCAs are relatively simple, but has also been done for more complex manufactured goods (for example, cell phones) and services (for example, savings accounts) that are more demanding in terms of data and methods.

The largest scheme by far in terms of number of products is the Carbon Reduction Label. It is operated by the Carbon Label Company (a subsidiary of Carbon Trust) in the UK, which since 2007 has certified 2800 products in 120 categories. The 12 remaining schemes have together calculated the carbon footprint for around 300 products, ranging in number from one to 100. Not all these footprints have been publicized, however. For example, Climatop performed GHG LCA studies for 70 products in order to label ten 'carbon champions' within nine product groups, while AB Agri GHG Modelling has not published the footprints it calculated for dairy products.

It was not possible to enumerate all users of the schemes. Carbon Reduction Label is used by, for example, PepsiCo (Tropicana brand juices), British Sugar, Adili Eco-Chic (clothing) and Tesco (UK retailer) (Carbon Label Company, 2009), while companies targeting or based in the German market, such as Voelkel GmbH (juice) and Platanera Rio Sixaola (bananas), have certified products to Stop Climate Change (Stop Climate Change, 2009). In the US, the Carbon Fund has certified 44 products to its Certified CarbonFree standard, including those produced by Motorola (cell phones), Monarch Beverages (energy drinks), Tandus (carpeting) and GBS Enterprises (mattresses)

(Carbon Fund, 2009), while the 100 products certified by CarboNZero in New Zealand include different brands of wine (CarboNZero, 2009).

The small numbers of products that have been footprinted to date reflect the youthfulness of the schemes, the costs and technical challenges involved in PCF and continued uncertainty among users about the benefits of PCF. Thus most users have only footprinted a small share of their product range, and often on a pilot basis. For example, the French retailer Casino has labelled less than 200 out of a planned 3000 own-brand staple food and drink products under its Indice Carbone Casino scheme; Tesco has carbon labelled between 100 and 200 products using the Carbon Reduction Label (and is targeting 500 products); while ten products sold by Migros, the largest retailer in Switzerland, have received the Approved by Climatop label. At the other end of the scale, Marshalls (UK) has published the footprints of all its 503 domestic landscaping products, using the Carbon Reduction Label. In general, when comparing these numbers with earlier statements made by users it is clear that many have fallen short of their initial targets.

Eight schemes offer carbon footprinting for all products irrespective of their country of origin, while three schemes only assess domestically produced products. One scheme (for fuel ethanol) only applies to producers in Brazil, while one scheme did not provide information on country of origin. Hence no strong bias against imported products was found in terms of this factor.

Carbon footprinting approaches and data

Poor access to technical documentation and the limited scope of this study prevent a comprehensive comparison of the scope and methodological rigour of the PCFs performed by the schemes. In lieu of a full technical evaluation, we discuss some key aspects of the PCF approaches used by the schemes.

Publication of methods and assessment results

Regarding the transparency of the assessments, seven schemes – Carbon Connect, Carbon Reduction Label, CarboNZero, Certified CarbonFree, Climate Conscious Label, Stop Climate Change and Verified Sustainable Ethanol Initiative use a written document (standard or description of methodology) published on their websites to guide the GHG assessments, but we stress that the quality and completeness of this documentation differ greatly. The Approved by Climatop scheme takes another approach by publishing the results of their assessments and the peer review reports of these, while CarboNZero publishes a summary of both the methods and the results of the assessment. This does not necessarily mean that the other schemes apply less rigorous or comprehensive methodologies, only that these are less accessible to the public.

Use of recognized standards for life-cycle analysis

All schemes relied on LCA for PCF calculations. The measurement methodologies of most schemes related, in one way or another, to recognized international or national standards for LCA-based GHG accounting. Six schemes referred to the ISO 14044, ISO 14064 or the WRI-WBCSD GHG-P (discussed above), without necessarily following these to the letter. Three schemes certified users to the PAS 2050 standard (or a variant thereof), published in October 2008, which 'builds on existing methods established through BS EN ISO 14040 and BS EN ISO 14044 by specifying requirements for the assessment of the life-cycle GHG emissions of products' (BSI, 2009). Finally, Indice Carbone Casino builds on the *Bilan Carbone* methodology for corporate GHG accounting, developed by the French l'Agence de l'Environnement et de la Maîtrise de l'Energie (ADEME) and which also follows ISO 14064 in several respects (ADEME, 2007, 85).

It is noteworthy that both the *Bilan Carbone* and the ISO standards are concerned with corporate or project-level GHG emissions, or both, rather than product-level ones. Moreover, ISO 14064 is mainly concerned with the transparency and management of GHG accounting and so it does not specify which methods to use for quantifying emissions or which emission sources or greenhouse gasses to include. The PAS 2050 standard, on the other hand, is designed for product-level GHG accounting and has detailed methodological specifications. It is accompanied by a Code of Good Practice (Carbon Trust, 2008), which guides users in their accurate and effective communication of PCF and PCF reduction claims.

Scope of GHG assessments

Regarding the scope (system boundary) of the PCFs, ten schemes claimed to include GHG emissions from all stages in the product life-cycle in the footprint calculation, while two schemes focused on the production stage and one let the scope depend on the client's preferences. However, 'all stages' clearly meant different things to the different schemes. For example, emissions from the production of capital goods are omitted in the PAS 2050 used by the Carbon Reduction Label, AB Agri and CarboNZero, while the similarly ambitious Stop Climate Change methodology includes this source but chooses to disregard the 'transport of the product to the consumer's house' stage. CarboNZero is the only scheme to publish detailed information of the system boundaries used in each case. Most schemes were less explicit about how they set the boundaries of their GHG assessments, preventing a meaningful comparison across schemes. A lack of consistent and transparent boundary setting obviously constrains the assessment and comparison of the carbon footprints of different products, especially among products footprinted by different schemes. For example, including the domestic use phase significantly affects the footprint of coffee; the brewing stage thus accounts for about 70 per cent of the total GHG emissions from a cup of black coffee and considerably more if the user does not behave in an economic way when brewing (Büsser et al., 2008).

Another important methodological choice is which GHGs to include in the assessments. This question was not explored in detail by the survey, but most schemes appear to include all the major GHGs, while one explicitly limits itself to considering only CO_2.

Data sources and quality

Data quality is a key factor for the validity of a PCF. An indicator for good data quality is the use of primary activity data in the calculation of energy and raw material use at the different stages in a product's life-cycle, in addition to secondary data sources (from databases and literature). All schemes claim to use both types of data sources, and cite a number of European and US LCA databases, but we were unable to assess the 'appropriateness' of the choice of data sources in each case. A few of the publicized standards used by the schemes are explicit on the use of primary and secondary data. For example, the PAS 2050 states that 'primary activity data shall be collected from those processes owned, operated or controlled by the organization implementing the PAS. The primary activity data shall not apply to downstream emission sources' (BSI, 2008, 17). The CarbonCounted Standard 1.2 is more flexible, stating that 'Initially, we will use an 80/20 practical approach to determining the footprint. If some data is not available, we should state this and provide a reasonable estimate for its contribution' (CarbonCounted, 2009).

Scheme scope and kinds of certification offered

Besides the calculation of PCFs, 11 schemes require meeting one or more additional climate change related criteria. The most common criterion is a commitment to reduce the carbon footprint at either the product or corporate level. The schemes operated by Timberland, Patagonia and Casino France all include reduction commitments at the corporate level, although these are often stated in a very general way. Commitments to reducing PCF over a specified time period are embodied in six schemes. Two schemes use economic incentives to 'encourage' such reductions. One, Certified Carbon-Free, offers financial incentives for users who can prove reductions of more than 10 per cent per year. In the other, Approved by Climatop, a product is certified as a 'carbon champion' if its carbon footprint is at least 20 per cent lower than the products (within the same product category) which it is compared to. Because certification must be renewed every 2 years, comparison between products in this scheme allegedly encourages producers to reduce their emissions. Comparing the carbon footprint with that of like products is an option in at least two other schemes – the Carbon Reduction Label and the Climate Conscious Label. Whether such comparative information is meant to directly incentivize users to reduce product footprints, rather than indirectly through consumer behaviour, remains unclear.

Secondly, two schemes require the PCF to be lower than a 'baseline' value: in the Verified Sustainable Ethanol Initiative, the 'field-to-wheel' emissions of the ethanol have to be 85 per cent lower than the 'well-to-wheel' emissions from petrol, while Approved by Climatop only certifies a few 'carbon champions' within each product category, as just mentioned. Thirdly, three schemes – Certified CarbonFree, CarboNZero and Stop Climate Change – require carbon neutrality at product level to be achieved through carbon offsetting. The two latter schemes have minimum standards for projects that qualify as offsets, while the former is silent on this aspect.

Altogether, the schemes show great variation in the actual content of their requirements. It is not possible to judge from this overview which general approach is 'better' from a climate change perspective; rather the diversity found points to opportunities for cross-learning and the need for work to identify 'best practices' suitable for different kinds of operators, users and countries. This level of diversity is not unusual during the first few years when standards emerge in a new area. Later diversity may become reduced through natural selection and pressures for harmonization.

Does the transportation stage get special treatment?

GHG emissions from the transportation of goods across long distances have been the subject of much debate in recent year; and in this context some retailers, standard-setting bodies and Northern farmer advocacy groups launched various initiatives to measure, label, restrict or 'green' the transportation of goods, especially food (AEA, 2005; Bolwig, 2008; Kasterine and Vanzetti, 2009). An example is Walmart's Food Miles Calculator that 'allows our buyers to enter information on each supplier and product, determine product pickup locations and select which of our 38 food distribution centres the product will reach. With this information, the calculator computes the total food miles, which the buyer can use when making buying decisions' (Walmart, 2009).

We have argued elsewhere (Gibbon and Bolwig, 2007; Bolwig, 2008) that focusing narrowly on emissions from transportation, rather than considering all stages in the product life-cycle, will discriminate against exporting nations. This is especially true for poor countries, which are often located at a distance from OECD markets and which typically have poor access to high-volume, more energy-efficient shipping systems. For example, the capacities of container ships serving West Africa range between 2000 and 3000 containers, while those landing at the major ports in the EU, the US and East Asia have a tonnage from 8000 to 12,000 containers (personal communication with Morten Nielsen, SAFE Shipping). Moreover, rail transport is poorly developed in many developing regions, especially in Africa, implying a higher dependence on road transport, which is less carbon efficient. Finally, less reliable and more expensive sea freight systems in poor countries mean higher dependence on air freight for certain products, especially fresh produce (Gibbon and Bolwig, 2007).

At the same time, LCA studies show that favouring locally produced goods does not guarantee a reduction in GHG emissions. This is because producers in distant locations may be more carbon efficient than those nearby, and this gain may outweigh the higher emissions from transportation (Edwards-Jones et al., 2008). It is has also been observed that the mode of transport – sea, air, road, rail – as well as the transport technology used within each mode can significantly influence the size of a PCF (Michaelowa and Krause, 2000). In this regard, the relatively high carbon efficiency of sea freight can in some cases advantage distant producers. For example, transporting broccoli 12,000 kilometres from Ecuador to Sweden by boat produces only 40 per cent of the emissions of trucking broccoli 3200 kilometres across Europe from Spain (Angervall et al., 2006).

All surveyed schemes except one include the transport stage in the calculation of the PCF, up to at least the stage of wholesale and in most cases up to the retail outlet. Some also include transport to the consumer's house. Assuming that these calculations also take account of the different modes of transport used, this suggests that the schemes at least do not under estimate emissions from transportation or disregard especially climate-unfriendly modes of transportation such as air freight and diesel-based trucking.[10] The survey also asked whether a scheme placed special emphasis on transport-related GHG emissions. Only one scheme, Patagonia's footprint chronicles, appears to do this, by displaying information on the website on the distance travelled by the product from the stage of raw material to garment delivery at the company's Nevada distribution centre. It is noteworthy that a draft version of the Indice Carbone Casino label highlighted, as the only source, GHG emissions from transport, while the final version shows emissions from all stages in the life-cycle. This development is mirrored in the evolution of the KRAV-Svenskt Sigill Climate Labelling of Food standard (Gibbon, 2009).

Altogether, the design and methods adopted by the schemes generally do not discriminate against products originating in distant countries. However, the users of the schemes may still decide to focus on reducing emissions from transportation through other climate change initiatives, which may disadvantage certain exporting nations. For example, through its climate change programme, Tesco will 'seek to restrict air transport to less than 1% of our products' (Tesco, 2009).

Conformity assessment

In all the schemes examined, the product GHG assessments are carried out by the scheme's own staff or by (other) consultants hired by the users or scheme operators to do so. The schemes can be divided according to, firstly, whether any independent verification is (required to be) performed of these calculations and, secondly, who is supposed to perform this verification where it is required.

No independent verification appears to be performed of the PCF assertions used by the user-operated Footprint Chronicle, Green Index Rating and Indice Carbone Casino schemes, although the general PCF methodology used by the latter has been validated by a public agency (ADEME). In the remaining ten schemes, the organization certifying the product is independent from the one producing or selling it. Within this group, third-party verification of the PCF, that is, where consultants or companies independent of those making the life-cycle calculations perform a check of these calculations, is required and/or practiced in five schemes (AB Agri, Approved by Climatop, CarboNZero, Carbon Reduction Label and Stop Climate Change). The remaining five schemes (Carbonlabels.org, Climate Conscious Label, Carbon Connect, Certified CarbonFree and Verified Sustainable Ethanol Initiative) do not require or practice such an independent stage of verification ('second-party' in Table 2.1), although in the last three schemes mentioned calculations are performed by listed consultants independent of the scheme operator.

Systems of accrediting consultants (other than the scheme operator) qualified to carry out both original PCF calculations and verifications of them generally lack transparency. In two cases, Stop Climate Change and Verified Sustainable Ethanol Initiative, approved consultants are ISO 14065 accredited, although in neither case is it clear that this is a requirement. In one scheme, AB Agri, verification is done by the Carbon Trust, while the verifier used by Approved by Climatop is accredited to ISO 9001:2000 (quality management). There also seems to be a general shortage of consultants accredited (in one way or another) to deliver independent verification of results of the standards used by the schemes. In recognition of this, the Carbon Trust is sponsoring a pilot accreditation scheme by the UK Accreditation Service with the aim of accrediting six auditing companies to certify to PAS 2050. Stop Climate Change and CarboNZero deal with this issue by training, authorizing and monitoring the consultants themselves. The remaining schemes either do not use external consultants or do not specify what is required of them.

Communication of product carbon information

The survey revealed great variation in the way the schemes and the users chose to communicate through text and graphics the product carbon information related to the certification. All schemes offer a carbon label or mark as a proof of certification, often in the form of a seal carrying a logo and the name of the scheme or the organization operating it. In seven schemes, the label also shows the actual value of the PCF, expressed in CO_2e per unit of product, while in one case – the Green Index rating – the footprint is placed on a scale from one to ten (where one denotes <2.5 kg and ten denotes >100 kg per pair of shoes). Two schemes show both the CO_2e value and its position on a scale. Some of the labels display additional information relating to the certification on the packaging; for example, the Carbon Reduction Label reads 'we have committed to reduce this carbon footprint' while the Indice Carbone Casino label states that 'Casino works for the environment in collaboration with its suppliers to reduce its GHG emissions' (our translation). Both these labels also carry a brief explanation of what a PCF is. Other labels for display on packaging carry simpler but not less powerful messages, such as 'certified carbon free' (Certified CarbonFree), 'climate friendly' (Stop Climate Change) or 'verified sustainable' (Verified Sustainable Ethanol Initiative). In most cases, the more complex information associated with the certification is displayed on websites, leaflets and in-store. For example, UK retailer Tesco distributed 1 million copies of the booklet 'How can we shrink our carbon footprint?' to support customers' understanding of its new carbon labels (Tesco, 2009).

Some users choose not to publicize any specific PCF information, such as Sainsbury's Dairy Development Group applying the AB Agri scheme, using it only internally for carbon management purposes. In the experience of the Carbon Label Company, this is the case for most of their clients.[11]

Consumer perceptions of and reactions to PCF

At least six studies of UK consumers, two of Swedish consumers, one of US consumers and one of UK and US consumers jointly have been carried out on climate change issues since 2006. Almost all deal with the climate change impacts of food. No recent studies of German or French consumers on this issue could be found.

Most of these studies deal with consumer decision-making, such as overall determinants of purchase decisions, decisions concerning choice of retailer and decisions concerning willingness to pay a premium. A number also or instead deal with consumers' perceptions of retailers and manufacturers, in relation to their overall credibility on environmental issues, whether they provide enough information in the climate area and whether the information that they do provide is considered trustworthy. A few studies also cover consumers' views on how GHG emissions from products should be labelled. The studies mostly take the form of reports on survey results. In a majority of cases these were obtained during so-called 'omnibus' surveys by market-research companies, that is, surveys covering a variety of unrelated topics. In most cases the sample size was between 1000 and 3000 respondents. A few focus group studies have also been reported.

The main conclusions can be summarized as follows. UK consumers are largely sceptical about the overall environmental and climate convictions of manufacturers and retailers. They, and Swedish consumers, are also interested in obtaining more information from manufacturers and retailers on the climate impact of specific products. However, neither in the US nor in the UK do they trust businesses to report this information accurately. Hence, they would prefer statements and claims in this area to be verified independently.

While there is interest among consumers in obtaining relevant information in this area, climate change concerns are unlikely to become a major driver of most consumers' buying decisions relative to factors such as price and food safety. All other things being equal (especially price), businesses that carry out carbon labelling and products that are carbon labelled are likely to be preferred over comparable businesses and products that do not or are not. But if they were required to pay more than 20 per cent extra for a product with a significantly lower PCF than a comparable one, less than 10 per cent of UK and US consumers, and 28 per cent of Swedish ones, would do so. These figures are considerably higher than the market shares represented, for example, by organic food sales, which on average also command a premium of roughly 20 per cent. Notable in this context is that the proportion of UK consumers reporting regular purchase of organic food is three times higher than the actual share of organic sales in total food sales.

Only very limited *ex post* information is available on consumers' reactions to products that have been PCF labelled. Timberland publishes quarterly information, direct or indirect, on sales of its Green Index labelled products. Up to 2009, this label had been applied to eight of Timberland's models within the Mios sandal and Outdoor Performance ranges. Sales of labelled products declined sharply during 2008, although according to Timberland this was mainly an effect of the phase out of the Mios range. It is not clear whether labelling positively affected the Mios range of shoes at an earlier stage (Timberland, 2009). The surveys show no consistent response on the type of carbon labelling consumers would prefer.

Discussion and conclusion

This chapter has discussed the rationale, context, coverage and characteristics of emerging product carbon footprint schemes and standards, and has reported on how consumers perceive carbon footprinting and labelling and companies' climate change policies in general. We found that PCF is dominated by private certification schemes operated by small for-profit and not-for-profit consultancy companies and in a few cases by large retailers and manufacturers. All schemes have been established within the last 2 years and globally there are only about 15 schemes operational as of April 2009, of which we provide detailed information on 13. Considering the sometimes high costs and technical challenges of PCF, it is therefore no surprise that only a small number of certified carbon footprinted products so far have found their way to retail outlets (whether labelled or not). While some schemes report strong interest in PCF from producers and retailers, and are expanding their clientele and product range, we could not identify any clear trends in these respects.

The investigated schemes display large differences in scale and product coverage, type of claim made and (where applicable) certification offered, GHG assessment methods, communication approaches, and levels and means of verification and transparency. A range of factors may account for this diversity: differences in ambition, technical competence and access to external support; differences in economic resources; different country and business contexts; and the absence of a dominant PCF standard.

Meanwhile, consumers show some interest in PCF information and would probably prefer carbon-labelled products and firms over others, other things being equal. It is also likely that a minority are, or would be, willing to pay a price premium for products with significantly lower footprints than like ones, not much different from the organic price premium. But consumers are also sceptical about the credibility of the 'climate-friendly' claims made by retailers and manufacturers and show a preference for third-party verification. This contrasts with the relatively weak verification systems currently used in PCF. All this indicates that there are limits to the direct commercial benefits from PCF in terms of increased sales, as opposed to benefits related to energy cost reductions and to compliance with climate change legislation.

National governments and international organizations have so far played a minor role in the development of PCF standards or in the establishment of PCF certification schemes (except in the case of biofuels). The main exception is the UK Department for Environment, Food and Rural Affairs (Defra), which supported the development of the first public PCF standard (the PAS 2050) as well as established the organization (the Carbon Trust) which has already certified a relatively large number of products to this standard. In New Zealand, government-sponsored research seems to have been important for the creation of the CarboNZero scheme, operated by a government-owned ('but not controlled') research institute (Landcare Research) on a not-for-profit basis. On a smaller scale, the French *Agence de l'Environnement et de la Maîtrise de l'Energie* (ADEME) has assisted the development of a scheme operated by the retailer Casino, based on its elaborate methodology for corporate GHG accounting. Finally, the Japanese government assisted the start-up of a PCF pilot project in April 2009. The international standards relating to carbon footprinting at the corporate and project levels are the WBCSD-WRI GHG-P and the ISO 14040 and 14064 standards series. These two organizations both commenced work to develop PCF standards in late 2008; while it is unclear how these two processes will relate to each other, the PAS 2050 will likely wield significant influence on both.

We have also examined factors that can help assess the potential effects of PCF on international trade. First, the lack of an international PCF standard could favour producers based in countries with national public standards (so far only the UK), with trusted and workable private standards, or with well-functioning, non-proprietary scheme operators (Canada, Germany, New Zealand, UK and the US). In this regard, only two scheme operators, Carbon Label Company and Landcare Research, certify products in overseas markets. Second, PCF calculation and certification is expensive and demanding on human resources (for data provision and effective communication of the PCF). This tends to favour large and resourceful producers, who may benefit from significant economies of scale (low cost of certification per product sold). This could exclude most companies in developing countries. Third, and unexpectedly perhaps, no bias was found in the way the GHG assessments treat long-distance transport relative to other emission sources, although we did not investigate this aspect in depth. Thus, only one scheme highlights the distance travelled by the product. Finally, the GHG assessment method of the PAS 2050 standard has an in-built bias against relatively labour-intensive production systems, which are typical of developing countries. Other schemes and standards may also contain such biases, in principle or in practice, but more in-depth research is needed to document this.

In sum, although PCF, because it is based on LCA, is likely to have a higher degree of credibility with consumers than any other sort of claim made by operators in relation to the climate change attributes of products, is also difficult and costly to perform and its impact on sales remains unclear. Therefore, whatever its implications for developing countries in principle, its adoption seems likely to remain limited for some time to come and therefore its impacts on trade and development seem unlikely to be substantial – at least in the short term.

The results presented here suggest the usefulness of research in three main areas. First, research is needed on the – present and potential – impacts of private PCF schemes and standards, in respect of: GHG emission reduction, cost of conformity and certification, energy cost savings and trade – particularly in the South–North direction. GHG-related impact analyses should consider not only whether carbon labelling induces more climate-friendly consumer choice, but also whether PCF is an accessible and cost-effective tool for improved corporate carbon management compared to, for example, measurement of GHG emissions at a corporate level. Second, if implemented on a large scale, how would PCF, being a voluntary and consumption-based approach to climate change mitigation, interact with climate change polices that measure and regulate emissions at the physical source? Can measurement of embodied carbon in products be a basis for implementing carbon taxes or border duties (substituting for, or supplementing, an international carbon tax)? How should such a system be governed? How can double-counting of carbon be avoided? The third area concerns the more technical issues of standard implementation. Even with sound international PCF standards in place, the expansion and credibility of PCF will depend critically on research that improves the accuracy and objectivity, and reduces the cost, of footprinting methodologies, especially concerning data availability and use.

Notes

1. Data limitations prevent us from examining the issues of cost of conformity and cost of certification.
2. The other categories are: other personal effects; household appliances; furnishings and other household goods; clothing and footwear; alcohol and tobacco; and books and newspapers.
3. Personal communication with Graham Sinden, Strategy Manager, The Carbon Trust.
4. Under this concept, ceilings are established for total emissions by covered emitters. Emitters are then assigned some proportion of allowable emissions, and must then reduce their actual emissions to those assigned to them or acquire offsets that will cover the difference. Offsets can be purchased on a special market from other regulated emitters who reduce their emissions over and above target, acquired through arrangements with unregistered emitters or earned through carbon sequestration.
5. It is estimated that the US market alone will be worth US$ 300 billion (Gray and Edens, 2008).
6. ISO 14064-3 uses the term validation in relation to project plans and verification in relation to claims about GHG emissions.
7. According to Braunschweig (n.d.), the standard here reflects a misleadingly narrow interpretation of managerial responsibility in that many organizational decision responsibilities are typically hidden in the 'other indirect emissions' category.
8. Because they were not yet operational, the review did not include the ISO and GHG-P product-level standards discussed earlier as well as the following country-level PCF schemes: Climate Labelling of Food and ICA Pilot Project (Sweden), METI Carbon Footprint System (Japan), Cool (CO_2) Label (Korea) and Carbon Label Promotion Committee (Thailand).
9. Landcare Research is based in New Zealand and operates also in Australia and the UK. The Carbon Label Company has PCF activities in a range of countries outside the UK, including Australia (www.carbonreductionlabel.com.au), Brazil, China, India, Israel, the US and several European countries.
10. It was outside the scope of the study to qualify this statement through examining possible biases caused by the choice of emission factors for different transport modes or the accuracy with which distance travelled with different determined transport modes and technologies is determined in each case.
11. In this light, the common usage (also by Brenton et al., 2008), of 'carbon labelling' as a generic term for PCF activities is misleading.

3
Institutional Capacity for Food Safety Conformity in Tanzania

Adam Akyoo and Evelyne Lazaro

Introduction

Safety standards imposed by importing countries are escalating to the extent that they may constitute non-tariff barriers to trade (Antle, 1999; Hoekman and Kostecki, 2001; Mitchell, 2003; Athukorala and Jayasuriya, 2004). The barrier effect is either related to high costs associated with standards compliance that are incurred in production and conformity assessment activities or lack of requisite technology to meet the requirements of standards (Aloui and Kenny, 2004; Humphrey, 2008; de Battisti et al., 2009).

For exporters, conformity assessment costs have two components. Firstly, the cost of certification, inspections and the like, entailed by the requirements of specific standards, and secondly, cost of testing for food safety attributes entailed in relation to the food safety requirements of importing countries. For exporting countries there are an additional set of costs associated with having a food safety system deemed capable by importing country governments of assuring that food safety requirements are observed in export sectors.

In the Tanzanian spice industry costs of inspection, certification and testing for food safety attributes are met by exporters. Interestingly, while local capacity is present, certification (to organic standards in this case) is done by a foreign agency while testing for food hazards is done abroad. In theory, use of local conformity assessment institutions is expected to result in lowered certification and testing costs. Besides enhancing market access by reducing costs and lead times, they may also provide greater transparency and opportunities for dialogue and (via feedback) learning for local exporters. It is therefore worthwhile understanding the reasons for the current situation in Tanzania and further to explore the lessons arising in relation to local capacity for assessing standards compliance.

Conformity assessment refers to any procedure, direct or indirect, that is used to determine whether requirements in technical regulations or standards are fulfilled (Stephenson, 1997). It covers four areas, namely: declaration of conformity (own assessment), testing of products (by independent laboratory), certification (by an independent third party evaluator) and quality system registration (by quality system registrars). Each of the four areas covered by conformity assessment activities can be carried out at three different levels. The first level is assessment or evaluation, the second is accreditation and the third is recognition. Assessment can be done by producers or manufacturers, laboratories, certifiers and quality system registrars and involves comparing a product or process to a given standard (ibid.).

Accreditation is a process of evaluating testing facilities for competence to perform specific tests using specified test methods (Stephenson, 1997). It involves evaluation and formal documentation of a facility's testing competence. It determines whether a particular testing facility has the required personnel qualifications, equipment and/or ability to perform tests. The presence of accredited facilities enhances the possibility of forging Mutual Recognition Agreements between international trading partners. The challenge of conformity assessment becomes clearer on recognition that acceptance of equivalence requires not merely the physical presence of institutions and organizations that are equipped to carry out necessary tests, inspections and certification.

Requirements in respect of accreditation may be more demanding than those in regard to putting in place the required physical and human infrastructure (equipment and staff) for these tasks. To attain recognition inspection bodies must be accredited to ISO/IEC 17020; certification bodies to ISO/IEC guide 62, 65 and 66; and laboratories (testing and calibration) to ISO/IEC 17025. The trend in accreditation is to establish a worldwide network of national or regional groupings of accreditation bodies which will, through Multilateral Agreements, ensure that the competence of certification bodies and laboratories are assessed on the same principle regardless of where in the world they are located. These assessments are based on the harmonized ISO standards (www.sanas.co.za).

This chapter describes Tanzania's capacity to assess conformity in relation to its major developed country trading partners' standards and the challenges they present. It should be pointed out that no coverage is presented of conformity issues in relation to Asian markets; the current destination for Tanzania's clove exports. This is because no specific standards appear to be applied in these markets. The findings are based on a survey of stakeholders carried out in 2005 and updated in 2007–08. The chapter is divided into four main parts. Firstly, the Tanzanian spice sector is briefly introduced. Secondly, standard and conformity assessment issues in regard to EU market access for spices are described. Thirdly, existing Tanzanian institutional capacity for conformity assessment of spices for the EU market is analysed. The final section concludes.

The spice sector in Tanzania

The Tanzanian spice industry is described in detail by Akyoo and Lazaro (2007). Its importance is related to its potential as an avenue for diversifying the country's agricultural exports away from traditional exports, in a high-value direction. Global markets for spices are concentrated in developed countries, with the EU and US combined commanding over 50 per cent of total spice imports (Jaffee, 2004). Apart from cloves (see below), the major market for Tanzanian spices is the EU.

Accessing high value export markets raises issues of supply chain dynamics and conformity with international standards. Currently, however, certified organic standards are the only international standard complied with by the Tanzanian spice industry. But issues of food safety conformity are also of concern as organic products are also subject to testing for food safety compliance (Twarog, 2006). Organic certification and food hazards testing are thus important elements in accessing the EU spice market.

Generally, the Tanzanian spices sector includes two distinct types of supply chain. The first type of chain applies to certified organic spices and takes the general form: *Farmer→ organic export company (local) → sister company (abroad) → high value market*. This sub-structure involves a series of well-defined and coordinated vertical stages from production to final consumer. The second chain is based on conventional spice production and takes the general form: *Farmer → local traders → urban markets → regional market/local consumers*. This structure is made up of numerous actors whose relationships are loosely coordinated through short- or long-term business transactions. Figure 3.1 presents the types of actors in the two chains and the inter-relationships between them.

Standards for spices

Tanzanian national standards

According to the Tanzania National Trade Policy (URT, 2003a), local standards for any export oriented product should be designed to match those of the country's major importers. Theoretically this principle should ensure that conformity to national standards represents a means towards conformity to international standards. The national standards for spices in Tanzania that were formulated in the 1970s and 1980s matched with the international standards of the time, where only quality and cleanliness standards were applied. There has been little subsequent development of national standards in the spice sector in Tanzania to match with the current developments in international standards. The only international standards currently complied with are those for (EU) certified organic production. An East African regional organic standard was established in 2007, but no Tanzanian spice exporters have yet been certified to it.

46 *Conformity Assessment Capacity*

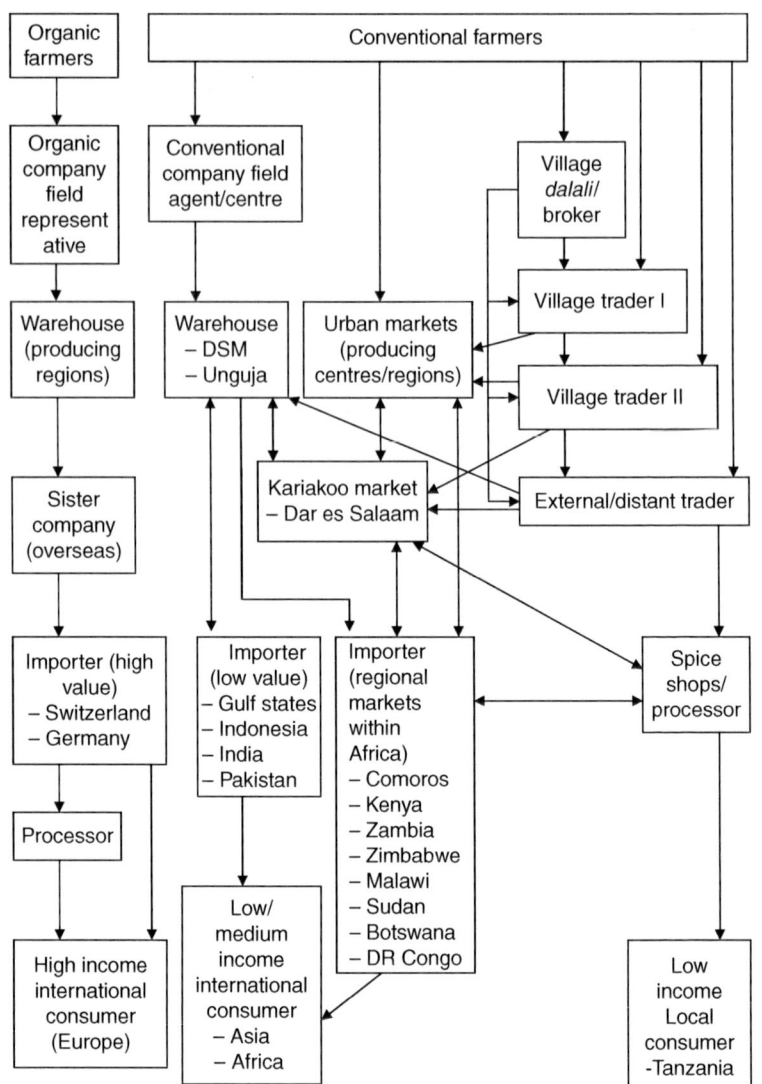

Figure 3.1 The supply chain(s) for Tanzanian spices.
Source: Akyoo and Lazaro (2007).

Initially, five national standards were formulated during the late 1970s and 1980s, namely: standards for black pepper (TZS 30:1979), chilies and capsicums (TZS 31:1979), curry powder (TZS 29:1979), ginger (TZS 47:1979) and turmeric (TZS 357:1987). Formulation of these involved setting limits for several parameters including colour and size of a mature crop, odour and flavour, freedom from fungi and insects, extraneous matter limits, limits for immature, marked or broken berries, fineness and chemical requirement limits. The last of these addressed five parameters, namely: moisture content, total ash, acid insoluble ash in hydrochloric acid, crude fibre and non-volatile ether extract. Table 3.1 summarizes the requirements

Table 3.1 Tanzania standard physical and chemical requirements for black/white pepper, chillies and capsicum

S. No.	Characteristics	Requirements for black/white pepper	Requirements for chillies and capsicums
1	Colour and shape of mature crop	Grey or black + wrinkled surface.	*Orange red – yellowish green, oblong, conical pods.*
2	Odour and flavour	Fresh and pungent, free from foreign odour or flavour including rancidity and mustiness.	*Characteristic odour causing sneezing but not disagreeable and free from mustiness. For chillies – acrid flavour, very strong, very pungent, and very persistent. For capsicum – acrid flavour, moderately strong, moderately pungent and moderately persistent.*
3	Freedom from fungi, insects etc.	Free from insect infestation, fungi, dead insects, insect fragments and rodent contamination visible to the naked eye.	*Free from insect infestation, fungi, dead insects, insect fragments and rodent contamination visible to the naked eye (for both whole and ground).*
4	Extraneous matter	Not more than 15% m/m for b/pepper and not more than 0.8% m/m for white pepper. Not more than 1.0% m/m of foreign matter not coming from the plant for whole b/pepper, or 0.5% m/m in whole w/pepper. Light berries less than 10% m/m, and pinheads $\leq 4\%$ m/m. Total defects (pinheads + light berries $\leq 15\%$ m/m.	*Non-conforming berries to be less than less tan 5%.*
5	Fineness	Ground pepper to pass through a sieve of 1.00 mm aperture size.	*Ground chillies and capsicum to pass through a 0.5 mm sieve.*

Table 3.1 (Continued)

S. No.	Characteristics	Requirements for black/white pepper	Requirements for chillies and capsicums
6	Chemical requirements		
	(i) Moisture % (m/m) max.	12.0	10.0
	(ii) Total ash % (m/m) max.	8.0 (whole b/pepper) 4.0 (whole w/pepper)	8.0
	(iii) Acid insoluble ash in HCL % (m/m) max.	1.4 (ground b/pepper) 0.2 (ground w/pepper)	1.25
	(iv) Crude fibre % (m/m) max.	17.5 (ground b/pepper) 6.0 (ground w/pepper)	30.0
	(v) Non-volatile ether extract % min.	6.8	12.0

Source: TBS (1979a; 1979b).

on these attributes for black and white pepper and chilli and capsicum. These standards are based upon unified American Spice Trade Association/US Food and Drug Administration (ASTA/FDA) criteria. Later in the 1980s other safety attributes were introduced, including a standard for microbiological specification (TZS 404:1988). In 1981, six other associated standards were established which related to acceptable sampling and analytical methods for microbiological analyses in general food stuffs (TBS, 1979a; 1979b; 1988).

Microbiological limits referred to five parameters, namely: mesophilic aerobic bacteria, *Salmonella*, *Bacillus cereus*, *Clostridium perfringens* and yeast and mould. The prescribed microbiological analysis was based on establishment of a total count of each micro-organism in a specified spice sample. The introduction of a microbiological specification standard for spices in 1988 (TZS 404:1988) was another step towards meeting the global trends in safety standards. According to Jaffee (2004), incorporation of health and hygiene specifications in commercial supply chains for spices started in the early 1990s. Before this period, it was only quality and cleanliness standards that were of concern. The publication of this standard meant that Tanzania national standard was not far from the requirements for the international safety standards in high value markets. For instance, a standard specification for zero tolerance to *Salmonella* was also a requirement in EU markets at this time. Table 3.2 shows the acceptable micro-organism limits for different spice types under the standard. However, Tanzanian national

Table 3.2 Limits of micro-organisms in spices (Tanzania national standards)

Spice type	Micro-organism type				
	Mesophilic aerobic bacteria (max. number per g)	Salmonella (max. number in 25 g)	B. cereus (max. number per g)	C. perfringens (max. number per g)	Yeast and moulds (max. number per g)
B/pepper + w/pepper	10^5	0	10^3	5×10^2	10^4
Chillies + capsicums	10^5	0	10^3	5×10^2	10^3
Cardamom	10^4	0	10^3	5×10^2	10^2
Curry powder	10^5	0	10^3	5×10^2	10^3
Cloves	10^4	0	10^3	5×10^2	10^3
Ginger	10^5	0	10^3	5×10^2	17×10^3
Turmeric	10^6	0	10^3	5×10^2	10^3

Source: TBS (1988).

Table 3.3 General microbiological specification – Germany and Netherlands

Parameter Germany	Standard value	Danger value
Total Aerobic Bacteria	1×10^5/g	1×10^6/g
E-coli	Absent	Absent
B. cereus	1×10^4/g	1×10^5/g
S. aureus	1×10^2/g	1×10^3/g
Salmonella	Absent in 25 g	Absent in 25 g
Netherlands		
Bacillus B. Cereus	Absent in 25 g	Danger values similar to those of Germany
Escherichia Coli	Absent in 25 g	
C. perfringens	Absent in 25 g	
S. aureus	Absent in 25 g	
Salmonella	Absent in 25 g	
Total aerobic bacteria	1×10^6/g	
Yeast and mould	1×10^3/g	
Coli form	1×10^2/g	

Source: Kithu (2001).

standards fell short of those applied in some of the major European spice markets, such as Germany and Netherlands. Table 3.3 shows the general acceptable microbiological limits in these markets. Differences in standards' stringency between member states within the EU on identical parameters for a particular product as depicted in Table 3.3 have always impacted negatively on LDCs' compliance efforts.

EU food safety standards

Food safety standards for spices in the EU are generally derived from general food standards. This is because there are no specific food safety standards for spices (Jaffee, 2004), excepting special requirements regarding chilli dating from 2005–09. Table 3.4 summarizes most of the standards which are currently applicable in the EU and provides details on the respective testing

Table 3.4 EU Food Safety Standards for Spices

Hazard type	Spice type	EU std/limit	Required conformity assessment investment	Indicative cost* per unit (USD)
Microbial Pathogens (*Salmonella* bacteria)	Black pepper, paprika, etc.	(i) Zero tolerance to Salmonella contamination (ii) Non-use of ETO (ethyl oxide) sterilization (iii) Non-use of irradiation procedures	(i) Autoclave (ii) Incubator (iii) Biological safety cabinet (iv) Water bath (v) Oven (vi) Stomatcher – –	10,000 6,000 15,000 2,000 4,500 3,000 – –
Aflatoxins[†]	Chillies, Paprika, Ginger, Nutmeg, etc	(i) 10 ppb (parts per billion) for aflatoxin (B1 + B2 + G1 + G2) (ii) 5ppb for aflatoxin B1. (iii) See Table 3.5 for individual country limits	High performance liquid chromatograph equipment (HPLC)	Modern HPLC model costs US$100,000
Pesticide residues • Cartap • Inorganic bromide • Hydrogen phosphide	Ginger All spices All spices	No MRLs set for spices at EU level (only individual country MRLs e.g., Germany and Netherlands) – See Table 3.6	Gas chromatograph equipment (GC) or Gas chromatograph mass spectrophotometer equipment (GCMS)	GSMS equipment model costs US$76,126

Table 3.4 (Continued)

Hazard type	Spice type	EU std/limit	Required conformity assessment investment	Indicative cost* per unit (USD)
Heavy metals	—	Unspecified	Atomic absorption spectrophotometer (AAS) equipment	AAS set costs US$120,000
- Mercury	All	5 mg/kg		
- Cadmium	All	20 mg/kg		
- Arsenic	All	10 mg/kg		
- Copper	All	50 mg/kg		
- Lead				
- Zinc				
Prohibited food additives Para red Sudan 1	• Turmeric, Chilli, Paprika, Cayenne Pepper • Ground chillies, Chilli and Curry powder	Zero tolerance to both additives	HPLC equipment (as for aflatoxins, the difference will only be on the certified reference materials needed for the detection.) Certificate stating absence of Sudan 1	As above Not known

*Figures for equipment costs were obtained from TBS and TFDA purchase records for 2007.
†Tracking of Ochratoxin levels in spices has also started in EU.
Source: Jaffee (2004) and Kithu (2001).

equipment required. A brief discussion of the general standards (and the chilli requirement) is presented below. All technical details, unless otherwise cited, are from Jaffee (2004).

Aflatoxins

The limits shown in Table 3.5 were established as a result of the 2001 amendment of the EU Commission's 1997 specific regulation on aflatoxins contamination in spices. In the amendment, aflatoxins were described as potent liver carcinogens in animals and hence probable human carcinogens. Aflatoxins B1, in particular, was branded a genotoxic carcinogen for which there is no lower threshold triggering harmful effects and therefore no admissible daily intake could be set (CEC, 2001). The EU Committee on Toxicity of Chemicals in Food, Consumer Products and the Environment (COT) held that aflatoxins contamination in spices should be reduced to the lowest level technologically possible.

Table 3.5 Summary of legislation on aflatoxins in developed spice-importing countries

Country	Permitted Levels	For which products	Comments
Austria	B1<1 ppb	All Food stuffs (except mechanically prepared cereals in the case of B1).	
Belgium	<5 ppb for Peanuts EU legislation is expected.		In Belgian law aflatoxins (and toxins in general) may not present in foodstuffs i.e. not detectable.
Germany	B1 + B2 + G1 + G2<4 ppb	All foodstuffs	
Denmark	B1 < 2 ppb		
Netherlands	B1 < 5 ppb	All foodstuffs	No controls on B2
Switzerland	B1 < 1 ppb	All foodstuffs (except maize)	
	B2 + G1 + G2 < 5 ppb	All foodstuffs	
United Kingdom	<50 ppb advisory level for chilly.		Only Aflatoxin Regulations on Nuts/Nut products Dried Figs/Dried Fig products, which when sold to the consumer must contain <4 ppb total Alfatoxin. No regulations on Spices/herbs.
Spain	B1 < 5 ppb		
	B1+B2+G1+G2 < 10 ppb	All foodstuffs	
Sweden	B1+B2+G1+G2 < 5 ppb	All foodstuffs	
Finland	B1+B2+G1+G2 < 5 ppb	All foodstuffs	
Italy + France	<10 pbb for B1		No regulations
U.S.A	<20 ppb	All foodstuffs	Guideline FDA

Source: Kithu (2001).

Maximum Residue Levels (MRLs)

Under the EU regulations there are no dedicated Maximum Residue Levels (MRLs) for spices. However, individual EU member states have set dedicated spice MRLs, particularly Germany and Spain which between them have about 30–40 MRLs for spices. In Spain for example, the limit for Ethion (an insecticide used in chillies) is set at 0.1 ppm (parts per million) and for Carbaryl in fresh pepper at 5 mg/kg (see Table 3.6 for details). However, the

Table 3.6 Maximum pesticides residues limits in Germany, Netherlands and United Kingdom

Active substance	Limit values in ppm		
	Germany	Netherlands	United Kingdom
HCH without Lindane	0.20	0.02	0.02
Lindane	0.01	0.02	–
Hexachlorobenzene	0.10	–	0.01
Aldrin & Dieldrin	0.10	0.03	0.01
Sum of DDT	1.00	0.15	0.05
Malathion	0.05	0.05	8.00
Dicofol	0.05	0.05	0.50
Chlorpyrifos	0.05	0.01	–
Ethion	0.05	0.01	–
Chlordan	0.05	0.01	0.02
Parathion	–	0.10	1.00
Parathion methyl	0.10	0.10	0.20
Mevinphos	0.05	0.05	–
Sum of Endosulfan	0.10	0.02	0.10
Phosalon	0.05	1.00	0.10
Vinclozolin	0.05	–	0.10
Dimethoat	0.05	0.01	0.05
Quintozen	0.01	–	1.00
Metacriphos	0.01	–	–
Heptachlor & -epoxid	0.10	0.21	0.01
Methidathion	0.02	–	–
Diazinon	0.05	0.05	0.05
Fenithrothion	0.05	0.05	0.05
Bromophos	0.10	–	–
Mecarbam	0.01	–	–
Methoxychlor	0.01	0.05	–
Omethoat	0.40	–	0.20
Dichlorvos	0.10	0.05	–
Phosmet	–	0.01	–
Methylbromide	–	–	0.10
Tetradifon	0.05	–	–

Source: Kithu (2001).

requirement to use only chemicals that are registered as acceptable pesticides is akin to a standard at the EU level.

Two complications in relation to MRLs for spices from the developing world have surfaced. A first complication relates to the absence of Extraneous Maximum Residue Limits (EMRLs) for persistent pesticides which are still found in soil and water though they are no longer in use. This complication becomes more serious when the list of accepted pesticides for use is frequently updated whilst their presence in water and soil persists over a longer period. A second complication concerns the magnification effect of pesticide residues in dried chillies due to dehydration. Proposals by some spice exporters from developing countries (especially India) and least developed countries to institute an adjustment factor of 10 to correct for this anomaly are yet to receive positive consideration in importing industrial countries (Jaffee, 2004).

Artificial colorants and additives

In recent years the EU's attention has been on the presence in spices of the prohibited red dye Sudan 1 and chemical dye Para red. They are both believed to be carcinogenic. Sudan 1 dye presence in Indian spice consignments was posted on the EU's Rapid Alert System of Food and Feed in May 2003 (Jaffee, 2004). A Para red dye alert was raised on 21 April 2005 following its detection in some spice seasonings in the UK (*Guardian Unlimited*, 3.5.2005). Both cases resulted in product recalls and withdrawal from supermarkets. More recently the EU introduced a requirement that all consignments of chilli imported to the EU shall be accompanied by an analytical report stating that there is no Sudan red dye in the product (see Broberg, this volume).

Pathogens

The major concern is with the presence of *Salmonella* bacteria contamination in spices. Individual member EU countries have specific concerns on this pathogen (Table 3.3). For example, whilst the Netherlands observes zero tolerance to both *Bacillus cereus* and *Staphylococcus aureus* in general foodstuffs, tolerance limits for the same hazards in Germany are 1×10^4/g and 1×10^2/g, respectively.

Heavy metals

Reference is sometimes made to spice contamination with Mercury, Lead and Cadmium (Henson, 2003; Jaffee, 2004). Many EU countries appear to have specified MRLs for Lead as well as for Arsenic, Copper and Zinc as shown in Table 3.4.

Local capacity for standards conformity assessment

Food hazard testing

Food hazard testing is a procedure to ensure that limits of micro-organisms are not exceeded in any food lot for conformity to any given food safety standard. Given the EU food safety-related standards presented above, requirements for conformity assessment would necessitate investment in the following equipment:

a) high performance liquid chromatograph for detection of aflatoxins;
b) atomic absorption spectrophotometer for detection of heavy metals;
c) gas chromatograph for detection of pesticide residues; and
d) diverse laboratory equipment (Table 3.7) for detection of microbial pathogens – and specifically for contamination with *Salmonella* bacteria.

If testing for anaerobic bacteria like *B. cereus* and *C. perfrigens*, such a laboratory would be required to make additional investments to acquire special incubators, special growth media and an anaerobic jar. This could amount to an extra US$10,000 worth of equipment.

Learning from the example of India (the largest spice producer and consumer globally, see http://www.caudilweb.com/triplestandards/en/Topic5aspx), the above safety-related investments are possible where there is a critical mass of exporters and where both industry and government collaborate effectively (Jaffee, 2004). Thus, over the period 1991–2003, total safety-related investment in the Indian spice industry amounted to

Table 3.7 Requisite laboratory equipment for Salmonella testing*

Name of equipment	Capacity of the equipment	Number of units required	Unit cost (USD)	Total investment cost (USD)
Incubator	400cc	3	6,000	18,000
Water bath	300cc	1	2,000	2,000
Autoclave	600cc	1	10,000	10,000
Oven	400cc	1	4,500	4,500
Stomatcher	–	1	3,000	3,000
Biological safety cabinet	–	1	15,000	15,000
Glassware	variable	variable	variable	30/piece
Total				52,530

*For a laboratory handling up to 10 samples per day.
Source: Laboratory Services Directorate, TFDA.

US$14.5 million, with three quarters of this being undertaken by the industry itself and one quarter by the public Spice Board. Investment in laboratories alone amounted to US$540,000. Of these costs 45 per cent was met through technical assistance from UNDP and ITC. The rest was met by industry and government (via the Spice Board). Meeting such challenges in the Tanzanian context, with low volumes, only a few exporters and a very weak institutional set up with minimal public sector involvement in the industry is bound to be difficult.

Testing capacity in Tanzania

No dedicated investment in laboratory testing equipment for safety-related risks for spices has been undertaken by either the private or public sectors in Tanzania. This is mainly explained by the factors just discussed, although it also relates to the change of direction in destination markets for clove, which is the major spice crop. If Tanzanian clove had continued to be traded in high value markets as was the case in the past (Akyoo and Lazaro, 2007), the position might be different today. Given its value, the volume traded and the significant (Zanzibar) government involvement in its marketing, it was probably the only spice crop that could justify the involved capital expenditure. The current prevalence of exports to Asian markets that demand no strict adherence to safety standards is, conversely, a significant disincentive for the sub-sector to engage in such costly investments.

Nonetheless, there are investments by the public sector that can potentially serve a variety of agro-food export industries, including spices. The Tanzanian Bureau of Standards (TBS), the Tanzania Food and Drug Authority (TFDA), the Tanzanian Industrial Research and Development Organisation (TIRDO) and the Government Chemist Laboratory Agency (GCLA) have all undertaken investments in this regard. These organizations, however, prioritize testing of imports and locally processed products. The capacities of each of these organizations are summarized in Tables 3.8 and 3.9 and then discussed in turn. Table 3.8 summarizes physical capacity in terms of available equipment whereas Table 3.9 summarizes personnel capacity in respect of professional staff for each laboratory.

Adequacy of human resource capacity is discussed here only in relation to the current activities planned and implemented by the agencies in question and not specifically in relation to testing of exports – which is not generally undertaken except in the case of NFQCL (see Table 3.9). It should also be underlined that, even in relation to imports and domestically produced goods aimed at the national market, the activities of most of these agencies are somewhat limited. Some do have documented surveillance programmes but these tend to be implemented only in relation to crisis situations such as reports of contamination or likely contamination. Furthermore, there is little or no monitoring of primary products.

Table 3.8 Summary of physical capacity for food safety testing by institution, 2008

Hazard	Test	Equipment necessary	Institutions having the equipment	Accred. status	Cost of test per sample
Salmonella	Laboratory test	Incubator, water bath, autoclave, oven, stomacher, biological safety cabinet	TBS, TFDA, TIRDO, GCLA, NFQCL	NFQCL only	TFDA and TBS: US$ 50; NFQCL is yet to set fees for services rendered to outside customers
Aflatoxins	High performance liquid chromatography (HPLC)	High performance liquid chromatograph	TBS, TFDA, TIRDO, GCLA	None	GCLA: US$ 30
Pesticide residues	Gas chromatography (GC)	Gas chromatograph	TFDA, GCLA	None	GCLA: US$ 45 per pesticide
Heavy metals	Atomic absorption spectrophotometry (AAS)	Atomic absorption spectrophotometer	TBS, TFDA, TIRDO, GCLA	None	GCLA: US$ 23 per metal
Artificial colorants and chemical dyes	High performance liquid chromatography (HPLC)	High performance liquid chromatograph (different certified reference material from those for aflatoxins)	TBS, TFDA, TIRDO, GCLA	None	No laboratory tests for these in Tanzania

Source: Author survey data, 2005–08.

Table 3.9 Summary of professional capacity for food safety testing by institution, 2008

Institution	Type of laboratory	Professional capacity		Additional staff required to carry out existing tasks
		Education level	Discipline	
TFDA	Chemistry Food microbiology	1 MSc	Food scientist	2 additional BSc level food scientists required
		1 MSc	Engineer	
		1 MSc	Chemist	
		1 Diploma	Technician	
		1 BSc	Food scientist	
		1 Diploma	Technician	
TBS	Chemistry Microbiology	1 MSc	Chemist	
		3 BSc	Food scientist	
		2 diplomas	Technicians	
		1 MSc	Microbiologist	
		2 BSc	Food scientist	
		1 diploma	Technician	
GCLA	Food Microbiology	1 MSc	Food scientist	2 additional BSc level food scientists and 2 additional BSc level microbiologists required
		1 BSc	Food scientist	
		4 Diplomas	Technicians	
		1 MSc*	Microbiologist	
		2 BSc	Microbiologists	
		2 Diplomas	Technicians	
TIRDO	Food microbiology	1 BSc	Microbiologist	No additional requirement in the short run
		1 BSc	Food scientist	
		4 Diplomas	Technicians	
NFQCL	Fish quality assurance	2 MSc + 1 BSc	Microbiologists	Unspecified staff deficit reported
		2 BSc	Food scientists	
		3 Diplomas + 2 certificates	Technologists/ Technicians	
TPRI	Pesticide residue Quality assurance	1 PhD	Chemist	6 additional PhD chemists + 1 MSc or BSc chemist + 10 technicians required
		1 PhD*	Chemist	
		1 BSc	Engineer	
		3 Diplomas	Technicians	
		2 MSc	Chemists	
		1 MSc*	Chemist	
		1 BSc	Chemist	
		2 Diplomas	Technicians	

*On-going programme.
Source: Authors' survey data 2007–08.

Tanzania Food and Drugs Authority (TFDA)

TFDA operates under the Ministry of Health and Social Welfare and is responsible for overseeing the quality and safety of food, drugs and related products. It was established under the Food and Drugs Act No. 1 of 2003 and started operations in July 2003. It issues certificates of registration subject to laboratory tests. Certification is provided on a consignment basis and the focus has mainly been on packaged processed foodstuffs. Spices have not been among the products that have been certified by TFDA. The argument is that, for a product to qualify for registration, its quality should remain unchanged over time and spices do not qualify on this basis, hence their exclusion.

The TFDA laboratory, as of June 2007, was under major renovation. The available equipment could only test for microbial pathogen contamination in food. However, customers requiring other tests for their samples were accepted and the samples were taken to the GCLA. The TFDA fee structure for various tests is summarized in Table 3.8 below.

A problem is that TFDA currently lacks accreditation[1] to register the results of its tests. TFDA was looking forward to applying for accreditation during 2008 after the new laboratory building was completed. Preparation of quality manuals (as per ISO/IEC 17025) was reported to have been completed.

Levels of professional capacity at TFDA suffice for its current operations.[2] The personnel profile in the chemistry laboratory is made up of three MSc holders (a food scientist, an engineer and a chemist) and one Diploma holder (a technician). Recruitment of two BSc holders (both food technologists) is required to improve the capacity to operate existing equipment but was reported to be limited by budgetary allocations. The food microbiology laboratory is staffed with only one BSc holder (a food technologist/scientist) and one Diploma holder (a technologist/technician). An additional two food technologists and one laboratory technologist/technician are required to improve the capacity.

Tanzania Bureau of Standards (TBS)

TBS is the sole standards body in Tanzania and was established under the Standards Act No.3 of 1975, subsequently amended by Act No.1 of 1977. Being a national standards body, TBS is a member of ISO. It is the national enquiry point for all matters pertaining to standardization and ISO. In the process of formulating standards, technical committees are established for which TBS forms the secretariat. Currently, there are 30 technical committees each comprising 12 members. Committee members are key stakeholders in the respective industries for which standards are to be formulated. Spices and Condiments is one of the technical committees of TBS and the national standards on spices are a result of its work.

TBS's laboratory can only handle tests for microbial pathogen presence and some aspects of heavy metal contamination. In the latter case, detection is only for lead contamination whereas mercury testing is hampered by lack of requisite kits. Capacity to test for cadmium and other heavy metals is doubtful as it was reported that such tests have not been attempted.

High Performance Liquid Chromatograph (HPLC) equipment to test for mycotoxins/aflatoxins was procured in October 2007. Gas Chromatograph equipment for pesticide residue (MRLs) testing is lacking. TBS's laboratory capacity deficit is reported to be more in regard to lack of necessary equipment than lack of trained staff.

TBS's microbiology laboratory is staffed with one MSc holder (a food microbiologist), two BSc holders (food technologists/scientists) and one Diploma holder laboratory technician. The chemistry laboratory had one MSc holder (a chemist), three BSc holders (food technologists/scientists) and two Diploma holder technicians. Both segments of the workforce were considered sufficient for existing operations at the time of survey. Toll fees for various tests at the TBS laboratory are shown in Table 3.8 below.

TBS's microbiological laboratory became accredited by SANAS[3] in December 2007 for *E. coli*, total plate count and coliform tests. *Salmonella* testing was not then accredited due to the absence of a biological safety cabinet. The cabinet has now been procured, thus an application for accreditation with respect to *Salmonella* testing is imminent.

Tanzania Industrial Research and Development Organization (TIRDO)

TIRDO is a parastatal organization which was established by Act No.5 of 1979 and became operational in April 1979. It was set up for the purpose of conducting industrial research and providing consultancy services to industry. TIRDO has three laboratory facilities covering food microbiology, energy and environment. The microbiology laboratory is capable of testing for *Salmonella, Vibrio cholera, S. aureus, Clostridium* spp. and *E. coli*.

TIRDO has HPCL equipment for aflatoxin testing but this was not in working order at the time of the survey due to software problems. An atomic absorption spectrophotometer (AAS) for heavy metal testing has been procured but was not yet in use at the time of survey. GC equipment is lacking so no testing for pesticide MRLs is possible.

TIRDO's microbiology laboratory is planning to apply for SANAS accreditation.[4] All the necessary quality manuals are ready and a pre-assessment has already been done. The laboratory is staffed with one microbiologist, one food technologist and four technicians. This workforce was reported to be adequate given existing operations.

Government Chemist Laboratory Agency (GCLA)

This is the most sophisticated laboratory facility in the country in terms of food hazards testing. It is well equipped to test for all of the four types of hazards of concern, in addition to antibiotic residues. It is also the sole laboratory facility in East and Central Africa that is capable of testing for Polychlorinated biphenyls (PCBs). However, Tanzanian exporters tend not to use this local facility, first because of delays in delivery of test results which often translates into loss of sales; and second because the laboratory, like those of TIRDO, TFDA and TBS, is not accredited, so test results would not be recognized in the EU market.

The existence of delays is conceded by GCLA but said to be an inevitable consequence of the necessity of sourcing most of its certified reference material from abroad. For instance, the process of obtaining certified reference material for aflatoxin from Europe may take up to 2 months. At times, given the toxic nature of aflatoxins, reference material suppliers may even decide to come and verify the need for these materials on the ground of fear of possible misuse, as aflatoxins are also potent raw materials for biological weaponry. If this occurs, further delays are likely to be encountered.

GLCA has also applied for SANAS accreditation and is now past the first stage, that is, registration for accreditation. In the first phase of evaluation, the current buildings were disqualified, thus new buildings are now under construction. The fee structure for GCLA test services on spices and herbs is as shown in Table 3.8.

GCLA is staffed with a total of five food technologists/microbiologists (one MSc holder, one currently undergoing MSc degree training and three BSc holders). The three BSc holders are serving in Mwanza branch. There is also a total of six technicians (four in the food laboratory and two in the microbiology laboratory). At the moment, there is a deficit of two BSc-holding food technologists and two BSc-holding microbiologists, to serve in the food and microbiology laboratories, respectively.

Tropical Pesticide Research Institute (TPRI)

TPRI was established in 1979 by an Act of Parliament. It is under the Ministry of Agriculture, Food Security and Cooperatives (MAFSC). It has two laboratories that fall under the analytical section of its technical services department. The laboratories are (i) a pesticide residue laboratory and (ii) a quality assurance and analytical laboratory.

TPRI is yet to start on food testing activities due to two major reasons. Firstly, its laboratories are ill-equipped for food hazards testing. The pesticide residue laboratory is deficient in equipment (MRLs cannot be tested for as a GC is lacking). The available AAS can only detect copper, chromium, zinc and manganese but not other heavy metals including cadmium, lead and mercury. Secondly, TPRI is specialized in pesticide formulation, so food testing is outside its main agenda. Pesticide formulation activities involve testing pesticide composition against given specifications for ensuring their authenticity, effectiveness and proper usage. The quality assurance laboratory is thus equipped with working HPLC, AAS and GCs. This equipment is not however used for food testing for fear of cross contamination of results.

TPRI's personnel profile also reflects the organization's specialization. The entire staff is made up of chemists and there are no food microbiologists or technologists. However, judging from the long experience with pesticides in general and the available personnel, TPRI could be a strong centre for MRL testing in future if the proper equipment were available and its mandate modified.

On the other hand, according to the analyst in-charge, current recruitment priorities are for more chemists, including four with PhDs, natural products chemist and a toxicologist and four diploma level technicians for the pesticide residue laboratory, as well as three additional analytical chemists (two of them at PhD level) and four Diploma level technicians for the quality assurance laboratory.

National Fish Quality Control Laboratory (NFQCL)

The NFQCL is situated at Nyegezi in Mwanza city, North Western Tanzania. It is owned by the government and operates under the Ministry of Natural Resources and Tourism. It is the government-designated fish quality control laboratory and caters specifically for the Lake Victoria Nile Perch industry. Fish quality and safety failures in the past resulted in EU import bans on Nile Perch from Lake Victoria. Recent government investment in the laboratory is thus a response to these shocks.

NFQCL food testing capacity is summarized in Table 3.8 feature of this capacity is its achievement of SANAS accreditation for *Salmonella* testing. This is the only laboratory in the country that has so far been accredited for testing this parameter. The lab however lacks capacity in testing for other food hazards – pesticide residues, heavy metals, aflatoxins and chemical dyes and colorants. NFQCL's personnel profile is summarized in Table 3.9. Deficits of personnel in each category were stated (an analytical chemist, an environmental chemist) but no precise figures were given.

In the short term, NFQCL's objective is to provide laboratory analytical services for fish and fishery products only. In the long run, the laboratory plans to offer such services for other food stuffs plus intensive involvement in research activities.

Conformity assessment for organic agriculture

Organic certification for export destined spices is currently carried out by a Swiss company, IMO (Akyoo and Lazaro, 2007). Initially, all work including inspection was carried out by this agency. Lately, most of the activities (especially inspection) have been externalized to staff from the local certification agency TANCERT[5] (Tanzania Organic Certification Association). This has been the trend in all the East African countries in matters pertaining to organic certification (Rundgren, 2007). But certification itself is still performed by IMO.

Costs for foreign-based certification are generally considered to be high, with charges per individual farmer ranging from US$10 to US$100 for typical Internal Control Systems (ICS) for 500 farmers and for 10–20 farmers, respectively (ibid.). The average cost of certifying an individual farmer as calculated from data for Tanzanian exporters ranges from US$9.3 to US$35.3 (author's survey, 2006–07). Accreditation of local agencies has always been thought of as a feasible way to reduce these costs.

However, the observed trend is that foreign-based certifying agents establish regional representation and forge ever closer cooperation with local bodies, rather than the latter obtaining EU accreditation in their own right. Conflicts of interest between the two camps (accreditation of a local body for certification purposes possibly means replacing a foreign-based one) may slow down the process.

TANCERT describes itself as a private organization of farmers that was established in 2003. It was founded by NGOs interested in organic-related activities and registered under the 1954 Societies Ordinance. It inspects and/or certifies spices on request. It is able to inspect for organic standards for almost all markets through its contract and cooperation with IMO. However, it plans to fully replace IMO in 2 years' time. Its accreditation application for international organic certification is being audited by IOAS (International Organic Accreditation Services).[6] TANCERT claims that local exporters are incurring high certification costs due to the absence of an internationally accredited local certifier. TANCERT is currently authorized only to inspect to regional organic standards. IMO and TANCERT fee structures for their different activities are shown in Table 3.10.

From the details of Table 3.10, marked differences in inspection and certification costs can be observed between the IMO and TANCERT. However, it is difficult to compare these on account of TANCERT's lack of international accreditation. Arguably, given the fact that TANCERT's jurisdiction is restricted to the domestic and regional markets whereas IMO caters for high value markets, such differences might be expected.

However, an ongoing point of contention concerns IMO's different charges for field inspections when these are done by junior or senior inspectors, respectively. This was also brought up by spice exporting companies in Zanzibar (Akyoo and Lazaro, 2007). The complaint is that the decision to send a junior or a senior inspector is the prerogative of the certifying agency. Since both scenarios (use of junior or senior inspector) lead to similar outcomes, the different charges (US$133 vs US$224 per day) are said to be unjustified.

Summing up

From the foregoing discussion, the following can be observed: that while there are no dedicated testing facilities for spices, there are a number of multi-functional testing facilities in Tanzania. However, none of these facilities performed any tests for spices. This is partly because of lack of international accreditation of most Tanzanian testing facilities, partly because of

Table 3.10 IMO* and TANCERT fees schedules

Application fees	Category	Level in USD or equivalent (TANCERT)	Level in USD or equivalent (IMO)	Explanations (TANCERT)	Explanations (IMO)
	Small individual farms	30	–	The fees are paid in a lump sum when applicants submit the forms to TANCERT. The application fee is not refundable.	No application fee. Prepayment of inspection costs required before start of inspection.
	Society/Association/Farm group	30	–		
	Operator with contracted farmers	25	–		
	Processor at small scale	30	–		
	Processor at factory level	50	–		
	Big farms	50	–		

Inspection fees	Category (Daily fees)	Level in USD or equivalent domestic market (TANCERT)	Level in USD or equivalent domestic market (IMO)	Explanations (TANCERT)	Explanations (IMO)
	Small individual farms	100	€250 ($350)	All levels are rated per day of inspection work.	Depending on the task, field re-inspection €95 ($133) conducted by junior inspector, €160 ($224) conducted by senior inspector, €370 ($518) for evaluation of ICS.
	Society/Association/Farm group	120	€95–€370 ($133–$518)		
	Operator with contracted farmers	150	€95–€377 ($133–$527.8)		
	Processor at small scale	100	€250 ($350)		
	Processor at factory level	150	€250 ($350)		
	Big farms	150	€250 ($350)		

Certification fees	Category	Domestic and regional market in US$ or equivalent (TANCERT)	International market in USD or equivalent (IMO)	Description (TANCERT)	Description (IMO)
	Small individual farms	50	€160–€830 ($224–$1162)	Per working day	Certification fee (lump sum payment) according to standard, to be paid for each standard certified against.
	Society/Association/Farm group	80	€160–€830 ($224–$1162)		
	Operator with contracted farmers	100	€160–€830 ($224–$1162)		
	Processor at small scale	60	€160–€830 ($224–$1162)		
	Processor at factory level	100	€160–€830 ($224–$1162)		
	Big farms	100	€160–€830 ($224–$1162)		

Notes: Other fees: the operator must meet transport and accommodation costs for the inspector as well as overhead costs during inspection like photocopying and printing. These will be worked out and agreed with TANCERT before an inspector is assigned to the inspection work. For IMO, travel costs and accommodation during inspection have to be reimbursed based on actual expenditure.
* IMO inspection and certification fees in Africa.

Source: TANCERT, 2008; IMO, 2008, personal communications.

specialization by some accredited facilities in other commodities and partly because exporters of spices (and many other products) avoid using these facilities due to inefficiency.

At the same time, there seems to be a lack of a coordinated national approach to capacity for food testing generally. This is reflected in the overlapping mandates of, and replication of efforts in equipment acquisition and test accreditation by, laboratories under different ministries' ownership. Many stakeholders attribute this to the absence of a food safety policy in the country. This results in underutilization of sophisticated and often very expensive equipment.

Some critical equipment is not yet working, out of order or not accredited for use. This is partly an indication of inadequate technical capacity to operate the equipment. Levels of professionally qualified staff for current food safety testing is generally not the main constraint, but specialized training to carry out specific tests, operation and maintenance of equipment is still needed. A major problem would appear to be dispersal of capacity between laboratories. Capacity would almost certainly be a more serious problem if a majority of institutions systematically implemented surveillance programmes.

Finally, for organics, IMO has a *de facto* monopoly in Tanzania although TANCERT may be an alternative in the future.

Concluding remarks

Despite the existence of multi-functional testing facilities in Tanzania, local exporters of spices to the EU are not among the users of these facilities. Tests and certification are invariably carried out abroad or by foreign actors, usually through the assistance of exporters' sister or partner companies (Akyoo and Lazaro, 2007). This can be explained, firstly, by delays in local service delivery due to inefficiencies in, for example, the procurement of necessary laboratory reference materials for various tests, or to laboratory equipment being unusable.[7] Secondly, it relates to the existence of testing facilities abroad which are more efficient and convenient to importers (exporters are not made to pay for tests directly upfront and in some cases appear to pay only for dispatch of samples). Whether or not testing facilities abroad are also cheaper could not be determined since efforts to obtain data on relative costs of testing in Europe and Tanzania proved unsuccessful. Thirdly, it relates to the fact that all surveyed laboratories are struggling to acquire comprehensive SANAS accreditation. Since accreditation is given on a test by test basis, the recent achievements in this area have not so far created significant benefits for the spices sub-sector. For instance, while the NFQCL laboratory is the only facility in the country that has acquired accreditation for *Salmonella* testing due to the importance of the hazard for the Nile Perch industry, the laboratory is not only far removed from spice production and marketing sites, but is also – at least for the time being – specifically reserved for the Nile Perch sub-sector. Moreover, there is no laboratory in the country which is accredited to test for aflatoxins, pesticide residues, heavy metals or artificial chemical dyes. Finally, in the case of organic certification, TANCERT goals to be accredited and recognized as an international organic certification agency are far from being achieved. It is one thing to be IOAS accredited and quite another to gain international recognition.

According to Tanzania's National Trade Policy (2003), the general approach in export promotion is to align local standards with those of the major importers. Local capacity for conformity assessment of exports is important for Tanzania, both in relation to the potential reduction in turn-round time and the possibility for more detailed informal technical interaction between actors. At the moment however, even conformity assessment of imports is patchy. One major challenge is better coordination between, and greater efficiency of, Tanzanian institutions. A second challenge is completing the necessary investments and gaining international accreditation by governments.

Theoretically, meeting local standards will prepare operators for participation in international markets. However, the documented local standards are not enforced, either in the domestic market or in regional markets within Africa and low value markets in Asia. It is only if an exporter wishes to export to the EU that he or she has to meet either local or international standards. In a context where exports to high value markets like the EU are still quite low (see Akyoo and Lazaro, 2007), both enhanced conformity and improved conformity assessment for spices are distant prospects (except in the case of organic certification). The small number of exporters and volume of exports, the current modus operandi in production and marketing, agencies' lack of experience with systematic surveillance programmes and the demanding nature of export conformity assessment techniques and accreditation requirements are not positive ingredients for further investment in domestic conformity assessment, whether it is dedicated to spices or indeed if it is for agro-food exports in general. However, if all potential export industries that require such safety assessment are factored in, such an endeavour could become at least economic.

Incomes in the developing Asian countries are increasing. These are the countries that form the major market for conventional spices from Tanzania. Since demand for food safety is a function of income levels, it is likely that these countries also will demand higher levels of food safety in the near future. In this sense, safety-related investments in Tanzania have a long-term justification.

Organic certification is currently the most demanding type of food safety-related conformity that the Tanzanian spice industry engages with. Lack of international accreditation of the local certification body is making compliance costs exorbitant. Again since TANCERT will certify for all export crops and the organic market is growing worldwide, there is a case for public support for its achievement not only of international accreditation but also subsequent efforts to secure practical recognition.

Formulation of a National Food Safety Policy that defines the role of the private and public sectors as well as each individual institution will go a long way towards harnessing the currently scattered efforts for building a stronger national conformity assessment capacity in Tanzania. Unified ownership of all public testing laboratories would as a first step enhance a common approach to building capacity. A second stage of such changes could be encouragement of private participation in testing laboratories.

Notes

1. Accreditation involves a multi-stage process that include: documentation → application → documents review→ feedback → pre-assessment → initial assessment → recommendation → accreditation. In this regard, TBS's metrology (scientific measurement) and microbiology laboratories are currently SANAS accredited (although not for *Salmonella*). SANAS (South Africa National Accreditation Service) is a member of both the International Laboratory Accreditation Cooperation and the International Accreditation Forum and it is recognized by the EU. TBS's food and chemistry laboratory is at the pre-assessment stage; and TIRDO's microbiology and chemistry lab is at the pre-assessment stage. DANIDA is financing the ongoing accreditation applications for all five laboratories.
2. Following procurement of HPLC and GCMS, TFDA laboratory staff were trained in Germany for three months to enhance their ability to operate the equipment.
3. Government Chemists in Tanzania and Uganda are applying for SANAS accreditation, whilst that in Kenya has opted for accreditation by UKAS (United Kingdom Accreditation Service).
4. Normally the total cost of completing an accreditation exercise, for any test, amounts to about US$9000. However, any applicant has to be cautious when applying because non-compliance at any single stage will render the whole exercise null and void and thus requiring a fresh start after the anomaly or anomalies are corrected. A fresh start attracts the same costs as initially, so many laboratories prefer to go through the pre-assessment stage before actual initial assessment to avoid such possible losses.
5. Besides IMO, TANCERT has cooperation agreements with other organic certifying agencies that are operating in Tanzania. These include CERES (Germany) and Bioinspecta (Switzerland). However, IMO is the major player in the spices sub-sector. Other agencies that are operating in Tanzania but are yet to enter into cooperation agreement with TANCERT include Ecocert (France/Germany) and SKAL (Netherlands).
6. This will not automatically qualify it for recognition by the EU as an authorized certification body however. Under EU regulation 834/07 this is subject to a further assessment by the EU Commission.
7. Major breakdowns are frequent due to erratic power and water supply. Exorbitant repair and maintenance costs for laboratory equipments are also significant challenges. Manufacturers and suppliers do not disclose all technical details in regard

to laboratory equipment supplied. This necessitates that laboratories obtain technicians from source to fix and repair. The exercise has so far proved very expensive and unsustainable. Donor funded equipment is more prone to this problem as each financier normally has its own preferred suppliers, a situation which leads to a large number of diverse suppliers and manufacturers per laboratory.

4
An Analysis of Organic Contract Farming Schemes in East Africa

Peter Gibbon, Adam Akyoo, Simon Bolwig, Sam Jones, Yumiao Lin and Louise Lund Rants

Introduction

As noted in a number of chapters in this volume, recent years have seen a substantial increase in African smallholder production to 'sustainability' standards. This reflects the dynamic growth of Northern markets for products certified to these standards and, in turn, the premium prices that this generates. All of the production concerned appears to be organized through a contemporary variant of contract farming. Like earlier African variants, this is donor-supported. But contracting for sustainability attributes is generally by private corporations rather than by government or public–private agencies and contracts are 'market based', in the sense that they tend to focus mainly on price and quality requirements rather than input supply, production calendars and so on.

Against this background, the chapter asks whether there are measurable economic benefits for farmers who participate in one variant of such schemes, namely those for certified organic produce. Secondly it asks whether, assuming such benefits can be established, these derive from initial differences in factor endowments or from factors integral to scheme participation, such as price premiums and access to different technologies. Thirdly, assuming that outcomes will not be identical across organic contract farming schemes, it poses the question of what scheme framework conditions are associated with optimization of farmers' economic benefits.

The chapter reports and analyses results from seven surveys of six organic contract farming schemes in East Africa (one surveyed twice) conducted between 2005 and 2009 by participants in the SAFE research programme. It is organized in seven succeeding sections. These review the relevant issues in contract farming and organic farming (second and third sections), provide an overview of the schemes surveyed (fourth section), describe in more detail the research questions addressed and methods used (fifth section) and present results (sixth section) and a discussion of them (seventh section).

The final section concludes. An appendix provides more detail in relation to the analytic methods employed.

Contract farming in Africa

Glover (1983; 1987) defines contract farming as an arrangement where a processor or exporter (or an agent combining these functions) purchases the harvest of independent farmers, on terms arranged in advanced and described in a contract. Such contracts are usually annual and in relation to a single crop. Typically, they also specify a given volume (minimum or maximum) to be delivered, crop quality requirements and price. Often there is provision by the processor or exporter of inputs and services. There is always reference to the contracting agent's right to reject produce, although the grounds referred to may be more or less narrowly defined. Glover and others distinguish this type of arrangement from similar contractual ones where farmers are not independent, such as sharecropping.

Contract farming in developing countries appeared first in the 1950s, in two main forms. Firstly, particularly in Asia and Latin America (and parts of West Africa), it emerged in the wake of the dissolution of plantation production for crops such as palm oil, rubber and cocoa. This occurred against a background of political independence and falling terms of trade for the crops themselves, and usually involved distribution of plantation land to former workers (Baumann, 2000, 11). A second form dating from this period, evident throughout Africa, was large state-sponsored rural development projects focussing upon a single export crop, established on land cleared for the purpose with farmers resettled from areas deemed to be overcrowded. These schemes normally had some private participation, either on the basis of a management contract or direct investment. But public investment usually dominated. Schemes were established for cultivating tea, sugar, tobacco, cotton, groundnuts and – less frequently – fresh produce. After the liberalization of export crop agriculture in Sub-Saharan Africa in the mid-1990s a number collapsed, while others were taken over by private companies. Most of the literature on contract farming in Africa published before 1995 reflects the experience of these schemes.

Since market liberalization, new 'second generation' contract farming schemes have continued to be organized in the horticulture sector (see IFAD, 2003 on Kenya and Zambia; Minten et al., 2007 on Madagascar; Maertens et al., 2007 on Senegal). These differ from earlier similar schemes in that they involve private companies making arrangements with already established farmers. However, they are identical in certain other respects, for example the often very detailed controls exercised over smallholder production. From around 2000, on the other hand, a further distinct generation of contract farming has also emerged, for production of traditional export crops to international 'sustainability' standards. In East Africa today, schemes of this kind exist for coffee, tea and cocoa in relation to standards such as organic, UTZ CERTIFIED and Fairtrade.

Both 'second' and 'third' generation contract farming can be interpreted as providing solutions for processors or exporters to the problem of securing determinate crop volumes and qualities while confining associated production risks to the farmer. This contrasts to the earlier generation of public schemes which – while also confining production risk to farmers – were mostly aimed at securing continuous throughput for *in-situ* crop processing (cf. Binswanger and Rosenzweig, 1986).[1] In both its recent forms, contract farming also potentially reduces processors' or exporters' transaction costs in supplying inputs and technical services – by creating economies of scale in distribution and by allowing input credit to be recovered through deductions in price at the time of crop purchase. However, input supply, especially on credit, is much less common in the third generation schemes associated with traditional export crops and sustainability standards. This is a result both of the presence of a large potential supply base absent in the case of horticulture and of clear opportunities for farmers to side-sell inputs and outputs.[2] From the standpoint of the farmer therefore, this type of contract farming scheme can be mainly interpreted as providing secure access to markets and – where prices or premiums (or both) are stated in contracts – with a reduction in price risk.

Donors were heavily involved in the promotion of the first generation of contract farming schemes between the 1950s and the mid-1970s, but, with a few exceptions such as the Commonwealth Development Corporation, seemingly lost interest in these arrangements over the next two decades. Since around 1995, they have become active supporters again in Africa. This has been against the background of growing public recognition of deficiencies in the market liberalization paradigm, including input market failures and apparently low smallholder access to higher-value markets. Thus, donors have been attracted to contract farming because of its perceived capacity to solve problems of 'missing markets' – including restoring the link between smallholders and remunerative export markets. This is despite the fact that the first generation of these schemes were heavily criticized for excluding the poor, not least as a result of selection criteria deliberately aimed at screening out less educated farmers or farmers with fewer assets (cf. Buch-Hansen and Kieler, 1983; Kennedy and Cogill, 1987; Glover and Klusterer, 1990; Little, 1994).

Two recent ways in which contract farming inclusiveness has been pursued are integration of group marketing mechanisms (Coulter et al., 1999) and group certification and similar arrangements where schemes involve production to sustainability standards. A contemporary survey of contract farming in developing countries even goes as far as identifying a new 'Multipartite' model involving both intermediary agencies and group marketing

Table 4.1 First and third generation contract farming in Africa

	End market characteristics	Local market characteristics	Contracting company	Corporate strategy	Contract content
First generation	Bulk, thick	Monopsonistic; fully inter-locked	Large, publicly backed	Multi-stage control over farmers	Detailed, strong focus on pre-harvest
Third generation	Niche, thin	Semi-monopsonistic with some competition; sometimes inter-locked	Variable in size, donor-supported	Price incentives and strict QC	Limited coverage, focus on post-harvest

arrangements, in opposition to the supposedly classic 'Centralized model' (Eaton and Shepherd, 2001).

Arguably however, the presence of such mechanisms is not the most important difference between earlier models and recent 'third generation' ones as defined above. In contrasting 'first' and 'third' generation contract farming, differences in the nature of the end markets served, in local market conditions, in types of contracting companies and their corporate strategies and in the content of the contracts typically used are equally important. For these parameters, some stylized differences between the first and most recent generation of contract farming are presented in Table 4.1.

The difficulty in enforcing monopsony following liberalization in traditional export crop sectors, even under contract farming conditions, has been already referred to – as has its corollary of contracting companies' reluctance to supply inputs and services on credit. In addition, the markets that contracting companies in third generation schemes typically sell into are both specialized and subject to discontinuous patterns of demand. This has implications for their strategies in relation to farmers. Ideally, in order to minimize their risks of participating in these types of markets, companies need to achieve levels of product quality that command premiums in mainstream as well as specialized markets. Together with reluctance to undertake the investments necessary for detailed control of the production process (compounded by the small size of some contracting companies[3]) this leads to a concentration of interventions around the point of purchase – by enforcing quality control criteria and providing price incentives aimed at rewarding conformity to them. This is reflected in the typical content of contracts, which provide detail mostly in relation to what quality attributes attract premiums while – as regards production requirements – referring simply to whatever international standard is being followed.

It is not obvious how these unique features of third generation contract farming affect the selection issue. The fact that contracting companies in such schemes are little involved in input provision suggests that they will have less incentive to select only farmers with greater resources. Another relevant factor concerns costs of certification, where this utilizes 'internal control schemes' (ICSs). Where ICSs are used, large economies of scale can be attained in farmer certification. Nonetheless, a relation still exists between scale of contracting and costs of farmer registration, so that some incentives for selection remain.

The economics of organic farming

Organic farming's distinctive features are its emphases on building soil fertility and controlling weeds, diseases and pests through rotations and encouragement and application of naturally occurring materials and organisms. Reliance on non-local inputs is reduced to a minimum and use of synthetic inputs is generally forbidden. Meeting the requirements of organic certification, on the other hand, mainly involves elimination of synthetic inputs rather than following a list of prescribed techniques. This reflects the fact that organic standards emerged in countries with widespread and heavy use of synthetic inputs. Here, yields would typically collapse in the absence of use of synthetics unless rotations and alternative soil fertilization methods were adopted. Hence there was no need to require these in standards.

Against this background, economic studies of organic agriculture in Northern countries focus mainly on trade-offs from replacement of synthetic-based practices by more labour-intensive techniques. Generally the literature finds that losses from lower yields and higher labour requirements are offset by reduced input costs and price premiums (for overviews of recent findings see Dmitri and Green (2006) for the US and Nieberg and Offerman (2003) for the EU). However, premiums are rather unstable and, at least in Europe, the profitability of organic farming also depends upon public support for the process of conversion (cf. Padel and Lampkin, 1994).

Only a handful of studies comparing organic with conventional farming in the tropics have been published (Lyngbaek et al., 2001; Bray et al., 2002; Damiani, 2002; Bacon, 2005; Van der Vossen, 2005; Eyhorn, 2007). Except of the study by Eyhorn, none report comprehensive farm budget-related survey data and most are based on sample sizes of 20 or fewer. A further limitation is that most of the report results from Latin America, where the conventional farming systems with which comparisons are made are relatively high-input ones. No studies are available from Africa, where chemical use amongst smallholders is much lower than in other tropical regions and has stagnated for some years (Kelly et al., 2005). As a result of the prevalence of low-input systems, most African smallholders can conform to the requirements for organic certification without making significant changes to their farming methods – and thus without incurring new costs (or savings).

On the other hand, public support of farming in Africa, including of organic farming, is almost entirely absent. Thus, while organic certification should be technically easy to obtain, in practice this occurs only in the context of donor financial support. Typically this is in the context of a smallholder contract farming package that also involves farmer training and in which certification is on the basis of an ICS -an apparatus for farmer registration, designation of internal inspectors and reconciling farmer sales against their production capacity. Training may include dissemination of specifically organic farming techniques, but contracting companies often chose to place greater emphasis on generic crop and field maintenance and post-harvest processing techniques. Thus, in addition to the classic confounding variable confronting the economic evaluation of contract farming schemes (selection), evaluation of organic contract farming schemes needs to take into account a second source of potential bias. This is that the farming methods utilized in these schemes need not necessarily be significantly more 'organic' than those used by 'conventional' African smallholders.

The organic contract farming schemes surveyed

This study reports the results from seven household surveys of six organic contract farming schemes (OCFSs) in Uganda and Tanzania, carried out between 2005 and 2009 (Table 4.2). All the schemes received technical assistance (TA) and financial support from a Swedish development assistance programme Export Promotion of Organic Produce from Africa (EPOPA), which ran from 1997 to 2008. EPOPA supported a total of 31 OCFSs in East Africa in this period, mainly in the form of developing ICSs, training company staff and field officers, setting up demonstration plots and quality management systems, commissioning market surveys and supporting attendance at international trade shows. Certification was also financed but only during the period of organic conversion (normally one year from registration where there was no history of chemical use). Other support was normally provided for a 3-year period. The companies supported by EPOPA typically received around US$100,000 worth of TA and financial support, of which about US$20,000 was allotted to ICS development and certification, after the fees received by the implementation agency were deducted (Agro Eco BV and Grolink, 2008).

In all areas where the schemes surveyed were located, chemical use was low or non-existent. Hence, organic conversion entailed farmers having to make few practical changes to farming systems. On the other hand, use of specifically organic farming practices prior to conversion was also quite rare, except for pineapple farmers' use of coffee husks for mulching and upland coffee farmers' use of soil conservation methods. It should also be noted that, in the areas surveyed, the crops that were certified were typically free of major plant health problems.

Table 4.2 Organic contract farming schemes surveyed, 2005–09

Crop(s)	Additional standards	Contracting company	Location	Date scheme started	Date of survey	N contracted farmers at survey date	Sample size, scheme members	Sample size, control group
Arabica coffee	–	Kawacom (U) Ltd	Mt Elgon, Uganda	2001	2006	3,870	112	48
Arabica coffee	Fairtrade	Gumutindo Cooperative	Mt Elgon, Uganda	2001	2006	2,134	102	50
Cocoa, vanilla	–	Esco (U) Ltd	Bundibugyo, Uganda	2001	2005	1,721	30	30
Cocoa, vanilla	–	Esco (U) Ltd	Bundibugyo, Uganda	2001	2009	6,950	90	82
Pineapple	–	Biofresh (U) Ltd	Luwero and Kayunga, Uganda	2004	2006	34	32	32
Black pepper	–	Tazop Ltd	Muheza, Tanzania	1999	2006	152	61	71
Chilli	–	Zangerm Ltd	Zanzibar, Tanzania	1995	2007	150	61	59

The OCFSs surveyed will now be briefly compared in relation to some of the characteristics of contemporary contract farming in Africa referred to earlier, that is with reference to the nature of local output markets, contracting firms and their strategies, and contract content and implementation. While all the schemes studied broadly share the stylized characteristics depicted for contemporary contract farming schemes in Table 4.1, some important differences in respect of these parameters were also evident.

Local output markets

Local output markets for crops produced in the schemes were generally dynamic. During periods of peak demand, between four and eight conventional buyers competed in each of the Kawacom, Gumutindo Cooperative, Esco (2005) and Biofresh scheme areas. Competition was partly on price but also in relation to product specification. Rival buyers were typically prepared to buy produce in a semi- or unprocessed state, or to offer farmers other incentives such as buying crop in the field and then harvesting it themselves.

In the Esco (2009) scheme area, there was not only competition from two or three conventional buyers but from another large international trading company that had registered over 3000 farmers in a geographically overlapping cocoa OCFS. Esco responded to this both by raising its prices and by buying cocoa throughout the year rather than only during traditional harvesting seasons when competition peaked.

The situation in respect of the two Tanzanian spice schemes was quite different. Although other traders were present in both areas, these did not appear to command significant resources and neither Zangerm nor Tazop faced serious local competition.

The contracting companies and their strategies

The contracting companies fell into three categories. Kawacom and Esco were Ugandan affiliates of multinational trading companies whose main businesses were in the conventional market and which had the resources to run large schemes in a professional way. Gumutindo Cooperative, though small relative to most Secondary Cooperative societies in East Africa historically, had a long-standing link to the largest UK Fairtrade organization, Twin Trading. Twin Trading provided 60 per cent of Gumutindo's annual crop finance requirements (enabling it to obtain the remainder on favourable terms) and in addition financed a cupping laboratory and training of a cupper. Gumutindo was also unusual in that its crop purchase and export marketing functions were hived off into a financially autonomous agency. The third category of company was made up by Biofresh, Tazop and Zangerm. All three were partnerships between local businesspeople and small-scale specialized organic distributors based in Germany or Switzerland. Their annual turnover was in a range between US$100,000 and US$150,000 only. In each case working capital was provided by the distributor.

Table 4.3 Descriptive statistics (means)

Row	Indicator	Unit	KAWACOM O	KAWACOM C	GUMUTIN O	GUMUTIN C	ESCO 2005 O	ESCO 2005 C	ESCO 2009 O	ESCO 2009 C	BIOFRESH O	BIOFRESH C	TAZOP O	TAZOP C	ZANGERM O	ZANGERM C
1	Age, h/h head	years	46.3	47.1	44.1	46.5	48.9	40.1†	48.6	38.1§	40.8	37.0†	55.9	52.1	45.1	44.2
2	h/h size	count	7.2	6.2†	6.5	6.4	10.0	7.5	8.0	7.9	8.9	7.3	6.3	5.0‡	8.0	6.5‡
3	h/h labour §	count	6.0	5.0§	4.9	4.8	7.1	5.5†	6.1	5.6	6.4	5.0	2.0	1.9	3.6	2.9
4	Whole farm size	hectare	1.1	1.0‡	5.3	4.7	2.4	2.1	2.5	2.5	3.6	3.2	2.8	1.8‡	0.9	0.7†
5	Prod trees/Plants	,000	0.65	0.31‡	0.52	0.44	1.25	1.20	1.35	1.33	29.64	28.47‡	0.71	0.38§	1.56	1.41
6	No organic practices	%	20.5	39.6†	15.0	42.0‡	30.0	86.7‡	56.0	61.0	16.0	18.0	96.7	100.0	100.0	98.3	NT
7	2 or more organic pracs	group	33.9	12.5‡	44.0	8.0‡	10.0	0.0‡	12.0	13.0	34.0	0.0‡	1.7	0.0	NT	0.0	0.0	NT
8	Total h/h revenue	,000 U/Tshs	1425	1236	1745	1499			2625	1117§	4152	3268†				
9	Total crop revenue	,000 U/Tshs	680	374†	1072	866	1438	961	2560	1032‡	3835	2653			525	564
10	Total cert. crop(s) rev	,000 U/Tshs	566	177‡	836	497†	1320	930					328	203	NT		

Table 4.3 (Continued)

Row	Indicator	Unit	KAWACOM O	KAWACOM C	GUMUTIN O	GUMUTIN C	ESCO 2005 O	ESCO 2005 C	ESCO 2009 O	ESCO 2009 C	BIOFRESH O	BIOFRESH C	TAZOP O	TAZOP C	ZANGERM O	ZANGERM C
11	Net cert crop(s) rev	,000 U/Tshs	519	155‡	712	400†	1149	582†	2427	882§	3527	1456*	246	113 NT	436	492 NT
12	Labour costs	,000 U/Tshs	33	18†	121	95*	132	288	135	139	154	458†	43	48	42	14†
13	Equipment costs	,000 U/Tshs	14	7‡	14	10	21	34	50	38‡	142	715†	18	20	17	28‡
14	Marketing costs	,000 U/Tshs	1	0‡	3	2*	18	26	16	12†	12	25	5	4	0	0
15	Yield per hectare	kg	836	630†	1681	1197	208	151					365	344	598	763*
16	Yield per tree	kg			0.8	0.7			0.7	0.5§						

Key: O: organic farmers, C: control group ($* = P < 0.10$; $† = P < 0.05$; $‡ = P < 0.01$, $§ = P < 0.001$). NT: significance not tested. All tests of significance used Chi square except for Tazop and Zangerm schemes (t-tests).

Notes: Row 3. Data for all schemes except Tazop and Zangerm refers to N household members 18–50. Rows 6–7. For list of organic practices see text. Rows 8–14. Results given in ,000 Ush for Kawacom, Gumutindo, Esco and Biofresh schemes and in ,000 Tsh for Tazop and Zangerm schemes. Data for Tazop and Zangerm schemes refers to N household members 6 years and over.

Exchange rates: 2005 Ush 1000 = $0.56; 2006 Ush 1000 = $0.55; Tsh 1000 = $0.82; 2007 Tsh 1000 = $0.83; 2008 Ush 1000 = $0.59.

Apart from Gumutindo, all of the schemes were bought direct from farmers rather than through Primary Cooperative Societies or other intermediaries. Otherwise, different types of contracting company tended to follow distinct scheme management strategies. Kawacom in 2006 and Esco in 2009 were buying the entire organic crop available, while using trained field staff to provide extension programmes aimed mainly at yield enhancement and improved on-farm processing. Their goal was to achieve crop quality attributes that were marketable at a premium in conventional markets when organic markets were in surplus. In 2005, however, Esco had been mainly buying organic crop against specific orders and was employing fewer field staff pro rata, although it still aimed at securing superior crop quality attributes. At this time it sought to cover its overheads by adding certification of farmers' vanilla crop to that of cocoa, while also buying vanilla only against orders.[4] In essence, the Biofresh, Tazop and Zangerm schemes operated in this way too, although none certified a second crop as Esco did. These companies tended to purchase only part of scheme participants' production on an unpredictable basis, reflecting variable export orders.

Gumutindo Cooperative's strategy differed from both these models. While it also only bought organic crop against orders, its integration into Fairtrade networks meant that orders were received at the start of each season and that their fulfilment could therefore be allocated on a pro-rata basis between the Cooperative's five Primary Societies. So, while only about 45 per cent of scheme members' crop could be sold as organic in the survey year, there was still an element of predictability for farmers concerning how much could be sold and when.

Contract content and implementation

There was a high degree of similarity between schemes in the contracts applied. Contracting companies agreed to buy all qualifying crop, 'subject to quality'. In most cases quality criteria referred not only to conformity to organic production rules, but also to other provisions. For Kawacom and Gumutindo the latter comprised supply of coffee in 'parchment' form, that is, wet processed, fermented and sun dried. In addition, Gumutindo scheme members' coffee had to have a moisture content below 13 per cent and be free of foreign matter and black pods. Esco required in 2005 that cocoa be fully fermented, sun dried and free of mould. By 2009, 'fully fermented and sun dried' was re-stated as a requirement to have a moisture content below 8 per cent. In 2005, Esco had not required any special quality attributes for its vanilla, only to find that it had to write off a large part of the purchased crop due to low vanillin content. In 2009, therefore, it accepted only crop that was fully ripe. Biofresh's criteria included that pineapple weigh between 1.2 and 1.6 kg 'crown on', be cut with a knife leaving a stalk between 25–40 cm and be packed into cardboard cartons. The referred to pineapple weight requirement had a different status from all other criteria stated here, since its attainment faced natural constraints. The average weight of the 'Sweet Cayenne' variety grown was more than 2 kg, even where farmers modified their crop spacing systems to eliminate very large fruit. As a result, only around a third of the pineapple grown by scheme members could potentially qualify for a premium. The two exceptions to requiring 'premium' quality attributes in addition to organic ones were Tazop, which required only that black pepper be delivered fresh, that is, unprocessed, and Zangerm. Like all conventional chilli buyers, Zangerm required that chilli be delivered after drying, but it did not provide a detailed specification.

Contracting companies all agreed to pay a premium for qualifying crop, although its magnitude was not stated in any contract. They also agreed to finance farmers' organic certification and provide them with unspecified technical assistance. In no case was there a written obligation to supply inputs, although most companies did so to a limited extent in schemes' first years. For their part, farmers were required to follow organic rules and in some cases other 'good agricultural practices'. In no case was there an obligation to sell all qualifying crop to the contracting company.

As indicated, only Kawacom and (in 2009) Esco bought all qualifying crop at the time of the surveys. The Esco cocoa and Biofresh pineapple premiums in 2005–06 were 30 per cent over the conventional prices for the same product specifications. The Esco vanilla premium at this time was 100 per cent. The coffee premiums offered by Kawacom and Gumutindo were around 15 per cent. Neither Tazop nor Zangerm offered a premium at all. By 2009, the Esco cocoa premium had fallen to around 15 per cent, although farmers who joined a company-sponsored savings society received one of 17.5 per cent. The Esco vanilla premium remained around 100 per cent.

While contracting companies observed commitments to supply TA to farmers rather unevenly, none could be said to provide it intensively. Either field staff imparted information through internal inspections, where all farmers were visited on their plots once or twice yearly, or they 'cascaded' information via 'contact farmers' who were responsible for relaying information to 50–100 scheme members through group training as well as conducting internal inspections. Outside of the schemes, on the other hand, there was virtually no provision of extension services.

Finally, considerable differences were evident between schemes in regard to enforcement of requirements on farmers. Roughly a quarter of original scheme members had been 'sanctioned' (de-registered) by 2006 in the case of Tazop and by 2009 in the case of Esco. Reasons for de-registration were not available for the Tazop scheme, but in the Esco scheme the commonest reason was non-sale to the scheme – despite this not having the formal status of a contractual requirement.

Research questions and methods

Research questions

On the basis of the considerations identified in the second and third sections above, three main research questions are investigated. Firstly, the extent to which positive selection into organic schemes has occurred is examined. 'Positive selection' is used here to denote a skewed outcome in the distribution of factor endowments between households participating in OCFSs and control groups, rather than the conscious use by a contracting company of one or more specific selection criteria.[5] A second question concerns the diffusion of organic farming practices amongst scheme members and control groups. To what extent are scheme members more likely to follow organic farming practices than control groups and what other factors (if any) are associated with their adoption? A third question concerns whether there are revenue effects of participation in OCFSs and, if so, from where these effects arise. In particular, what is the respective contribution of participation in contract farming as such, and of use of organic farming methods? Further, if there are revenue effects from contract farming regardless of adoption of organic farming methods, from what do these arise?

As noted, the issue of farmer selection already featured as a policy question in the first generation of literature on contract farming. Quite aside from this, there are methodological grounds for examining it, since in order to determine whether participation in contract farming has genuine revenue effects it is necessary to control for whatever selection bias into schemes can be established. The same goes for determining whether use of organic farming methods has any revenue effects, since unless biases influencing their uptake are controlled for it will not be possible to isolate their impact.

The issue of the revenue effects of contract farming is surprisingly less central in the existing literature (and policy discussion) than that of selection. Only four studies (Warning and Key, 2002; Simmons et al., 2005; Benfica et al., 2006; Maertens and Swinnen, 2006) deal with this question while controlling for selection of scheme participants – with findings pointing in no consistent direction. On the other hand, revenue issues were widely discussed, albeit mostly using before-and-after recall data and at best on the basis of descriptive statistics, in the pre-1995 literature (Buch-Hansen and Kieler, 1983; Glover, 1983, 1987; Kennedy and Cogill, 1987; Sithole and Boeren, 1989; Little 1992, 1994). A recurrent but often downplayed finding in this literature was of positive revenue effects from scheme participation. This finding was then qualified by the argument that such benefits tended to decline over time – a thesis termed 'agribusiness normalization' by Glover and Ghee (1992). The evidence for 'agribusiness normalization' tended to be sketchy. Comparison of the data from the two Esco surveys will be relevant to the assessment of this thesis.

Diffusion of explicit organic farming methods can be considered as a question of technological diffusion. Strangely, diffusion of farming technologies through contract farming also occupies a minor role in both the contemporary and earlier literature. Only one study, by Goveneh and Jayne (2003), examines the impact of technological diffusion through contract farming while controlling for selection into schemes. This study examines the relationship between commercialization of cotton production under contract farming conditions in Zimbabwe and output and productivity of scheme members' food crop production. Contrary to claims in the earlier literature that contract farming for cash crops poses dangers for food security, the authors show a positive impact of technologies used in cash crop commercialization, at least on food crop productivity. However, the study assumes the adoption of specific technologies as the mechanism by which this process occurs, rather than directly measuring either the extent of uptake or the consequences of using them. In that adoption of organic farming methods is measured directly, the results reported here make a new contribution to the literature.

While it should be underlined that no attempt is made to consider the totality of technology diffusion occurring within OCFSs, adoption of one other farm technology will also be considered in relation to the coffee and cocoa schemes surveyed. This is recommended post-harvest processing techniques. The price premium offered in these schemes could only be obtained for crop that had been subjected to these techniques. However, this implies that revenue attained and adoption of these techniques are endogenous, and that the latter cannot therefore be considered as an independent variable in the same way as use of organic farming practices. Use of such processing technologies will thus be considered in relation to the interpretation of the results on revenue rather than as an independent variable.

Survey methods

The surveys referred to in the fourth section collected data on household demographics and factor endowments (including farm area, area under the certified crop and tree or plant stock), farm expenditure, farm revenue and use of organic farm practices. In each case, except the Biofresh Pineapple scheme, they were based on two-stage random samples for both scheme participants and control groups. Scheme participants were randomly sampled in a number of villages or parishes chosen purposively to reflect the range of agro-ecological conditions in scheme areas. Sampling of scheme participants used lists provided by the contracting company. Sampling of control groups was performed randomly, from lists prepared by village leaders in villages or parishes nearby schemes, chosen to match the (range of) agro-ecological conditions represented in the sampling frame for scheme participants. In the case of the very small Biofresh pineapple scheme all members were surveyed except two who had been sanctioned. The pineapple control group was sampled randomly from lists prepared by local leaders in two separate locations chosen to match the agro-ecological conditions represented in the sampling frame for scheme participants.

Variables and indicators

Farm revenue was considered in terms of net revenue from the crop(s) subject to certification in the respective OCFS. This operationalization was chosen in preference to total household revenue, gross household farm revenue or net household farm revenue since it was considered to be most sensitive to the changes likely to be induced by participation in OCFSs. On the other hand, it does not allow the capture of possible spill-over effects of participation on production of non-certified crops and it is less relevant to evaluation of more general household welfare benefits than say, use of a total household revenue measure. These issues are not, however, the main focus of this chapter.

Net revenue was defined as revenue from the crops concerned, less expenditure entailed by their production, processing and marketing. This was in turn defined as expenditure on purchase and transport of planting materials; purchase and transport of soil fertilization, mulching or plant health treatment materials; hire of farm labour, either in cash or in kind (including for crop processing); purchase or hire of farm equipment; and marketing costs. Revenue was operationalized in terms of value of crop sales and value of sales of planting material. Investment in and income from sale of land was not included in these calculations as such investments are normally financed from savings over long periods. Neither was expenditure of household labour measured, due to the greater difficulties of recall implied, as well as those associated with attributing accurate time values to tasks such as supervision and with devising a metric covering both adult and child labour.

Organic practices were operationalized in terms of a range of specific farm interventions recommended to members of OCFSs during inspections and training. In the subsequent analysis, non-use of synthetic inputs was treated as a condition qualifying such interventions to be recorded rather than an organic practice in itself. Lists of qualifying positive interventions varied slightly from scheme to scheme but all included use of organic fertilization methods, mulching, plant health treatment methods and soil conservation methods. Adoption of post-harvest processing methods was operationalized in terms of the proportion of sales of the certified crop qualifying for the premium attached to use of the processing method concerned.

Data analysis

A first stage of analysis using descriptive statistics will be presented in relation to each research question. For all schemes, except Tazop and Zangerm, a second stage of data analysis using econometric methods is also presented. Two null hypotheses (of no significant effects) will be tested with farmer revenue as the dependent variable and participation in OCFSs and use of organic farming practices as explanatory variables. In this process, regressions for participation (in the scheme and in organic practices) are undertaken, followed by regressions for the outcome variables under consideration. In the latter, potential sources of selection bias are taken into consideration. Further details of the empirical strategy are outlined in Appendix I.

Results

Selection into schemes

Survey results on selection into schemes are presented here in two stages. Firstly, descriptive statistics are reported on the factor endowments of scheme participants, relative to control groups. Farmers' age, and by implication experience, and size of household (and particularly count of household members of working age, that is, over 6 years) are technically demographic characteristics but also have the status of factor endowments. Only statistics collected in common across all schemes are reported. Secondly, Probit regressions are reported for the schemes where these have been carried out.

Three conclusions can be drawn from an examination of the descriptive statistics relevant to selection (Table 4.3, rows 1–5). Firstly, on all five indicators where comparisons are made, there are significant differences in favour of organic farmers in two or more of the six schemes. Secondly, there are no significant differences in factor endowments in favour of conventional farmers on any indicator in any scheme. Thirdly, while there are significant differences in favour of scheme members on at least two factors in four of the schemes, there is one scheme where no selection bias at all is evident (Gumutindo). Overall this suggests that selection according to factor endowment advantages is common but not invariable.

In the binomial Probit regressions used to model participation in the Kawacom, Gumutindo, Esco (both 2005 and 2009 surveys) and Biofresh schemes, several factor endowment variables additional to those referred to in Table 4.3 are included. The results are presented in Table 4.4, with exact descriptions of the indicators provided in notes to the table. The results support the earlier conclusion of common but not invariable positive selection (indicated by a statistically significant 'Constant' variable). There is evidence of a substantial and significant impact on selection from farm altitude, tree stock and construction materials in the Kawacom scheme, indicated by a statistically significant Beta. In the Esco scheme, stock of vanilla vines is similarly important in both surveys, as is (more modestly) farmer age. Certain other variables (notably extent of off-farm economic diversification)

Table 4.4 Profit models for scheme participation

Independent variable	KAWACOM		GUMUTINDO		ESCO (2005)		ESCO (2009)		BIOFRESH	
	Beta	Standard error	Beta	Standard error	Beta	Standard error	Beta	Standard error	Beta	Standard error
Farm size	0.06	0.19							−0.01	0.07
Farm size (log)	0.39†	0.16	0.15	0.19	0.39	0.44	−0.34	0.34	0.00	0.00
Trees/plants (N)			0.02	0.14	0.00	0.00	0.03	0.02†		
Trees/plants (log)										
Trees/plants (sq rt)					−0.08	0.06				
Van. vines (sq rt)					0.05†	0.03	0.24	0.04		
P/apples planted									0.00†	0.00
Farm altitude	5.79†	1.73	0.70	1.78			−0.01†	0.00		
Farm geog									−0.28	0.47
F-headed h/hs									−0.22	0.56
Farmer age	−0.02*	0.01	−0.02	0.01	0.05†	0.02	0.03	0.01	0.00	0.02
Farmer education	0.00	0.04	0.03	0.04			−0.00	0.36		
H/h size	0.07	0.06	−0.04	0.04						
H/h labour count					0.29†	0.10	0.01	0.06	0.04	0.08
Dependency ratio					1.67	1.50	−0.99	0.76		
Ratio off-farm rev	−0.63†	0.27	0.07	0.27						
% off-farm wkrs					0.19†	0.07				
H/hs w/out off-fm					3.91†	1.32				
Building material	0.47*	0.26	−0.42*	0.25					0.81*	0.46
Exp. school fees							−0.09	0.07		
N cattle owned							−0.04	0.03		
N goats									0.00	0.00
N chickens									0.12	0.08

Table 4.4 (Continued)

Independent variable	KAWACOM		GUMUTINDO		ESCO (2005)		ESCO (2009)		BIOFRESH	
	Beta	Standard error	Beta	Standard error	Beta	Standard error	Beta	Standard error	Beta	Standard error
Meat/fish cons pc					−0.55	0.46	0.42	0.43	−0.03†	0.01
Savings soc/bank							0.57*	0.30		
Major assets										
Constant	12.42‡	3.53	−2.48	3.95	−6.62‡	1.93	2.23	1.89		
Intercept									0.02	0.93
N	147		149		56		171		54	
Log-likelihood	−66.7		−91.11		−25.2		56.36		−26.9	
Pseudo R sq	0.23		0.03		0.35		0.52		0.46	
Chi-sq	40.7‡		6.52		31.0§		124.03§		see notes	

* = P < 0.1, † = P < 0.05; ‡ = P < 0.01, § = P < 0.001. Robust (Huber/White/Sandwich) standard errors given. Samples exclude missing observations and outliers, defined as households with net revenue from main crop +/− 5 standard deviations from the sample mean. Calculations using Stata 8 except for Biofresh (SAS 9.1). Because of the use of SAS for the Biofresh analysis, it has not been possible to calculate a chi sq for this scheme.

Explanation of variables. Pineapples planted: N pineapples planted in 2005; Farm geog (pineapple only): whether farm was situated in Luwero or Kayunga district; H/h labour count: N household members aged > 6 years; Dependency ratio: N persons in household aged < 6 years; Ratio off-farm rev: ratio of non-farm revenue to total household revenue; % off-farm workers: off-farm workers as % of household adults; H/hs w/out off-fm: households without off-farm income sources or without persons employed off-farm; building material: whether farmhouse has brick walls; exp. school fees: household expenditure on school fees in 2005; meat/fish cons pc: meat and fish consumption per capita; savings soc/bank: household head is a member of a savings society or bank; Major assets: households own farm in another village, house in town; television/DVD player or generator.

contribute to selection in more than one scheme, but not in a consistent direction.

Use of organic farming practices

In a majority of OCFSs, scheme members followed significantly more organic farming practices than control groups (Table 4.3, rows 6–7), but in all these cases use of organic practices by scheme participants was moderate to low. In the cases where there was no significant difference between participants and the control group, use of organic farming practices was low or negligible for both groups. Although the samples used were different in each case, the two Esco surveys do not suggest increased adoption by scheme members over time. Thus, diffusion of organic farming technologies was generally weak.

In the Poisson regressions used to model the number of organic farming practices used in the Kawacom, Gumutindo, Esco (both 2005 and 2009 samples) and Biofresh schemes, scheme participation is shown to influence adoption in three cases (Table 4.5). However, neither in the Esco scheme, in 2009, nor in the Biofresh scheme is this the case. In the Biofresh scheme no variables appear to influence adoption significantly, while in the Esco scheme in the 2009 survey the only significant relationship identified is with chicken ownership – possibly relating to supply of manure that this provides.

Revenue effects of scheme participation

Survey results on revenue outcomes of scheme participation are again discussed in two stages. First, descriptive statistics are reported from all the surveys conducted comparing different components of revenue between scheme participants and control groups. Secondly, regression results on different components of revenue are reported for all of the surveys except those of the Tazop and Zangerm schemes.

Table 4.3 (rows 8–14) provides descriptive statistics showing scheme participants receiving significantly higher mean net revenues from certified crops than control groups, for all the schemes surveyed except those operated by Tazop and Zangerm. In neither of these two latter schemes was a test of significance performed on the results obtained (see below); in the Zangerm scheme it may be noted that the control group had higher mean net revenues than scheme participants. Revenue effects across schemes at the level of gross crop revenue and gross household revenue are also broadly in favour of scheme participants, but with less consistent significance.

In two of the schemes, where net revenue for participants was significantly higher than for non-members (Esco [anno 2005] and Biofresh), it appears that lower expenditure on labour by scheme members contributed to this outcome. The most plausible explanation for control groups' higher expenditure on labour in these schemes relates to differences in age of household heads between participants and non-participants (see Table 4.3, row 1).

Table 4.5 Poisson models for organic farming practices

Independent variable	KAWACOM		GUMUTINDO		ESCO (2005)		ESCO (2009)		BIOFRESH	
	Beta	Standard error	Beta	Standard error	Beta	Standard error	Beta	Standard error	Beta	Standard error
Farm size	0.02	0.09							-0.01	0.07
Farm size (log)			0.18	0.97*	0.28	0.44	-0.11	0.30		
Trees/plants (N)	-0.08	0.08			-0.00	0.00	-0.00	0.01	0.00	0.00
Trees/plants (log)			-0.30	0.65						
Trees/plants (sq rt)					0.03	0.05				
Van. vines (sq rt)					0.02	0.02	0.20	0.02		
P/apples planted									0.00	0.00
Farm altitude	-0.10	0.68	-0.15	1.0			0.00	0.00		
Farm geog									-0.17	0.28
F-headed h/hs									0.05	0.34
Farmer age	0.01	0.00	-0.00	0.00	0.01	0.01	-0.00	0.01	-0.01	0.00
Farmer education	0.01	0.02	-0.03	0.02			-0.36	0.32		
H/h size	0.01	0.03	0.04	0.02*						
H/h labour count					0.05	0.07	0.02	0.04	0.03	0.05
Dependency ratio					2.36*	1.42	0.74	0.62		
Ratio off-farm rev	-0.16	0.15	-0.05	0.15						
% off-farm wkrs					0.00	0.06				
H/hs w/out off-fm					0.32	1.15			0.00	0.29
Building material	0.01	0.12	0.01	0.14						
Exp. school fees									0.00	0.00
N cattle owned									0.05	0.03

Table 4.5 (Continued)

Independent variable	KAWACOM		GUMUTINDO		ESCO (2005)		ESCO (2009)		BIOFRESH	
	Beta	Standard error	Beta	Standard error	Beta	Standard error	Beta	Standard error	Beta	Standard error
N goats							0.08	0.04		
N chickens							0.05†	0.02		
Meat/fish cons pc					0.21	0.55	0.30	0.21	0.00	0.01
Savings soc/bank							−0.12	0.22		
Major assets					1.78‡	0.59	0.04	0.38	0.30	0.30
Scheme participation	0.43†	0.19	0.74§	0.19						
Inspections	−0.02	0.07	0.06	0.33*						
Constant	0.44	1.42	−0.49	0.62	−4.43†	1.89	−3.29	0.98§	0.32	0.61
Intercept									54	
N	147		149		56		171			
Log-likelihood	−231.6		−231.47		−45.0		−158.50		−49.6	
Pseudo R sq	0.02		0.10		0.25		0.11		0.37	
Chi-sq	9.9		60.14§		34.8§		57.32§		see notes	

* = $P < 0.1$, † = $P < 0.05$, ‡ = $P < 0.01$, § = $P < 0.001$. Robust (Huber/White/Sandwich) standard errors given. Samples exclude missing observations and outliers, defined as households with net revenue from main crop +/− 5 standard deviations from the sample mean. Calculations using Stata 8 except for Biofresh (SAS 9.1). Because of the use of SAS for the Biofresh analysis, it has not been possible to calculate a chi sq for this scheme. *Explanations of variables*: see notes to Table 4.4.

These differences suggest the control groups were at an earlier stage of farm development than participants, where expenditure on land clearance, preparation, planting and (in the case of pineapple) spreading of coffee husks was being incurred. Thus, gross revenue from certified crops in these schemes is not significantly higher for participants than for non-members. The overall pattern is therefore one where scheme participants enjoy higher incomes than non-participants, though with some exceptions.

As indicated in the fifth section of the chapter, different approaches were adopted for determining the extent to which differences in revenue can be explained by scheme participation, or by (a combination of) other factors. In the case of the Tazop and Zangerm schemes, mean revenue outcomes were crudely controlled for scale of production by re-expressing them on a per hectare (under the certified crop) basis rather than in absolute terms. On this basis, net revenues of participants in the Tazop scheme are no longer higher than those of non-members. The mean net revenue of participants in the Zangerm scheme expressed on a per hectare basis is significantly *lower* than that of non-members.[6]

In relation to all other schemes, regression-based estimates using OLS and Heckman models (FIML or Two Step) are reported (Table 4.6). The results show, controlling for other variables, a positive relation between participation and net revenue from the crop(s) subject to certification that is significant and consistent across schemes. Only in the case of the Gumutindo scheme is a result found (in the FIML model only) which is not significant. However, in the case of this scheme there is no evidence of selection bias, so that the modest positive coefficient from the OLS can be considered meaningful.

With respect to organic practices, a significant positive relation to net certified crop revenue is found for more than one scheme or survey – namely, the Kawacom and Esco (anno 2005) schemes. However, the coefficient for this variable is rather low for the Kawacom scheme and, in regard to the Esco scheme, the relation is not found in the 2009 survey. Thus, looking across the results, it appears that it is scheme participation *per se* that is the main determinant of revenue from certified crops, conditional on other covariates. Use of organic farming techniques plays at best a modest role in some schemes.

Turning to the magnitude of the estimated revenue effects of scheme participation, that is, the treatment, these are hardly negligible. Taking the Kawacom, Esco (2005 survey) and Biofresh schemes, we find a 75 per cent increase in revenue for the Kawacom sample (scheme participants and non-participants combined), a 62 per cent increase for the Esco sample and a 46 per cent increase for the Biofresh sample. The average incremental treatment effect for use of organic practices was considerably lower in the Kawacom and Esco (2005 survey) schemes, at around 9 per cent and 30 per cent, respectively. In the Biofresh scheme there was no treatment

Table 4.6 Regression results for net revenue from certified crop(s)

Independent variable	KAWACOM OLS Beta (Std error)	KAWACOM FML Beta (Std error)	GUMUTINDO OLS Beta (Std error)	GUMUTINDO FML Beta (Std error)	ESCO (2005) OLS Beta (Std error)	ESCO (2005) Heckman Beta (Std error)	ESCO (2009) OLS Beta (Std error)	ESCO (2009) FML Beta (Std error)	BIOFRESH OLS Beta (Std error)	BIOFRESH Heckman Beta (Std error)
Farm size (log)	0.12 (0.09)	0.11 (0.09)	0.02 (0.10)	0.37 (0.11)	−0.06 (0.30)	−0.10 (0.31)	0.44§ (0.12)	0.45§ (0.12)	0.06 (0.05)	0.05 (0.05)
Trees/plants (log)	0.71‡ (0.08)	0.65‡ (0.08)	0.63§ (0.67)	0.63§ (0.77)			0.03§ (0.06)	0.02§ (0.01)	0.36* (0.17)	0.48‡ (0.14)
Trees/plants (sq root)					0.15‡ (0.04)	0.16‡ (0.04)				
Van. vines (sq rt)					−0.01 (0.01)	−0.01 (0.02)	0.01 (0.01)	0.00 (0.01)		
Farm altitude	−2.27‡ (0.70)	−3.02‡ (0.80)	−2.37‡ (0.84)	−2.31* (0.94)			−0.00 (0.00)	−0.00 (0.00)		
Farm geog									0.04 (0.20)	−0.01 (0.19)
Farmer age	0.00 (0.02)	0.00 (0.02)	0.01* (0.00)	0.01* (0.00)	−0.01 (0.01)	−0.02+ (0.01)	−0.01 (0.00)	−0.01 (0.00)	0.00 (0.01)	0.00 (0.01)
Farmer education	0.02 (0.02)	0.02 (0.02)	0.03 (0.02)	0.02 (0.02)			−0.31 (0.13)	−0.31* (0.12)		
H/h size	−0.02 (0.02)	−0.02 (0.02)	0.02 (0.02)	0.16 (0.02)			0.00 (0.01)	0.01 (0.01)		

Table 4.6 (Continued)

	KAWACOM		GUMUTINDO		ESCO (2005)		ESCO (2009)		BIOFRESH	
	OLS Beta (Std error)	FIML Beta (Std error)	OLS Beta (Std error)	FIML Beta (Std error)	OLS Beta (Std error)	Heckman Beta (Std error)	OLS Beta (Std error)	FIML Beta (Std error)	OLS Beta (Std error)	Heckman Beta (Std error)
H/h labour count					0.04 (0.04)	0.02 (0.05)			0.01 (0.03)	0.00 (0.03)
% off-farm wkrs					0.01 (0.02)	0.01 (0.01)				
H/hs w/out off-fm									−0.26 (0.21)	−0.36+ (0.20)
Organic practices (N)	0.09* (0.05)	0.09* (0.05)	0.04 (0.05)	0.04 (0.05)	0.28* (0.15)	0.26* (0.15)	0.07 (0.07)	0.07 (0.06)	0.18 (0.24)	0.21 (0.24)
Scheme participation	0.78‡ (0.16)	1.31‡ (0.27)	0.28* (0.14)	−0.05 (0.35)	0.67* (0.27)	1.12* (0.55)	1.09§ (0.14)	1.19§ (0.27)	0.49‡ (0.20)	0.94* (0.39)
Constant	10.85‡ (1.46)	12.30§ (1.69)	13.62§ (2.03)	13.49§ (2.10)	9.41‡ (0.74)	9.36‡ (0.75)	12.84§ (0.59)	12.33§ (0.59)		
Intercept									10.63‡ (1.66)	9.48‡ (1.37)
Lambda		−0.49* (0.19)		0.21 (0.21)		−0.31 (0.33)		−0.07 (0.16)		−0.33 (0.26)
N	147		149		56		168		52	
Log likelihood	−160.4	−225.4		−244.68				−220.91	−89.47	−123.72
F stat	24.66‡	205.8‡	29.72§	146.36§	13.2‡	11.3‡	31.28§	251.83§	32.83§	28.65§
R sq	0.61		0.52	–	0.66	0.66	0.62		0.48	0.56

Note: Lambda refers to Heckman's lambda (inverse Mills ratio) calculated from Heckman first stage selection regressions not reported here but available from authors. * = P < 0.1, † = P < 0.05; ‡ = P < 0.01, § = P < 0.001. Robust (Huber/White/Sandwich) standard errors given. Samples exclude missing observations and outliers, defined as households +/− 5 standard deviations from the mean of the dependent variable. For explanations of variables see note to Table 4.5. Calculations using STATA 8, except for Biofresh (SAS 9.1).

effect for use of organic practices. While undue stress should not be placed on the precision of these results (since in all three surveys referred to, the Heckman/FIML scheme participation coefficient is significant only at the 90 or 95 per cent level), their direction broadly confirms the regression findings.

Interpretation

Discussion in this section will focus on the results obtained in regard to the two (null) hypotheses considered, namely, that there is a generally strong relation, broadly consistent across schemes, between membership of OCFSs and net revenue from certified crops. On the other hand, there is only a modest relation between adoption of organic farming practices and net revenue, which is not consistent across schemes.

Differences in net revenue from certified crops, controlling for other factors, are likely to reflect a combination of differences in prices received and in productivity. The two schemes where the coefficients for scheme membership as a determinant of net revenue are highest (and their standard errors lowest) are the Kawacom scheme and the Esco scheme (2009 survey). Referring back to the fourth section, it is worth noting that while the premiums offered by these schemes at time of survey were lower than in some other cases, they were in both instances available for all crop produced by scheme members, provided it met a clear quality specification. This could not be said of any of the other schemes surveyed, including the Esco scheme in 2005. Continuous availability of premium according to clear criteria can be considered as effectively reducing the disincentives attached to conducting the extra activities necessary to meet 'organic-plus' quality specifications. These disincentives relate to shrinkage of the crop as a result of processing, additional investments of time and/or money, as well as deferral of receipt of revenue while processing is undertaken. By the same argument, where premiums are not offered continuously for the entire crop, or not offered at all, disincentives will be correspondingly greater and extra activities will be more limited. In addition to these disincentives, engaging in processing for coffee and cocoa entails a price risk unless organic premiums are guaranteed on a continuous basis. While price premiums are also available in the conventional market for quality crop, these tend to be lower than organic ones and subject to greater fluctuation. A comparison of farmer processing behaviour as revealed in the surveys of the Esco scheme in 2005 and 2009 supports this argument. In 2005, when the premium was not available continuously, scheme members sold 24.6 per cent of their cocoa by weight in an unprocessed state. In 2009, when it was, they sold only 1.6 per cent of their cocoa by weight in this form.[7]

This argument is further substantiated by a review of the cumulative distribution of the proportions of the coffee crop fully processed by Kawacom scheme members and the control group. Figure 4.1 shows that only

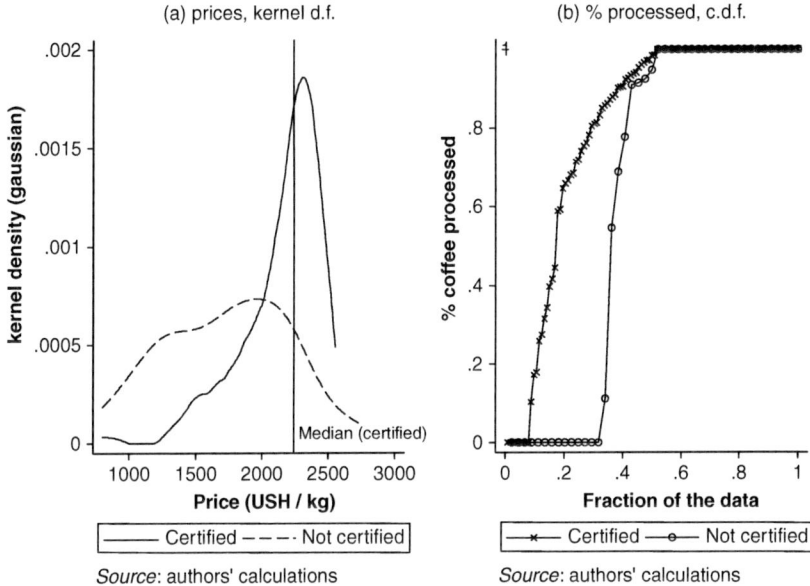

Figure 4.1 Distributions of (a) average prices received and (b) proportion of coffee crop processed for certified organic farmers and non-organic farmers

10 per cent of scheme members were processing no coffee. On the other hand, 30 per cent of the control group undertook no processing. The distribution of processing between the two groups is also quite different, with a smooth distribution for scheme members and a highly disjointed one for the control group (suggesting that in the control group, processing was confined to the larger producers).

The continuous availability of premiums in the Kawacom and Esco (anno 2009) schemes reflects a number of factors including the financial resources of these companies, their presence in the differentiated conventional as well as the organic market and relatively high levels of competition for crop around the scheme areas (see the fourth section). Other operators either lacked these resources, a presence in the differentiated conventional market, local competitors or all three.

Uptake of organic farming methods (cf. Table 4.3, rows 6–7) appears to have been lower and patchier than uptake of processing technologies such as fermentation in the schemes under consideration. This may relate to lower commitment to their diffusion on the part of contracting companies but it may also relate to farmers' assessment of benefits from their adoption in relationship, for example, to yields. Descriptive statistics comparing yields of scheme members and control groups were collected for all schemes except Biofresh (since crop on this scheme was sold by the piece rather

Table 4.7 Regression (FIML) results for yield per tree (log), Kawacom and Esco (2009 survey) schemes

Variable	KAWACOM		ESCO	
	Beta	Std error	Beta	Std error
Farm size (log)	0.12	0.08	0.20†	0.10
Trees/plants (log)			−0.28§	0.01
Trees/plants (N)	−0.40‡	0.06		
Van. vines (log)			−0.00	0.01
Farm altitude	−2.51‡	0.69	−0.00	0.00
Farmer age	0.00	0.00	−0.00	0.00
Farmer education	0.02	0.01	−0.32‡	0.11
H/h size	−0.03	0.02	0.01	0.01
Organic practices (N)	0.07	0.04	0.07	0.06
Scheme participation	1.01‡	0.23	0.54*	0.29
Constant	4.22‡	1.46	0.12	0.52
Lamda	−0.49†	0.19	0.08	0.18
N	147		171	
Log likelihood	−200.6		−202.14	
F stat	57.5§		62.64§	
R squ		0.37		

Note: Selection equations omitted but are available from authors. * = P < 0.1, † = P < 0.05; ‡ = P < 0.01, § = P < 0.001. Robust (Huber/White/Sandwich) standard errors given. Samples exclude missing observations and outliers, defined as households with net revenue from main crop +/ − 3.5 standard deviations from the sample mean of the dependent variable. Calculations using Stata 8.

than by weight) (Table 4.3, rows 15–16). Yield is significantly higher for scheme members only in relation to the Kawacom and Esco (anno 2009) surveys.

Regressions were run for yield in relation for these two schemes (Table 4.7). These show scheme membership having a large and very significant impact on yield in both schemes. The only other common significant impact is somewhat surprisingly a negative one from number of trees. Number of organic farming practices adopted does not have an impact that is significant in either scheme. Thus, both presumed components of higher net revenue (premium price and yield) derive primarily from contract farming *per se*.

Conclusion

This chapter reports results from household-level surveys of six OCFSs in East Africa, conducted in 2005–09 and including one scheme which was surveyed twice in this period. The surveys and subsequent analysis focused upon selection into schemes, revenue effects from scheme participation, uptake of technologies by scheme participants and the impact of organic farming practices on revenue.

The results show that scheme participation is somewhat skewed towards farmers with superior factor endowments, although this tendency is not systematic across factor endowments or schemes. The most important selection biases relate to farmers' stocks of the trees or plants from which certified crops are produced, and to farm altitude (a factor also relevant to coffee productivity).

Scheme participants received significantly higher mean net revenues from certified crops than control groups in four of the six schemes. In one of the remaining schemes, the control group's mean revenue was higher when results were expressed in terms of net revenue per hectare. In the four schemes for which net revenue was higher for scheme members, net revenue was regressed against a number of exogenous variables. The results across these schemes show that, controlling for other factors, participation *per se* and tree and plant stock had the greatest impact on net revenues. The results for participation are slightly less consistent than for tree and plant stocks but the coefficients are generally higher.

Use of organic farming practices by scheme members was generally significantly higher than for the control group, and when this was regressed against a number of exogenous variables it was participation that proved to have the greatest impact on number of organic farming practices used. But use of organic farming practices even by scheme participants was at best moderate and in the case of the scheme surveyed twice (in 2005 and 2009) there is no evidence of increased adoption. The regression results for revenue show number of organic farming practices used having a modest impact on revenue, but only in some schemes. Regression results for yield also show use of organic farming practices having at best a weak impact.

'Treatment effects' for net revenue from certified crops were calculated using the results of three of the surveys. These show scheme participation to be associated with increases in revenue of between 46 per cent and 75 per cent by scheme. There were also treatment effects for number of organic practices used in two of the schemes, although these were again modest.

It is argued that the mechanism linking scheme participation with higher net revenue is the presence of predictable price premiums on a continuous basis. This reduces the risks that farmers run in conforming to the 'organic plus' quality requirements that are a necessary condition for selling to the contracting companies in most of the schemes. Where premiums were not offered on a continuous basis, scheme participation had a lower impact on revenue outcome, and in the two schemes where no premiums were offered there were no positive revenue effects. In turn, the schemes where premiums were offered on a continuous basis were those run by contracting companies with relatively substantial financial resources and a presence in differentiated conventional as well as organic markets. These were also schemes where there was a relatively high level of competition for the certified crop from conventional buyers and in one case another large organic buyer. Where these conditions are present, Glover's 'agribusiness normalization' thesis appears to be refuted.

These results suggest that OCFSs, where price premiums are provided, generate measurable benefits for scheme participants. This holds true even when selection bias into schemes is controlled for. However, it is the contract farming rather than the organic element of OCFSs that is decisive in this respect. This underlines the importance of distinguishing between well-functioning and poorly functioning schemes. In a context of 'market-based' contract farming with loose and fairly narrow (rather than systematically interlocking) contracts, the preconditions for schemes to work well for both contracting companies and participants appear to relate to contracting company resources and market orientation, and to the presence of local competition.

Appendix: analytical strategy

As indicated in the text, one of the main difficulties involved in evaluating the effects of contract farming schemes refers to the possibility of selection bias. For detailed discussion of these issues see Blundell and Costa Dias (2000, 2002). This can arise if, for example, the most able or productive farmers select into the scheme based on knowledge of its potential benefits. Consequently, the counterfactual outcomes for these farmers, that is, their performance in the absence of the scheme cannot be correctly estimated from observations taken from the control group. Note that we refer to the treatment group as those participating in the policy intervention, which is the contract farming scheme of interest.

Excluding randomized evaluations based on pre- and post-intervention surveys, various techniques exist for dealing with this selection problem. The first assumes that selection into the scheme is 'strongly ignorable' conditional on observed covariates such as household characteristics and factor endowments. This means that treatment effects can be consistently estimated from the observed data, as long as a robust set of controls is included. The second approach is more conservative and uses (quasi) instrumental variables techniques as per the Heckman selection model (Heckman, 1979) to address unobserved selection bias.

Formally, consider the *observed* outcomes for farmer i under treatment and 'no treatment' states, given by y_{1i} and y_{0i}, respectively:

$$y_{1i} = x'_i \beta_1 + u_{1i}$$
$$y_{0i} = x'_i \beta_0 + u_{0i}$$

where the vector $x' = (1x_1)$ defines a set of structural regressors affecting both the outcome and the decision to participate and u_i are error terms. These can be combined to give:

$$y_i = x'_i\beta + t_i\alpha + u_{0i} + t_i(u_{1i} - u_{0i}) = x'_i\beta + t_i\alpha + \varepsilon_i$$

where t_i is a dummy variable taking the value of 1 for treated households and zero otherwise. In the case of selection on observables, it is appropriate to estimate the equation by ordinary least squares (OLS). This is because the aggregate error term (ε_i) is independent of treatment status in expectation conditional on the vector x'. Heckman selection models do not make this assumption; rather, they estimate both a selection or participation equation *and* an outcome equation. This is either undertaken simultaneously, as per the Heckman FIML (full information maximum likelihood) estimator or in two separate stages (Two step). By doing so, a correction for selection bias is estimated and is indicated by the lambda term given in Table 4.6. Where this is insignificant, the OLS results can be taken as consistent.

As the precise nature of any selection bias in not known, empirically we proceed by estimating both OLS and Heckman models (see Table 4.6). To investigate the latter, however, as a first step we also estimate (stand alone) selection equations based on a binomial Probit model, in the case of contract farming, and a Poisson model in the case of the number of organic practices employed (Tables 4.4 and 4.5).

Note that the robustness of the Heckman model is assured both through the inclusion of instruments that do not appear in the outcome model and by additional tests. These include collinearity and heteroscedasticity tests. In no estimate do these give cause for concern.

Notes

1. For this reason, contracts in such schemes typically specified dates for planting and harvesting. Detailed inter-locking contracts of this kind are still present in a few locations in Africa but are more common in developing countries outside of Africa, with parastatals, international and nationally owned companies as contracting agents. For Asia see, for example, Simmons et al., (2005) on Indonesia.
2. Side-selling is noted as a problem of contract farming almost from the beginning of a specialized literature on the subject (cf Nyoro and Whittaker, 1986).
3. Some, if not all, of the donor programmes referred to target smaller locally owned companies for support, resulting in contracting companies having much more diverse levels of corporate resources than was the case in the earlier period.
4. Despite this, vanilla never became a major export crop in the Esco scheme. Although its cultivation remained much more common amongst scheme members than other cocoa farmers in the area, few farmers sold more than 20 kg of the crop annually. As vanilla prices remained fairly high, the reasons for this are unclear.
5. Of the schemes considered, probably only Kawacom was located with maximization of supply as an aim. Esco (U) Ltd's cocoa scheme was taken over from its original

designer after he had abandoned it (following activity in the area by insurgents). Biofresh's pineapple farmers were mostly members of a local NGO who canvassed an exporter through the Ugandan national organic movement NOGAMU, and were hence self-selecting. Gumutindo's participants were also self-selecting.
6. Members of the Tazop Black Pepper scheme had mean annual net revenues from the crop of Tsh 252,024 per hectare, as against Tsh 271,699 for non-members. The difference is not significant. Members of the Zangerm Chilli scheme had mean annual net revenues from the crop of Tsh 1,064,695 per hectare, as against Tsh 1,446,548 for non-members. This difference is significant at the $P < 0.001$ level (t-test).
7. The corresponding figures for the control groups were 52.1 per cent (2005) and 29.1 per cent (2009).

5
Challenges and Opportunities of Organic Agriculture in Tanzania

Emmanuel R. Mbiha and Gasper C. Ashimogo

Introduction

This chapter provides an account of challenges and opportunities of organic agriculture in Tanzania. A brief introduction on organic agriculture's setting and its development in Tanzania is followed by a more detailed review of the development of the country's organic production, processing and marketing systems. It is observed that export demand far exceeds the supply. This implies that there is need to circumvent production constraints to meet the demand. It is further noted that while promotion of organic agriculture in Tanzania has received great support from development agencies and NGOs, the contribution of the government has lagged behind. As the government has now expressed a desire to promote the sector and as further efforts are put into the development of awareness and knowledge of both producers and consumers, it is expected that organic agriculture has a promising future.

Background

Agriculture in Tanzania is dominated by small-scale farmers owning on average less than 2 ha. Most production is low technology-based. The use of yield enhancing inputs and mechanical implements is minimal. The farming technology used is the one that has been passed down from generation to generation (URT, ASDS). Beginning in the 1950s, agro-chemicals were introduced to enhance output through increased soil fertility and control of pests, respectively. Pesticides were mainly applied to exported crops particularly coffee and cotton[1]. In the 1970s, promotion of staple grains output included subsidization of chemical fertilizers. Most fertilizers were applied on maize in the Southern Highlands (Hawassi et al., 1997).

Tanzania is endowed with a range of natural resources and a favourable climate that allows a range of crops to be grown (Mlambiti and Isinika, 1997; Food Studies Group, 1992). The major crops are grains (maize, rice, sorghum and millets), legumes (beans, cowpeas) tubers (cassava, sweet potato, round potatoes, carrots), vegetables and fruits (tomato, leafy vegetables, onions, citrus fruits, pineapples), fibers (cotton and sisal), beverages (coffee and tea) and spices.

Agriculture is the leading economic sector in terms of number of people employed in it. Over 80 per cent of the population lives from agriculture. For many years it was the leading contributor to GDP and export earnings, contributing about 50 per cent of GDP and 75 per cent of export earnings. According to the National Bureau of Statistics, the agriculture sector now contributes only about 26 per cent of GDP. The shift in proportional contribution has been caused by increased production in other sectors such as mining, fisheries and tourism (BOT, various years).

Crop switching and diversification in the agriculture sector is also a notable development. Traditionally the major crops serving as large cash income sources were coffee, cotton, tea, sisal, pyrethrum, cashew nut, tea, sugarcane and oilseeds. Various reports by the government of Tanzania such as the Economic Survey and analyses by the Bank of Tanzania show that the major market for these crops was and remains the export market. The other crops such as maize, rice, beans, fruits and vegetables were regarded as food crops and contributing less to cash income. As a result of crop switching and diversification the composition and importance of crops in Tanzania have changed. Non-traditional export crops have emerged including fruits and vegetables, spices, specialty crops and organically produced crops. This has led to farmers' resources being invested in these alternative crops and in some cases at the expense of the traditional crops. Regardless of these changes, such production is still geared for export. In the internal and regional market rapid urbanization and population growth will increasingly be a source of demand for food crops in particular.

Organic agriculture is embedded within the sustainable agriculture movement. While aiming to produce high quality products, it also supports the enhancement of a well balanced and continuous agro-ecosystem (Grolink, 2004). Unfortunately the advocated principles of sustainable agriculture as well as the organic standards are not in conformity with some of the traditional methods of promoting agricultural productivity through application of synthetic chemicals. Agricultural development initiatives in Tanzania are more dominated by the promotion of the use of agro-chemicals. The cost of agro-chemicals has been a major issue though and without subsidies adoption has therefore been minimal. Many farmers have been unable to afford these inputs and where they are accessible sub-optimal use and cost has resulted in still poor revenues. According to Mahundaza et al. (1992) and Hawassi et al. (1997), before the removal of fertilizer subsidies in the mid-1990s, fertilizer use per unit area in Tanzania ranged from 4–9 kg/ha of cropped land. As a result of market liberalization and removal of subsidies in the early part of the 1990s fertilizer prices increased drastically. Currently the estimated use of fertilizers is about 2 kg/ha (FAO, various years).

In 2002, at the end of the first phase of EPOPA[2] there were 17 organic schemes covering about 14,000 ha in Tanzania. The number of organic schemes, farmers and crops has continued to increase and the Tanzania Organic Agriculture Movement (TOAM) estimates that there are currently about 89,000 farmers employed in the sector with approximately 65,000 ha under organic production. However, this is only about 1 per cent of the total arable land for agriculture. In total there are currently more than 30 certified operators (for example, companies or organic schemes) and many more projects that are not yet certified but are in the process of conversion (Table 5A.1). In Uganda, EPOPA was also very instrumental in promoting organic agriculture. Commercial companies began to engage in organic agriculture in the mid-1990s, which is around the same period for organic development in Tanzania. Interest in organic agriculture in Uganda was, however, preceded by awareness about sustainable agriculture. According to Taylor (2006), this awareness which had been promoted by NGOs and the government helped to quicken adoption of formal practices of organic agriculture. However, the formation of EPOPA further speeded up this process. Most organic projects in Uganda received support of one kind or another from EPOPA. It should, however, be noted that unlike in Tanzania, the Ugandan government showed an early interest in organic agriculture. A good example is coffee, whereby the government targeted at least 10 per cent of coffee production to be organic (Nagawa et al., 2007; EPOPA, 2008). While development of a national organic policy was initiated in 2005 in Uganda, in Tanzania development of a similar policy (National Organic Agriculture Development for Tanzania) was initiated only in 2008 (EPOPA, 2008).

Developments in organic production, processing and marketing in Tanzania

Development of organic agriculture has been driven mainly by growing international demand for organically produced products in industrialized countries. The premium price received by farmers also contributed to fast adoption at a time when farmers were receiving unfavourable prices for conventional crops in the international market. Poor revenues for farmers due to falling conventional crop prices encouraged farmers to diversify into alternative enterprises. This market opportunity was taken up by private individual farmers with assistance from promoting organizations. The most significant support to organic farming development in Tanzania was spearheaded by EPOPA.

Table 5A.1 provides a non-exhaustive list of firms and farms involved in organic agriculture in Tanzania. The list contains certified operators as well as those which are in the process of conversion. Both traditional export products and non-traditional exports are involved. For both traditional and non-traditional exports the premium price was a major reason for conversion to organic. A majority of products under the EPOPA programme for example have benefited from organic or quality-related premium prices (EPOPA, 2008). However, producers and exporters usually have the possibility to sell on the organic market or on quality-oriented segments of the conventional one. In addition, some producers have acquired other certifications, for example Fairtrade certification in the case of coffee in Kilimanjaro.

Value chain structures in the Tanzanian organic sector

A typical organic farming scheme consists of an export firm or buying company, farmers' group, a facilitating agency linking farmers with the exporter and a certifying agency for organic products. According to Akyoo and Lazaro (2007), the organic market chain for spices is closely coordinated with well-defined vertical steps unlike the conventional spice chain which is said to be loosely coordinated. Exporting companies have contractual arrangements with out-growers (contract farming) whereas promoting agencies such as EPOPA facilitate the link between the two through organizing farmers' groups, technical support and financial support during conversion to organic production. Support to farmers by exporting firms and facilitating agencies is mainly in terms of guaranteed markets, extension and training. Some firms also extend credit in kind or as cash advances aimed at facilitating production. Some credit and produce selling transactions are thus interlocked. Forward arrangements for sales are also essential to marketing and hence the need for contracts.

Most produce is exported in a raw or semi-processed form. Little processing is undertaken. Processed products find it difficult to penetrate export markets in particular while on the local scene there is stiff competition between locally processed products and imports. Processed products are mainly sold in the local market while raw or semi-finished products are exported (Mwasha and Liejdens, 2004).

While there are distinct supply chains for organic and conventional produce, some participants in these chains deal in both organic and conventional products. This is particularly the case for small-scale farmers who usually produce at least more than one crop type. Large-scale farmers, on the other hand, may specialize in a single crop. Some of these farmers produce a single conventional crop and diversify into organic production to take advantage of a niche market.

Buyers and traders too can handle both organic and conventional produce. For example, Premier Cashew Industries, whose case will be presented below, deals in both organic and conventional cashew nut. The same applies to Dabaga Fruit and Vegetables Canning Company. This organization procures organic pineapple from contracted farmers but at the same time is involved in canning conventional vegetables and other products.

The organic chain is much shorter compared to the conventional chain. In the case of organic produce the buyer is a particular company which has organized a buying source by contracting farmers to supply the organic produce to the firm. On the other hand, for conventional produce, farmers can sell to a multiplicity of buyers: traders originating within the locality, distant traders, direct sale to the urban market or sale through cooperative arrangements. There is a wide range of intermediaries between the final consumer and the farmer. These traders are spread along the market chain. Some are in contact with the farmer directly (village trader), while others are those based in urban centres acting either as wholesalers (buy from village traders or even directly from farmers) or retailers.

Efforts to promote and facilitate growth of the sector

Organic export promotion programmes have played a great role in the development of organic farming in Tanzania. At the start of certified organic farming in Tanzania, farmers were largely disorganized with little knowledge of organic technologies and market opportunities. Efforts mainly by the private sector and NGOs facilitated the development and growth of organic farming in a number of ways. The major aim was export promotion, concentrating on identifying and linking exporters to the final markets in Europe, America and Japan. Due to the infancy of the sector, export promotion had to go hand in hand with the introduction of organic agriculture principles. In many cases exporters, in order to obtain the produce they require, had to organize farmers into supply groups and then obtained group certification through setting up 'internal control systems' (ICSs).

Interventions along these lines helped to increase and expand the production of organic produce, both raw and processed. As already mentioned above, EPOPA turned out to be the most influential organic agriculture promoting program providing a range of services to exporters as well as farmers and farmer groups. These services included management assistance, staff training, farmer mobilization and training, provision of seed money to procure inputs, product quality management, market surveys, product development, sharing in certification costs and so on (Van Elzakker and Rundgren, 2008).

The companies that became involved included ones owned by local entrepreneurs, expatriates, local–foreign joint ventures, international trading houses and cooperatives, selling to importers and distributors, health shop chains or supermarkets. The companies organized the production and certification. They paid for certification and thus 'owned' the certificate. This way of organizing production is well known also from conventional contract farming and out-grower schemes. The training that farmers receive is normally strictly connected to a specific crop or line of production. Related to the fact that farmers do not own the certificate, they remain highly dependent on the company owner and the success of the specific business.

In the early phase of the development of the organic sector in East Africa, the local market was largely absent, and any certified production not exported (or perhaps unexportable due to lower quality) was sold on the local market as conventional produce with no premium price. Later, in both Tanzania and Uganda, national institutions begin to appear. Local organic demand increased and interest groups or associations emerged. This has led to the establishment of East African organic standards and certification systems (East African Community, 2007). Government policy in Tanzania and Uganda has come to recognize the role of organic agriculture and in both countries commissions developed recommendations for an organic agriculture policy. In the export sub-sector this later stage has also seen the marketing of non-traditional and processed crops as well as traditional ones. Local markets are still limited, but dedicated outlets have been set up and supermarkets are beginning to sell organic products.

When the East African Organic Conference launched the East African Organic Products Standard in 2007 the main aim was to allow producers to certify at a lower cost than applies for international certification, so that they could benefit from regional market opportunities. Many producers have usually felt that the market for certified organic products is very complex and that the opportunities and requirements associated with the certification programmes are not always clear. Initially producers did not know if the requirements were compulsory (created as an official law or regulation in the importing country) or voluntary (which means that producers or exporters may choose to comply with the requirements or not). They also did not know the advantages and limitations of different types of certification. Furthermore, the large number of import requirements established by different countries made it even more complicated for producers who wanted to export.

Of the East African countries, the local market is most developed today in Kenya. Kenya also has examples of large-scale organic agriculture and of more commercialized smallholder organic production in the Rift Valley. Both are predominantly export oriented within horticulture, fruits, coffee and tea. However, the Rift Valley also enjoys excellent connectivity to the Nairobi consumer market.

An account of selected organic agriculture development schemes

Golden Food Products, Arusha – a privately owned producer of non-traditional crops[3]

Golden Food Products (GFP) started its activities in 1998 as a grower of a range of herbs and spices. It later expanded into procurement from farmers. It procures pepper, lemon grass, ginger, cloves, cardamom, cinnamon and cocoa in Muheza district and turmeric in Korogwe district. Initially it had 600 contract farmers and today has more than 1000. In 2006, it exported its first consignment through Tanga port to Holland and plans to expand its destinations to Austria and the USA. It is certified by IMO to both American (NOP) and EU standards, using a group certification scheme. Initial contacts were made when the entrepreneur personally visited a number of trade fairs in Europe, the designated export point, where some commission agents were identified.

The major costs of the operation relate to the management of the ICS. Costs include salaries for field officers, documentation, updating of internal inspection manuals, preparation of growers' lists and external inspection. The company is also involved in training and mobilizing farmers. Farmers do not pay directly for costs of certification for production activities. At the processing and marketing levels company certification has enjoyed external support. For example, during the first year of operation, EPOPA paid certification costs in full and during the following year it paid 50 per cent (ca. €5700) of certification costs. In future, however, annual deductions (Tshs 100/kg sold) from farmers will be used to pay for external certification. According to GFP's management, the major problems the company has encountered include strong competition for produce, demands involved in building up market confidence in relation to the high levels of quality required and low bargaining power *vis-a-vis* importers.

Premier Cashew Industries Ltd – a private processor and exporter of traditional crops

Premier Cashew Industries (PCI) was established in 1999 for cashew nut processing in Tanzania. Previously cashew nut processing was undertaken by public owned processing factories. The government set up 10 processing factories in the 1980s. These could not compete in the world market and in the mid-1990s the introduction of economic liberalization and structural adjustment policies led to their closure. Most were left idle but some were sold to private investors. PCI was the first private company to start processing raw cashew nuts. Now more new factories have been established mainly by Indian investors. Since its establishment, PCI has grown and currently processes about 50 tons per day. PCI exports over 95 per cent of its processed cashew kernels to countries such as South Africa, USA, Canada, the EU, Japan, India, Pakistan, South Korea and Dubai. Some exports are also carried out to Kenya and Uganda. It procures cashews mainly from Mkuranga district in Coast region, 40 km south of the city of Dar-es-Salaam.

Beginning in 2001, PCI diversified into organic cashew with support of EPOPA. In the 2003/2004 season, PCI was certified to EU and US (NOP) standards by KRAV (Sweden) – certification was later transferred to IMO. In this first season PCI handled about 610 tons of raw organic cashews from 164 small farmers. While EPOPA helped the company with capacity building and finance for certification, PCI embarked on modification of its factory layout and operating procedures in order to comply with the organic standards. By 2005/2006, 30 per cent of all raw cashew nuts bought were organic.

Field officers employed by PCI are stationed in villages where they procure cashews and provide extension services. In addition to farmer training, government extension officers in the area were also trained by EPOPA on organic agriculture. The cashew trees owned by certified farmers are sprayed with sulphur at the time of flowering. Sulphur is an approved fungicide used to treat powdery mildew disease. Another activity has been the renovation of cashew trees. Most cashew trees were very old (40–50 years). It was necessary to train farmers in improved farming practices (pruning, spacing, ventilation, use of a cover crop, scouting of disease and effective use of sulphur). This was done to reverse the trend of low yields that had been experienced after many years of neglect of the crop due to low market prices (EPOPA, 2008).

Kilimanjaro Native Cooperative Union (KNCU) – a secondary cooperative union[4]

Two cooperatives (KNCU and Kagera Cooperative Union) have been involved in promotion of organic agriculture in the coffee sector, driven by volatile and declining world prices, rising input costs and loss of local market share to private traders. Organic and Fairtrade markets were seen as offering better prices than conventional markets, by-passing input price problems and enabling a reconnection with primary producers. The cooperative structure is made up of a union under which there are varying numbers of primary societies. Through primary societies it is possible to reach individual farmers and extend information and knowledge.

KNCU promoted organic coffee through the Kilimanjaro Fairtrade Organic Project beginning in 2003 with initial support by EPOPA. KNCU commands a membership of 120,000 smallholder farmers organized into 90 primary cooperative societies. The organic project first operated with a few farmer volunteers within seven primary cooperative societies.[5] In all, approximately 2929 households cultivating an average of 0.5 ha are now involved. At first some farmers were skeptical about making a profit without high doses of synthetic fertilizers and pesticides and therefore would not adhere to required standards. Two of the primary societies dropped out because of violation of required conditions. Three more societies are being brought into the project through a project financed by Oxfam in Belgium.

Usually it takes 3 years for farmers to convert to organic production. However, since use of chemical fertilizers has been declining, 1 to 2 years of close observation are now considered sufficient for conversion. The first organic crop was exported in 2004 to Royal Coffee in the US. Farmers enjoy both organic and Fairtrade premiums.[6] As a result, during 2007/2008, organic farmers were paid TShs 3000/kg compared to TShs 2000/kg paid to conventional farmers. EPOPA paid part of certification costs, trained KNCU's technical staff, facilitated establishment of the internal control system and linked KNCU to markets through provision of information and sponsoring attendance at trade fairs.

According to KNCU, adoption of organic agricultural methods has made farmers feel more responsible for their farms and it has made KNCU more competitive against private traders. However, KNCU also recognizes several major problems or challenges confronting its initiative. These include difficulties in enrolling more farmers because of scepticism, lack of inclusion of poorer farmers, farmers dropping out of the project because of poor communication between members and the farmers' groups in relation to issues such as delayed payments and price differences between the farmer groups and high monitoring costs to maintain segregation and integrity of product.

Global Service Corps (GSC), Arusha – an NGO promoting organic farming for the local market

GSC is an American NGO that started operations in Tanzania in 1991. Its work covers HIV-AIDS education, targeting primary and secondary school youths, nutrition and 'bio-intensive agriculture' (BIA)[7] (mainly horticulture). Of late it has also focused on the development of cultural tourism in relation to organic farming. BIA is advocated because of acute land shortage in Arusha which makes extensive agriculture impossible. The programme started off with three groups in Arusha district. More recently, the programme has taught farmers from over 50 farmer groups in Arumeru district, via on-farm training. The farmer groups have different committees, including ones dealing with marketing and quality control, and are associated under an umbrella association known as MUWAKIHA (*Muungano wa wakulima wa kilimo hai Arumeru*).

GSC has also provided farmer groups with 'start-up funds' (approximately US$2000–3000) for purchase of farm inputs and tools. Demand for output produced under the scheme largely comes from expatriates and better-off local consumers, although developing other outlets such as schools and tourist lodges has also been attempted (with the assistance of other NGOs). Product is certified to the East African organic standard. Maintenance of product segregation and integrity has been a problem which GSC is seeking to address by adopting a 'Participatory Guarantee System' – a variant of internal control systems based on peer-group assessment and pressure.

Problems, prospects and future outlook of the organic sector

Constraints and challenges of the organic sector

Organic agriculture faces many challenges that have been documented in many countries both developed and developing. In East Africa, a study by Gibbon (2006) in Uganda and various reports by EPOPA provide an outline of some of the key constraints and challenges to organic agriculture development. These can be considered in relation to problems faced by exporters and farmers, respectively.

In respect of exporters, developing markets and maintaining product quality are major challenges. Another problem is that of value addition. Opportunities for local value addition are limited, especially for traditional export crops. In relation to all crops, moreover, entry barriers posed by technologies and capital requirements tend to be difficult to surmount. Where value addition in the form of processing is undertaken, most processors face limited availability of organic raw materials supplies, especially in the early stages of processing projects. Companies and processors also face fragmented supply from smallholder farmers adding to higher costs of transactions with farmers. Many operations are at 10–40 per cent capacity.

Organic ingredients or components such as organic sugar and enzymes are locally unavailable and therefore expensive. Most of these ingredients are imported and processors report that they have in some cases experienced delivery delays. Lack of export-quality packaging materials for processed products is another difficulty. The above constraints and the long lag time before full capacity utilization may lead to local processing being uncompetitive.

In respect of farmers, a major challenge is dependency on exporters for market access and certification. This is reinforced by the low level of development of local and regional markets. Thus farmers are left vulnerable to reduced commitment from exporters and/or the erosion of price premiums.

As regards challenges for government, it is clear that policy towards agriculture development is still geared towards the promotion of conventional agriculture. In some cases some policy decisions are directly at variance with the needs of organic agriculture. Examples include re-introduction of synthetic fertilizer subsidies and promotion of spraying of DDT to control malaria in Uganda and Tanzania. Thus, government faces the challenge on how to reconcile the interests of conventional and organic production.

Prospects and future outlook of the sector

The local market

Today, Tanzanian organic retail outlets are mainly found in Dar-es-Salaam and other major cities such as Arusha and Mwanza (Mjunguli, 2004). These outlets stock a range of organic products: vegetables, jams, spices, cereals, drinks, edible oils and medicinal products. Most supply sources to these outlets are internal with a small amount being supplied from other countries, especially South Africa. Organic product prices are generally higher than those of conventional products.

Only around 10 per cent of customers are Tanzanians of African descent. These include health conscious clients and those who can afford the relatively higher prices. Others are responding to medical problems especially diabetes and high blood pressure (Mwasha, 2007). Further market growth is limited not only by income but also by lack of awareness of organic products and their attributes. According to a survey by Sogn and Mella for Envirocare, about one-third of respondents failed to identify what organic production involved (Envirocare, 2007). Amongst the remaining two-thirds there are different perceptions regarding what organic products are. This implies a need for more awareness creation among the population.

Foreign markets

Export data for organic products is not available in a systematic form. However, EPOPA's experience indicates that a number of exporters do well. Several projects have expanded. An example is Premier Cashew Industries. It increased the output of cashew exports and has expanded into organic sesame and cocoa. However, the viability of others fluctuates with market demand. An example is the main project for organic cotton in Uganda whose fortunes have oscillated alongside the fluctuation in the overall world organic cotton market.

The wider context

Organic agriculture may represent an interesting opportunity for many producers in East Africa and may become an important tool to improve the quality of life and income of farm families. Producers shift to organic agriculture for a variety of reasons. Some feel that the use of agro-chemicals is bad for their health and environment, while some producers are attracted by the higher prices and the rapidly growing market for many organic products in recent years. Changing to organic may be easier for some producers depending on whether they use agro-chemicals intensively, own their land or have access to labour, organic fertilizers and other permitted inputs.

Organization of farmers to meet organic standards through an internal control system managed by an interested exporter or buyer in many cases may lead to the strengthening of organized farmer groups and hence facilitate links between the farmers and other market participants. Farmers can thereby participate in a more integrated market chain that exposes them to better management practices implemented by exporters. Ultimately many of the benefits go beyond the receipt of better prices. Organic agriculture promotes increased understanding and appreciation of farming technologies and environmental values.

Conclusion

The development of organic agriculture in Tanzania owes much to the intervention of promotional agencies involved in providing free technical support. Organic agriculture, however, still forms only a very small percentage of agriculture output in the country. Its practice could be enhanced by changing attitudes towards established conventional methods in agriculture and promoting consumer awareness of its environmental and health benefits. Farmers have been encouraged to respond to rising demand on the basis of assurance of a market for their produce and a premium price. Since organic markets have to be retained, the need to follow prescribed rules is foremost. This is required at the primary production level as well as during processing. Value addition and processing require further attention if they are to become more general.

Appendix

Table 5A.1 Tanzania: organic producers, products and area under production

S/N	Main product	Other products	Name of the farm/firm	Location	Product description/output (2008 data)	Area, ha. (2008 data)	No. of contracted farmers (2008 data)	Organic status
1	Bananas		Selian Agricultural Research Institute	Arusha and Kilimanjaro	Organic bananas from tissue culture		500	Not certified
2	Beef		Kisolanza Farm					Not certified
3	Cashew	Cocoa Sesame	Premier Cashew Industries Ltd –	Mkurunga District, Coast Region	Vacuum packed cashew kernels (2458 tons)	3045 ha. (168520 trees)	463	Organic
4	Cashew		The Dutch Connection	Masasi				Organic
5	Cashew	Cocoa	Tanzania Organic Food Trade Ltd (exporter)	Dar-es-Salaam				Organic
6	Cocoa		FidaHussein Co. Ltd	Turiani	Cocoa (790 tons)	332	429	Organic
7	Cocoa		Biolands International Ltd	Kyela	Cocoa (2500 tons)		20000	Organic
8	Cocoa		HAI Tanzania Ltd	Kyela	Cocoa (2000 tons)	2600	11000	Organic
9	Coffee		LIMA	Tukuyu				
10	Coffee		Tanganyika Instant Coffee Co. Ltd	Bukoba	Instant coffee			

#	Crop	Other crops	Company	Location	Product	Area (ha)	Farmers	Type
11	Coffee		TANICA–Dar-es-Salaam Processing and exporter	Dar-es-Salaam	Spray dried instant coffee			
12	Coffee		Mara Coffee Ltd	Tarime	Hard coffee arabica (320 tons)	237	572	Organic
13	Coffee		Kilimanjaro Native Cooperative Union (KNCU)	Kilimanjaro region	102 tons	Range 0.5–1 ha. Per farmer	2929	Organic
14	Coffee		Kagera Cooperative Union, (KCU)	Bukoba	500 tons		14 primary societies (3377 farmers)	Organic
15	Coffee Compost		ZAREC Ltd	Mbeya Zanzibar	85 tons Compost		3768	Organic
16	Cotton	Sesame, Moringa trees, yellow gram and soya beans	Biosustain	Singida	Cotton – 1100 tons lint Sesame – 500 tons	4500	2100	Organic
17	Cotton		BioRe Tanzania Ltd	Meatu		4800	2410	Organic

Table 5A.1 (Continued)

S/N	Main product	Other products	Name of the farm/firm	Location	Product description/output (2008 data)	Area, ha. (2008 data)	No. of contracted farmers (2008 data)	Organic status
18	Cotton	Chicken peas, sunflower, groundnuts, maize, sorghum, cowpeas, green gram and sesame	Busangwa Organic Farming Association (BOFA)	Kishapu, Shinyanga	Seed cotton, 120 tons and lint 41 tons	2225	250	Organic
19	Fruits		UNAT Fruit Processing Ltd	Morogoro	Fruit juice concentrate	0.5–2 ha per farmer	5000	Not certified, Trial processing
20	Fruits		Matunda Mema, Karagwe	Karagwe	Dried pineapples, banana, papaya, chamomile and peppermint		230	Organic
21	Fruits		Mikese Organic Farm	Morogoro	Mangoes, lime, citrus	250	n.a.	Organic

No.	Category	Company	Location	Products	Quantity	Type
22	Fruits	Dabaga Vegetable and Fruit Canning Co. Ltd	Iringa	Canned pineapple (196 tons)		81	Organic
23	Green beans	Rotian Seed Company	Arusha	Green Bean Seeds	800 per farm	7	Organic
24	Herbs and spices	Kibidula	Mafinga	Herbs			
25	Herbs and spices	Agrotex Ltd	Zanzibar	Bananas, pineapples, papaya, mangoes, jackfruits, yams, breadfruits, cassava, coconut, oranges and sweet basil			
				Cloves, cinnamon, lemon grass, vanilla, black pepper, ginger, turmeric, cardamom and essential oils (1200 tons)	782	3000	Organic
26	Herbs and spices	ZanGerm Enterprises Ltd	Zanzibar, Tanga, Kigoma	ginger, pepper, lemon grass, and so on		700	Organic
27	Herbs and spices	Kimango Farm	Morogoro	Chilli, paprika, lemon grass, hibiscus; neem, egg plants	700	n.a.	Organic

Table 5A.1 (Continued)

S/N	Main product	Other products	Name of the farm/firm	Location	Product description/output (2008 data)	Area, ha. (2008 data)	No. of contracted farmers (2008 data)	Organic status
28	Herbs and spices	Fruits	Golden Food Products (Processing for export done at Arusha)	Arusha Muheza	Pepper, lemon grass, ginger, cloves, cardamon, cinnamon, cocoa, oranges, mangoes, coconuts	1186	550	Organic
29	Herbs and spices		Tanzania Organic Products Ltd (TAZOP)	Zanzibar, Tanga, Kigoma	Cloves and other organic spices (300 tons)	800	250	Organic
30	Herbs and spices		Agricultural Development Project (ADP)	Isangati District	Turmeric			
31	Honey		Tabora Bee Keepers Association				Coops, Rufiji District	Not certified
32	Honey		Honey Care Africa					
33	Leather		Asilia Co. Ltd	Arusha	Leather processing			
34	Mushroom		Agro Products Ltd	Dodoma				
35	Neem tree		Osho	Arusha	Pesticides			

#	Product	Company	Location	Notes		
36	Oils	Clove Stem Oil Distillery	Pemba	Essential oils, lemon grass oil, eucalyptus oil, sweet basil oil		
37	Peanuts	Fairshare Ltd	Sumbawanga		1072	
39	Peanuts	TanPro	Dar-es-Salaam			Organic
40	Pyrethrum	Mansoor Daya Chemical Co. Ltd	Dar-es-Salaam	Pesticide		Organic
41	Rock Phosphate	Minjingu Co. Ltd	Arusha	Fertiliser		
42	Sesame	Lumumba Farm	Morogoro	Sesame, vegetables		
43	Sesame	Chogo Farm	Handeni	Sesame ginger		
44	Sesame	FidaHussein Co. Ltd	Rufiji	Sesame (75 tons)	800	
45	Tea	Mufindi Tea and Coffee Company Ltd	Luponde Tea Estate, Njombe	Coffee, chamomile, peppermint		Organic
46	Tea	Tanzania Tea Packers Ltd (TATEPA)	Dar-es-Salaam		330	Organic

Table 5A.1 (Continued)

S/N	Main product	Other products	Name of the farm/firm	Location	Product description/output (2008 data)	Area, ha. (2008 data)	No. of contracted farmers (2008 data)	Organic status
47	Tea		Bombay Burmah Trading Co. Ltd	Soni, Lushoto District	Fairtrade organic tea			Organic
48	Tea		Herkulu Estate	Usambara				
49	Tea		Balangai Tea Estate	Korogwe				
50	Tea	Baby corn, Vegetables	Gomba Estate	Arusha	Tea, baby corn, vegetables	4,000		Not certified
51	Vanilla	Rosella, bananas and mushrooms	Mayawa	Bukoba	Cured vanilla	314	750	Organic
52	Vegetables		Mshikamano Women Group	Mukuranga				Not certified
53	Vegetables	Maize	Global Service Corps (GSC) – NGO	Tengeru	Vegetables, maize			Not certified
54	Vegetables	Spices	Floresta (NGO)	Moshi Same	Vegetables and spices	0.25–.5 ha per farmer		Not certified

Sources: (1) Personal communication with Tancert, TOAM and individual companies (2) Agro Eco B. V. and Grolink (2008).

Notes

1. According to Mlambiti and Isinika (1997), coffee and cotton have been the main users of fungicides, insecticides and herbicides.
2. Export Promotion of Organic Products from Africa (EPOPA) is a programme which was funded by the Swedish International Development Agency (SIDA) with the aim of improving the livelihoods of African smallholder farmers through developing exports of organic products from Tanzania, Uganda and Zambia, while also exposing these countries to sustainable agricultural practices. The programme worked well in Uganda and Tanzania but did not take off in Zambia. The programme's first phase in Tanzania ran from 1993–2002. 2002–2008 was the second phase.
3. Material based on direct discussion with Mr Ayo, Managing Director of GFP.
4. KNCU was founded in 1929 and is the oldest cooperative in Africa.
5. Inevitably this led to a situation where farmers, some practicing organic agriculture and some conventional farming, operate side by side. This led to segregation and integrity problems. However, continuous checks by farmer organization officials and use of peer pressure minimized such cases.
6. However, since 2006, some of the costs of certification have been deducted from farmers' prices.
7. This system uses intensive cultivation where application of organic practices and inputs such as farm yard manure, use of double dug beds, companion planting, maintenance of heirloom seeds and so on are encouraged.

6
Sustainability Standards and Agro-Food Exports from East Africa

Evelyne Lazaro, Lone Riisgaard, Fredy Kilima, Jeremiah Makindara and Raymond Mnenwa

Introduction

This chapter deals with private sustainability standards and their application in the agro-food export sector in East Africa. It covers three firm or industry-level case studies: (1) Arabica coffee plantation production to the UTZ CERTIFIED standard in Tanzania; (2) GlobalGAP-certified production of fresh vegetables using smallholder contract farmers in Tanzania; and (3) Large-scale cut flower production in Tanzania and Kenya, certified to various 'social' standards focusing on worker conditions. Table 6.1 provides basic information on the case studies.

The case studies thus cover large farmer or plantation as well as contracted smallholder examples of UTZ and GlobalGAP certification, and large cut flower farm examples of the Flower Label Programme (FLP) and other social standards. The geographical focus is on Tanzania and the region's major agro-food exporter, Kenya.

The presentations of the different cases are each organized around three groups of questions:

1. Who adopts standards on the ground? What categories of operator participate in the different initiatives?
2. How are standards implemented in practice? Are there standards provisions that are only partly implemented and if so, why? Does incomplete implementation relate to measurement problems pertaining to the variables covered (for example, discrimination in relation to social standards)? Are there also aspects of these standards that are poorly adapted to local conditions (social, economic and environmental) and therefore not implemented? What are the consequences of specific instances of 'bad fit'?
3. What have been the economic and social costs and benefits of standard adoption in each case and what are the more general opportunities and threats that these standards bring with them?

Table 6.1 The case studies

Standard	UTZ CERTIFIED	GlobalGAP	Ethical standards
Crop	Coffee	Fresh vegetables	Cut flowers
Fieldwork date	2005/2006	2007/2008	2006
Site	Kilimanjaro region, Northern Tanzania	Arusha and Kilimanjaro regions, Northern Tanzania	Kenya and Tanzania
Cases	• Two UTZ CERTIFIED and one non-certified coffee plantations • Two UTZ CERTIFIED millers • Two coffee exporters	• One certified vegetable exporter • Five large-scale famers (three certified to GlobalGAP standards), • Six medium-scale farmers (all uncertified) and • 105 smallholder farmers (49 certified to GlobalGAP standards).	• All (10) export flower farms in Tanzania and • Ten (out of approximately 150) farms in Kenya

The chapter is organized in six following sections. The second section introduces the topic of sustainability standards. The third section describes the three (groups of) standards considered and their adoption in East Africa. The fourth, fifth and sixth sections review the questions just listed in relation to the three (groups of) standards, while the final section concludes.

Sustainability standards

Assurance of environmental and social 'sustainability' has become a key differentiator for marketing agricultural products. As a result, private voluntary standards have been formulated that seek to operationalize and codify this concept. Giovannucci and Purcell (2008) argue that the emergence of sustainability standards is also a result of a situation where existing food safety standards and international conventions on environmental and social issues are perceived by consumers as inadequate in their content and/or their implementation.

Generally, sustainability standards cover both environmental and social requirements. Examples include standards for organic agriculture, Fairtrade, Rainforest Alliance, UTZ CERTIFIED and GlobalGAP. Sometimes, these standards are referred to as process standards, although they are perhaps better understood as management ones. They cover management processes the whole length of the value chain.

However, despite these similarities, sustainability standards, labels and certifications are quite varied with respect to the functions they perform and their potential impacts. Ponte (2004) indicates that one of the motives for actors to engage with them is often to earn higher margins, especially when products can be sold at a premium. However, price premiums paid to both exporters and farmers vary considerably and in fact many initiatives, including UTZ CERTIFIED, do not offer a guaranteed price premium although a *de facto* premium is sometimes paid. Relevant questions are whether revenues from sale of certified sustainable products cover compliance costs and are equitably shared among chain actors.

Mazzocco (1996) and Henson et al. (1998) also identify access to markets as a benefit of adoption of such standards, for example through securing preferred supplier status in closed supply chains. Other benefits for African farmers from adopting such standards may include spill-over effects on farm management and thus improvements in farm productivity as well as household health and nutrition. Assessing the costs and benefits of compliance with sustainability standards is difficult because many such potential impacts are indirect and long term in nature.

Concerning labour issues, these standards are particularly controversial. One major concern is whether private standards can deliver the intended outcomes for workers – and, if they do, whether this is for all workers or only some. Some groups, particularly trade unions, fear that private labour standards are not able to guarantee fundamental rights such as that of organization and that they are being used to side-step unions (Justice, 2002; Spooner, 2004).

Others have raised the concern that sustainability standards as a category might constitute new non-tariff barriers for developing-country producers particularly small producers (Giovannucci and Reardon, 2000; Reardon et al., 2001; UNCTAD, 2007). This overlaps with concerns that these standards reflect a Northern agenda in relation to Southern producers and workers and are thus poorly adapted to local conditions (Barrientos and Smith, 2007; Blowfield and Dolan, 2008). Experience shows that it is difficult for many African farmers to achieve conformity to these standards, or at least to take full advantage of the market opportunities resulting from compliance. Furthermore, if farmers cannot achieve conformity to at least some standards they risk being excluded from remunerative markets altogether. Thus, a major challenge is how to ensure that the implementation of sustainable standards does not widen the gap between larger commercial farmers and smallholder farmers producing primarily for home or local consumption.

Low levels of human capital in many African countries limit farmers' ability to apply the prescribed production and management protocols and maintain the appropriate level of documentation required by sustainability standards. Another dimension of this challenge is the lack of adequate or well-managed infrastructure to facilitate cost-effective but credible quality and safety assurance mechanisms (Akyoo and Lazaro, this volume). These and other challenges are examined empirically in the three cases that are presented in the following sections.

The standards and their local adoption

UTZ CERTIFIED coffee

UTZ CERTIFIED,[1] formerly known as UTZ Kapeh, is an industry-led certification programme established in 1997 by the Ahold Coffee Company together with a number of coffee producers. The standard aims to secure 'responsible production' and seeks to address consumer concerns about industrial food production methods and their impact on people and the environment. The UTZ code covers environmental protection including pesticide management, water use, waste management and worker health and safety and certain other social conditions. UTZ CERTIFIED provides no guarantee of a premium price to farmers, although as already noted a *de facto* premium is often paid.

Conformity to the standard requires that coffee is registered through the UTZ Foundation sales announcement process and is traceable. The foundation certifies producers and millers and facilitates the matching of registered producers with traders and roasters through a web-based tracking and tracing system. In Tanzania, UTZ certification started in the early 2000s but has so far only been adopted by coffee plantations with at least 50 ha of Arabica coffee. Thus, in 2006, there were only three compliant operators: Kilimanjaro, Machare and Uru estates in Kilimanjaro region. These firms were certified in 2005.

The UTZ foundation was originally focused on coffee certification but in 2007 it expanded its programme to include other agricultural commodities including cocoa, palm oil and tea. Also, while UTZ standards were initially aimed at large coffee estates, subsequent efforts were made to develop guidelines that accommodate smallholder groups. Furthermore, the UTZ code has been regularly updated to maintain equivalence with what was originally called the EurepGAP protocol (now GlobalGAP-version 3, General regulations, Control points and Compliance criteria).

GlobalGAP

GlobalGAP is a set of standards designed to embody Good Agricultural and Good Manufacturing Practices (GAP and GMP). It is owned by a European based trade organization whose members today comprise growers, food manufacturers and retailers. For consumers and retailers, the GlobalGAP standard provides assurance that food reaches acceptable levels of safety and quality, and that has been produced sustainably, respecting the health, safety and welfare of workers, the environment and in consideration of animal welfare concerns.

GlobalGAP currently covers production of fruit, fresh vegetables, combinable crops, green coffee, tea, flowers and ornamentals, livestock, feed, nursery stock and aquaculture. The GlobalGAP protocol defines Good Agricultural Practices (GAP) in relation to integrated crop management, integrated pest control, quality management, hazard analysis and critical control points (HACCP), worker health, safety, welfare, environmental protection and conservation management. It also requires crop traceability to lot and agricultural site levels. A GlobalGAP option 2 for smallholder production was unveiled in 2005.

In Tanzania, two large-scale fresh producer–exporters (Seregeti Fresh and Gomba Estates) were certified to what was then EurepGAP in 2003. Today, the two exporters obtain most of their produce from out-growers who produce under contract. To ensure compliance with this standard, the exporters provide technical support to out-growers in regard to pesticide application (in this case by undertaking crop protection functions), crop husbandry and hygiene. The companies supply inputs, mostly on credit deducted from crop payments. They also collect produce from out-grower farms for transport to a central pack house. Contract farmers supply land for production and labour for most operations, including farm management.

Product prices are set by the estate based on their sales prices, allowing for deductions for input costs, packaging, transport and overheads. Some negotiations between the estate and farmers on farm level prices now occur, following complaints from farmers concerning their margins. The contract is binding for farmers on production practices and to a certain extent on volume of production and timing of delivery.

Social standards in the cut flower sector

Cut flower exports from Sub-Saharan Africa (led by Kenya) increased from approximately US$13 million in 1980 to almost US$300 million in 2007, representing one of Africa's most significant cases of non-traditional export development during the past two decades.[2] The sector in East Africa is an example of how tightened quality requirements and increasing concerns with social and environmental issues have created a highly regulated industry. The Dutch flower auctions have historically been the most important channel through which flowers are distributed to European wholesalers and retailers. But lately the proportion of flowers imported into the EU that goes through the auctions has diminished and direct sourcing by large retailers is increasing. For producers participating in value chains driven by large retailers, adopting social and environmental standards is a requirement, and it is not unusual for producers to comply with half a dozen different standards (cf. Barrientos et al., 2003; Riisgaard, 2009).

In all, at least 16 different social and/or environmental standards (international and national) exist for cut flower exports (CBI, 2007; Riisgaard, 2009).

International standard initiatives in this sector include that of the Fairtrade Labelling organization (FLO), the Dutch Milieu Programma Sierteelt (MPS, which has an additional social standard MPS-SQ), the German Flower Label Program (FLP), the British Ethical Trading Initiative (ETI) and the international Fair Flowers Fair Plants (FFP) standard as well as the International Code of Conduct for Cut Flowers (ICC).

UTZ CERTIFIED coffee in Tanzania

Implementation in practice

UTZ compliant producers are required to prepare manuals to guide farm operations and documented programmes for water use and water treatment. These manuals must reflect the protocol, but producers can adapt this to suit their unique farm situations, provided that they observe and implement all major requirements as prescribed. For example, the code indicates that native tree (shade) species should be used to provide required levels of canopy for coffee plants, without specifying which species.[3]

Value chain restructuring and standards compliance

The value chain that handles UTZ Arabica coffee from Tanzania is a buyer-driven one. Coffee destined for UTZ buyers (international traders and roasters) normally moves from plantation as green bean to certified millers in Moshi for milling, grading and storage before it goes to dedicated storage facilities in the main export centre(s). Although lower grades of certified coffee have to be exported via buyers bidding at the national coffee auction in Moshi, there is a parallel and distinct structure that handles most certified coffee. Thus, the value chain for UTZ coffee excludes many actors in the conventional chain, for example, smallholder farmers and conventional coffee buyers.

Unlike in other countries, smallholder coffee farmers in Tanzania have not been able to adopt this standard, partly because the national coffee regulations state that the lower grades of coffee produced by most smallholders have to go through the auction, and partly because most smallholder farmers are not aware of this standard. Furthermore, there are no local collective initiatives, for example through the cooperatives under the Kilimanjaro Native Cooperative Union (KNCU) to support smallholder compliance. Possibly, however, smallholder farmers could develop capacity for conformity (and producing the grades allowed to be exported directly) through support from larger certified firms to assist them upgrade their practices and to fulfil other social and environmental requirements. Our field experience in Kilimanjaro supports this view as one of the certified plantations was successfully supporting farmers in the nearby villages to reduce soil erosion and conserve wetland areas.

The new value chain strands for certified coffee have somewhat reduced the influence of certain national and local institutions such as the Tanzania Coffee Board and KNCU both at the production and processing levels, as the production and processing of certified coffee occurs independently of the farmer extension, farmer organization and export regulation systems.

Compliance costs and benefits

Our comparison of costs and benefits for compliant and non-compliant plantations over 4 years (2004–07) shows that, on average, the additional net earning over conventional coffee on sales by certified producers was approximately US$0.52/kg. According to the interviewed exporters, this extra earning could not be mainly attributed to a *de facto* UTZ price premium but primarily reflected the price differential between all coffee sold in the Tanzania auction and all coffee exported directly. There was a good deal of variance from year to year in the level of this premium.

Analysis indicated that major components of compliance costs included: (i) changes to farm infrastructure, (ii) waste disposal and environmental conservation measures and (iii) certification and inspection. Compliance costs averaged in aggregate 28–29 per cent of all productionand marketing costs. Whereas compliant producers had average annual total costs of US$913/ha, non-compliant producers had costs of US$626/ha. This indicates that, while standards compliance entailed higher costs compared to non-compliance, there were also considerable benefits (direct and indirect) from compliance.

Threats, opportunities, lessons learned

According to interviews with the certified firms in Kilimanjaro, the incentive to comply with UTZ seems to be to reduce market risks, especially price shocks, rather than meeting a requirement for market access. This is because UTZ compliant producers retain the option to sell through both the conventional bulk and conventional high-value chains. Superior grades of UTZ certified coffee (grades AA, A and PB) can be exported directly to conventional buyers if demanded in the export market, as under regulations set by the Tanzania Coffee Board (TCB) such coffee can by-pass the auction. On the other hand, even when sold through the UTZ chain a premium is not guaranteed as this depends on direct negotiation between the parties involved and the basic principle in determining coffee price remains the quality of coffee delivered as revealed in cup and chemical tests. Potts (2007) reports that certified producers can realize higher prices, but only when they are reliable suppliers and if the quality of their products is consistent.

The limitation of UTZ in Tanzania is its restriction to plantations. Its economic and environmental benefits would be greater if it was extended to smallholders. To an extent, some such benefits are already evident since changes appear to have occurred in agricultural practices and perceptions about sustainable agriculture among non-certified farmers in the immediate neighbourhoods of certified plantations in Tanzania. This demonstrates smallholders' willingness to learn and adapt to new practices (for example, conserving wetland and reduced use of chemicals) from certified firms.

GlobalGAP certified vegetables in Tanzania

Implementation in practice

Implementation of GlobalGAP schemes can be in accordance with any one of the following options:

(i) Option 1: an individual producer applies for GlobalGAP certification and becomes the certificate holder.
(ii) Option 2: a producer group applies for GlobalGAP group certification, and – as a legal entity – becomes the certificate holder.
(iii) Option 3 and 4: benchmarking – owners of another standard can apply to GlobalGAP for benchmarking (equivalence). If equivalence is determined, then producers certified to this standard will be also considered certified to GlobalGAP.

Smallholder producers in the case study are certified under Option 2 – as opposed to large-scale producers in Kenya, who are mostly certified under Option 1. The smallholders are organized in a producer marketing organization (PMO) comprising several cooperatives linked to a GlobalGAP-certified exporter. Of a total of seven smallholder fresh vegetable cooperatives linked to the exporter, three had acquired GlobalGAP certification. At the time of the research, the other four were producing vegetables for markets which do not require a GlobalGAP certificate. The certification process starts with sensitization of farmers intending to join the GlobalGAP out-grower scheme. Following this, interested farmers are registered with the exporter and agreements are drawn between the exporter and producers. These stages are followed by training on group formation and crop husbandry.

GlobalGAP has two sets of requirements. The first set is classified as 'major musts' and the second set is classified as 'minor musts'. The 'major musts' include requirements on record keeping, site management, soil erosion control, fertilizer usage and storage, quality of water for irrigation, use and handling of chemicals, product handling during harvesting, post-harvest treatment, worker health, safety and welfare and other environmental issues. Their implementation requires investment in infrastructure and upgrading of human resources. Examples of investments that are required include:

(i) construction of chemical stores, chemical mixing areas, water taps and toilets;

(ii) purchase of modern equipment for chemical application; and
(iii) construction of facilities for grading, cooling, storage and disposal.

According to our field work, most of these infrastructural investments are in practice only required for large-scale vegetable producers. Smallholders are not required to invest individually in construction of stores, toilets and water taps. Some of the smallholder farmers were found owning spray pumps, but these were not used in production of certified crop as crop protection was usually undertaken by the exporter. Similarly, smallholder investments in grading, cooling and storage facilities were not called for because the products were collected by the exporter just after harvesting. In contrast, for medium- and large-scale farmers investment in these facilities was necessary, though the level of investment varied depending on the size of their operations.

Expenditure on labour and in some case also on infrastructure was required from smallholders for land preparation, soil management and crop maintenance. For improved crop husbandry, land had to be adequately cleared and tilled including putting in place cross linings and planting pest control plants around the plots. Weeding and construction of plant support materials were also required.

Critical for compliance with GlobalGAP standards is proper use of chemicals, particularly fertilizers and pesticides. As noted, the GlobalGAP protocol insists on integrated crop management and integrated pest management, including the use of natural predators. However, the need to ensure freedom from pests, diseases and blemishes, coupled with the heavy pest pressure in humid tropics, means that pesticides are also used for fresh vegetable production without exception. Because farmers were observed exceeding recommended rates of application, arrangements were made by exporters to spray all the smallholder plots under contract themselves. The cost of this service is deducted from the farmers' proceeds when selling to the exporters. Fertilizer application activities are also closely supervised by exporters.

Value chain restructuring and standards compliance

For exporters and farmers in Tanzania the main objective of certifying to GlobalGAP has been to maintain market access. The two large exporters' main market is retailers in the UK and other EU markets. The exporters have contacts or understandings with their GlobalGAP buyers covering price, quality, conformity to specification, timing of delivery, delivery mode, packaging, sharing of expenses and payment mode. Some costs of conformity with these contractual conditions are passed on to out-growers. Meanwhile, the exporters also retain access to markets for uncertified products. Most of the excess certified produce or uncertified produce goes to wholesalers and processors in Europe who do not insist on the GlobalGAP certification.

When the exporters studied here were first established, they primarily depended on their own production of vegetables. However, over time they extended outsourcing. Hence, GlobalGAP certification in Tanzania has been associated with a lengthening rather than a shortening of the value chain. However, the exporters have retained nuclear farms of their own. Serengeti Fresh for instance has 70ha of own production that guarantees a minimum volume of quality vegetables year round.

Exporters ensure consistently high quality through multiple quality checks, sorting, grading, packing and transporting in refrigerated fleets of trucks for export through Nairobi, Dar-es-Salaam and/or Kilimanjaro airport (KIA).

Thus the adoption of GlobalGAP standards has resulted in profound changes to value chain structure in Tanzania, but in rather an unexpected direction. As a result of GlobalGAP Option 2, certification of smallholders became possible: albeit under conditions of high levels of vertical coordination. The value chain is characterized by a high level of monitoring of out-growers by exporters owing to the low capabilities in the supply-base to meet the requirements of the standard.

Compliance costs and benefits

Participation in GlobalGAP had provided important opportunities for smallholder farmers including the knowledge and skills necessary for production for export. Farmers have been trained, among other things, on good production practices, storage and handling of produce, health and sanitary requirements and protection of the environment. Many of these skills and areas of knowledge can be applied to non-GlobalGAP production. A second opportunity is for smallholder farmers to access the UK fresh vegetable market. This allows certified farmers to get higher prices compared to alternative markets. For instance, certified vegetable producers in the study areas were getting $0.85/kg for fine beans and snow peas and $1.40/kg for baby corn as compared to less than $0.60 and $1.10 for uncertified sales of the same crops. Farmers have also been accessing credit in the form of inputs and/or cash for agricultural production. Introduction of new crops to the production systems allows rotation and diversification of agricultural production. GlobalGAP vegetable production has also been associated with intensification of agricultural production. Most of the vegetable crops for export take only about three months to mature. Farmers reported that this allows for three crop cycles per season and therefore high land productivity. In the study areas, certified smallholder farmers got as much as 10 per cent and 16 per cent higher yields per hectare than uncertified farmers for baby corn and fine beans, respectively, and 32 per cent higher for snow peas.

As a result of these factors, net horticultural revenue for certified farmers exceeded that for uncertified farmers. Net revenues for certified farmers from baby corn and fine beans, computed on a per hectare basis, were respectively

10 and 24 per cent higher than those for non-certified farmers. However, for snow peas net revenues per hectare for certified farmers exceeded those of uncertified farmers by only 3 per cent.

It is important to note however that the figures reported here do not take into account costs of the development of the smallholder quality management system necessary for certification, farmer training or farm certification. These were all financed by the EU's COLEACP/PIP programme. An additional contribution to training was made by DANIDA's Tanzania Small and Medium Enterprise Competitiveness Facility. The farmer groups received further support from the African Development Bank's Agricultural Development Facility and from the Kilimo Trust for group-level infrastructure (office and stores), while part of the exporter's infrastructure costs and working capital were financed through a World Bank loan.

Threats, opportunities, lessons learned

High costs of compliance and inadequate technical know-how are typically identified as the most important bottlenecks facing exporters and farmers in Tanzania, with respect to standards compliance. Other constraints that are always mentioned in relation to high-value exports include inadequate cargo capacity, finance and institutional support. More recently, Tanzanian exporters mention inadequate airport facilities for vegetables rather than cargo capacity problems.

Currently, most of the perishable produce air-freighted out of KIA is carried by KLM, landing daily. The cargo capacity of the plane is approximately 18 tons. Since July 2004, MK Airlines has added to the airfreight capacity at KIA by landing a narrow-bodied cargo plane once a week, collecting 7–10 tons of cargo most weeks, with the highest uplift being just under 13 tons (still below the targeted break-even level for the service). The rates that were being charged were US\$1.88/kg to the UK and US\$1.84/kg to Amsterdam, which are comparable to rates charged out of Nairobi. However, due to KLM's inadequate facilities for vegetables, high rates of produce spoilage were reported.

There are also constraints that are associated with incorporation of smallholder farmers in certified fresh vegetable production for export. For example conditions are not conducive to sorting at farm level. As a result all produce is transported to the pack house where sorting is done. This denies farmers an opportunity to sell in the domestic market or use for home consumption produce that does not meet export standards. This creates dissatisfaction among participating farmers in that the volume collected at the farm is normally higher than the volume that they are paid for, due to high level of rejects.

The proliferation of standards is one of the challenges for exporters from developing countries. Exporters to the UK from Tanzania are required to comply with one, two or a combination of three standards namely

GlobalGAP, Tesco's Natures Choice (TNC) and British Retail Consortium (BRC). To obtain BRC certification, in addition to GlobalGAP, the exporter has to meet a separate set of pack house handling requirements.

The role of donor support in smallholder GlobalGAP certification referred to above underlines perhaps the most profound threat, namely that of the questionable sustainability of this value chain in the absence of such support. As the GlobalGAP standard continues to evolve in a more stringent direction, it seems that new training as well as investment costs will continuously rise, along with increasing costs of certification itself.

Social standards in the cut flower industries of Kenya and Tanzania

Implementation in practice

Provisions included in those sustainability standards applied to cut flowers differ considerably, amongst other things, in the ease with which they can be monitored. Some requirements, like provision for pesticide storage, sanitary facilities and even payment for overtime, are relatively easy to check using a combination of physical observation, document review and interviews. Other requirements however, such as freedom from gender or ethnic discrimination and workers' freedom to organize, are inherently more difficult to check and this often leaves decisions about the presence or absence of compliance up to the personal judgement of the auditor. These observations, based on interviews, are confirmed in a comprehensive study conducted by Barrientos and Smith (2007) who distinguish between outcome standards and standards referring to process rights.

Process rights such as those just mentioned describe principles of social justice that enable workers to attain wider objectives such as negotiation of wages, working hours, health and safety policies, health insurance and pensions provision or even comprehensive collective bargaining agreements. In a comprehensive study of the effects of social standards amongst suppliers to retailer members of the ETI,[4] it was found that while standards were having an effect on variables referred to in outcome standards, they were having little or no impact on process rights and furthermore failed to be applied to more marginal (often female) workers including casual and subcontracted workers (Barrientos and Smith, 2007; see also Nelson et al., 2007 for similar findings).

Value chain restructuring and standards compliance

In cut flowers, standard coverage is very much related to the channel through which the flowers are sold. The Africa–Europe cut flower value chain entails two distinctive strands. The Dutch flower auctions[5] have historically been the most important channel through which flowers are distributed to European wholesalers and retailers. But lately the percentage of flowers imported into the EU directly by large retailers and importers has increased, although the auction still accounts for the larger part (Thoen et al., 2000). This applies to Tanzania and Kenya alike. An estimated one-third of Kenyan exports in 2004 were direct, but most of the larger operations still supply both the auctions and the EU supermarkets (Tallontire and Greenhalgh, 2005). In Tanzania, roughly 75 per cent of exports went to the auctions in 2006, while the remainder was supplied directly to wholesalers and/or retailers, mostly in Germany, Norway, the UK and Sweden.

For producers participating in direct sales to large EU retailers, adopting social and environmental standards is a requirement while producers selling through the auctions are not faced with such a demand. Thus, a strong association exists between the nature of the value chain and producer motivations for adopting standards. In buyer-driven strands, standards form part of the governance structure operated by retailers and are hence a market access requirement. But in the market-based auction strand, if standards are adopted at all, this is as a reputation enhancer or simply as a management tool.[6] Moreover, buyer expectations are also highly country specific. For example, MPS is employed largely for flowers aimed at the Dutch auction system whereas FLP caters mostly for flowers bound for the German market and ETI is specific to UK retailers.

However, in the case of some chains there are other reasons for adopting standards. Especially for Kenyan producers, standard compliance is important to rebut public criticism both locally and in buyer markets. Additionally, adoption of a recognized standard decreases the risk of a buyer suddenly requiring new proprietary sustainability conditions.

Adherence to sustainability standards forms part of the requirements imposed by the large buyers along with specific requirements concerning price, quality, volume, logistics and so on. Adherence to sustainability standards thus only form one of many capacities required for entering the direct export market and producers do not regard it as the main challenge they face.

In terms of market coverage, social and environmental standards have become mainstream. A rough estimate puts 50–75 per cent of flowers imported into the EU as adhering to one or more standards. However, the vast majority of these standards are of a business-to-business kind (governed by business and not communicated to the consumer). Secondly, where social clauses are included in such standards, these mostly focus on outcome standards, not process rights. Social standards that are communicated through a consumer label characterize a much smaller portion of the market (no exact figures exist, but an estimate puts their EU market share at 5–10 per cent depending on the country). These tend to focus on process rights, although in the US market even consumer labels tend to focus more on outcome standards.

Compliance costs and benefits

As noted, while all sustainability initiatives applied in the East African cut flower sector include some elements related to labour, these mostly have a peripheral status. Moreover, they range along a continuum from mere endorsement of workers' basic rights to requiring the participation of unions and NGOs in monitoring. They therefore also differ markedly in their potential to create opportunities for labour and for local labour organizations.

The focus of the case study was on interactions between compliance with social standards and gains made by local labour organizations (including both trade unions and NGOs). One finding was that interpretation of standards' provisions by inspectors and national representatives of standard-setting organizations has an important bearing on the degree to which the standards in practice provide opportunities for labour and local labour organizations. Another was that the way in which social standards are actually used by labour organizations depends to a large degree on the context in which their local implementation takes place and the strategic priorities of different labour actors.

Unionization in the flower sector has increased considerably in Tanzania from two out of eight farms in 1998 to six out of ten in 2006 covering two-thirds of all flower workers. In Kenya, unionization has remained relatively low with only around 3400 unionized flower workers out of approximately 50,000. To a major extent, the positive development in Tanzania has come as a result of how local labour organizations have engaged with standards and managed to use them as a platform to organize and build capacity at farm branch level. This has occurred particularly through constructive interaction between the owners of the FLP standard and the Plantation and Agricultural Workers Union of Tanzania (TPAWU), with FLP seeking confirmation from the union that freedom of association and collective bargaining rights are complied with before certifying farms. Assurance of these rights resulted in collective bargaining agreements on the two largest farms which, according to TPAWU, opened the door for them to the Tanzanian flower sector in general. Regarding wages, a comparison between (three) certified and (seven) uncertified farms in Tanzania revealed higher average wages for employees on certified farms.

Labour's approach to standards in the Kenyan flower industry differed markedly from that in Tanzania. Unions at the national level positioned themselves against standard initiatives and refused to engage with any apart from Max Havelaar. It was reported that the national representative for Max Havelaar had been influential in pushing for a collective bargaining agreement on one of the largest farms. The Kenyan labour NGOs, on the other hand, very actively seek to influence how standards are adopted and renegotiated in Kenya.

Threats, opportunities, lessons learned

In sum, the cut flower case found that labour organizations may use (at least some of the more rigorous) standards to (1) enhance union organization and obtain collective bargaining agreements; (2) obtain better insight into the operations of cut flower markets; (3) get a seat at the table when business discusses social issues; and (4) exert a watchdog function in relation to non-compliant businesses, backed by a threat of exposure in consumer markets. Realization of these possibilities, perhaps optimistically, presupposes that labour organizations are accountable to their constituencies and work for the good of the workers they represent. Where labour organizations (and particularly trade unions) actually do so, the more stringent private social standard initiatives can be used to further their influence.

Conclusion

Sustainability standards in coffee, vegetables and flowers enhanced the possibility for producers to undertake direct exports, increased their security of contract and had measurable financial benefits for them. In two of the three cases (fresh vegetables and cut flowers) compliance to sustainability standards is a condition for access to large retailers in the UK and other EU markets. On the other hand, all cases showed that compliant producers also maintained access to markets for uncertified products. All, moreover, sold certified products into 'conventional' markets, indicating excess supply in chains demanding compliance.

Smallholder farmers are not compliant except for fresh vegetables in Tanzania through donor-supported contract farming. Such participation is rather untypical internationally (cf., *inter alia* Kenya and Senegal) and may be only temporary. But, where smallholders comply, there are benefits including significant increases in farmer revenues. Labour also benefits from sustainability standards but again under restricted conditions, namely where these have a content that is both stringent and clearly formulated, and where both EU retailers and local labour buy into them.

Referring to Jaffee and Henson's (2004) classic distinction between standards as barriers and opportunities, the overall picture is ambiguous. The new generation of standards are a barrier, particularly for smallholders, but also – where a range of facilitating factors are present – a major opportunity.

Notes

1. www.UTZcertified.org.
2. Data from UN COMTRADE.
3. In this particular process certain new risks may be inadvertently introduced. The introduction of certain native species may lead to increased incidence of pests and diseases, and competition for soil nutrients and sunlight.

4. The ETI (Ethical Trading Initiative) is a UK 'multi-stakeholder' initiative to promote and improve the implementation of corporate codes of practice which cover supply chain working conditions.
5. The Dutch auctions function as a distribution centre, absorbing large quantities of flowers that are re-packed and sold to buyers around the world. The system is based on a public price discovery system and a cooperative organization structure. There are seven cooperative flower auctions in the Netherlands with total sales amounting to US$1.9 billion in 1998. During the mid-1990s, Oserian/East African Flowers opened the Tele Flower Auction, a private auction. For a detailed description of the auction system see Thoen et al. (2000).
6. Lately there has been a marked increase in social standards adoption amongst those exporters, particularly Dutch ones, who sell through the auctions. This is related to the introduction of a new standard scheme named Fair Flowers Fair Plants. For details see Riisgaard (2009).

7
Localizing Private Social Standards: Standard Initiatives in Kenyan Cut Flowers

Lone Riisgaard

Introduction

As a response to the emergence of Northern-based social standards in the cut flower export industry, a range of Southern social standard initiatives have emerged. In this chapter, I analyse two Kenyan standard initiatives in the cut flower sector – a business initiative and a multi-stakeholder initiative. I investigate how international social standard requirements are 'localized' and the results of this localization for different stakeholders. The analysis shows that when the standards are negotiated and applied, the power relations that exist both between local stakeholders and along the global value chain (GVC) for cut flowers are reproduced. Placing local standard initiatives in the context of GVC governance, this chapter also illustrates how they can be seen as indirectly playing into the governance agenda of retail buyers, because local standards (particularly multi-stakeholder standards) offer better insurance against conflict and create necessary consensus and 'back-up' from critical voices, both locally and in buyer markets.

Private Social Standards (PSSs) covering the employment conditions of Southern producers exporting to European markets have multiplied rapidly since the 1990s. Multinational Enterprises (MNEs) and large buyers have increasingly adopted labour standards along global value chains (GVCs), such as the right to form trade unions and prohibitions on discrimination, child and forced labour. PSSs, however, remain highly disputed, particularly since their intended impacts are by no means guaranteed. Amongst other things, standard initiatives have been criticized for being Northern driven, for implementing a Northern agenda on Southern producers and workers, for not being sensitive to local specific conditions and for not including local stakeholders (Barrientos et al., 2003; Utting, 2005; Blowfield and Dolan, 2008).

Most PSS initiatives have been designed in the North. Lately, however, a range of Southern standard initiatives have emerged in the African horticultural industry. These local initiatives are most often run by producer associations, although a few multi-stakeholder initiatives have also appeared.[1] The Kenyan horticultural industry provides an interesting case, since no less than four local standard initiatives exist in parallel, including two business association standards (Kenya Flower Council (KFC) and the Fresh Produce Exporters Association of Kenya (FPEAK) standards), and a multi-stakeholder initiative (Kenyan Horticultural Ethical Business Initiative (HEBI)). Additionally, the Kenya Bureau of Standards (KEBS) has also developed a standard for the national horticultural industry. Kenya thus provides an interesting case for exploring what happens when international pressure for minimum social standards is translated into local standard initiatives.

In this chapter, I address developments in the governance structures of PSSs in the cut flower industry and particularly focus on Kenyan efforts to localize PSSs and the results of these efforts. I argue that the move towards 'localizing' PSSs cannot uncritically be seen as automatically furthering the interests of the intended beneficiaries of social standards (workers, their families and communities) nor as necessarily representing a 'Southern' agenda as opposed to a 'Northern' one. Through case studies of KFC and HEBI, this chapter investigates how the introduction of PSS requirements are 'localized' and how standards are 'played' in different ways by different stakeholders in order to gain influence and forward specific goals. Therefore, I analyse local standards against the background of local power relations. But local PSS initiatives also operate in the context of GVCs, particularly buyer-driven value chains, where lead firms govern the activity of other firms in the chain (Barrientos, 2003; Gibbon and Ponte, 2005; Riisgaard, 2007; Tallontire, 2007). Thus, in this chapter, the Kenyan PSS initiatives are also placed in the context of the GVC for cut flowers, particularly the strand of the value chain that is driven by large European retailers. This enables an analysis of how local standard initiatives fit into the governance mechanisms employed by powerful buyers and a discussion of whether these local initiatives from a value chain governance perspective create contested terrains.

To carry out the examination of local PSSs, I employ an analytical framework that combines explorations of horizontal interactions between stakeholders at the local level with vertical interconnections with stakeholders related to and involved in the GVC for cut flowers. Global Value Chain analysis is employed as an overall frame and used to situate the local PSSs in vertical relations of power. Particular attention is paid to the governance mechanisms employed by large retailers. The local level of PSSs constitutes the second level of analysis. In the forefront here are relations of power and negotiation.

For this purpose, I draw selectively on the conceptual framework developed by Tallontire (2007) to analyse developing country private standard initiatives in agro-food value chains. Tallontire also brings into play GVC analysis, but expands the understanding of governance by adopting concepts from convention theory and from analysis of regulation. I focus on the parts of Tallontire's framework that deal with legislative governance (who makes the rules and how) and judicial governance (how conformity is assessed). Underlying the analysis is an understanding of standards as socially mediated and therefore neither objective nor unbiased. Conversely, standards are always embedded in particular systems of social relations, and standard outcomes often reflect differences in power between different actors (Busch, 2000; Hatanaka et al., 2006).

The chapter is based on fieldwork I carried out in 2006 covering ten export flower farms in Kenya. Additionally, a range of interviews were conducted with industry organizations, industry consultants, local and international standard initiatives, labour NGOs and trade unions at national as well as district- and farm-branch levels. Follow-up interviews with key stakeholders were carried out in May 2008 (for interview reference key see notes[2]).

In the next section developments in the global flower value chain, including developments in PSSs and in the Kenyan context, are discussed. In the third section, I turn to the Kenyan PSS initiatives focusing on legislative and judicial governance, the motivation and strategies of the different stakeholders, as well as the relation to GVC governance. The fourth section concludes by reflecting on how power inequalities are played out in the localization of PSSs in Kenya and how local standard initiatives can be seen as indirectly playing into the governance agenda of retail buyers.

Private social standards and cut flowers in Kenya

Reorganizing production

Private social standard (PSS) initiatives, both international and local, operate in the context of GVCs. The production strategies of MNEs have changed substantially since the 1970s. At present, they are often characterized less by direct foreign investment and more by indirect sourcing through GVCs linking them to networks of suppliers in developing countries (Dicken, 2007). This shift has been described at length in the GVC literature, which traces the linkages between production, distribution, retailing and consumption. This body of literature highlights the ability of some lead firms[3] to govern the activity of other firms in the chain (for instance, Gereffi and Korzeniewicz, 1994; Gibbon and Ponte, 2005). Setting rules and conditions of participation are the key operational mechanisms of GVC governance (Gibbon and Ponte, 2005) and PSSs can therefore be seen as forming part of the mechanisms used to govern GVCs by lead firms.

Governance is defined by Gereffi as 'authority and power relationships that determine how financial, material, and human resources are allocated and flow within a chain' (1994, 97). Governance thus refers to the process of organizing activities with the purpose of achieving a certain functional division of labour along a value chain. It results in specific distributions of benefits, and sets terms of participation and of exclusion (Ponte, 2008). Gereffi originally distinguished between buyer- and producer-driven[4] value chains to describe two distinct forms of overall chain governance. Producer-driven chains are usually found in sectors with high technological and capital requirements; and here chain governance is exercised by companies that control key technology and production facilities. Buyer-driven chains, such as the retailer-driven 'strand' of the cut flower value chains, are generally more labour intensive and information costs, product design, advertising and advanced supply management systems constitute the entry barriers to chain leadership. In these chains production functions are usually outsourced and retailers and brand name companies exercise key governance functions (Gereffi, 1994).

In general, a move towards buyer drivenness[5] in GVCs can be observed particularly in GVCs led by branded manufacturers and retailers (Gereffi et al., 2005; Gibbon and Ponte, 2005). In buyer-driven GVCs, a movement can be detected from direct control to more indirect or 'hands off' mechanisms of governance. This includes a heightened explicit role for quality within a framework of 'control at a distance' and the increased importance of standards and auditing technologies and methods (Power, 1997; Gibbon and Ponte, 2005). The heightened importance of quality (broadly defined) relates to a shift from an economy of quantities to an economy of qualities (Callon et al., 2002), where quality is becoming a central component of economic competition and where private quality standards and their ability to differentiate products therefore are becoming increasingly important (Hatanaka et al., 2006). This shift is mirrored in GVCs by an extension of governance mechanisms to wider issues, such as management standards, environmental standards and, more recently, social standards that are observed by suppliers (Reardon et al., 2001; Nadvi K and Wältring, 2004; Gibbon and Ponte, 2005; Hatanaka et al., 2006; Tallontire, 2007; Nadvi, 2008).

Restructuring the cut flower value chain

The move towards buyer drivenness is evident in the cut flower value chain, where structural shifts in distribution channels in EU markets are taking place, with the growing importance of supermarkets sourcing directly from suppliers in developing countries, cutting out wholesalers and the Dutch auctions[6] (Thoen et al., 2000; CBI, 2007). The world market for cut flowers has grown consistently since the early 1980s, but has experienced a slowing of growth in demand over the past 5 to 10 years, especially in the EU. At the same time, increases in production (especially in developing countries) have led to a downward movement in prices. Consumers in EU markets are demanding greater variety and are increasingly interested in the environmental and social dimensions of production. This is leading to a proliferation of social and environmental standards in the industry (Thoen et al., 2000; CBI, 2007).

The Kenyan–European cut flower value chain entails two distinctive strands (the direct strand and the auction strand). The Dutch flower auctions have historically been the most important channels through which flowers are distributed to European wholesalers and retailers. But lately the proportion of flowers imported into the EU from East Africa that goes through the Dutch flower auctions has diminished and direct sourcing by large retailers is increasing. The auctions still remain the most important world market outlet for cut flowers, however, and the main way that cut flowers from East Africa reach European wholesalers and retailers (Thoen et al., 2000). Since standards are a requirement only for producers participating in the 'direct' strand of the GVC, which is driven by large retailers, in this chapter I focus on this particular strand (hereafter simply named the flower GVC).

The increase of direct sourcing by large retailers is having a significant impact on governance (due to the retailers' considerable market power) as well as creating an increasing demand for compliance with social and environmental standards. More complex consumer demands and a more demanding regulatory environment faced by retailers have led to changes in how retailers manage their value chains, aimed at both avoiding negative publicity and differentiating their products. One way that retailers have achieved this is by codifying the knowledge required to meet quality specifications in standards and grading systems. Social and environmental standards are an extension of this process and one way in which retailers seek to reduce risks and govern their value chains (Barrientos et al., 2003). In cut flowers, PSSs therefore form part of the mechanisms that are used by retailers to govern the GVC. The direct strand for flowers is highly driven by supermarket buyers, particularly UK retailers.

Private social standards in cut flowers

Critique in consumer markets of appalling working conditions in factories and plantations in developing countries producing consumer goods for the Northern markets spurred the formulation and adaptation of PSSs. The nature of cut flowers and the character of the flower trade have created the context for some highly criticized working conditions in the industry. The Kenyan flower industry in particular has been one of the favourite targets for campaigns, both locally and in Europe, demanding better environmental and social conditions. Export of cut flowers from East Africa is an example of how tightened quality regulations and increasing concerns with social and environmental issues have created a highly codified industry. For producers participating in value chains driven by large retailers, adopting social and environmental standards is a requirement, and it is not unusual for producers to comply with half a dozen different social and environmental standards (cf. Collinson, 2001; Barrientos et al., 2003).

Social standards differ significantly in origin (both in terms of geography and actors involved) as well as in content, implementation and monitoring procedures. Initially, these standards mostly took the form of unilateral business initiatives, but later they have also included broader business and multi-stakeholder initiatives. The majority of standard initiatives were conceived and formulated in Europe, but in recent years a variety of standard initiatives have also been initiated in producer countries. Cut flower export trade associations in Kenya, Uganda, Zambia, Zimbabwe and Colombia have all developed their own social standards (CBI, 2007; Dolan and Opondo, 2005). In all, at least 16 different social and or environmental standards (international and national) exist for cut flower exports (CBI, 2007; Riisgaard, 2007). The first standards that emerged in the industry were mainly set by buyers or producer groups and tended to be weak on social issues and rely mainly on first- or second-party monitoring. During the 1990s, there was a development towards the use of third-party monitoring and the emergence of new multi-stakeholder initiatives. Standards, furthermore, have tended to broaden from only covering cut flowers to including pot plants and foliage.

With the demand for standards also comes a demand for auditing and certification. Depending on the individual standard, different actors qualify (and often compete) to carry out services in the audit and certification market. Furthermore, standard creation, adoption and implementation affect terms of inclusion and exclusion in value chains. It is therefore of importance to examine who sets these standards and what issues are subjected to standardization and how. As argued in Brunsson (2000, 9): 'the creation of standards can seldom be seen as natural, straight forward or harmonious processes. Rather many factors are important: which actors are able to participate or allowed to do so, how the decision processes are designed, and so on.' Standards are thus not objective and neutral mechanisms, but socially mediated and embedded in particular systems of social relations and power (Busch, 2000; Hatanaka et al., 2006). Studies by Hughes (2001) highlight that when all costs of complying with social standards are borne solely by suppliers, then PSSs can actually reinforce an already adversarial supply chain relationship and retailer dominance. In this way, as Freidberg (2003) puts it, 'cleaning up down South comes cheap' and PSSs can be seen as reinforcing existing power imbalances and as a new mechanism of control through self-control. Additionally, when PSSs touch down in local settings, they invariably interact with local relations of power and politics and should not be viewed as neutral market tools (Hatanaka et al., 2006; Riisgaard, 2007;Ponte, 2008). Local PSS initiatives therefore need to be seen as sites of struggle and contestation, which might reinforce or change roles and inter-relationships (du Toit, 2002; Tallontire, 2007). Thus, the emergence of local standard initiatives needs to be addressed in the context of power relations both within the GVC and between the local stakeholders. Before proceeding to explore how this unfolds in Kenya cut flowers, a critical discussion of developments, potentials and limitations of PSSs is presented.

The potential and limitations of PSSs

The benefits of PSSs remain highly disputed. PSSs are almost exclusively limited to export industries and reviews have highlighted that many are weak in content, especially in terms of workers' right to organize and bargain collectively, as well as in relation to gender issues (Barrientos et al., 2003; Blowfield and Frynas, 2005; Barrientos and Smith, 2007). Recently, the adverse effects of corporate buying strategies (particularly price cuts, short lead times and rapid turn around) on labour conditions have been highlighted and there is growing recognition of the limits of PSSs as a means of improving working conditions in global production and particularly as a means of altering the power relations between labour and capital (du Toit, 2002; Barrientos et al., 2003; Utting, 2005; Barrientos and Smith, 2007; Riisgaard, 2007; Blowfield and Dolan, 2008).

Serious inadequacies have been reported in the way standard compliance is monitored by companies and by the burgeoning social auditing industry. Auditors have tended to rely heavily on management information, with little involvement of workers and the organizations representing them. Additionally, audits have focused most attention on the more visible aspects of standards, such as health and safety and working hours, rather than more embedded issues such as discrimination (Barrientos and Smith, 2007). Research has shown that the use of a participatory social audit methodology[7] is more likely to build trust, promote dialogue and expose sensitive workplace issues but the method is also more challenging and costly to apply (ibid.; Dolan and Opondo, 2005; Blowfield and Dolan, 2008). Even so, elements of participatory auditing seem to have been incorporated along with an increase in multi-stakeholder initiatives (Riisgaard, 2009).

A related point is highlighted by Barrientos and Smith (2007), namely the distinction between outcome standards and process rights. Process rights, for example the principles of freedom of association and no discrimination, describe intrinsic principles of social justice that enable workers to claim their rights. These process rights provide a route to the negotiation of and access to other entitlements and specified conditions of employment, such as a health and safety policy, minimum wages, working hours and provision of benefits such as health insurance and pensions. These entitlements and specified conditions of employment are labelled outcome standards. Most PSSs are now based on ILO core conventions and thus are comprised of both outcome standards and process rights. Nevertheless, in a comprehensive study of the effects of PSSs amongst suppliers to members of the ETI,[8] it was found that while PSSs were having an effect on outcome standards, they were having little or no effect on process rights (Barrientos and Smith, 2007; see also Nelson et al., 2007 for similar findings).

That PSSs have more impact on outcome standards than process rights relates to auditing methods and reflects the dominance of a technical compliance perspective. Checklist-based auditing and self-assessment have been the main ways of monitoring PSS implementation. This system is compatible with other forms of technical and financial auditing, and is often carried out by companies who also specialize in those activities. While technical social auditing is able to identify outcome standards, such as health and safety provisions and wage levels, it has proved less capable of identifying process rights (Barrientos and Smith, 2007). This in turn reflects a general tension between a focus on PSS as a technical tool to achieve social compliance based on outcome standards and a focus on PSS as a means of enhancing the process through which workers claim their rights. In multi-stakeholder initiatives, to which I will turn shortly, this tension often plays out as a tension between civil society and commercial actors.

In the cut flower industry, most standards still focus on outcome standards, not process rights. In terms of market coverage, social and environmental standards have become mainstream in flowers. A rough estimate puts between 50 and 75 per cent of flowers imported into the EU as adhering to one or more social and or environmental standard. However, the vast majority of these standards are business-to-business standards (governed by business and not communicated to the consumer). While most of these standards now use third-party monitoring and mention rights such as the freedom of association and the right to collective bargaining, most still focus on outcome standards, not process rights. The standards that focus on process rights are mainly collective standards with consumer labels operating in niche markets. The standards that are communicated through a consumer label characterize a much smaller portion of the market (no exact figures exist, but an estimate puts their market share at 5–10 per cent depending on the country).[9] However, the share of consumer-labelled flowers has been rising quite rapidly over the last years (sales of Fairtrade flowers, for example, increased by 66 per cent from 2006 to 2007; The Fair Flowers Fair Plants (FFP) initiative is also growing rapidly).[10]

Multi-stakeholder initiatives, Southern initiatives and issues of power and representation

Retailers have responded to criticism by creating alliances with the very groups that criticize them in so-called multi-stakeholder initiatives where NGOs, multilateral and other organizations encourage companies to participate in fora that set social standards, monitor compliance, promote social reporting and auditing and encourage stakeholder dialogue and social learning (Utting, 2002). Multi-stakeholder initiatives, however, are also open to criticism. There are important questions about representation. Who is included? Who is excluded? Who speaks on behalf of workers, especially more marginalized informal workers, many of whom are women? (du Toit,

2002; Barrientos, 2003; Dolan and Opondo, 2005; Tallontire, 2007; Blowfield and Dolan, 2008).

Furthermore, tensions can easily arise between different stakeholders, who are representing or reflecting different interests and occupy different positions of economic power linked to the global value chain (Hughes, 2001). As argued by Utting (2002), corporations might encourage multi-stakeholder initiatives and other forms of collaboration with NGOs as a means of (a) accommodating threats to their dominance that derive from civil society activism and (b) exercising what Gramsci has referred to as 'moral, cultural and intellectual' leadership as a basis for rule via consensus as opposed to coercion (Levy, 1997). In GVC language, this argument touches upon the potential role of multi-stakeholder standard initiatives as a tool that indirectly reinforces the governance agenda of buyer-driven value chains, because they enable cooperation and consensus while securing against conflict.

Another criticism concerns the fact that many multi-stakeholder initiatives and PSSs in general have been developed in the North, and there is concern that these fail to incorporate Southern stakeholders and the concerns of workers in developing countries (Barrientos, 2003; Tallontire, 2007; Blowfield and Dolan, 2008). Southern initiatives have emerged to counter this trend. According to Barrientos (2003), Southern initiatives reflect a move away from a Northern-based focus towards local engagement in how standards and standard implementation can more genuinely address and improve the needs and rights of workers. In this view, Southern initiatives are better able to address worker needs at a local level and in the specific local context. Discrimination based on gender or race may, for example, be embedded in social norms and, thus, require different strategies in one context compared to another. Furthermore, local initiatives can address more context-specific and more complex issues on an ongoing rather than an on-off basis (ibid.).

Blowfield and Dolan (2008) highlight how African standard initiatives, like Northern initiatives, are not formulated by the workers they purport to benefit. It is also questionable exactly how local the local initiatives actually are. Do they represent a new position that in any substantial way contests existing Northern initiatives or the dominant position of Northern buyers? The following sections will show that local standards can, to some degree, play into the governance agenda of buyer-driven value chains.

Kenyan social standard initiatives

Analytical framework and background

In this part of the chapter, I turn to an analysis of relations of power, contestation and negotiation in local PSSs in Kenya. The analysis is based on the understanding that the content of standards and how they are applied is often the outcome of strategic actions and negotiations between involved stakeholders reflecting existing power differences (Juska et al., 2000; Bingen and Siyengo, 2002; Hatanaka et al., 2006). Each stakeholder has its own agenda and ideas about quality (in this case, ideas about what constitutes acceptable social conditions) that it seeks to implement, and standards are used to further this agenda. Thus, the way standards are negotiated and used may reflect and reproduce power relations that exist both between local stakeholders and along the GVC.

As recommended by Tallontire (2007), I start by analysing the rules which are being developed and implemented through the PSSs. A next step is charting the evolution of the PSS opening up for discussions about who makes the rules and how (what Tallontire refers to as 'legislative governance'). This concerns the origin of the standard, the extent to which it draws on international standards or includes locally specific criteria, the links it has with other standards, both in the public and private domains, and identification of who is involved and who may be excluded. This is particularly pertinent in relation to worker representation, as new forms of worker representation are legitimized through NGO advocacy. Attention is also given to what Tallontire terms 'judicial governance', referring to the way compliance is monitored and assessed. This issue is particularly relevant since the initiatives differ substantially in this area. Finally, the initiatives are set in the context of governance of the cut flower GVC and the important question of whether these local PSSs actually represent a form of 'control at a distance' on the part of lead buyers.

Focus is on the KFC and HEBI standards, the two initiatives developed explicitly for the flower industry. These two standard initiatives provide appropriate grounds for comparison, since they are substantially different both in relation to their structure as initiatives and in the methodologies they employ for assessing compliance. Two other local standard initiatives (FPEAK and KEBS) were not specifically designed for cut flowers, but contain general standards for horticultural products. The FPEAK and KEBS standards are not analysed in this chapter, but since they are relevant in relation to both KFC and HEBI, they are briefly introduced in the following together with a short overview of other relevant local stakeholders.

The development of local PSSs in Kenya

Kenya is one of the top players in the world cut flower industry (the fourth largest) with a value of US$313 million out of a total export value of US$354 million from Sub Saharan Africa (the global value was US$5.5 billion in 2007).[11] The export flower industry in Kenya started to take off in the late sixties and cut flowers are now the nation's second largest source of foreign exchange in agriculture (after tea), providing employment to an estimated 50,000 workers. Although there are an estimated 150 export flower farms in Kenya, a tendency can be seen towards concentration, with three-quarters of the exports supplied by about 25 large- and medium-scale operations (Opondo, 2002; Omosa et al., 2006).

The Kenyan flower industry has been one of the favourite targets for campaigns both locally and in Europe demanding better environmental and social conditions. Since the 1990s, producers (particularly producers supplying EU retailers) have adopted a range of social and environmental standards (see also Riisgaard, 2007) and four local standard initiatives have emerged (all the Kenyan standards are named 'codes', so in the following codes and standards are used interchangeably). The first local standards were launched by the Fresh Produce Exporters Association of Kenya (FPEAK) in 1996 and Kenya Flower Council (KFC) in 1998. KFC has about 50 members representing more than 70 per cent of Kenyan flower exports. FPEAK has around 70 flower exporters as members. Compared to KFC, which counts many of the largest flower growers, FPEAK caters more for medium- and smaller-size flower exporters (Thoen et al., 2000; www.fpeak.org). Both the FPEAK and KFC standards relate mainly to good agricultural practices but also cover environmental management and occupational health and safety of workers.

In 2002, the Kenya Bureau of Standards (KEBS) launched the 'KS1758 Code of Practice for the Horticulture Industry'. Although KEBS is a statutory organization and the national standards body,[12] it did not develop the standard. The forces behind the establishment of the KEBS standard were FPEAK and KFC. Together they drafted a harmonized standard based on their own standards. This document was handed over to KEBS, which merely corrected the format and sent it to the Standard Council for approval (interviews St2/St7/St8 2006).

At the time of its approval (on Valentine's Day 2002), local NGOs launched a public campaign criticizing the failure of existing social standards to protect workers' rights (Hale and Opondo, 2005). As a direct outcome of this critique, the multi-stakeholder Kenyan Horticultural Ethical Business Initiative (HEBI) was formed in 2003 and the HEBI code, which deals exclusively with social issues, was released (ETI, 2005; Hale and Opondo, 2005). The board of HEBI has representatives of NGOs as well as employers' associations (FPEAK and KFC) and individual producers (Hale and Opondo, 2005; www.hebi.org). In 2004, a second edition of the KEBS standard was approved (interview St7, 2006). The 2004 version was aligned to EurepGAP (now GlobalGAP) and incorporates provisions on worker health, safety and welfare from the HEBI standard (KEBS, 2004). Both KFC and FPEAK have endorsed the HEBI standard. In the following sections the KFC and HEBI standard initiatives are examined in turn.

The Kenya Flower Council (KFC) code of practice

Rules and genealogy

In 1998, KFC was created by five of the largest farms as a reaction to a flurry of negative media attention in the UK and pressure from NGOs in Kenya as well as abroad (Hughes, 2001). The KFC standard was motivated by a wish to 'clean up' the image of the flower export industry and in this way accommodate critical civil society voices, both locally and in buyer markets, while at the same time accommodating new retailer demands. The KFC code of practice details the standards to be met in environmental, social, health and safety and good agricultural practices by all KFC members. The authors of the standard are the KFC Council Directors, comprising eight financial and production managers of the major farms. The standard, now in its seventh edition, is based on European standards (particularly UK retailer standards) for good agricultural practices and social and environmental performance, but with references to Kenyan legislation.

All KFC members have to comply with the KFC Silver standard within 1 year and can choose to move up to the optional Gold standard thereafter (interview St2, 2006). Members are mostly large Kenyan flower growers, while associate members are EU importers, UK retailers and Dutch auctions (Hughes, 2001; www.kfc.org). Apart from a yearly certification and six monthly surveillance audits, KFC also carries out unannounced audits in 10 per cent of the member farms every year. The Silver standard is audited by KFC's own auditors. However, due to changing demand from international buyers, since 1999, KFC audit procedures are evaluated by accreditation bodies that are qualified and recognized by the International Accreditation Forum, such as SANAS or BVQI (Hughes, 2001).[13]

Integration, recognition and accreditation

In June 2005, KFC became the first national growers' association to achieve benchmark status with the EurepGAP (now GlobalGAP) Ornamentals Scheme (UNCTAD, 2007).[14] After being awarded equivalence status to GlobalGAP, KFC started the process of aligning the KFC Quality Management System to ISO guide 65. This is necessary in order to be accredited to certify to internationally recognized standards such as GlobalGAP. If successful, this means that when certified to the KFC standard, members will for a small amount be able to become certified to GlobalGAP without further auditing (interviews St2/St4 2006, http://www.kenyaflowers.co.ke/audit.htm, accessed March 2008).

In 2006, KFC reached a recognition agreement with the largest UK supermarket chain, Tesco, which carries out an ongoing assessment of KFC's standard and audit procedures in order to ensure that the procedures of the KFC standard are compliant with the Ethical Trade Initiative (ETI) requirements, which TESCO adheres to.[15] Apart from these accreditation and recognition agreements, KFC also cooperates with local standard initiatives. As mentioned earlier, KFC is a board member of HEBI and has together with FPEAK been the driver in establishing the KEBS standard.

Integration with international and national standard initiatives through accreditation, recognition and cooperation has constituted an important tactic for KFC since its first code was drawn up in 1998. Alignment with international standards serves the purpose of keeping members up-to-date with buyers' standard demands and thus helps members to remain competitive. At the same time, it makes the KFC standard more attractive (and less costly) to flower growers by offering a 'one off' audit (interview St2, 2006). In turn, this allows KFC to capture a larger chunk of the auditing and certification market. Alignment with international standards is moreover necessary to gain reputational recognition amongst buyers.

KFC participates in HEBI at board level, thereby engaging at the institutional level with the NGOs, which have been the main critical voice in the country. This way, they accommodate critical voices both locally and abroad and are able to 'contain' some of the negative publicity (this is considered in more detail in connection with the analysis of HEBI below). At the same time, the involvement with HEBI plays into the existing conflict between NGOs and unions in the sector. Thus, KFC effectively recognizes labour NGOs as preferred partners when discussing labour rights issues and social standards in the industry.

Localization and relation to GVC governance

While KFC founders had some autonomy in drafting the code, it was powerfully shaped by UK supermarket standards and audit procedures. Global institutions like the ILO and WHO have formulated the conventions that form the background for the writing of standards in the area of chemical use and labour standards. National level legislation informs many of the specific requirements laid out in the code, especially with regards to labour issues, but also on the use of chemicals (the standard demands relevant licenses, for example a license to store chemicals obtained by the Pest Control Products Board and certificates from the Department of Health and Safety). UK legislation shapes the recommendations on other issues, like the storage of pesticides (Hughes, 2001; Kenya Flower Council code seventh edition).

The KFC social standard to some extent represents a localization move due to its reference to specific parts of the national legislation. However, this is not unambiguously a process towards local sensitivity and empowerment. On the contrary, the KFC initiative can be seen as a move towards alignment with international standards and audit procedures which focus on documentation and traceability and employ a technical checklist approach to measuring standard compliance. In this way the KFC standard, as most other PSSs, can be presented as a technical tool to achieve social compliance based on outcome standards as opposed to a means of enhancing the process through which workers claim their rights.

Both legislative governance (who makes the rules and how) and judicial governance (how compliance is assessed) of the KFC standard is strongly shaped by the demands of retailers. Furthermore, the standard in no way contests the power of large buyers in the value chain. In other words, what is agreed upon in the KFC standard is already accepted and increasingly demanded by EU flower buyers. Even though the standard initiative is local, it is shaped around the same managerial audit culture of buyer standards. The emergence of the KFC standard can therefore be seen as a move towards 'self-regulation' by producers in developing countries, and in this way it plays into a general governance move towards more indirect forms of governance in buyer-driven value chains. By being local the standard is helping to avoid conflict through its ability to detect and address non-compliance and disputes at an early stage and in a continuous way. In this way the local standards can indirectly aid buyers in creating the necessary 'back-up' from critical voices both locally and in the buyer markets.

Perhaps somewhat paradoxical is the fact that even though pressure from civil society at both ends of the value chains was influential in bringing about the KFC standard, civil society did not participate in standard setting and is not involved in monitoring. The realms of both legislative and judicial governance are exclusively confined to the largest producers and EU buyers (the most important of which are associate members of KFC).[16] In this way, both smaller producers and all other stakeholders are excluded from this process as well as from implementation. So, even though the KFC standard represents a localization move, the standard caters to business interests to the exclusion of the end-beneficiaries or organizations purporting to represent them.[17]

The Horticultural Ethical Business Initiative (HEBI)

Rules and genealogy

The HEBI code, released in 2003, draws on established African and international standards but resembles most closely the ETI Base Code. It includes provisions on child and forced labour, discrimination, regular employment, living wages, health and safety as well as freedom of association and the right to collective bargaining (www.hebi.or.ke/hebi-code.htm). However, what sets the HEBI standard apart from most other social standards are detailed instructions concerning implementation and auditing using participatory social auditing methods. This methodology is based on thorough participation in the audit process by all groups of workers as well as unions and NGOs. The methodology includes as key elements the use of participatory interview techniques (such as, for example, focus groups or the use of drama, storytelling or problem ranking) and an 'awareness day' prior to the audit involving both workers and management. The methodology also involves independent auditing and audit shadowing by (and consultation of) trade unions and NGOs (HEBI, 2005; HEBI, n.d.). The HEBI initiative thus falls within a tradition of focusing on PSS as a means of enhancing the process through which workers claim their rights.

As mentioned, HEBI was a response to the perceived shortcomings in the PSSs that were introduced in the Kenyan industry from the mid-1990s. The NGO campaign publicly launched on Valentine's Day in 2002 by the Workers' Rights Alert (WRA – a loose coalition of workers rights NGOs)[18] criticized the failure of these standards to protect workers' rights. This campaign successfully raised public awareness in Kenya and highlighted the poor conditions for workers in the flower export industry. This was followed by an international conference in May 2002, which the UK-based labour NGO and ETI member Women Working Worldwide (WWW) attended. An increasingly large percentage of Kenyan flowers were being bought directly by UK supermarkets that signed up to the ETI initiative. Therefore, it was possible for WRA through WWW to use the procedure in ETI that enables NGOs or trade union members to report violations of the ETI code. The companies in question have an obligation to investigate the situation and take appropriate action. Following the ETI investigation in Kenya, the multi-stakeholder initiative HEBI was formed and officially recognized in 2003 (ETI, 2005; Hale and Opondo, 2005). The board[19] of HEBI include three NGO representatives, three employers' associations (KFC, FPEAK and AEA – the Agricultural Employers Association) and three individual producers, with seats also available for representatives of the Kenya Plantation and Agricultural Workers' Union (KPAWU) (Hale and Opondo, 2005).

So far, HEBI has resulted in the development of the HEBI social base code. HEBI has conducted pilot audits on ten farms and a secretariat has been set up using grants provided by ETI and other donors. HEBI offers specialized training programmes in participatory social auditing to individuals and firms within the horticultural industry and has a pool of about 30 local social auditors who have been trained in the participatory social auditing methodology. It is yet to be decided if and how certification to the HEBI code will be carried out in practice, but it has been decided that official audits against the HEBI code have to be authorized by HEBI and shadowed by auditors trained and approved by HEBI (www.hebi.org; interview St2/St3, 2008). It seems, however, that HEBI activities have been somewhat halting in the last few years. At the moment, activities are confined to occasional board meetings and maintaining an available pool of auditors trained in the specified participatory methodology (interview St1/ St2/ St3, 2008). According to several board members, the performance and long-term viability of HEBI is questionable, particularly due to lack of funds since external donors have pulled out (interview St1/St2/M1/M8, 2006; St1/St2/St3, 2008). The HEBI secretariat, which previously had its own office and a project manager, is now reduced to temporarily borrowing a room in the KFC office (interviews St1/St2/St3, 2008).

Motivation and power – a stakeholder analysis

As mentioned, HEBI was formed because – despite the existence of initiatives that address labour standards on cut flower farms – a number of workers' rights violations persisted on these farms (ETI, 2005; interviews St3, 2008). The main problem seemed not to be the content of the standards, but the way in which compliance was assessed. At this time, many organizations were using their own auditors (leading to potential conflicts of interest particularly regarding standards governed by industry associations), with little transparency or involvement of external, independent stakeholders. Additionally, very few had established ongoing links with local trade unions and NGOs and none were using a participatory audit methodology (ETI, 2005).[20]

The mandate of HEBI was to develop a participatory social audit system that would be able to remedy these shortcomings while being acceptable to all stakeholders, including retailers in the North. HEBI was to develop detailed terms of reference for the audit of flower farms, raise funds to finance the audit process and appoint and contract independent auditors and approve the audit process (ETI, 2005; www.hebi.org). An important aspect of HEBI was at the same time to ensure dialogue amongst former adversarial stakeholders and contain damaging press coverage. The different stakeholders in the flower industry, however, had diverse and sometimes opposing motivations for participating (or not participating) in HEBI as well as diverging agendas for the desired performance of HEBI. The local stakeholders invited to participate in HEBI comprised trade unions, companies, industry associations and labour NGOs. Their agendas and stances will be discussed in turn.

The Kenyan trade unions have never participated in HEBI and this has raised questions about inclusiveness and representation. But neither Kenyan stakeholders, nor ETI members, have been able to build contacts between the established trade unions and HEBI (ETI, 2005). This situation needs to be seen in the broader context of a highly problematic relationship between labour NGOs and unions, both purporting to represent workers. NGOs claim that since only 3400 (out of around 50,000) flower workers are unionized and since unions are tailored to service male permanent workers, they cannot adequately represent the flower workers (which are often female and non-permanent). Unions, on the other hand, contend that NGOs have no right to stand in as worker representatives in labour market conflicts. The NGO–union relation seems to have grown worse with the introduction of private social standard initiatives, because these cooperate with NGOs but rarely with the unions (Hale and Opondo, 2005; Riisgaard, 2008). COTU (the Central Organisation of Trade Unions) has categorically declined to fill the seats available to them in HEBI due to the presence of labour NGOs (interview UN3, 2006; see also Riisgaard, 2007).[21] The unions have chosen to position themselves against the initiative and thereby refuse to attribute legitimacy to it. Also, at the international level, the global union federation representing agricultural workers' unions (the International Union of Foodworkers and Allied – IUF) does not endorse the HEBI initiative. According to the IUF Africa representative there are already too many standards; and the IUF has chosen to lobby for standard harmonization through the international Fair Flowers Fair Plants (FFP) initiative (interview Ex3, 2006).

The rejection of HEBI by the Kenyan trade unions does not only mean that the trade unions are not represented in the HEBI initiative. It also means that when buyers, employers and employer associations choose to endorse the initiative, they at the same time play into the conflict between NGOs and unions and effectively recognize labour NGOs as preferred partners when discussing labour rights issues and social standards in the industry.

As for producers and their organizations, HEBI was set up in a situation of heightened awareness of the significance of labour issues and this led several of the largest producers to immediately join the initiative (Hale and Opondo, 2005). Also, the industry organizations KFC and FPEAK were swift in joining and both endorsed the HEBI code. However, it remains unclear how (and if) this endorsement has any positive implications (interview St1, 2006; St2/St3, 2008). For both the large flower farms and the industry associations, participation was strongly encouraged by their main UK buyers. In addition, public allegations in Kenya compelled producers to move beyond industry-centred solutions into dialogue and cooperation with their usual adversaries. The producers had an interest in silencing the damaging press coverage for which the labour NGOs were responsible. While this changed the traditionally conflictual relationship between NGOs and producers, at the same time it reinforced the conflict between NGOs and unions in the industry and, thus, to some degree reinforced the divide among worker advocates. Producer participation in HEBI plays a powerful legitimizing role and helps satisfy critical voices (both national and international). However, producers and producer organizations also have an interest in not yielding influence over business procedures to NGOs. Particularly there is an interest in not adopting practices that complicate auditing by being more costly, more time-consuming or which potentially lead to more profound changes in the relationship between employees and employers.

Three labour NGOs participate in HEBI: Kenya Human Rights Commission (KHRC), Kenya Women Workers Organization (KEWWO) and Workers Rights Watch (WRW). Although they differ in focus (KHRC focuses on human rights broadly, KEWWO focuses specifically on woman workers, while the focus of WRW is on workers in general), they all fight for the rights of workers and they have a tradition of being activist and very critical of the cut flower industry conditions as well as of existing social standards.

Through HEBI, they have tried to push local standard practice towards a more participatory framework by promoting participatory social auditing. But the HEBI initiative also yields other benefits for the participating labour NGOs. By getting the industry players to engage in HEBI, they have gained recognition and influence. In HEBI, they have an influential position as the only labour representatives and as industry watchdogs with connections to solidarity groups in consumer countries. Through HEBI, they engage the biggest business actors in the industry at board meetings and potentially gain access to part of the audit economy by conducting audits against the HEBI code and by offering training and awareness-raising activities. In this way they have managed to be accepted as relevant stakeholders that merit active engagement (although as we shall see, the active engagement seems to be diminishing over time). Thus, the labour NGOs can to some extent claim to have succeeded in influencing the local standard agenda. Kenyan NGOs thus actively play the standards agenda and the mechanisms inherent in social standard initiatives to gain influence. In getting the industry players to engage, the labour NGOs exploited their indirect connections to the market (through ETI members), as well as their ability to damage the local industry reputation. At the same time, they indirectly outmanoeuvred the trade unions. What they give in return for gaining influence is (relative) silence.

An important aspect of HEBI concerns the aim to resolve problems through dialogue, thereby diminishing critical media attention that damages the industry. All board members and observers have signed a confidentiality agreement which prohibits them (in their individual capacity) from releasing sensitive information such as audit results (Dolan and Opondo, 2005; interview NGO3/NGO4, 2006). According to several HEBI representatives, in practice this confidentiality is interpreted in different ways amongst the stakeholders. The first serious test of what business actors within HEBI had hoped would be an alliance for dealing with criticism (avoiding damaging press coverage) occurred in early 2006, when one of the NGO representatives on HEBI publicly criticized conditions on flower farms without notifying the board of HEBI (interviews, St2/St4/NGO3/NGO4, 2006). A board meeting was called immediately after to sort out the situation, and at this meeting the position of the NGO representatives (including the HEBI Chairman) was that if the board could not solve problems, then the NGOs would use other channels, like the press, thereby retaining their activist leverage point (interviews St2/NGO3/NGO7, 2006). Another conflictual situation was being played out in 2008, where audits against the HEBI code carried out by the NGO Africa Now[22] were seen by civil society representatives of HEBI as being compromised because they had neither been authorized by HEBI nor shadowed by auditors trained and approved by HEBI. These allegations were the subject of internal discussions within the board of HEBI, but they were also communicated to UK retailers and the ETI. In this way the NGO representatives of

HEBI try to activate support and pressure from the buyer end of the value chain (interviews St2/St3, 2008).

HEBI can thus be seen as an initiative where conflicting interests are at play and where the different stakeholders have different degrees and types of leverage. The labour NGOs exploit their indirect connections to the market (through ETI members) as well as their ability to damage the local industry reputation. In return for gaining influence, they award their (relative) silence. The trade unions in Kenya have not been able or willing to pull the lever of damaging the sector's reputation abroad, and thus they have not proved as important for the flower producers to cooperate with (or to be seen to cooperate with). The more traditional source of trade union power, namely the threat of disrupting production, has not been employed by the Kenyan trade unions, whose members account for only around 6 per cent of the flower workers. Business actors in HEBI award legitimacy and influence to former NGO adversaries by recognizing them as actors with whom to cooperate on social issues. However, as illustrated in the next section, in terms of standard content the flower producers only accommodate what is already expected by ETI member buyers, while at the same time they satisfy critical voices at home and in buyer markets by being seen to cooperate at an institutional level with critical local civil society representatives.

Integration

HEBI has chosen specific ways of promoting its standard. Like the other Kenyan initiatives, the strategy of integration has been particularly important, and all stakeholders seem to agree on the need to link up to other local standards. Particularly, efforts have been put into incorporating the HEBI standard into the KEBS standard (a government standard). The 2004 version of the KEBS standard does include the general provisions of the HEBI standard, although with far less detail.[23] However, so far HEBI as an institution has been side-stepped in the process of standard creation and monitoring. Only the business associations (FPEAK and KFC) were involved in setting up the KEBS standard and, more importantly, the KEBS standard does not mention the participatory auditing procedures even though this can arguably be considered the most important aspect of HEBI.

In discussions about private social standards, critical voices highlight their voluntary nature and advocate more mandatory measures, often via integration with public regulation (for example, Utting, 2005). The incorporation of the HEBI standard provisions into the KEBS standard is an example of such a move. However, as the KEBS standard is neither a legal requirement nor (at the moment) monitored by government inspectors, this link with public regulation is largely symbolic.[24] KFC has made an agreement allowing them to audit compliance to the KEBS standard among KFC members. This means that among KFC members there is potentially some enforcement of the KEBS standard – however, to the exclusion of HEBI as an institution and its participatory auditing methods.

While the HEBI code has been endorsed by both FPEAK and KFC, it is unclear what this means in practice. It appears that the endorsement does not entail adoption of the participatory auditing methodologies developed by HEBI. Indeed, the auditing procedures of FPEAK and KFC remain modelled on international technical audit procedures, which are not participatory in nature.

The KFC representative (when asked what it means in practice that KFC endorse the HEBI standard) explained that it means that they work with HEBI, they find it a suitable standard for the industry and in the KFC standard they make reference to the HEBI code and say that it is a good and useful document (interview St1, 2008).[25] However, when talking to NGO representatives from HEBI and when looking at the KFC's description of its auditing, it appears that adoption of the HEBI participatory auditing methodology is selective at best (interview St2/St3, 2008). On the website of KFC, there is no mention of any participatory techniques in auditing (such as for example focus groups or alternative interview techniques), an awareness day prior to the audit is not mentioned and no audit shadowing or consultation of trade unions or NGOs are included.[26] The KFC does not consistently employ independent third-party auditing either. All these elements are included in the HEBI participatory auditing methodology (www.kfc.org; HEBI, 2005; HEBI, n.d.). Civil society representatives[27] from HEBI claim that the current auditors of KFC have not been trained by HEBI (although KFC did send three auditors for training, these are not the ones currently listed as KFC auditors). According to them, KFC continues to employ a technical auditing method, where workers are asked a range of yes-no questions, and they have refused to use HEBI auditors to audit the social aspects of their standard (interview St2/St3, 2008).

In sum, it appears that when the HEBI code is integrated into or endorsed by other standard initiatives it is to the exclusion of HEBI as an institution and to the exclusion of at least key aspects of the HEBI participatory auditing methodology. As mentioned, HEBI is currently not very active and has not lived up to the expectations of either donors or HEBI members (interviews St1/St2/St3, 2008). While the reasons for this are complex, according to civil society representatives some actors are trying to eliminate HEBI slowly by not using it, by being reluctant to participate in meetings and by saying that they endorse HEBI while in practice only adopting small parts of its code (interviews St2/St3, 2008). Lack of funds also seriously weakens the functioning of HEBI, and one could argue that multi-stakeholder initiatives inherently are prone to conflict and difficult to move beyond mere dialogue. Certainly participatory social auditing is inherently more complex and time-consuming than more technical social audits and therefore also more challenging to implement. Another reason for the difficulties facing HEBI is that in terms of private standards, social standards are not the only or even main concern to local producers. Particularly good agricultural practices are of uttermost importance if wanting to export; and this is reflected in the accreditation or alignment to GlobalGAP of the KFC, FPEAK and KEBS standards alike.

Localization, representation and GVC governance

Critical voices have questioned the wider legitimacy of HEBI as a multi-stakeholder initiative (Dolan and Opondo, 2005; Hale and Opondo, 2005; Blowfield and Dolan, 2008). First of all, not all stakeholders are called to the bargaining table and it can be argued that HEBI represents a selected group of stakeholders to the exclusion of small- and medium-sized producers, trade unions (although invited) as well as the workers themselves. As stated by Dolan and Opondo (2005, 95), '[i]n fact, workers are the most marginalised group of primary stakeholders within HEBI as it is assumed that their interests are adequately served by the civil society organisations representing them.' The representation that is effected through the HEBI initiative is one of NGOs speaking on behalf of workers. One way that HEBI does seek to award some form of direct representation to the end beneficiaries is through the participatory auditing process but, as mentioned, this particular element of the HEBI initiative has found it hard to survive.

In spite of this criticism, the HEBI initiative does represent a move towards greater sensitivity to local issues and inclusion of, and ownership by, local stakeholders, especially in comparison to KFC. The HEBI code has borrowed heavily from the ETI Base Code, but it also contains additional and more specific clauses. For instance, it states that 'pregnant and breastfeeding mothers shall not be assigned duties which would expose them, or their babies to risk'. It is also specific on sexual harassment as a form of discrimination, entitles three months of maternity leave and extends coverage to seasonal and casual labourers under the Compensation and Regular Employment sections (Dolan and Opondo, 2005; Hale and Opondo, 2005; www.hebi.org). The extension of coverage to the seasonal and casual labourers is particularly important and constitutes a significant improvement compared to most other standards in the industry. But most of all, it is the participatory social auditing techniques that means that HEBI is more than just a copy of existing initiatives in the sector. Paradoxically, even though HEBI was initiated exactly because of deficiencies in the way compliance to social standards was assessed, participatory social auditing is precisely the element that does not seem to survive when the HEBI standard is endorsed or incorporated into other local initiatives.

Seen from a GVC governance perspective, the HEBI initiative (even when including its participatory auditing principles) like most PSSs does not contest the power structure of the retailer-driven GVC (such as for example addressing buying practices which lead to and uphold adverse working conditions). What it does, however, is to indirectly offer retailers some safeguard against conflict, create necessary consensus and 'back-up' from critical voices locally (and in buyer markets) and, thus, present a means of governing at a distance. For local business, the participatory social auditing mechanisms represent a contested terrain, because the adoption of these methods is laborious and potentially leads to more profound changes in working conditions and employer–employee relationships. But as shown, this 'obstacle' seems to have been quite effectively circumvented by local inter-standard cooperation deselecting this particular element of the HEBI initiative.

Conclusion

In this chapter, I have analysed how PSSs are localized in the Kenyan cut flower industry and illustrated how this localization process reproduces existing power inequalities (both local and in the GVC).

Analysing the legislative governance (who makes the rules and how) of the two Kenyan standard initiatives reveals a business association standard which is strongly shaped by international standards and demands from retailers. Although with references to local legislation, the KFC standard is an image of existing international standards and inclusion of local stakeholders is limited to larger producers. HEBI, on the other hand, does in several areas go beyond conventional international social standards and includes local civil society stakeholders (although workers are still not directly represented in the initiative). Through HEBI, civil society organizations have gained better access to workers in the industry and engaged in critical dialogue with business actors. At the same time, new forms of worker representation are legitimized through NGO advocacy. This may have positive implications for women workers and other marginalized groups. However, the conflict between NGOs and unions has intensified and the unions face challenges to their legitimacy as worker representatives and in relation to the traditional tripartite industrial relations structure.

The judicial governance (the way compliance is monitored and assessed) of these standards has proved particularly contested and interesting, not least in relation to integration and inter-relations between local standards. While the KFC standard mainly employs a technical audit methodology, HEBI employs participatory social auditing methods; and this is where HEBI distinguishes itself from other Kenyan standard initiatives. The KFC initiative can be seen as a move towards alignment with international standards and audit procedures that focus on documentation and traceability and employ a technical audit approach to measuring standard compliance. Thus, the KFC standard falls within a tradition of seeing PSSs as a technical tool to achieve social compliance based on outcome standards as opposed to a focus on PSSs as a means of enhancing the process through which workers claim their rights (as advocated by HEBI). In other words, one could say that the way quality (in relation to social concerns) is defined, differs substantially between civil society actors focusing on process rights and commercial actors focusing on outcome standards. In the ongoing negotiation of the HEBI initiative this tension is reflected most clearly in the fact that when the HEBI standard is integrated into, or endorsed by, other local standard initiatives it is to the exclusion of HEBI as a multi-stakeholder institution as well as key aspects of the HEBI participatory auditing methodology – the main vehicle through which process rights are promoted.

The analysis provided in this chapter shows how stakeholders entered HEBI with different agendas and different power leverages. These power asymmetries to some degree determine what issues are negotiated and whose interests count; and partly explain why it is the participatory social auditing method that seems not to have endured cooperation and integration with other Kenyan standard initiatives. In these processes of integration and endorsement, existing power relations are reproduced. Seen in this light participating in multi-stakeholder dialogue with conventional adversaries comes cheap for the Kenyan producers.

Placing the local standard initiatives in the context of GVC governance illustrates how local standard initiatives can be seen as indirectly playing into the governance agenda of retail buyers. First of all, the standards are not contesting the power of retailers. Secondly, by reinforcing demands already posed by retailers the standards constitute a move towards 'self-regulation' by producers in developing countries. Thirdly, by being local the standards are helping to avoid conflict through their ability to detect and address non-compliance and disputes at an early stage and in a continuous way. In this way local standards can aid buyers in assuring producer compliance to social standards. Lastly, local standards, particularly multi-stakeholder standard initiatives, can enable consensus and cooperation while securing against conflict and criticism (by critical voices locally and in buyer markets) which could potentially disrupt sales. In this way the localization of standards can be seen as indirectly playing into the governance agenda of buyer-driven value chains, where the lead firms now endorse (and at times actively promote) local standard initiatives not least because they offer better insurance against conflict, create necessary consensus and 'back-up' from critical voices locally and in buyer markets and present an effective means of governing at a distance.

Notes

1. Southern multi-stakeholder initiatives in the field of labour codes of practice in Africa include the Wine Industry Ethical Trade Association (WIETA) in South Africa, the Agricultural Ethics Assurance Association of Zimbabwe (AEAAZ) and the Horticulture Ethical Business Initiative (HEBI) in Kenya.

2. The Chief Executive Officer of KFC as well as three board members from the HEBI were interviewed by phone in May 2008. Various documents concerning HEBI were also reviewed in 2008. All other interviews were conducted in 2006. For interview codes and a list of how interviews were distributed, see table below:

Union officials, national level and district level (UN)	9
Union officials, farm level (UF)	6
Representative from works councils, joint bodies or other worker committees (Wc)	5
Farm management (M)	17
NGOs (NGO)	7
Standard representatives (St)	11
Experts (Ex)	4
Total	59

3. 'Lead firms' refer to a group of firms in one or more functional positions along a value chain who are able to 'drive' it.
4. The distinction between buyer- and producer-driven chains describes only one aspect of governance. GVCs can actually move from one category to the other (Ponte, 2008). Furthermore, actors external to the chain can have an important say in how a GVC is governed – these actors can be NGOs, trade unions, 'experts', certification bodies and/or providers of support services (see Herod, 2001; Riisgaard, 2007; Coe et al., 2008; Ponte, 2008).
5. 'Drivenness' is a measure of power and describes degrees of capability to determine the functional division of labour along the value chain, to set quality and other demands, and to dictate the terms of participation or exclusion, as well as the distribution of rewards from participation (Raikes et al., 2000; Ponte, 2008). The degree of drivenness can differ significantly ranging from highly driven GVCs to GVCs that are not driven.
6. The Dutch auctions basically function as a distribution centre, absorbing large quantities of flowers that are re-packed and sold to buyers from all over the world.
7. A participatory approach to codes of labour practice puts greater emphasis on involvement of workers and workers' organizations in the process of standard implementation and assessment. It is based on partnerships between different actors (companies, trade unions, NGOs and preferably governments) in developing a locally sustainable approach to the improvement of working conditions. This approach is sensitive to uncovering and thus addressing more complex issues such as gender discrimination and sexual harassment. A participatory approach can be developed at different levels. At a minimum, it involves the use of participatory tools in the process of social auditing. At its broadest level, it involves the development of local multi-stakeholder initiatives forming an independent body able to oversee implementation and monitoring (Auret and Barrientos, 2004).
8. The ETI is a UK initiative to promote and improve the implementation of corporate codes of practice which cover supply chain working conditions. It was developed in 1998 by a consortium of companies, trade unions and NGOs. Supermarket members of the ETI are: ASDA, the Co-Op Group, J Sainsbury, Marks & Spencer and Tesco. They are applying codes to all their 'own brand' products,

including fresh produce. ETI has a base code and provides a generic standard for labour practices. All corporate members are required to submit annual progress reports on their code implementation activities (ETI website, 2008).
9. This estimate is based on figures from the Flower Label Programme (which has a 3 per cent market share in Germany) as well as on estimates provided by representatives from Fairtrade Labelling Organization and Union Fleurs (interviews 7 and 19, 2008).
10. www.fairflowers.net/flowers.html accessed July 2008. The forecast potential of FFP is based on a rapid increase in FFP participants (with a 414 per cent increase from 2007 to 2008). FFP listed 3587 participants in October 2008. Of these, 165 were producers, 235 traders and 3187 sales outlets. The forecast is also based on the following: FFP certified products can be traded through the Dutch auction system; and FFP is backed by very influential industry actors (Flower News 12, 2008).
11. Data from UN COMTRADE, HS 2002, product category 0603.
12. KEBS develops and acts as custodians of Kenyan standards (like, for example, the Diamond seal of product quality excellence) but KEBS also certify to system standards like ISO 22000-2005, ISO 9000-2000, ISO 14000 and HACCP (interview St7 2006, and-http://www.epzakenya.com/UserFiles/File/Presentation%20by%20KEBS%20-%20Mr%20Masila.pdf date accessed 20 August 2007).
13. The Gold Standard audit is carried out by an independent third-party auditor like BVQI or SGS (www.kenyaflowers.co.ke/).
14. The KFC silver standard has the status of a provisionally approved standard (i.e., a standard that has already completed the benchmarking procedure). All benchmarking documents have undergone the assessment process and have been acknowledged as a GlobalGAP equivalent. The corresponding benchmarking agreement has already been signed. The only missing link here is the formal accreditation of the responsible certification bodies (http://www.globalgap.org/cms/front_content.php?idcat=31 accessed March 2008).
15. KFC had provisional recognition as of September 2006 but it is unclear whether this is still in effect (http://www.kenyaflowers.co.ke/audit.htm date accessed March 2008).
16. Associate members are: Aalsmeer Flower Auction BV, Agrotropic AG, East African Flowers BV, Flora Holland, Flower Plus Ltd, K. N. Airlink, Marks & Spencer PLC, Omniflora Blumen Centre GmbH, Sainsbury's, Tesco, World Flowers Ltd and Van Beek Bloemen BV (http://www.kenyaflowers.co.ke/members/associates.php date accessed 17 July 2007).
17. The lack of civil society involvement can be partly explained (but not excused) by the fact that it is primarily a technical code with social additions rather than a social code *per se*.
18. The WRA coalition consists of Kituo Cha Sheria (a legal rights NGO pursuing individual and group worker cases in civil courts), Kenya Human Rights Commission (KHRC), Kenya Women Workers Organisation (KEWWO) and Workers' Rights Watch (WRW) (interviews NGO3/NGO4, 2006).
19. The board members are: KFC, Homegrown, FPEAK, Workers' Rights Watch (WRW), Kenya Women Workers' Organisation (KEWWO), Karen Roses, Kenya Human Rights Commission (KHRC) and Shera Agency (via Martin Ole Kamwaro), also representing the Agricultural Employers' Association (AEA) (Interviews St1/St10, 2006).
20. Examples of problems listed in the ETI report from 2005 include: workers unaware of their rights, very few workers selected for worker interviews, workers

interviewed in the presence of management, little contact between auditors and local trade union and NGO representatives, only permanent workers interviewed and too few female auditors (ETI, 2005).
21. In late 2005, COTU agreed to nominate a representative to the board (the deputy secretary general). However, in practice the unions have never attended any meetings (interview St1/UN1/UN2, 2006).
22. The three NGOs represented on the HEBI board have a very activist approach, while Africa Now (an NGO observer to HEBI) has become more substantially involved in the economy of social auditing in close cooperation with business. The UK-based ETI member Africa Now has an 'Ethical Business Services unit' that offers ethical audits to businesses (www.africanow.org). They have conducted audits for amongst others Finlays and Homegrown.
23. For example, the KEBS standard does not recommend 3 months maternity leave nor spell out how regular employment shall be provided (KEBS 2004).
24. It is unclear how widely the KEBS standard has been implemented (interview St7/St8, 2006).
25. Asked about the participatory auditing methodology developed by HEBI, the KFC representative explained that they endorse all of HEBI, including the participatory methodology. In practice, for example, they require gender and health and safety committees on the farms and this, according to the representative, facilitates participatory auditing. Furthermore, the KFC auditors have been trained by HEBI. Unfortunately, I was not allowed to see the KFC auditing procedures since these are regarded as internal documents (interview St1, 2008).
26. At the time of fieldwork in 2006, there was no audit shadowing or consultation of trade unions or NGOs.
27. Two out of three representatives were interviewed (the third NGO representative had only just started and was not interviewed).

8
Food Safety Standards and Fishery Livelihoods in East Africa

Reuben M.J. Kadigi, Ntengua S.Y. Mdoe, Ephraim Senkondo and Zena Mpenda

Introduction

The export fishery industry in East Africa has experienced a number of important challenges over the past two decades, most dramatically those associated with the new generation of food safety standards imposed by Northern countries.[1] Closely associated with this has been the challenge of increasing competitive pressures in global fish markets. The combined effect of these challenges might seem likely to marginalize weaker economic players in the sector, including small businesses, artisanal fishers and boat owners. In fact, this has not occurred.

Because of the EU's so far restricted interpretation of what stages in the value chain need to implement HACCP requirements in full, the most important of the East African fisheries (that for Nile Perch from Lake Victoria) has remained predominantly artisanal. However, HACCP has had to be applied in full at all stages of the chain from the lakeshore forward (landing sites, processing plants, post-process handling and transport). Successful conformity at these stages of the chain means that the riparian countries remain a part of the global fish value chain into the EU. The current situation is therefore that the artisanal part of the chain benefits from participation in a demanding global value chain without having incurred radically increased costs.

Nonetheless pessimistic views concerning the development of the fishery still dominate the public debate. On the one hand, there is the viewpoint which maintains that the new generation of food safety standards have been, are and will always remain a barrier to high-value agro-food exports from this and other low-income regions (see for example Rahman, 2001; Otsuki et al., 2001; Zaramba, 2002; Wilson and Otsuki, 2003). On the other hand, there is the view that where exports do continue, this is associated with highly skewed benefits, such that around the Lake deterioration occurs in living standards, the environment and even in food security. This position is taken by Jansen (1997), Abila (2000) and Bokea and Ikiara (2000), although it is most comprehensively incarnated in the award-winning documentary *Darwin's Nightmare*.[2]

The position outlined in this chapter is more in line with that of Buzby (2003), Unnevehr (2003) and Jaffee and Henson (2004) who argue that emerging food safety standards work as a catalyst for modernization and contribute to the creation of competitive advantages, resulting in increases of exports as well as improvements in the livelihoods of local communities. They further conclude that the picture for developing countries as a whole is much less pessimistic than that widely presented by the standards-as-barriers perspective. The twist in our own argument is that livelihoods improve much more generally where, as on Lake Victoria, standards are not only complied with but are implemented in ways that preserve the inclusion of small-scale producers in export chains (cf. Namisi, 2002b; Odongkara et al., 2005; Henson et al., 2005; indirectly, Geheb et al., 2008[3]).

This argument is supported here by showing the generally superior livelihood conditions pertaining for participants in the artisanal segment of the Nile Perch global export chain – as opposed to participants in other fishery chains also based on Lake Victoria but *not* linked to global markets through conformity with EU food standards. The former situation represents one of inclusive conformity to EU market access requirements while the latter represents one that is also inclusive, but where there is no global market access. It needs to be emphasized from the outset that 'other fishery chains' include some strands of the Nile Perch chain itself, which are oriented to domestic rather than global consumption.

The argument is demonstrated using evidence from a survey conducted in 2006 on the Tanzanian shores of Lake Victoria, with a total sample size of 522 (generating 484 usable responses). The sample was made up of participants in both the Nile Perch and other Lake Victoria fishery value chains, including those indirectly employed such as boat-builders, net-menders, cooks in fishing camps, porters and transporters. The sample's breakdown by category of operator and fishery is given in Table 8.2. In addition, interviews were conducted with key informants including Fisheries Department officials and leaders and members of Beach Management Units. Data has been analysed using a 'Livelihoods Analysis and Change in Net Income (CNI)' approach (cf. Ellis, 2000). This takes household-level income and household livelihood portfolios as its units of analysis. Thus, unless indicated otherwise, all data presented in the chapter refers to income or expenditure at the household level.

The second section of this chapter provides an overview of the development of the Nile perch value chain in East Africa since the 1980s. The third section presents a detailed account of household-level assets, income portfolios and incomes for participants in the different Lake Victoria fishery chains. The final section concludes.

The development of the Nile perch value chain in East Africa

In the early 1980s the Nile Perch fishery on Lake Victoria was of secondary economic significance to those for other species such as Tilapia, Haplochromis and *Dagaa* (Rastrineobola argentea). It was based on the lakeshore alone and characterized by low levels of fishing effort and low levels of asset concentration. On landing from artisanal craft, fish were mostly sold by boat owners to small-scale shore-based processors, who smoked or dried the fish whole before selling it on to traders from the immediate region or from markets in urban centres in Tanzania. A small part of output was exported in a whole sun-dried form to other countries in the Great Lakes region. The value chain in this period is depicted in Figure 8.1.

The fishery began to change following an apparent large biomass increase in the late 1970s and early 1980s and rising demand for white fish fillets in the EU following the depletion of the North Atlantic cod fishery. These factors drove the emergence of fish processing factories, mainly owned by Kenyans, and an increase in the volumes of Nile perch traded in distant export markets. With these changes, the volume of fish going into the domestic market declined but exports of sun-dried fish to neighbouring countries also increased.

The emergence of the factories and the global export trade set in motion a series of far-reaching changes in the organization of the fishery. In contrast with developments in other sectors in Tanzania these proceeded rapidly, aided by the fact that the sector had never been subject to state ownership or detailed market regulation. Firstly, the factories contracted boat owners and collectors to fish on their behalf, supplying them with gear and boat engines. Secondly, there were new entrants to the boat owner category including local businessmen and former civil servants and politicians. Correspondingly, several 'large fishermen' owning between 30 and 90 artisanal craft emerged by the mid-1990s. Thirdly, fishing effort increased, as did competition between the factories and thus prices (which reached about US$0.80/kg on the Lake around the same time). As the number of vessels fishing for Nile Perch rose, the larger motorized fishing fleet owners moved offshore, setting up camps on the islands on the Lake to exploit untapped resources. Alongside these changes emerged new categories of specialist labour serving the fishery. Besides boat builders, who had always existed, Nile Perch fishing camps came to include net-menders, mechanics, cooks (sometimes doubling as prostitutes) and even operators of radio and sonar equipment (Gibbon, 1997).

On the shore, traditional artisanal Nile Perch processors were marginalized from the trade and shore-based artisanal processing became confined to fish that, for one reason or another, could not be sold to the factories. Meanwhile, new categories of artisanal processor emerged who bought and re-processed waste materials discarded by the factories. In addition a

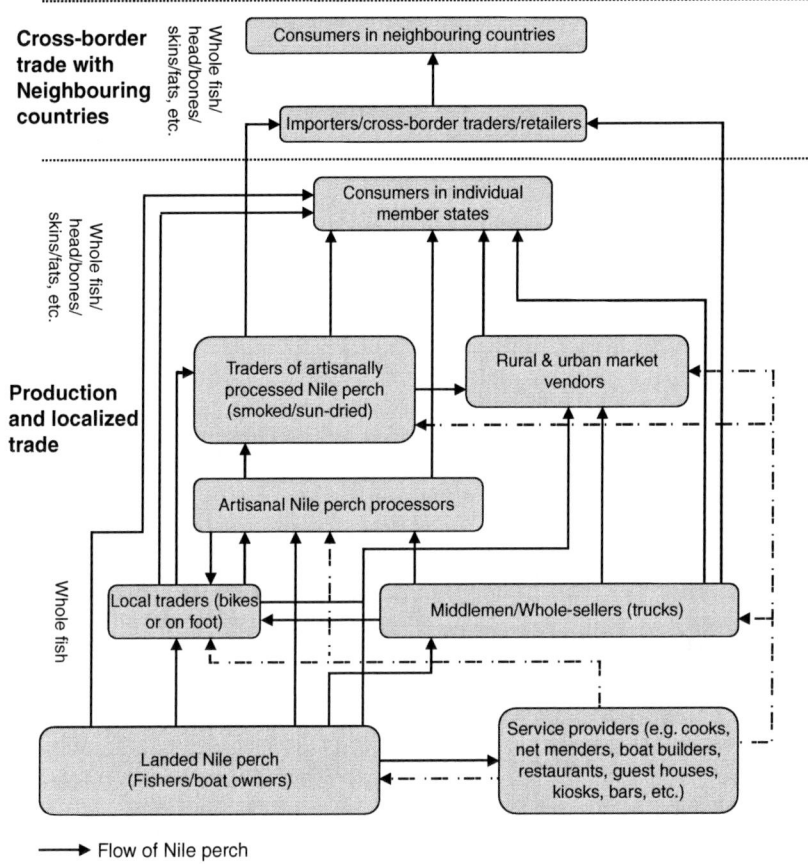

Figure 8.1 The Nile perch value chain in East Africa before the start of exports

specialist and higher-value trade in dried Nile Perch gas bladders (*mabondo*) emerged – destined for the Far East market (Gibbon, 1997).

Further changes in the value chain occurred after the intermittent import bans of fish and fishery products from East Africa by the European Commission between 1997 and 2000, requiring Lake Victoria riparian countries to adopt more stringent food safety standards (see Chapter 9 for details). In particular, the factories were compelled to invest in new infrastructure and quality management systems. While as a result their numbers shrank, those that remained were larger and better capitalized. Other segments of the chain experiencing forced upgrading were fish collection and transport from fishing sites to the factories. Related to this, some new institutions were established (for example Beach Management Units).

Nonetheless, the artisanal character of the fishery was preserved throughout the entire period. This was partly because of regulation by the Tanzanian government banning trawling from the Lake (said to have been enacted in order to obtain UNEP funding) and partly because the factories saw little reason to incur the heavy investment costs entailed by trawling while the artisanal fishery functioned reasonably smoothly.

The Nile perch value chain today

Today's Nile perch value chain in the riparian states of Lake Victoria is a complex system with three main strands, all of which however share a common artisanal fishing base (Figure 8.2):

- Localized trading within the Lake zone and markets in other parts of the riparian states;
- Cross-border trade between the riparian states and neighbouring countries, for example Zambia, Sudan and the Democratic Republic of Congo (DRC); and
- Global exports to the EU and other developed countries' markets as well as the Far East and Middle East.

Tanzanian actors in the Nile perch global export value chain can be grouped under the following major categories:

- Fishers or crews and fishing boat owners or operators who catch fish and deliver them to the landing sites;
- Factory agents and their assistants or independent collectors, who purchase fish at the landing sites for delivery to the processing plants;
- Artisanal processors;
- *Mabondo* collectors and traders; and
- Workers in and owners of the processing plants.

The last of these categories will not be discussed in this chapter. A brief description of the other four categories is provided below.

Fishers and boat owners

A majority of boat owners sell their landed catch at a home beach close to where they are settled or camped. Fishers and crews constitute a mixture of local people living in the villages close to the landing sites and migrants from distant areas. Most fishers more or less permanently operate from the same camps. A few of those surveyed (4 per cent) shifted their camps away from their main base in April to October (the season of low catches) before returning during the rainy season, which coincided with the period of high catches (that is, from October or December to February or March).

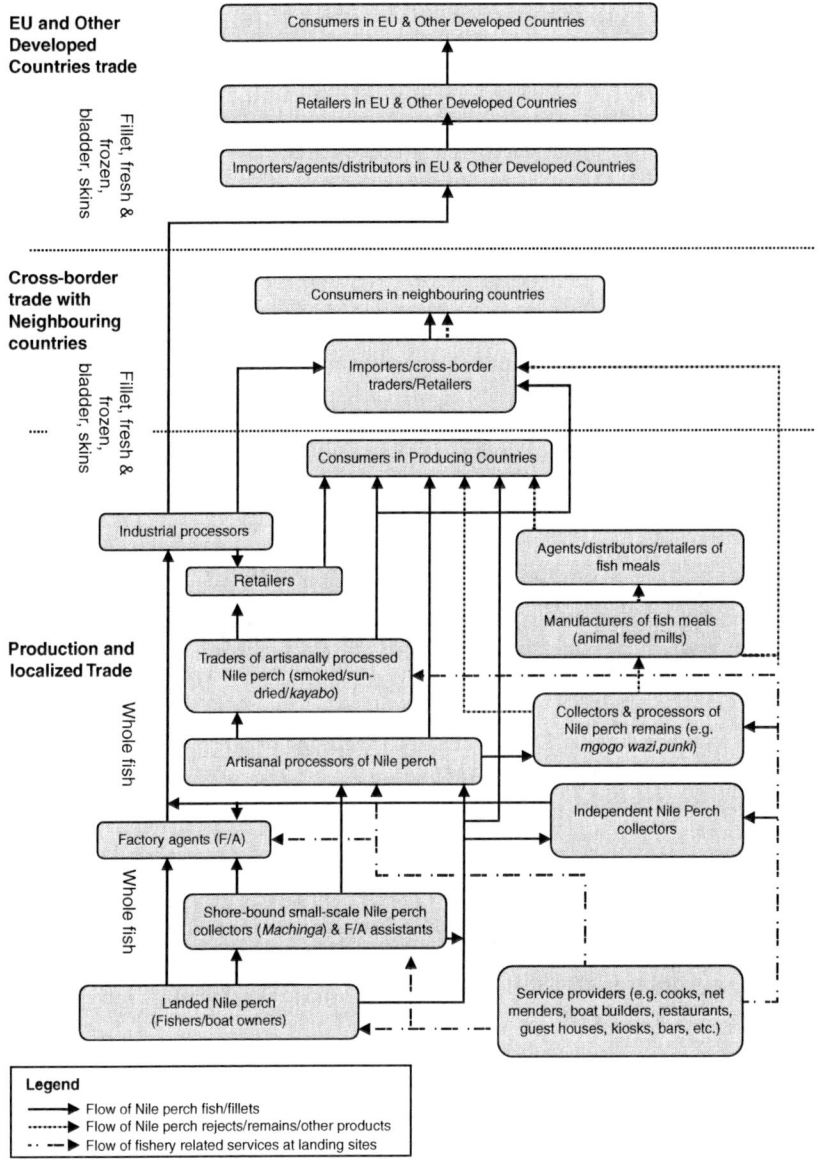

Figure 8.2 The contemporary Nile perch value chain in East Africa

Most boat owners, especially those owning more than a handful of boats, are tied to individual factories through contracts interlocking credit for nets and engines with delivery of fish. However, it appears that ownership of artisanal craft has become less concentrated over the last decade. This may be related to the liberalization of other sectors of the Tanzanian economy and a resulting growth in alternative investment opportunities.

Nile perch agents and collectors

The value chain for fresh Nile perch involves either the direct supply of fish by fishers and boat owners to factory agents or (for a smaller part of the catch) via independent collectors. Most factory agents are provided with a truck (usually a four ton one) by the factories they enter into contracts with. Using their own capital, they then buy Nile Perch. They normally employ supervisors or sub-agents (both men and women) responsible for most of the 'front-line' collection of Nile perch, both from the factory's tied vessel owners and from anyone else they can buy from.

Independent collectors are actors with varying scales of operation, including shore-bound small-scale collectors (famously known as *machinga* on the Tanzanian side of the Lake), as well as those who use either their own or hired fish vans or small collector boats with ice containers and sell directly to the processing factories.

Processors and sellers of Nile perch rejects and remains

Nile perch catches that are not exported (factory rejects, small fish or fish remaining when a collector fails to buy) are either traded locally in a fresh form or artisanally processed. Two basic artisanal processing methods for Nile perch were reported. The first was smoking, for 8 to 16 hours under a papyrus mat in multi-rack kilns built of earth and usually set over a mound, to produce *sangara moshi* or *vibambara vya sangara*. This type of processed fish is mostly traded within Tanzania. The other method is dry-salting to produce *kayabo* (dried salted steaks). This type of fish is mostly traded in African export markets, particularly eastern DRC. Frying of fresh fish is practised to some extent for Tilapia but seldom for Nile perch.

Since large-scale factory production has emerged, a large number of people are also engaged in purchasing, processing and selling Nile Perch remains, either the frame or skeleton (*mgongo wazi*) or the head, famously known as *punki*. These products are mostly traded in Northwest Tanzania only. This processing largely occurs in urban areas, rather than near to the main landing sites.

Mabondo collectors and traders

Mabondo (see above) is also processed and exported. It is believed that some factories extract it from the whole fish that they purchase and export it direct. Persons touring the camps and buying from processors of reject fish or from camp cooks also collect *Mabondo*. Other collectors simply stay in the main settlements and hang fliers reading '*mabondo* bought here' on their huts. Some of the larger collectors are agents of specialist export companies and either work for a commission on capital advanced by these companies or supply *mabondo* in part-repayment of personal loans from the exporter.

Livelihood dimensions

The concept of livelihood is widely used in contemporary writings on poverty and rural development, but its meaning may appear elusive, either due to vagueness or to different definitions being encountered in different sources. Its dictionary definition is a 'means to a living', which straight-away makes it more than merely synonymous with income since it directs attention to the way in which a living is obtained, and not just the net results in terms of income received or consumption attained. A popular academic definition is that provided by Chambers and Conway (1992) wherein 'a livelihood comprises the capabilities, assets (stores, resources, claims and access) and activities required for a means of living'. The term 'capabilities' in the foregoing definition refers to a combination of capacities that individuals need to realize their potential (that is to be adequately nourished, educated and free of illness) and conditions that allow them to do so (that is, to exercise choices, develop skills and experience, participate socially and so on) (Sen, 1997).

In this chapter, we use the definition provided by Ellis (2000), wherein a livelihood 'comprises the assets (natural, physical, human, financial and social capital), the activities, and the access to these (mediated by institutions and social relations) that together determine the living gained by the individual or household'. According to Ellis (2000), the terms 'livelihood' and 'income' are not synonymous but they are inextricably related, since the composition and level of individual or household income at a given point in time is the most direct and measurable outcome of the livelihood process. Using Ellis's definition, livelihood dimensions of participation in the Nile Perch global export chain are examined by comparing the asset status, livelihood portfolios and incomes of actors in this chain (that is, a *with* inclusive compliance scenario) with those of actors who are in other strands of the Nile perch chain or other fishery chains entirely (that is, a *without* compliance scenario).

Asset ownership and livelihoods in Lake Victoria

Current understandings of poverty place considerable emphasis on the ownership of, or access to, assets that can be put to productive use. These thus serve as building blocks, by which the poor can find ways out of poverty (Moser, 1998; World Bank, 2000). In this respect, successful asset accumulation is of special interest since it should allow greater and more sustainable movement away from poverty. This may involve 'trading-up' assets in sequence (for example, from goats to cattle to fishing gears; or, cash from fishing to farm inputs to higher farm income and then to land or to livestock). High asset holdings reduce vulnerability and are based upon paths of accumulation that strengthen livelihoods over time. The findings presented here illustrate the extent in the Tanzania case to which such processes have emerged, for actors in the Nile perch global export fishery and for those in other fisheries on Lake Victoria.

Table 8.1 reports values for fishing assets, land area, livestock holdings, human capital and other assets owned by the households of fishers and crew and boat owners in the Nile perch export and other fisheries. Most of the different asset categories referred to in the table are self-explanatory but notes are necessary on those referring to human capital and 'other assets'. The first human capital variable, 'average years of schooling' refers to the household member interviewed only. The other human capital variable, 'adult labour equivalent' is a percentage referring to total adult labour equivalents as a proportion of all household members (counting adult males and females aged 15–60 as 1, males over 60 years as 0.67, females over 60 years as 0.60 and children aged 10–14 as 0.25). 'Other assets' refers to the aggregate value of all cars or motorbikes, bicycles, farm equipment, radios, television sets, furniture and cooking utensils owned by the household.

The results in Table 8.1 show that households of participants in the Nile perch export fishery have assets of consistently higher value than those of participants in other Lake Victoria fisheries. These differences are significant at a 95 per cent level in most cases. Households of participants in the Nile perch export fishery have roughly double the level of fishing assets by value than others, and roughly 50 per cent more land. Households of boat owners in the Nile perch export chain also have significantly greater human capital assets than their counterparts.

From a poverty perspective, it is also important to understand how assets are distributed between different participants' households within the same fisheries. As is clear from Table 8.1, households of boat owners have significantly higher asset holdings than those of fishers and crew for all asset categories and across all Lake Victoria fishery chains. The remainder of this section presents more detailed findings on household asset ownership, reporting results for additional categories of participants both in the Nile perch global export chain and in other chains.

Figure 8.3 shows that household fishing assets of the category of collector most integrated into the global export chain, namely those with fish vans, have more than six times the value of those owned by small-scale shore bound collectors.

Turning to household land assets, Figure 8.4 further indicates that households of those categories of operator most closely integrated into the Nile perch global export chain (factory agents, owners of boats integrated into factory delivery systems, collectors with four-ton vehicles and collectors with motorized vessels) have the greatest assets. Exactly the same pattern is repeated for household ownership of 'other assets' (Figure 8.5). However, this

Table 8.1 Mean value of household assets (Tsh) of participants in the Nile perch export and other fisheries. (Average exchange rate 2006: US$1 = Tsh 1286, www.oanda.com.)

Type of asset	Value of asset				Mean difference	Mean value for pooled sample
	Nile perch export		Other fisheries			
	N	Value	N	Value		
Fishing assets (Tshs):						
Fishers and crews	134	25,005	29	12,753	12,252†	21,612
Boat owners	17	2,703,298	74	1,033,500	1,669,798†	2,240,892
Land owned (ha):						
Fishers and crew	134	2.4	29	1.7	0.7*	1.88
Boat owners	17	3.5	74	2.8	0.68*	2.88
Land cultivated (ha):						
Fishers and crew	134	1.9	29	1.4	0.5013*	1.65
Boat owners	17	3.8	74	1.8	2.0011*	2.8
Livestock holdings (TLUs):						
Fishers and crew	134	1.3	29	1.2	0.0998*	1.3
Boat owners	17	3.7	74	3.8	−0.1006	3.7
Human capital (average years of schooling)						
Fishers and crew	134	4.3	29	4.2	0.0656	4.2
Boat owners	17	6.8	74	6.1	0.6879*	6.6
Human capital (% adult labour equivalents)						
Fishers and crew	134	51.1	29	51	0.1028	51.1
Boat owners	17	68.4	74	62.3	6.1002†	66.7
Other assets (Tshs):						
Fishers and crew	134	398,800.00	29	345,677.00	53,122	384,089.00
Boat owners	17	1,172,460.00	74	776,347.00	253,013	1,077,568.00

Note: Test of significance: Independent samples t-test. Key: *Significant at $P < 0.05$ level. †Significant at $P < 0.01$ level.

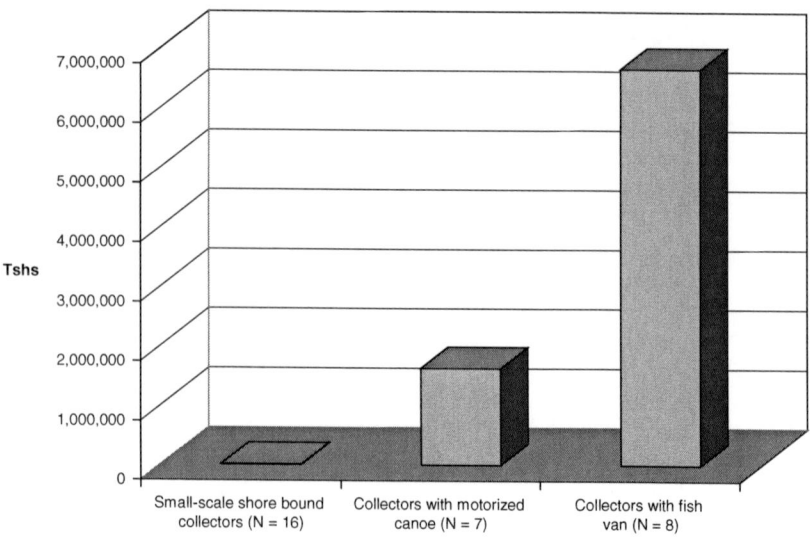

Figure 8.3 Mean value of household fishing assets, Nile perch collectors (for exchange rates see Table 8.1)

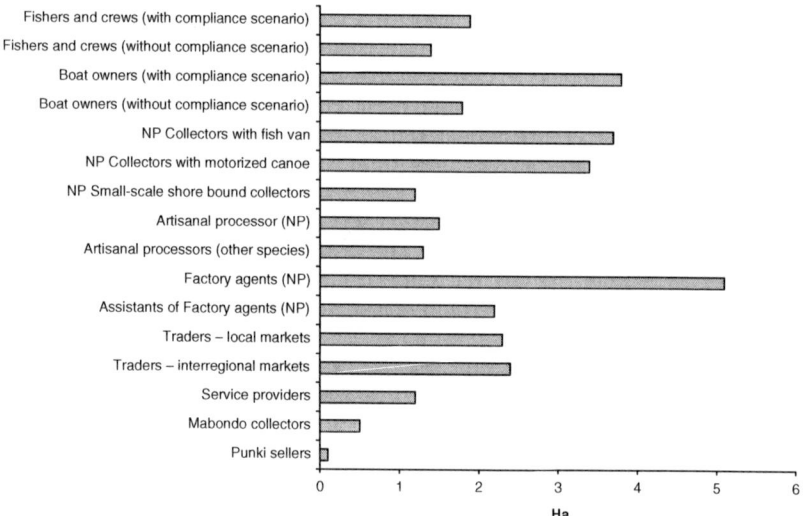

Figure 8.4 Mean household land holdings, Lake Victoria fishery participants (for exchange rates see Table 8.1)

pattern is not repeated with the same consistency in relation to household livestock ownership (Figure 8.6) and not repeated at all in relation to mean household human capital endowments, where there is only slight variance between categories (Figure 8.7).

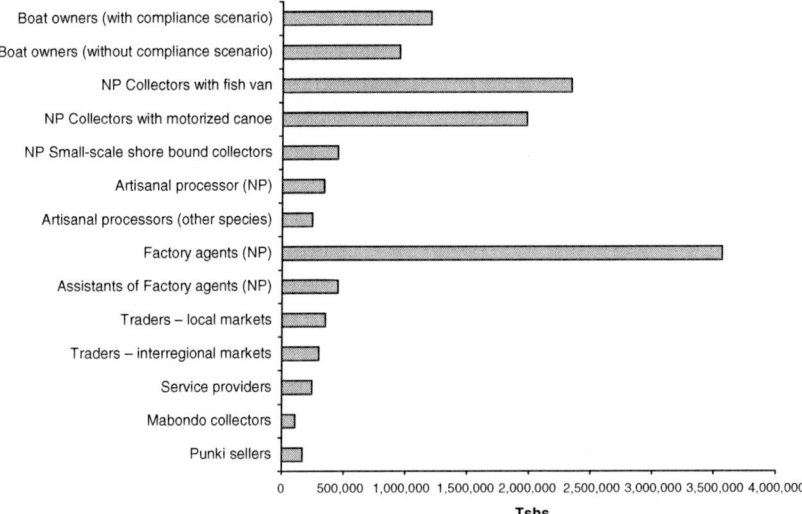

Figure 8.5 Mean value of households' other assets, Lake Victoria fishery participants (for exchange rates see Table 8.1)

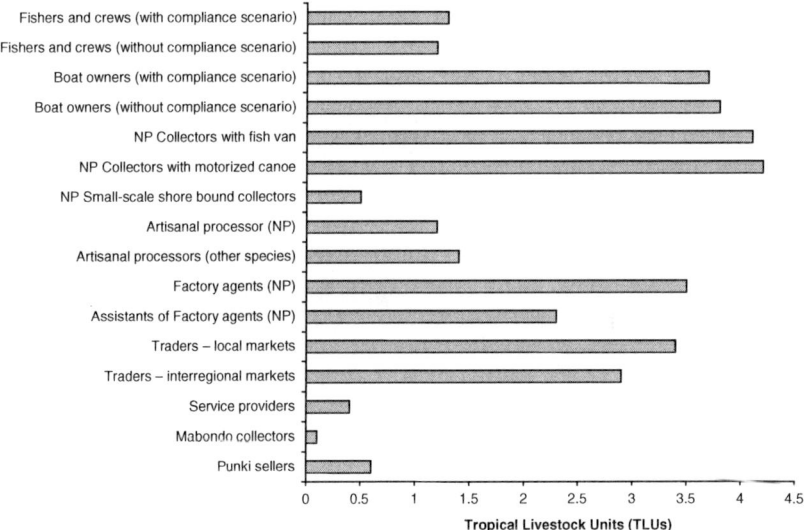

Figure 8.6 Mean household livestock holdings, Lake Victoria fishery participants

Summing up, it is clear that households with members most closely integrated in the Nile perch global export chain are generally more likely to have greater asset holdings than those less closely integrated in this chain (for example, service providers), those participating in other strands of the

174 *Standards and Fishery Livelihoods*

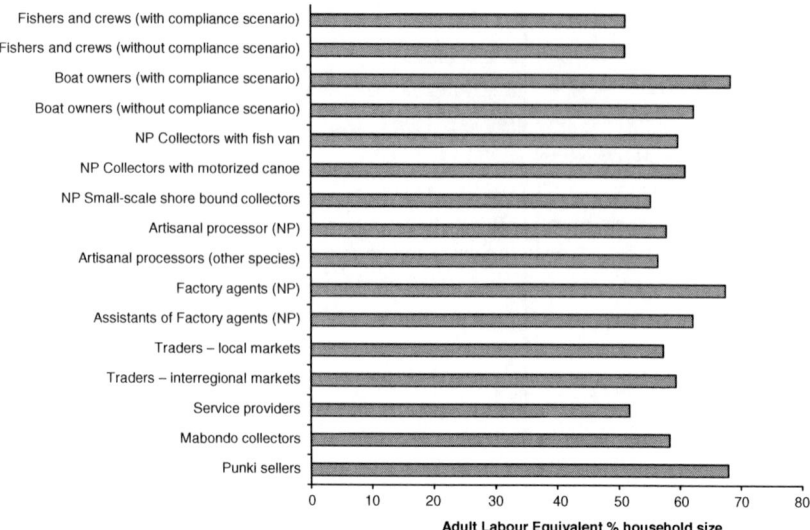

Figure 8.7 Mean household adult labour equivalent level, Lake Victoria fishery participants

Nile perch chain (artisanal processors, sellers of *punki* and *mabondo* collectors) and those participating in other fishery chains entirely. On the other hand, it is not possible to say whether this finding is reporting a cause or an effect of participation in the Nile perch global export chain (or both).

Livelihood activities and net income portfolios of fishery actors

Although activities within fisheries dominate the net income portfolio of fishing households, households follow livelihood strategies that include farming and micro-enterprises. Diversification is a key feature of livelihood strategies in rural areas in the developing world, being defined as the process by which rural families construct a varied portfolio of activities and social support capabilities in order to survive and improve their standards of living (Ellis, 1998). This helps them reduce the risk of losing all income sources simultaneously as a result of climatic, economic or other shocks (Ellis, 2000; Start, 2001).

The livelihood activities and net income sources of actors in the Nile perch and other fishery chains in the Tanzanian part of Lake Victoria are presented in Figures 8.8–8.11. As the figures show, farming (crop and livestock production) accounts for a mean 10–22 per cent of household net income, depending upon whether these households included members that were

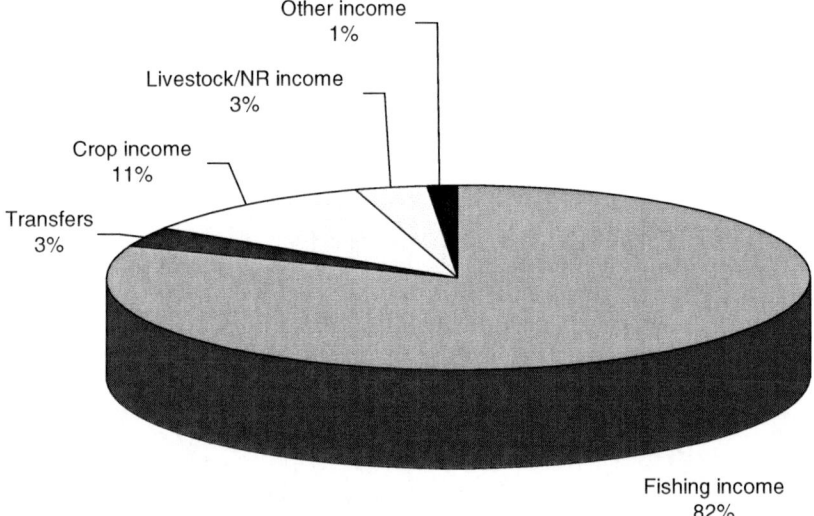

Figure 8.8 Net income portfolio for Nile perch fishers and crew

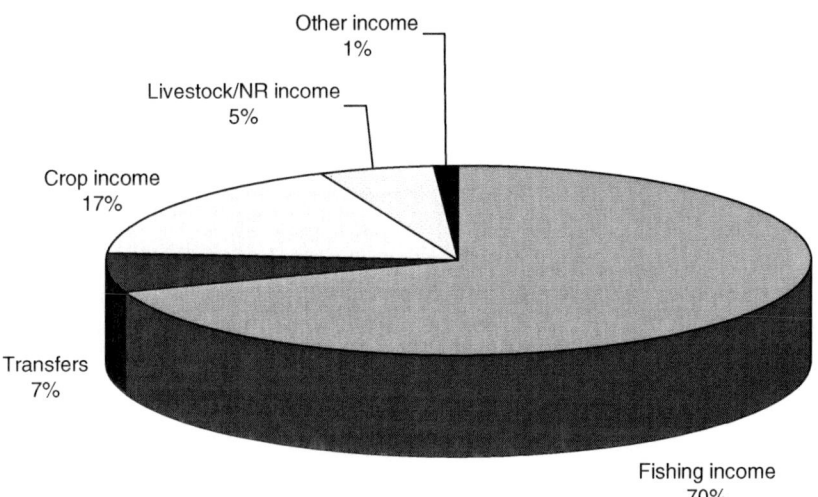

Figure 8.9 Net income portfolio for fishers and crews in other fisheries

fishers or boat owners and upon which fisheries chain these activities were carried out in. The figures also show that specialization in fishing activity is considerably greater for households involved in the Nile perch, irrespective of whether they are fishers or boat owners.

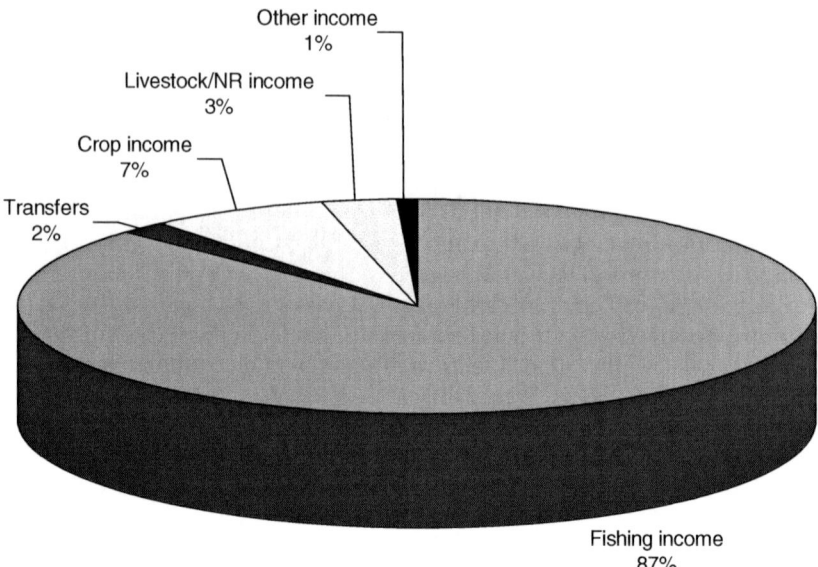

Figure 8.10 Net income portfolio for boat owners in Nile perch fishery

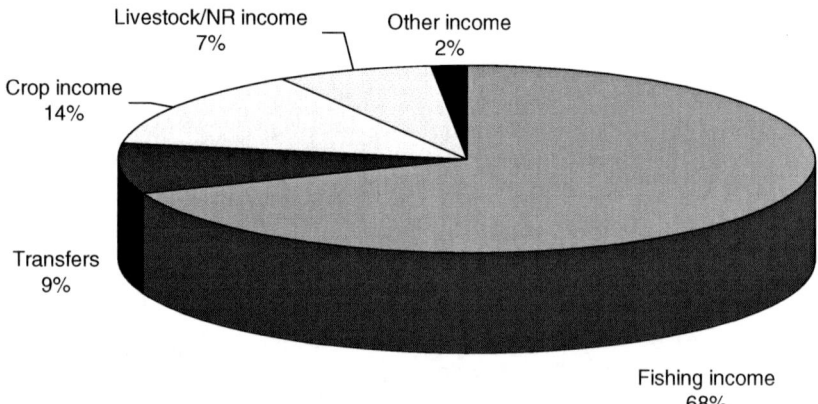

Figure 8.11 Net income portfolio for boat owners in other fisheries

Gross and net incomes

The description of household income portfolios just presented is based upon the more comprehensive mean household net income data presented in Tables 8.2 and 8.3 below. These show, once again, a clear hierarchy in outcomes, with households that include members in the roles most closely integrated into the Nile perch global export chain enjoying the highest net

Table 8.2 Mean annual household net income for different groups of actors in the Nile perch and other fishery value chains (Tsh) (for exchange rate see Table 8.1)

Actor category	N	Fishery	Transfers	Crops	Livestock	Other Activities	Total Net Income	Fishery income % Total income
Fishers and crews (*with compliance scenario*)	134	1,533,708	65,000	210,569	65,000	25,900	1,900,177	81
Fishers and crews (*without compliance scenario*)	29	800,949	75,010	199,560	60,000	12,500	1,148,019	70
Boat owner (*with compliance scenario*)	17	5,372,163	120,500	450,005	185,000	56,500	6,184,168	87
Boat owner (*without compliance scenario*)	74	1,832,820	234,090	363,060	190,000	43,015	2,662,985	69
Collectors with fish van (*with compliance scenario*)	5	12,402,108	0	650,950	205,000	237,890	13,495,948	92
Collectors with collector boat (*with compliance scenario*)	10	9,047,360	0	490,250	210,000	598,500	10,346,110	87
Small-scale shore bound collectors (*with compliance scenario*)	16	180,459	240,000	250,680	25,000	14,050	710,189	25
Processors – (*Kayabo, vibambara vya sangara*)	23	294,284	155,050	350,770	60,000	33,700	893,804	33
Processors – Other species	5	121,552	104,015	211,809	70,000	40,124	547,500	22

Table 8.2 (Continued)

Actor category	N	Fishery	Transfers	Crops	Livestock	Other Activities	Total Net Income	Fishery income % Total income
Factory agents (*with* compliance scenario)	7	16,374,982	0	750,505	250,901	143,570	17,519,958	93
Assistants of factory agents (*with* compliance scenario)	24	570,122	124,012	211,560	115,000	65,809	1,086,503	52
Traders – local markets (*without* compliance scenario)	34	379,016	120,450	390,501	170,000	96,890	1,156,857	33
Traders – interregional markets (*without* compliance scenario)	12	890,980	0	560,560	200,500	114,098	1,766,138	50
Service providers (e.g., cooks, accommodation, foods)	59	183,456	240,125	178,150	120,450	68,908	791,089	23
Mabondo collectors	13	78,684	110,234	120,505	51,981	30,768	392,172	20
Punki sellers	22	411,776	112,005	254,043	14,852	8,791	801,467	51

Table 8.3 Tests of significance for paired comparisons of mean annual household net income from fishing activities

Actor category	Fishermen/crews		Boat owners		Collectors with van	Collectors with boat
	With compliance	W/out compliance	With compliance	W/out compliance	With compliance	With compliance
Net revenue (year)	1,900,177	1,148.019[†]	6,184,168	2,662,965[†]	12,402,108	9,047,360

Note: Test of significance: Independent samples t-test. *Key*: *significant at $P < 0.05$ level; [†]significant at $P < 0.01$ level. For exchange rates see Table 8.1.

incomes, both from fishing-related activities and in aggregate. Secondly, the fishery-related mean household net incomes of all groups in the Nile perch global export chains are substantially higher than those for groups occupying corresponding roles in the chains for other fisheries – in the case of fishers and crews and boat owners significantly so. Both the households of Nile perch fishers and boat owners have fishery-related net incomes more than double those of households of fishers and boat owners of Tilapia, *Dagaa* and so on (Table 8.3). A third point relates to the uneven distribution of mean household net income from fishery activities *within* the Nile perch global export chain. Within this chain, net incomes of households with boat owners are three times greater than those of households of ordinary fishers, while net incomes of households with collectors using fish vans are four times greater and those of households with factory agents are ten times greater.

Higher net incomes in the Nile perch global export chain reflect the superior prices paid by the factories for fresh Nile perch. In 2006 the average price for fresh Nile perch on the Tanzania side of Lake Victoria was Tsh 1450/kg when sold by fishers or boat owners and Tsh 1900/kg when sold by a factory agent. By contrast the average prices of *Dagaa* were Tsh 534.60/kg (for fishers and boat owners) and Tsh 796.20/kg (for local traders). Odongkara et al. (2005) report similar Nile perch prices in Kenya in 2004 – with fishers and boat owners receiving the equivalent of US$1.00/kg and factory agents receiving US$ 1.10/kg. In Uganda, Namisi (2002a, b) also reported significantly higher prices for Nile perch compared to other fish species. In 2001–02, the highest beach or on-water price for Nile perch was Ushs 1700/kg and the lowest was Ush 1200/kg, with Ush1500/kg being the most common price. Tilapia, the next most important commercial fish in Lake Victoria, had a maximum beach price of Ush 1000/kg and a lowest of Ush 300/kg with the price mostly varying considerably between Ush 500/kg and Ush 1000/kg.

Meanwhile artisanal processors of Nile perch (*sangara moto* or *vibambara vya sangara*) received an average of Tsh 440.63/kg in 2006, while traders in these products received an average of Tsh 648.00/kg in bulking markets such as Kirumba Mwaloni in Mwanza. These prices were almost identical to those for smoked Tilapia (*vibambara vya sato*) in the same locations. The average selling price for Nile perch in its *kayabo* form averaged Tsh 793.75/kg when sold by processors in camps and Tsh 1271.43/kg when sold to traders from other countries in the Great Lakes region in Kirumba Mwaloni.

The mean household net incomes from fishing presented in Table 8.2 are derived from an analysis of household-level gross fishing revenues and fishing operating costs, presented in Table 8.4. Operating costs for fishers and crew (except for the taxes levied specifically on them) are in practice typically financed by boat owners. They are then deducted in kind from the share of catches earned by crew. Such costs have been monetized and counted as fishers and crew operating costs in the Table. Likewise, the share of boat owners' costs that are clawed back in this way are not included in boat owners' costs as recorded here.

Operating costs included the costs of registration for fishing vessels. Boat owners interviewed at Bwiro (Ukerewe district) reported annual registration costs of up to Tsh 34,000. In addition, Ukerewe District Council also collected an annual levy of Tsh 30,000 for boats using fishing nets and Tshs 20,000 per annum for boats using longlines (*migonzo* or *ndoano*). Owners also pay a local tax of Tsh 30/kg for fish landed.

Table 8.4 shows that the significantly higher household net fishing incomes for fishers and crew and boat owners in the Nile Perch export chain reported in Table 8.3 are earned in a context where these operators also incur significantly higher operating costs than is the case for their counterparts in other Lake Victoria fishery chains.

Table 8.4 Mean household gross income, operating costs and net income from fishery activities (Tsh)

Actor category	Fishermen/crews		Boat owners		Collectors with van	Collectors with boat
	With compliance	W/out compliance	With compliance	W/out compliance	With compliance	With compliance
Gross revenue (week)	97,245	53,317*	295,390	147,958†	15,766,000	14,302,545
Operating Cost (week)	58,473	32,185*	173,161	89,720†	12,594,625	11,807,492

Note: Test of significance: Independent samples t-test. *Key*: *significant at $P < 0.05$ level; †significant at $P < 0.01$ level. For exchange rates see Table 8.1. Operating costs reported are exclusive of investment costs.

An estimate of part of the total direct welfare benefit from the Nile perch global export chain was obtained by extrapolating from the data collected in this survey, on the basis of figures for total vessels, total number of fishers and crews and average numbers of vessels owned by each boat owner reported in Frame Survey National Working Group (2006). Aggregate net income in 2006 for all households with members participating as fishers or boat owners in the Tanzanian Nile perch global export chain was Tsh 221.2 billion or around US$17.5 million.

Comparative findings

In Uganda, the study by Odongkara (2002) conducted in 2001–02 reports similar results with mean monthly earnings for Nile perch fishers (at Ush 279,473) more than double those of Tilapia (at Ush 129,278) and *Dagaa* fishers (at Ush 207,742).[4]

Henson et al. (2005) in a study of two landing sites in Kenya, a major export site and a site less integrated into the Nile perch export chain, concluded that both fishers and artisanal processors and traders in the major export site had significantly higher household incomes than the same groups on the site less integrated into the export chain for Nile perch.

In addition to the income impacts in fishing communities, these studies show that the processing factories have provided better prices and guaranteed cash payment on delivery. They again also indicate that the export industry directly and indirectly supports the livelihoods of many groups including not only those mentioned in this chapter but also owners of and workers in kiosks, bars, eating places, tailoring businesses and video halls.

Overall, the results in Tables 8.2–8.5 and the evidence from Kenya and Uganda show that although participation in the global export chain is

Table 8.5 Estimate of aggregate net income per annum for fishers and boat owners in the Tanzanian part of Lake Victoria

Target species	Number of Crafts	Annual Net Income (Billion Tshs)*		
		Fishers	Craft owners	Total
Nile perch (with compliance scenario)	25,313	85.02	136.16	221.19
Other species (without compliance scenario)	7,216	15.76	13.23	28.99
Nile perch and other species (Tilapiines)	377	1.06	1.36	2.42

*For 2006 exchange rates see Table 8.1

associated with higher costs, actors in it obtain significantly higher net incomes than comparable groups in other fisheries. As expected, net incomes are also distributed unequally between groups. Groups with more assets (collectors with fish vans, collectors with motorized boats and boat owners) obtain higher incomes than groups with inferior assets, whether these are within the same chain or in other chains.

Conclusion

Over the past two decades, the fishing sector in East Africa has experienced important changes including greater investment, increasing fishing effort, booming exports and a new generation of food safety standards. These developments have acted together to mould a novel fisheries value chain in the region, namely the global export chain for Nile perch. The chain has registered a significant success in combining ongoing access to high-value markets with inclusiveness.

The results of the analysis indicate major impacts in terms of income and welfare, despite the challenge of compliance with the new generation of standards. This has been demonstrated relative to the outcomes associated with chains not linked to global markets. While there are important differences in the asset stocks of those participating in these two different types of chain, given the fact that exports have been taking place for well over a decade it seems probable that differences in asset levels also reflect the benefits of participation.

All this suggests that it is worth supporting the maintenance of compliance to EU food safety standards in the Nile perch value chain in order to avoid loss of markets and to thus forestall any reversal of the positive impacts on the livelihoods that have been witnessed so far. At the same time, there is an apparently continuing increase in fishing gears and in the number of fishers raising concerns, particularly in relation to the sustainability of the fish stock. It is therefore important to ensure that efforts to maintain compliance with standards are accompanied with measures to ensure sustainable fishing (see Chapter 9). We suggest a need for more effective and coherent planning in order to safeguard the future of the fishery sector in East Africa. This will involve adopting an appropriate regulatory framework and strengthening the capacity of the stakeholders to manage the resource sustainably, while at the same time maintaining a broadly based fishery.

Notes

1. For EU food safety standards generally see Chapter 10; for EU standards specific to the fisheries sector see Chapter 9.
2. *Darwin's Nightmare*, directed by Hubert Sauper (2004, France/Austria/Belgium) depicts the Nile perch fishing industry on Lake Victoria in Tanzania. For a critical review, see Molony et al. (2007).

3. Geheb et al. (2008) in their study on gender, status and food in 44 fishing communities in Uganda, Tanzania and Kenya suggest that there is no direct relationship between Nile perch exports and the high rates of malnutrition observed along the Lake – contrary to what is argued by the authors cited earlier. Geheb et al. (2008) consider gender-based inequality as hindering more positive impacts on nutrition in these communities and underscore the issue of 'cash redistribution' within households (or lack thereof) as the problem – not fishing *per se*.
4. The mean earnings for fishers concealed a large difference between those working on motorized boats (Ush 436,530) and those on non-motorized boats (Ush 187,223). See also the later surveys reported in Namisi (2002a, b) and Odongkara (2002, 2005).

9
When the Market Helps: Standards, Ecolabels and Resource Management Systems in East African Export Fisheries

Stefano Ponte, Reuben M. J. Kadigi and Winnie Mitullah

Introduction

This chapter examines the role that standards and management practices play in maintaining a rewarding and sustainable export fish industry in East Africa. It does so by analysing two separate but interconnected mechanisms: (a) how the industry matches food safety standards set by the EU; and (b) how it applies regulations, standards, ecolabels and fishery management systems to ensure the sustainability of the resource.

The case study of fish in East Africa provides insights in relation to several key debates explored in this book. First, it provides nuance to a series of dual characterizations of standards that are prevalent in the literature: private versus public; product versus process; and risk management versus product differentiation standards. Second, much of the literature examines compliance and impact of individual sets of standards in specific industries. However, the reality is that industry operators normally face several sets at the same time – with objectives that may be aligned or that contradict each other. On Lake Victoria, successful conformity with food safety standards created incentives for maximum extraction of fish that made attainment of sustainability standards and related management practices more difficult. But subsequently, an unexpected turn in the market (a drop in European demand for small fillets) provided a fortuitous opportunity to solve this dilemma. This suggests not only that a holistic approach is needed to understand the role of standards in specific industries, but also that following developments over time is important.

The chapter is structured in two logical steps that build upon the findings presented in Chapter 8 of this book, where it was shown that the fish export industry in East Africa has had a positive impact on incomes of households around the Lake; such findings suggest that when fish prices decrease and/or the volume of fish extracted from the lake decreases, livelihoods will be affected negatively.

In the *first* and main step carried out in this chapter, we examine which standard compliance and management systems are necessary for maintaining a sustainable and remunerative industry in the Lake Victoria region. Particular attention is paid to three aspects and to the interactions between them: (1) the importance of continuously complying with food safety standards, especially those set by the main fish importer from Lake Victoria, the EU; (2) the adoption of effective fishery management systems *vis-à-vis* the incentives and pressure to maximize fish extraction from the lake for exporting; here we focus on two recent initiatives – a voluntary system by export processing plants aimed at banning the purchase of undersize fish; and the start of community-based co-management through the establishment of Beach Management Units (BMUs); and (3) the potential role and limitations that ecolabelling of fishery products can have in facilitating market access, addressing the negative international image that has beset the industry (Molony et al., 2007), supporting fishery management and matching new standard content.

Specifically, we argue that at this particular historical conjuncture, the type of market demand for Nile perch in importing countries is favouring the implementation of effective fishery management measures. While until a few years ago, high demand for small Nile perch fillet made difficult enforcing rules against fishing and processing undersize fish, recently European markets (the main destination of exports from Lake Victoria) have been flooded with cheaper, smaller fillets of Pangasius from Vietnam – especially in the frozen segment. Total exports of Pangasius fillets from Vietnam to all destinations increased from virtually nil in 2001 to almost 300,000 tons in 2006 – 43 per cent of which are imported into the EU (EU Fish Processors Association, 2007, 11–12). In other words, and as reflected in the title of the chapter, at the moment the (export) market may help sustainability efforts.[1]

In the *second* step, we reflect upon the case study to advance the state of discussions on agro-food standards and draw some conclusions on the challenges facing the Nile perch export industry in East Africa.

Meeting food safety standards

The Nile perch export industry in East Africa is relatively new. The first recorded exports to Europe and the Far East go back to the late 1980s (NRI and IITA, 2002, 86), although some exports of Tilapia had taken place in the 1950s from Lake George. Increased market demand for Nile perch in the last 20 years has been partly created by declining stocks of Cod and Haddock in Northern hemisphere waters. Although Nile perch is a fresh water fish, it competes directly with other species in the market for so-called 'white fish' (or 'groundfish') of neutral flavour. Salmon has also become a direct competitor with Nile perch following the dramatic increase in farmed Salmon production and concurrent decrease in its price (Anderson, 2003).

Previous to 1991, much of the factory-based fish processing that was taking place on Lake Victoria was based in Kisumu and Nairobi, Kenya. The Kenyan plants were sending insulated trucks with ice to landing sites in Uganda and Tanzania to collect the raw material. By the late 1980s and early 1990s, some plants had sprung up in Tanzania and Uganda as well. The expansion of the industry saw facilities established nearer landing beaches in an attempt to reduce transport costs and maintain quality. Processing capacity continued to expand in the early 1990s in Kenya (Bokea and Ikiara, 2000). At the same time, the Ugandan and Tanzanian governments placed bans on the export of unprocessed fish, thus further stimulating investment in local processing capacity (Ogutu-Ohwayo, 1999; Gibbon, 2001). In the early days, Nile perch was exported in fillet form and sometimes headed and gutted (H&G) – all blast frozen. At that time, the main market was Australia, where Nile perch was sold as *bora mundi*. Hygiene certificates were needed for export, but the product and the processing plants were never really monitored. In the early 1990s, fish was first exported chilled on ice to the EU.

As we can see from Table 9.1, the value of fish exports from Kenya, Tanzania and Uganda to all destinations skyrocketed from US$27 million in 1992 to US$132 million in 1996, stagnated as a result of the EU ban on imports, then started growing again from 2000 onwards, reaching a peak of US$328 million in 2005.

The fish quality management system currently in place in the three riparian countries is the result of adjustments made in the late 1990s and early 2000s in response to successive import bans placed by the EU between 1997 and 2000. In 1991, the EU promulgated EC Regulation 91/493 on the 'Production and placing on the market of fishery products for human consumption.' This regulation required the introduction of systems of inspection and control to ensure human consumption safety both in EU countries and in countries willing to export to the EU. These measures included compliance with 'Good Hygiene Practices' (GHP) and the application of HACCP procedures. In addition, competent authorities in third countries needed to demonstrate adequate control. The EU has now integrated these regulations in the so-called 'hygiene package' that came into force in 2004. Its main features are: (1) third countries need to have health and sanitary regulations that are at least equivalent to the ones required within the EU; (2) they need to have competent authorities that can guarantee effective implementation of the relevant regulations through inspection, monitoring and sanctioning systems; and (3) business operators need to apply specific sanitary and health practices in catching, handling, processing and packaging fish and

Table 9.1 Exports of Nile perch to all destinations (chilled and frozen fillets, gutted and headed) from Lake Victoria (1992–2007; million USD)

Country	1992	1993	1994	1995	1996	1997	1998	1999	2000	2001	2002	2003	2004	2005	2006	2007
Kenya	14.6	21.2	26.9	21.9	43.9	43.0	30.0	34.2	34.2	50.4	50.2	50.9	52.0	61.1	54.5	44.6
Tanzania	5.7	6.5	8.9	13.1	52.3	54.8	65.7	51.9	49.8	79.5	82.5	104.5	87.5	123.2	127.5	150.1
Uganda	6.4	8.8	14.8	25.9	39.8	28.8	29.7	36.6	34.4	79.0	87.6	86.3	102.9	143.6	137.0	116.2
TOTAL (REGION)	26.8	36.4	50.6	70.0	132.0	126.7	125.4	122.8	118.4	209.0	222.3	241.7	242.5	327.9	313.1	310.9

Source: Adapted from Lake Victoria Fisheries Management Plan, 2008.

fishery products, and a system of risk management based on HACCP (see Chapter 10 for details).

In the early days of Nile perch exports, and even after the promulgation of EU regulation on fish safety in 1991, East African processing plants did not have operational HACCP plans in place. In the period preceding the 'mad cow disease' scare, the EU was not strict in enforcing food safety standards and a phase-in period was granted to third countries. There was no organized system of inspections by the competent authorities in East Africa. The first import ban took place in 1997 as a result of reported instances of high bacterial contamination, including *Salmonella*, in some Nile perch exports from Lake Victoria to Spain and Italy (Henson and Mitullah, 2004, 40). The ban was limited to these two countries. The second ban was imposed for 7 months in 1997–98 as a result of an outbreak of cholera in the three riparian countries and Mozambique. On this occasion, the EU banned the import of fresh fish and imposed mandatory tests on frozen fish on the basis that the competent authorities were not applying sufficient measures to control the outbreak (Waniala, 2002, 2).

The third ban of 2000 (which lasted 4 months) was initially a self-imposed export ban by Uganda. It started in response to local press reports on the death of a Ugandan child from fish poisoning. Poisoning was linked to the alleged practice of fishing by dumping pesticide in the Lake. The Uganda competent authority, at that time the Uganda National Bureau of Standards (UNBS), declared that it could not guarantee the safety of fish exports and pleaded with the EU for time to solve the problem. The EU, however, immediately applied its own import ban and extended it to Kenya and Tanzania as well – even though the allegations were never proven (cf. Rudaheranwa et al., 2003). Successive missions carried out by the EU to assess the state of health control and monitoring in the three riparian countries identified a number of problems in the regulatory system that was in place at that time.[2]

The EU import bans had wide-ranging effects. In addition to lower fish exports and loss of export revenue, negative repercussions were felt in fishing communities, among fish processors and in related service industries (packaging, transport and so on). As a result of the bans, several plants closed down completely and the rest worked at much lower capacity. At the same time, the bans and the feedback provided by the EU missions led to the streamlining of the regulatory and inspection systems, and a revision of food safety procedures and guidelines, and of monitoring and inspection systems. An internationally accredited private laboratory was established in Uganda, thus it became possible to carry out some tests locally instead of shipping samples to Europe or South Africa. In all three countries, the public laboratories of the competent authorities were also upgraded.

At the landing sites, over the years, improvements included basic requirements such as fencing, paving, constructing fish shades, supplying portable water, fish handling equipment and construction of toilets. In isolated cases, major improvements such as upgrading of access roads, construction of landing jetties, cold rooms, supply of electricity and ice making plants were undertaken as well. At the factory level, compliance with HACCP, Good Manufacturing Practices (GMP) and Good Hygiene Practices (GHP) necessitated changes in the layout of plants, the establishment of new procedures, training of personnel and forming of quality control teams. Despite assistance from the EU, this came at a high cost to the industry. However, it is generally agreed that the bans provided the stimulus for an important process of upgrading in the industry (Hensen and Mitullah, 2004; Ponte, 2007). Finally, regional efforts started for the harmonization of handling procedures in the three countries sharing Lake Victoria.

The ban was finally lifted in 2000 as a result, among other changes, of competent authorities having developed standard operating procedures, having achieved more transparency and having installed document control systems. This was done in close collaboration with the industry, especially in Uganda and Tanzania. In 2000, Tanzania was placed back on the EU list that allows imports from a third country without special permission,[3] followed by Uganda in 2001[4] and Kenya in 2004.[5]

A second round of EU inspections took place in 2006, in all three countries. The reports of these inspections highlighted: (1) the need for fine-tuning of regulations and standard operating procedures (in all three countries); (2) a lack of upstream food safety procedure controls on the Lake (Uganda); (3) the need for landings for export to take place only at approved sites (Tanzania); and (4) deficient inspections of landing sites and deficient conditions in some landing sites and fishing vessels (Kenya).[6] One of the major fears preoccupying fish authorities (that the EU would demand complete traceability to the level of the individual fishing boat) proved to be unfounded. The current level of areal traceability (to the group of islands where a transport boat has operated) is reputed to be sufficient.

In comparison to the previous inspections, the issues raised are of less immediate concern and gravity, although they may create problems if unaddressed. Of particular concern is the issue of icing and handling on fishing boats and the quality of ice holds on transport boats. Given that it is fished at night and usually collected by the transport boat after a few hours, the first few hours after the fish is caught do not have a major impact on freshness. This, in any case, could be solved technically in fairly inexpensive ways (by carrying one or two washable crates on the fishing boat). An alternative way of addressing early handling issues is to minimize the time from the death of the fish to the point of icing – this could be solved by promoting longlines, instead of gill nets, where the fish remains alive longer and thus spoils less quickly. At the same time, transport boat ice holds are thought not to live up to EU standards and are difficult to clean properly. On average, installing a proper hold would actually cost more than the value of the vessel itself.

Participant observation carried out by the authors at landing sites in the three countries suggests that there is still a large gap between what is chronicled in the food safety 'paperwork' and what actually takes place on the ground. For example, having a documentation system that certifies boat-level inspections is not the same as actually carrying out such inspections (which almost never occur). But, all in all, it seems that the East African Nile perch industry has to a large extent solved the issue of food safety; or at least it appears to 'perform' it in a way that is acceptable to the EU. Still, this also suggests that the literature on agro-food standards may be over-blowing the argument when it insists that process standards are becoming more important than product standards. While processes have indeed become more systematized, streamlined in apparently coherent frameworks and documented more thoroughly, in East African fisheries instances of non-compliance tend still to be caught in the 'old way' – when product tests fail to match minimum (or maximum) levels set by the EU. And even when this happens, 'quiet' remedial action by the public authorities in the region (reasonably, given the history of reaction by the EU in the 1990s) and/or private commercial remedy (a discount on the price of the consignment) seem to be more common resolutions than the destruction of a consignment, as EU regulation would have it.

These developments imply that the burning issue in terms of maintaining viable livelihoods around Lake Victoria is now the sustainable management of the stock, where improvements (whether 'performative' or real) have been far less satisfactory than in the case of food safety standards. Strong demand and healthy export prices until recently militated against discussions on how to limit the amount of fish extracted from the Lake. However, changes in demand specifications (a fall in demand for smaller fillets in particular) is now providing new incentives to take sustainable fishery management more seriously in the region, together with signs that stocks may have reached a critically low point.

These observations suggest that analyses focusing on only one set of standards and related management systems may miss important problems of compliance that are related to other sets of relevant standards faced by an industry. They also suggest that alignment and/or contradictions are far from static overtime, and that fortuitous changes need to be exploited quickly by the industries concerned.

Sustainability and fishery management systems

Nile perch was introduced into Lake Victoria from Lake Albert in the 1950s. It is a predator that feeds on other fish and the idea behind its introduction was to 'convert' Haplochromine species that are small in size into a more commercially exploitable fish of larger size (Ogutu-Ohwayo, 1999, 32). Nile perch was first noted in fish catches in the early 1960s (O'Riordan, 1996, 40–41). Stocks of Nile perch started to increase rapidly from the early 1980s, followed by an increase in catches and the reduction or disappearance of many native species (Ogutu-Ohwayo, 1999).

The high rates of growth of fish exports from the three riparian countries from the late-1980s were accompanied by a number of concerns regarding the environmental sustainability of the resource base (Ogutu-Ohwayo, 1999, 11). These concerns related to: (1) overfishing and resource depletion; (2) loss of biodiversity with the introduction of exotic species; (3) effluent pollution from fish processing and other industries; (4) degradation of shoreline ecosystems; and (5) deficient resource management due to different environmental standards in the riparian states.

In the last few years, a recovery in biodiversity (Balirwa et al., 2003) and a decrease in Hyacinth presence along the shoreline[7] have meant that most of the sustainability discussion has centred on increased eutrophication (due to space constraints, we are unable to discuss this issue here), on how to avoid resource depletion and on the effective implementation of regionally harmonized fishery management standards. A recent study assessing biological changes in the fish stock in Lake Victoria, including a review of trawl surveys, acoustic surveys and catch assessment surveys, suggests that 'the Nile perch stocks are under pressure and the fishery may have reached, or even exceeded, its limit' (LVFO, 2007a).

A number of standards and regulations have been agreed regionally to address dwindling stocks, such as licensing of fishers, trading bans on small size Nile perch, prohibition on using destructive gear and control of illegal fishing. Most of these, in different forms, have existed for many years, but until recently have been implemented, when at all, exclusively through 'rule-and-punish' systems. This entailed occasional busts and military-style operations involving the sequestration and public destruction of illegal gear. On-water patrolling was almost non-existent and bans on trading of undersize fish were almost never implemented (see Ponte, 2007 for details). Processing factories (with a few exceptions) only became serious about fisheries management in the very recent past – prior to the mid-2000s, management-related measures were driven by conservationists, researchers and to some extent LVFO. Yet, because the demand for small Nile perch fillet has decreased, there is now a market incentive for processing companies to leave small fish in the lake until they grow. In the following sub-sections, we look first at the implementation, starting in late 2007, of a self-monitoring system on minimum fish size by export processing plants; and second, at the establishment of Beach Management Units around the lake.

Self-monitoring system on minimum fish size at export processing plants

Since late 2007, a self-monitoring system geared towards banning the processing for export of undersize fish has been operational in the three East African countries. The process was initiated by the Uganda Fish Processors & Exporters Association (UFPEA) in September 2007, following a series of meetings amongst members including an extraordinary meeting held to adopt resolutions on the matter. The same system was adopted by the respective associations in Tanzania in October 2007 and later on in Kenya, after the violence that followed the December 2007 elections subsided.

Essentially, the industry association in Uganda started by setting up a team of independent inspectors, funded by the industry itself, which monitors the size of fish used in the members' processing plants (all plants are members of the association). At the start, a ban on accepting fish under the size of 40 cm was applied, later the minimum size was increased to 45 cm and finally to the statutory 50 cm as per regulation. Sanctions, however, are applied by the competent authority, not by the private team of inspectors, under a memorandum of understanding between the industry associations and the relevant fishery authorities. A first instance of non-compliance (with a 3–5 per cent tolerance level depending on the country) attracts a one-week closure of the plant; a second instance a 1-month ban; and a third instance a 3-month ban. Plants can go back to the starting point if no instance of non-compliance re-occurs within a 6-month period. By January 2009, all three East African countries had moved to zero tolerance, and currently no factory is supposed to process any fish outside the required minimum size.

In Uganda (as of February 2008), there had been only a few instances of first non-compliance; in Tanzania (as of May 2008), plant closures took place in four cases, once in two instances; in Kenya (as of late 2008), there had been no reported instances of closure of plants, but a factory manager was reportedly sacked for violation of the stipulated minimum size. A cynical view of such a development would suggest that ways have been found around the inspections at the plant level; however, participant observation and interviews at landing sites and with processors in all three countries suggest that undersize fish is not landed in any significant quantity at export landing sites. To the extent that this information is reliable, the initiative can be seen as a resounding success.

This is an instance in which a regulation that includes a public standard (minimum fish size), and a related monitoring and compliance system which existed on paper but was not actually implemented, are now being applied by a private entity (the industry association). This entity hires a private team of inspectors (often, former public fish inspectors), but in case of non-compliance the application of the sanction (the closure of the plant) is delegated to the public regulatory body. It is hard to separate public and private here. What can be said, however, is that the *content* of the standard was set by the public authority; that private *management and monitoring* of the standard has been more effective than the previous system of public management; and that, in contrast, public *sanctioning* is likely to have been more effective than had it been left to a purely voluntary and private mechanism.

However, that undersize fish do not seem to be accepted by the export processing plants does not mean that it is not fished. Press reports and direct observation of fishing activities on the lake suggest that undersize fish is landed at other sites and finds its way into local and regional markets (from Uganda, it goes especially to the DRC and Sudan), but at a lower price than the one commanded in exports to EU markets. This means not only that the resource is still likely to remain over-exploited, but also that the positive impact on local economies is reduced. Stopping undersize fish from being extracted from the lake is a complicated issue, relating to what gear is used in the Nile perch fishery, the costs and incentives of using alternative gear, and the type of fishery management and monitoring systems that are more likely to promote change in the direction of sustainability. We explore these issues in the next sub-section.

Advantages and limitations of community involvement in fishery management

Top-down fisheries management tools are usually built upon the estimation of Maximum Sustainable Yields (MSY) and direct or indirect control of gear type or size restrictions on fish. Two main criticisms have been levied against this approach. The first questions whether, in small- and medium-sized water bodies (but perhaps also in bigger ones such as lake Victoria) the MSY-based approach is the best way of managing fisheries resources, and whether management is needed at all. According to this argument, environmental fluctuations explain much of stock variability in some freshwater lakes in Southern Africa (Jul-Larsen et al., 2002; see also Kolding et al., 2005). Those who take this position highlight that fishing effort has impacted on the sustainability of the resource only where it was investment-driven (this could apply to Nile perch in Lake Victoria), not where it was population-driven (ibid.). They also question whether mesh size regulations, prohibitions on use of certain gear and minimum fish size regulations are necessary and/or useful, given the general lack of enforcement and the limited status of knowledge on the links between stock dynamics and fishing efforts.

A second line of criticism is based on the observation that traditional top-down approaches to fisheries management (government fishery officials posted at the local level) do not deliver as local communities are either not involved or not given formal recognition (Geheb, 2000). Partially as a result of this second criticism (and especially as a result of the kinds of management projects operating on Lake Victoria that have been funded in the last decade or so), the three East African countries have moved towards the direction of community-based solutions through the establishment of

Beach Management Units (BMUs). This approach follows what in the fisheries management literature is known as co-management – power sharing between state and local communities, and a shift of responsibilities from the former to the latter.

However, community-based fisheries management also has its limitations, since it relies on how collaboration between communities and local government takes place in practice, given the relatively authoritarian systems that communities are used to (Geheb and Sarch, 2002). It cannot be assumed that (different) communities are actually able and/or willing to take up these responsibilities. Indeed, often these 'participatory' processes are donor-driven and attract little interest locally (see Allison, 2003; Nielsen et al., 2004).

A total of 1069 Beach Management Units (BMUs) were established in the three riparian countries of Lake Victoria between 2004 and 2007: 281 in Kenya, 433 in Tanzania and 355 in Uganda (LVFO, 2008b). BMUs, among other tasks, register fishing boats, license fishers and record landings. All in all, local community involvement in monitoring and applying regulation on gear in East Africa has increased with the establishment of BMUs (Lwenya et al., 2007; LVFO, 2007c). However, in our interviews with BMU representatives around the Lake, a number of clear problems are also evident: (1) lack of resources to carry out patrolling on the Lake to sequestrate illegal gear and impose sanctions; (2) conflicts of interest – as the chairpersons that carry out the patrolling are voted by the same fishers that they are supposed to confiscate gear from and apply sanctions to; (3) security concerns: even with armed patrolling, chairpersons still go back home after a patrol and are vulnerable to retribution; (4) after a spurt of activity and optimism following the establishment of BMUs, local communities are puzzled about what they 'get out of them'; partly, this is related to community-level misunderstandings of what function a BMU has (it has no subsidized or priority access to financing or gear) and partly due to the lack of clear mechanisms through which fishers are supposed to access new and improved gear; and (5) a clash of mandate between BMUs and fisheries officials – at the time of establishment, some BMU officials assumed that they were an extension of government and would be doing the work of fisheries officials which could attract an income.

The BMU system could be an improvement over the *rule-and-punish* system based on fishery inspectors and the occasional and military-style operations that characterized previous top-down fishery management (although some military-style operations are still taking place). Evidence from survey data shows that communities are today more informed on the existence of rules, their logic and the benefits that can arise from their collective enforcement (Lwenya et al., 2007; LVFO, 2007c). At the same time, several prominent processors have argued that market instruments, together with some monitoring, can be the most effective means of stopping fish from being extracted from the lake. We label such an approach *market-and-punish* (although a more precise denomination would be 'the market punishes').

In this respect, they find that it could be more effective to control the trade of undersize fish than to patrol the Lake and destroy gear. Their claim is that if it is made sufficiently difficult to trade in undersize fish because of controls in local markets and border posts, it will become more difficult for fishermen to dispose of undersize fish, thus obliging them to switch to larger mesh nets and/or abandon the use of seine nets, which are the most destructive to the resource because the very small mesh size that captures large quantities of Nile perch fingerlings. This approach, however, does not take into consideration the interests of traders who carry out these kind of activities and the network of contacts that benefit as a result.[8] It also underplays how difficult it is to sustain such controls seriously in the long term. While at the height of such operations the trade does indeed stop, it tends to re-surface as soon as the pressure eases (the so-called 'Operation Clean' in Uganda in 2005 followed exactly the same dynamics). In other words, while processors have been successful through a 'market-and-punish' system in stopping the export trade of undersize fish, suppressing the regional and local trades is a much more complicated process.

We argue that rather than spending resources on tackling the regional trade, a successful solution to the undersize fish problem needs to take into consideration the constraints under which fishers operate. While for larger operators switching gear may not be a financial problem, smaller operators (who own only their own boat, for example) would incur a substantial expenditure. In this situation, it is more logical for them to risk a penalty (requisition does not mean that one cannot get out of a situation with a bribe or 'buy back' the very same gear) than to invest in nets with larger mesh sizes which will lead to lower catches, at least in the short term – this is the evidence that emerged from our interviews anyway. No discussion has been advanced in any of the three countries of a system of incentives, subsidies or swap mechanisms that would address these concerns, although one company has attempted a subsidized net swap with mixed results (on Lake Kyoga). Rather, fishermen are portrayed as villains and outlaws, both in government and ministerial pronouncements and in the popular press. We think that this does not bode well for sustainable management of fisheries on the Lake.

Ecolabelling

Ecolabelling in fisheries

Another market-based approach that can facilitate sustainability efforts is ecolabelling. Eco-labelled fishery products are a small but growing segment of the fish industry. Their rise relates not only to increased concern with environmental issues, but also to increased competition in the retail sector, and the consequent search for additional properties in products to add profitability and/or market share. Ecolabelling schemes are increasingly perceived as a way of simultaneously maintaining the productivity and economic value of fisheries while providing incentives for improved fisheries management and the conservation of marine biodiversity (Deere, 1999; Rotherham, 2005).

Potential environmental and economic benefits have been associated with ecolabelling (Deere, 1999; Wessells et al., 2001; Enviro-Fish Africa, 2005; Ward and Phillips, 2008a, b). The main argument for ecolabelling has been that it could provide the needed economic stimulus for better long-term stewardship and availability of natural resources important for national welfare. However, the evidence to back such a strong argument is still inadequate (see Agnew, 2006; Ponte, 2008). On economic benefits, Deere (1999, 21) notes that if fisheries management improves in response to efforts to comply with the standards that are embedded in the ecolabel, the potential benefits to fisheries could go beyond the possible higher revenues which ecolabelled products may generate. In line with this argument, Wessells et al. (2001, 54) highlight the following potential commercial benefits of ecolabelling: gaining access to new premium markets; adding value to existing products; expanding one's presence in existing markets; maintaining the market share in competitive markets; achieving product differentiation and export earnings; providing opportunities for attracting capital investments and new joint venture in developing countries; and maximizing long-term competitiveness (see also various chapters in Ward and Phillips, 2008a).

As in the case of environmental benefits, the literature has so far treated only the potential rather than the empirical economic benefits of ecolabels in fisheries (Ponte, 2008). And despite the acknowledged opportunities that ecolabelling could provide, serious concerns have also emerged. These include: possible lack of transparency and participation in standard setting; underlying protectionist motives; high potential costs of complying with required management practices and data collection; high costs of certification in developing countries which rely on expensive foreign experts; inadequate institutional and technical implementation capacity in developing countries and the *de facto* nature of ecolabels as barriers to market access when a majority of market players require them (see Deere, 1999; Wessells et al., 2001; Ponte, 2008; and various contributions in Ward and Phillips, 2008a).

The Marine Stewardship Council (MSC) ecolabel

The history of voluntary labels before the advent of the Marine Stewardship Council (MSC) initiative was limited to two single-issue labels (neither of which was third-party certified), aiming at reducing by-catch of Dolphin in Tuna fishing (Bonanno and Constance, 1996) and of Turtles in Shrimp fishing. In both cases, the main issue was not one of over-fishing and over-capacity, but of animal rights and the protection of endangered species (Allison, 2001, 945). Current efforts in developing organic certification of fishery products are mainly focused on aquaculture (Mansfield, 2004). But in recent years, a number of other certifications and ecolabels have emerged (Ward and Phillips, 2008b list 13 ecolabels in total related to wild-capture fishery products), though MSC remains the only one with a significant market share.

MSC was established in 1996 as a joint initiative of the World Wildlife Fund for Nature (WWF), the world's largest private non-profit organization, and Unilever, at the time the world's largest frozen fish buyer and processor.[9] MSC became an independent initiative in 1999. The idea behind MSC is to address the world-wide decline in fish stocks by awarding sustainably managed fisheries with certification to a label that could be affixed to retail products.

MSC certification partly depends upon a chain of custody system that keeps 'sustainable' and 'other' fish separate from each other all the way from catch to supermarket shelf or ice display. MSC argues that it allows, via its logo, consumers to promote sustainable fishing through a market-based (rather than regulation-based) mechanism by choosing the labelled product over the unlabelled product (Johnston et al., 2001; Roheim, 2003, 2008; Jaffry et al., 2004). Yet, many of the fishery management systems that need to be in place to achieve certification are heavily reliant on public regulation and publicly funded research.

Certification is granted against a specific standard called the 'Principles and Criteria for Sustainable Fishing'. Assessment is carried out on a voluntary basis by accredited third-party certification bodies. At the catch level, certification is awarded to a 'fishery', not to individual operators. Individual operators in the trade, processing and retail sectors can apply for chain of custody certification and for the use of the MSC logo.

A thorough analysis of the features and limitations of the MSC system has been carried out elsewhere and will not be replicated here (Ponte, 2008). What needs to be highlighted is that MSC until recently had failed to pay attention to the specific needs of artisanal fisheries in developing countries, and least-developed countries in particular. Although this is now being partially addressed by a pilot programme seeking to simplify the data and scientific research needs for the certification process, doubts remain on its potential to lift barriers to certification of fisheries in LDCs.

Ecolabelling initiatives on Lake Victoria

In this sub-section, we draw on existing experiences with fishery ecolabels around Lake Victoria to assess their potential to support sustainability. Through LVFO, the three East African countries are conducting a pre-assessment exercise to evaluate whether to apply for MSC for certification.

At the same time, two individual operators have been involved in other ecolabelling initiatives. One label, 'Kyoga Wild' has been developed by a Uganda-based exporter. The other, sought by a Tanzania-based exporter, is being developed with Naturland, a German organization involved in organic and sustainability standard setting and labelling.

In interviews and discussion or workshop documents three main motivations to move towards ecolabelling have been highlighted in the East African Nile perch industry : (1) to counteract the negative image portrayed by the documentary *Darwin's nightmare* (see Molony et al., 2007); (2) to spur both a more active engagement from government and the political system and collective private sector commitment to sustainable fishery management, given the perilous state of the stock; and (3) to stimulate a process of value addition, possibly open up market niches and/or obtain higher prices for 'sustainable fish' exports, given that the volume of the exportable resource is likely to decrease.

Despite the fact that there are reservations on whether Nile perch can even be considered for certification,[10] ecolabelling discussions have provided a focus for serious debate on fishery management measures. Consideration of the possibility of MSC ecolabelling started at a regional fishery stakeholder workshop held in Nairobi in October 2006 (LVFO, 2006a), where it was decided that ecolabelling would be a suitable strategy to address the challenges of Nile perch fishing and to provide a focus point for improving fishery management on Lake Victoria. From then on, LVFO took over the coordination of the initiative and put together a task force with representatives of the three fish processing/export associations and fisheries regulatory agencies around the Lake. A pre-assessment exercise (financed by GTZ) was then started in order to evaluate whether to formally apply for MSC certification. The results of the pre-assessment were not yet available at the time of writing. But LVFO officers argue that the process of pre-assessment can by itself provide stimulus for fish biologists to work more closely with fishery management people, and to speed up the adoption of input from other existing projects (such as LVFO's database building efforts or other efforts trying to integrate the results of fish stock assessments into fishery management decisions). However, for the time being, these are more statements of intent than a reflection of actual results.

In response to criticism highlighting the difficulties of LDC artisanal fisheries elsewhere in obtaining MSC certification (see Ponte, 2008), LVFO experts said that the volume of resources generated by the Nile perch industry should be sufficient to offset the costs of compliance and certification, even though the costs and challenges of monitoring thousands of small fishing boats are indeed a problem. Reasonable data on stock trends in Lake Victoria are apparently available, having been collected under a series of donor-funded projects. Enough resources, it is argued, should also be available to continue information gathering after donor funding ends.

Because the three industries are forming a regional body with legal status at LVFO, they should be able to use their pressure to extract resources from governments, the argument goes.

In parallel to this regional initiative, ANOVA (the main Nile perch fish importer into Europe), Vicfish (a processing and export company based in Tanzania) and GTZ initiated a pilot project aimed at certifying the Nile perch landings of Vicfish according to Naturland standards on 'sustainable capture fishery', which were adopted in late 2006.[11] Naturland has certified farms and companies involved in meat, milk, potatoes, cereals, coffee, tea, fruits, forestry and aquaculture products against organic standards. Their ecolabel on capture fisheries (named 'Naturland Wildfish') includes components on social and ecological responsibility and economic viability. The argument put forward for such an initiative is that while MSC would be able to address environmental and fishery management issues, it did not cover social issues (GTZ, 2008).

The pilot project in Tanzania involves the identification of landing sites from where 'sustainable' Nile perch will be procured via registered and contracted agents and sub-contracted fishers, and the establishment of an Internal Control System for managing documentation and traceability. Vicfish intends to procure all its fish from sustainable sources and to implement these procedures from all the seven or eight landing sites from where it usually buys fish. All suppliers and fishermen are to be registered and required to use specific gear. In terms of motivations and expectations, the Tanzanian export company acted under strong encouragement from ANOVA and other fish importers on the understanding that within 2–3 years from the start of the process, many buyers will be interested in ecolabelled fishery products due to increasing demand. Although there were no specific orders in place at the time of interview (January, 2008), the Tanzanian company was expecting a premium to be paid by buyers for such a fish.[12]

The process of preparation for certification, supported by a consulting company with GTZ funding, involved the identification, adaptation and implementation of social standards, improvement of hygiene and handling procedures and co-management with the local BMU (GTZ, 2008). The content of the project-specific standard was adapted to the issues that concern inland open-access fisheries, and was accepted by the Naturland board in April 2008.[13] Inspections at landing sites and the processing plant in Tanzania took place in January 2009 and resulted in a number of recommended corrective measures to be dealt with before certification is granted.[14]

In Uganda, a separate ecolabelling initiative was attempted by Greenfields, a processing and export company based in Entebbe, for a range of sustainable products under a project called 'Kyoga Wild' (supported by SIDA through EPOPA). Contrary to the Naturland case above, this was a 'first-party' label in the sense that Greenfields developed both its own set of standards and a label. The original purpose of the initiative was to catch Tilapia and Nile perch in Lake Kyoga using selected hooks and gillnets of the recommended size to prevent resource depletion. The project included a net swap system where fishermen were provided with recommended size nets at subsidized prices. Boat owners were registered and given an individual identification number and boats were painted in a specific colour for easy identification. The first exports started in early 2006 under the label 'Kyoga Wild Sustainable Tilapia/Nile perch' to the Swiss Coop retail chain. According to the general manager of Greenfields, however, the volume of demand was low and no price premium was paid for the fish. Also, their effort was covering a very small proportion of the catch from that lake, which meant that most fishing contined to be unsustainable (due to the poor level of fishery management on Lake Kyoga). This combined with high demands on managerial and financial resources (even with donor support) did not justify continuing the initiative, although the company says that it is still committed to work in areas where the BMUs are serious about sustainability.

The experience of ecolabelling on Lake Victoria suggests at least three important lessons for the discussion on standards: (1) although it is not yet clear if ecolabelling necessarily leads to positive environmental impacts through better fishery management, it is more likely to do so through collective initiatives targeting a fishery as a whole, rather than individual initiatives targeting a small part of a fishery – although at the same time, individual efforts may provide practical examples of 'best practice' and generate political support for collective efforts; (2) the outcome of ecolabelling (i.e., certification) is perhaps less important than the management processes it generates; at the same time, lack of explicit financial benefits (for example, a premium for 'sustainable' fish) can undermine the long-term buy-in of both industry and governments; and (3) while potential ecolabelling on Lake Victoria could be seen as providing a mainly 'product differentiation' function (Henson and Humphrey, 2008), it is actually performing a major risk management function as well, both for producers (to ensure the long-term availability of supply) but also for buyers (minimizing the risk of supply failure of Nile perch for fish importers and retailers in Europe).

Conclusions

In this concluding section, we briefly highlight two sets of reflections. First, we reflect upon the East African experience with fishery standards, labels and management systems in relation to some of the key themes explored in this book. Second, we underline the importance to Kenya, Tanzania and Uganda of continuing to meet food safety standards and of sustainably managing the Nile perch fishery to ensure the viability of livelihoods around Lake Victoria.

The case study of the Nile perch industry provides insights in relation to several key debates on standards. First, it highlights that different sets of standards interact with each other with sometimes unexpected consequences and with dynamics that change over time. As a result, it is not sufficient to examine one set of standards in detail in an industry, or even more than one set independently of each other, but it is also essential to explore the interactions between them. Failures to comply with a standard do not necessarily arise from failures in the compliance system for this standard; conversely, compliance with a standard may occur through mechanisms that are unrelated to the expected path of compliance. This is not just an analytical question, it has implications for the long-term sustainability of meeting the objectives that standards are trying to promote. Most standards are developed and applied in practice as if they were 'sealed systems', while they should be designed and implemented bearing in mind potential interactions with other sets of standards that may apply to a particular industry or a specific location.

Second, this chapter challenges the general argument in much of the literature on agro-food standards that suggests a clear movement from public to private forms of standards and managements. In fisheries, while the private sector indeed is playing a heightened role, it often does so by borrowing and adapting systems developed in public regulation. Specifically in relation to East Africa, it has become harder to distinguish between private and public forms: a regulation that includes a public standard on minimum fish size (and a related monitoring and compliance system which existed on paper but was not actually implemented) is now being monitored by a private entity (private inspectors hired by the industry associations). However, in case of non-compliance, the application of the sanction is delegated to the public regulatory body. In short, we have a situation here where the *content* of the standard was set by the public authority, the control of *conformity* with the standard is delegated to the private sector and where *sanctioning* reverts back to the public sector.

Third, while process standards and attached management systems are indeed becoming more widespread and systematized, product standards still play a key role, especially as it is fear over falling supply of the product itself that is spurring fishery management reforms around the Lake in ways that have not been seen before.

Fourth, much emphasis in the standards literature has been placed on whether actors in the South are able to comply with standards, with what costs and benefits, and what the impact of compliance is on selected indicators (social, environmental, on food safety and so on). In relation to the experience of ecolabelling in fisheries, however, arguments have been made by LVFO officers that the *process* of preparing for compliance may be as important as its end result. Even though the establishment of BMUs pre-dates the discussions that took place among stakeholders around Lake Victoria in relation to exploring the possibility of MSC certification for Nile perch, such discussions have provided more immediate focus to the fishery management debate in the region and a higher level of political commitment (or at least visibility). Whether these will translate into actual practices that will improve sustainability of the fishing effort on the Lake remains to be seen.

Fifth, the ecolabelling experience suggests that the distinction between risk management and product differentiation standards may be more blurred than previously thought (see Aragrande et al., 2005; Henson and Humphrey, 2008; Riisgaard, 2009). According to Henson and Humphrey (2008, 18), the main role of *risk management* standards is to 'provide a level of assurance that a product is in compliance with defined minimum product and/or process requirements'. They function to ensure that 'buyers have sufficient control over production processes in order to ensure that critical levels of product and process attributes are attained' (ibid., 19). *Product differentiation* standards, on the other hand, are 'mainly aimed at differentiating the firm and/or its products in the "eyes of the consumer"' (ibid., 18). They enable firms to 'supply blends of product and process attributes, and to communicate these to consumers, that set them apart from their competitors' (ibid., 21). The distinction is said to be critical because as the bar set by risk management standards rises, the space for product differentiation becomes compressed until new ways of differentiating are found. During these reconfigurations, power asymmetries along a value chain are challenged and comparative advantages reshuffled (Riisgaard, 2009).

While ecolabelling (including fishery ecolabelling) is usually placed firmly in the realm of product differentiation standards (see Henson and Humphrey, 2008: Table 2), it actually serves a dual function. From the viewpoint of the consumer (and retailer), it indeed serves a function of product differentiation by signalling that such fish has been sourced from stocks that are certified as not in danger of collapsing and/or that are properly managed. At the same time, it is also a risk management standard that helps reduce two specific kinds of risk. First, by stimulating improved management practices, as seen above, ecolabelling may help fish importers and retailers make sure that they have access to enough volume of fish in the future to match product demand (supply risk). Second, as an unintended consequence, it may also minimize another major risk at the level of producing countries – that of failing local livelihoods in case a fishery collapses.

This chapter has also shown that maintaining a viable and sustainable fishery that has positive implications for livelihoods around Lake Victoria (see Chapter 8) impinges on complying with two sets of standards and management systems: first, food safety standards have to continue being followed in ways that are acceptable to the main importer of Nile perch (the EU); and second, fishery management systems need to be in place so that enough fish can be extracted from the Lake without undermining its ecological balance and the sustainability of the fish stock.

In relation to food safety standards, we have seen that the three East African countries to a large extent have fixed the problems that beset them in the 1990s. Even though there are still some important aspects that could be improved upon, the EU seems to be satisfied with the state of things in the three countries – or at least it is accepting their performance of food safety systems as being reasonably appropriate.

In relation to sustainable fishery management, however, the situation is much more problematic. Without strong action, the industry may be in danger of collapsing. Fortunately, the market (or at least the export market) can help in this particular conjuncture. Up to the recent past, maximum extraction of Nile perch from Lake Victoria was encouraged both by industry and governments, due to healthy export prices and strong demand in the North. However, the sudden emergence of competition from small Vietnamese Pangasius fillets in Europe has wiped out much of the market for small Nile perch fillets (especially in the frozen sector). But because Nile perch can grow to a much bigger size than Pangasius (and many other competing species, both from wild capture and aquaculture), there is now a clear incentive for the export industry to stimulate fishery management systems that punish the fishing of small Nile perch from the lake.

Although standards on minimum fish size and the kind of gear that is allowed for the fishing of Nile perch have been in the regulation books for a long time, compliance was at best erratic. In the export sector, the recent emergence of a voluntary system of monitoring minimum fish size by processing plants seems to have been effective in cutting down undersize fish purchasing dramatically. The passage from a 'rule-and-punish' to a 'market-and-punish' system of monitoring is *per se* worthy of attention.

However, this has not yet stopped the fishing of undersize fish itself, which now finds its way in local and regional markets. Although politicians, governments and export operators have been vociferous in calling for a clamp down on the domestic and cross-border trades of juvenile fish, we argue that the key to assuring stock renewal lays in reducing the incentives that are behind this fishery at their source. First, this involves clarifying and revising the roles and mandate of BMUs, together with appropriate financing of their activities; and second, it involves setting up incentives for fishers to swap destructive gear with 'legal size' gear: this is unlikely to be successful unless a publicly funded fish net swap is established. Setting up ad hoc roadside controls to clamp down on the domestic trade, blaming fishers and carrying out occasional military-style campaigns for the destruction of gear are not going to solve the problem.

Notes

1. Information on changes in fishery management systems, food safety standards and ecolabelling was gathered mainly through fieldwork by Kadigi (in 2006–08,

Tanzania), Ponte (in 2004 and 2007–08, Uganda) and Mitullah (in 2004 and 2008–09, Kenya). Fieldwork included focus groups and key informant interviews with all key stakeholders in the three countries – fishers, transporters, artisanal processors, industrial processors and exporters, fisheries and other government officials, industry associations, the Lake Victoria Fisheries Organisation (LVFO) and Beach Management Units (BMUs).

2. See EC (1998; 1999a and 1999b; 2000a and 2000b).
3. Commission Decision 98/422/EC.
4. Commission Decision 2001/633/EC.
5. Commission Decision 2004/39/EC.
6. See EC (2006a, 2006b and 2006c).
7. A new weed, Hippo Grass has surfaced and has almost eliminated the Hyacinth. A Kenya Marine and Fisheries Research Institute official noted that the weed is a stronger species of grass and seems to overpower the Hyacinth. The weed has a tendency to rot, sinking into the lake, and is currently affecting Nile perch fish stocks. Its positive elements include water purification, that it can be used as fodder for cattle and that it attracts other fish species.
8. The military and prominent politicians have been accused of being behind this trade in Uganda (see *The New Vision*, 4 January 2008).
9. However, Unilever has since sold off major portions of its European seafood business.
10. The argument against Nile perch is that it is not a species endemic to Lake Victoria, having been introduced into the Lake in the 1950s. Others, however, argue that Nile perch was endemic in Lake Victoria, becoming extinct when the Lake dried up in the Miocene period (Beadle, 1962). An argument for allowing Nile perch to be considered for possible ecolabelling was put forward by at least one of the regulatory agencies around the lake to the FAO during the technical discussions on the drafting of ecolabelling guidelines for inland waters. The argument was that even if it was a (re)introduced species, the ecological imbalance that it is alleged to have created was also due to other environmental and cyclical factors. Thus, Nile perch should be considered for ecolabelling provided that an appropriate management system is in place. This is still under discussion within FAO's Committee on Fisheries. But eventually it will be down to MSC's own board to decide whether they will accept Nile perch from Lake Victoria, given its poor image internationally (although this has not discouraged MSC from certifying New Zealand Hoki or South Georgia Patagonian toothfish which also had bad sustainability records, see Ponte 2008).
11. Source: http://www.naturland.de/naturlandwildfish.html.
12. Interviews with Vicfish manager, 9 January 2008 and 18 June 2008.
13. http://www.naturland.de/8496.html.
14. At the landing sites, the most pressing of these were the lack of a 'sanctioned fishermen and boat owners list' and of a policy for inclusion in such a list, inadequate assessment of volumes of fish landed and lack of identification of approved fishers when landing fish. At the level of processing plant, issues related to social standards for casual workers. The applicability of such standards to fishers also arose (source: http://www.naturland.de/8496.html).

10
European Food Safety Regulation and Developing Countries' Regulatory Problems and Possibilities

Morten Broberg

Introduction

A large number of developing countries are highly dependent upon exports of agricultural products and for many of these countries the European Union is the primary export market. For decades, however, the EU's market for agricultural products was protected by high tariff barriers. These barriers were vigorously criticized; not least due to their adverse effects on developing countries' exports. Today the tariff barriers have been lowered, but in their place a regime of stringent food safety requirements ('sanitary and phytosanitary' or 'SPS' requirements) has taken shape (Ramaswamy and Viswanathan, 2007, 124).

This chapter provides a legal analysis of some important aspects of the EU's food safety regime and its consequences for developing countries. The objective is twofold, namely to identify those legal measures that cause the most problems for developing countries' exporters of food products and to point to possible solutions.

In the second section, the chapter provides an outline of the EU's food safety regime. Next, in the third section, the barriers to imports of foodstuffs from developing countries created by the food safety regime are identified. The chapter goes on, in the fourth section, to examine different ways of overcoming the barriers. Finally, perspectives for the future are considered.

The EU's food safety regime

The EU's food safety regime essentially prohibits food that is unsafe – for example injurious to health or otherwise unfit for human consumption – from being placed on the market. However, when a food product has been produced in compliance with specific EU provisions for food safety, the product will be deemed to be safe (Regulation 178/2002, Article 14(7)). This in itself is a strong incentive for food businesses to comply with the food safety regime, since in this way they can avoid liability.

Moreover, it is the responsibility of the food business operator, that is, the person controlling the food business, to ensure compliance with the applicable food law requirements. The obligation of ensuring that food products are safe is thus firmly placed with the food business operators, not public authorities.

EU food safety requirements have been established in a European context. This means, for example, that limit values for naturally occurring toxins (for example, mycotoxins) are normally set according to what can be required from a European food business operating in a European climate, that certification requirements are based on the premise that businesses have easy access to accredited laboratories – which is not always the situation in developing countries – and that the level of administrative competence of food businesses as well as public authorities is fairly sophisticated.

In order for imported food products to be marketed in the EU, they must comply with its food safety requirements or with conditions recognized by it to be at least equivalent (Regulation 178/2002, Article 11). Although the Member State authorities and the EU have the power to carry out control inside the EU, they do not have such power regarding food businesses in third countries. The EU therefore has either to rely on the food safety control carried out by the third country authorities (Regulation 882/2004, Article 47) or to require the food products to be controlled upon importation (see for example Regulation 882/2004, Chapter V). When a third country has presented information substantiating that its national food safety control complies with or is equivalent to the EU's food safety requirements, the European Commission may carry out official controls in the third country to verify 'the compliance or equivalence of third-country legislation and systems with Community feed and food law and Community animal health legislation' (Regulation 882/2004, Article 46).[1]

When a EU food business operator imports food products, the importer may presume these to be safe if the exporting third country has been formally recognized as having a food safety control system that either complies with or is equivalent to the EU system. In this situation the fact that the food product originates in a third country is immaterial. In contrast, if the third country has not been so recognized, Article 17 of Regulation 178/2002 requires the EU importer to ensure that the food products satisfy the relevant requirements of food law, and to verify that such requirements are met (Graffham, 2006, 5).

Identifying the barriers

Overview

In the following we set out to identify the most important barriers to imports from developing countries to the EU. First, the requirements that apply to the composition of the food product as such are considered. This is followed by an examination of the requirements regarding the processes under which the food is produced. Next, the examination turns to the authorization requirements that may apply and then to some more technical requirements regarding the control of imports of food products which may pose substantive hindrances. Finally, the issue of private food safety requirements is briefly considered.

Composition of food – setting the limit values

Most food products are made up of several different ingredients. Conventional ingredients with a history of safe use in the EU may be used freely. Other food product components may only be used to the extent that it has been considered safe to do so. To this end, the EU has established extensive legislation.

Any food product may contain components that are partly or wholly undesirable. Broadly speaking, two categories of such components may be distinguished: on the one hand, we have additives such as colours, sweeteners and flavourings that are intended to be part of the final food product. On the other hand, we have naturally occurring toxins such as mycotoxins, pathogenic bacteria such as salmonellae and residues of, for example, pesticides or veterinary drugs which all are unwanted in the final product, but which may be difficult to avoid completely. Originally, limit values for these types of components were laid down by the individual Member State, but over the years further limit values have been established by the EU. Whilst the early EU limit values often appeared to be rather arbitrary, the contemporary limit values are scientifically founded.

When setting limit values, an important objective is always to secure that the food product is safe for the consumer. When a food safety issue is covered by an international standard, the EU takes this into consideration, unless it finds the standard to be ineffective or inappropriate (Regulation 178/2002, Article 5(3)).

The EU applies slightly different methods for establishing limit values with regard to the different types of unwanted components, but in general the following approach is applied. First, an *acceptable daily intake* (ADI) must be identified, that is, the highest daily dose of the component in question that a human may consume without suffering any adverse effects when viewed over a lifetime. Normally, to establish the ADI, experimental animals are used to establish what is termed the *no observed adverse effects level* (NOAEL). The NOAEL value will then be adjusted by an appropriate safety factor to take into account the difference in sensitivity between the experimental animal and humans as well as the difference in sensitivity between different individuals (see for example Regulation 429/2008, Annex II, para. 3.2.3.1). For pesticide residues, the NOAEL will usually be divided by 100 to establish the ADI (van der Meulen and van der Velde 2008, 369).

The ADI relates solely to a specific unwanted substance such as a pesticide or veterinary drug. However, the ADI must be translated into *maximum residue limits* (MRL) for the different food products. An MRL is established by the authorities for those food products where the unwanted substance may appear. When setting the MRLs for different food products, a consumer's combined total intake of the unwanted substance must not exceed the ADI. To this end the authorities base themselves upon consumer intake models, which take into account the type and quantity of the different food products consumed by Europeans (as well as by the various national populations and sub-populations in Europe). This leaves a fair margin of discretion to the authorities. For example, if the combined MRLs surpass the ADI for the substance, it will be necessary to lower the MRLs for one or more products – and in this respect it may seem natural for the authorities to take account of industrial policy considerations when deciding which product(s) must comply with a stricter MRL.

If the combined MRLs fall below the ADI, it could be argued that there is room for increasing the MRLs for certain products without harming the consumer. However, the EU applies a 'double barrier' when laying down its limit values. This means that in addition to calculating the MRLs of unwanted substances in various food products it also identifies the *as low as reasonably achievable*-level (ALARA) for these products; this is typically the level that can be achieved when the farmer applies *good agricultural practices* (GAP) when using the substance. Therefore, even if in principle the ADI allows for an increase of some MRLs, the Community will not make such increase if it means exceeding the ALARA-level (Regulation 1881/2006, recital 4).

The consequences of changing a limit value may be significant. For example, in 2001, the European Community drastically reduced the MRL for a pesticide commonly used for de-greening pineapples. Ghanaian exporters did not take notice of this change and so their pineapples were rejected at point of entry to the European Community. Had the shipments arrived just a few days earlier, the pineapple would have been allowed to be imported and sold in the Community (Graffham, 2006, 18).

Applying both an ALARA and an ADI (MRL) requirement may help prevent the European consumer being exposed to unhealthy levels of the various components, but at the same time it may constitute a real problem for developing countries: the limits are based upon what is possible in a European context. Thus, it may be that in Europe it is only necessary to use a limited amount of a given pesticide whereas in the tropics a higher dose is required, leading to a higher residue level. If the EU's limit value is difficult to meet for a tropical producer, this may hinder exports to the European market – even if the intake by Europeans of the unwanted substance from the imported product together with the intake from the consumption of other food products would fall well below the ADI – that is, the level that gives rise to toxicological concerns.

In cases where a food product contains a component for which no limit value has been established and where the component is not a conventional one with a history of safe use within the EU the maximum residue level is set by default at the *limit of determination*; LOD (Cerrex, 2003, 34). Essentially, the 'limit of determination' is equivalent to the application of 'zero tolerance', since the food product may not be marketed in the Community if the substance is detected. Frequently, setting the MRL at LOD will preclude the use of the substance on the crop in question (Hirst, 2001; Willems et al., 2005, 16). The problem is, however, that since developing countries are less attractive markets for pesticide manufacturers than the EU, manufacturers have much less incentive to carry out the required trial work to establish (or to increase) the MRL for pesticides to be used on developing country crops (Jooste et al., 2003, 268). This lack of commercial incentive to bear the costs of trial work for establishing MRLs is particularly apparent with regard to the older, generic pesticides. But it is precisely these pesticides that are most likely to be used by poor farmers. Consequently, for a number of pesticides, the MRLs have been set at LOD with respect to a wide range of tropical crops (Hirst, 2001; Wilson and Abiola, 2003b, xxxvii).

Further problems arise when different export markets apply conflicting limit values; or apply diverging process requirements, as illustrated in the following section.

Process requirements

With the increased focus on food safety has come a shift towards process requirements (Josling et al., 2004, 104). This shift is clearly reflected in the EU food safety regime, which to an appreciable extent lays down stringent rules on managing the production, processing and distribution of food products, primarily through hygiene obligations and the duty to establish a traceability system. These requirements place a very considerable burden on all food businesses; a burden that is particularly felt by small businesses in developing countries (Bernauer and Caduff, 2006, 91; Wilson and Abiola, 2003b, xxxix; see also OECD 2006, 30).

For years, the EU has imposed extensive hygiene requirements on producers of animal origin food producers. In 2004, extensive hygiene requirements were also applied to food products of non-animal origin through the adoption of the so-called 'hygiene package', a common regulatory framework providing measures and conditions to control hazards in the production of food and to ensure that foodstuffs are fit for human consumption. The 'package' lays down specific requirements, based on good manufacturing practices, which food businesses must satisfy at all stages of production, processing and distribution if food products are to be sold in the EU.

Perhaps the most important part of the 'hygiene package' is that it requires all food business operators, with the exception of primary producers, to 'put in place, implement and maintain a permanent procedure or procedures based on the HACCP principles' (Regulation 852/2004, Article 5). HACCP is a systematic preventive approach aimed at identifying potential food safety hazards so that certain predefined actions can be taken to reduce or eliminate the risk of a hazard arising.

The EU's HACCP system requirements encompass the following seven steps:

- Identifying any hazards that must be prevented, eliminated or reduced to acceptable levels.
- Identifying the critical control points at the steps at which control is essential to prevent or eliminate a hazard or reduce it to acceptable levels.
- Establishing critical limits at critical control points, which distinguish acceptability from unacceptability for the prevention, elimination or reduction of identified hazards.
- Establishing and implementing effective monitoring procedures at critical control points.
- Establishing corrective actions when monitoring indicates that a critical control point is not under control.
- Establishing procedures which shall be carried out regularly to verify the effective working of the measures outlined above.
- Maintaining documents and records commensurate with the nature and size of the food business to demonstrate the effective application of the above measures.

Food business operators in the EU must be able to provide evidence of compliance with the HACCP procedures to the competent Member State authorities (Regulation 852/2004, Article 5(4)). As already noted, primary producers are not obliged to put into place a HACCP system (Regulation 852/2004, Article 5(3)); instead they must comply with some less far-reaching hygiene provisions (Regulation 852/2004, Annex I).

Hygiene requirements constitute a particularly heavy burden, not least on small and medium-sized enterprises in developing countries (Schillhorn van Veen, 2005, 494–495; Jaffee and Henson, 2005, 99; COLEACP-PIP, 2005, 67; Wilson and Abiola, 2003a, xx and xxi; Nyangito et al., 2003, 52). Moreover, there are reasons to assume that the marginal costs of implementing HACCP are higher in developing countries than in industrialized ones (Unnevehr and Jensen, 1999, 632). Equally, a developing country food producer is likely to find it more burdensome to comply with different systems of food safety requirements – for example, different public standards in the United States and Europe or differences between public and private standards – than a food producer in an industrialized country (Wilson, 2002, 438; see also Wilson and Abiola, 2003b, xxxv–xxxvi). Compliance with food safety procedures may therefore impose prohibitive costs on developing country food producers and governments (Wilson and Abiola, 2003a, xxiii; Wilson and Abiola,

2003b, xxxviii–xxxix; Roberts et al., 2004, 339) and in countries where it is not possible to certify HACCP systems, or where it is otherwise not possible to meet the process requirements, production of food products for export may be discouraged (Unnevehr and Jensen, 1999, 632; Jaffee and Henson, 2005, 103). Costs of compliance may, however, vary widely between firms according to prevailing standards and firm size (Henson and Jaffee, 2006, 605–606).

If a food business operator discovers a hazard, it is required to take corrective action. For example, this is the case under the HACCP procedure when a critical control point is not under control. If, however, the hazard requiring corrective action is only uncovered after the food product has been passed on in the food chain, the potentially unsafe product must be traced in order to be able to recall it from the market (European Commission, 2000c). To this end, Regulation 178/2002 requires that all food business operators are able 'to trace and follow a food, feed, food-producing animal or substance intended to be, or expected to be incorporated into a food or feed, through all stages of production, processing and distribution' (Regulation 178/2002, Articles 3(15) and 18(1)). Thus, each food business operator must have in place a system to identify any supplier of a food stuff, feed stuff, food-producing animal or substance that is to be incorporated into a food or feed product as well as to identify the other businesses to which the business operator's products have been supplied. In other words, all food businesses in the food chain must know from where they have obtained all supplies and to whom they have sold any products that may be used in a food or feed product. Moreover, the food business operators must have in place systems and procedures which allow for this information to be made available to the competent authorities on demand.

Maintaining a traceability system fulfilling these requirements places an appreciable burden upon food business operators (Wijnands et al., 2006, 90). However, the EU Standing Committee on the Food Chain and Animal Health has held that the traceability requirement only applies from entry into the EU (Standing Committee on the Food Chain and Animal Health, 2004, 11 and 27). Formally speaking, the requirement therefore is only a burden to EU food business operators. Nevertheless, the onus that the new food safety regime places on food business operators arguably means that EU importers of food products will only buy from third country food businesses that can guarantee product traceability (Graffham, 2006, 6; Cerrex, 2003, 31–32).

Authorization requirements

In a number of situations marketing of foodstuffs requires prior authorization from the authorities. Such authorization may relate to the ingredients of the food product (that is the product as such), or it may concern those producing the product (that is the processing of the product).

Product authorization

As observed earlier, conventional ingredients with a history of safe use in the EU may be used freely. For other ingredients authorization must first be obtained, however. This means that it is only possible to export food products containing such ingredients if authorization has been obtained.

The EU has established so-called positive lists regarding additives (antioxidants, preservatives, colours, sweeteners and so on) and food supplements (vitamins, minerals and so on). These lists set out which additives and supplements may be used in what food products and they frequently also set the maximum level for the additive or supplement. The lists are exhaustive, meaning that if an additive or supplement is not on the relevant list, it may not be used. In order to be added to one of the positive lists, an additive must first undergo a safety assessment by the European Food Safety Authority (EFSA), whereupon the EU legislator must amend the relevant list (Directive 94/35, Article 7; Directive 94/36, Article 5; Directive 95/2, Article 6). In contrast, a supplement can be added to the positive list through a much more accessible procedure than for additives – and a safety assessment by EFSA is not required unless the product can have an effect upon public health (Directive 2002/46, Articles 5(4), 13 and 14). Hence, if a food business wants to use an additive or supplement that is not on the positive list, it must apply for authorization. The authorization requirement necessarily constitutes a barrier to sales – albeit presumably not a significant one for developing country food businesses, first, because the use of additives and supplements is more widespread among food businesses in industrialized countries and, second, because authorization of an additive or supplement is generic in nature – meaning that when the additive or supplement has been added to the positive list, all producers may use the additive or supplement in accordance with the conditions laid down in the positive list in question.

Also, so-called novel foods, which are regulated by the Novel Food Regulation (Regulation 258/97, see particularly Article 1(2) og 3(1)), require prior authorization before being marketed in the EU. 'Novel' in this context not only means food products that are the result of technical innovation, but also refers to food products that may have been known and consumed for centuries, but which are new to the EU. Therefore, food products that may have a long history of safe use in a third country may not be exported to the EU without a prior safety assessment followed by an authorization. Hence, in order to market 'exotic' food products such as noni juice from Southeast Asia (European Commission, 2003), authorization must first be obtained. The noni juice decision took 3 years, and the scientific assessment included laboratory animal studies for toxicity, genotoxicity and allergenicity; in other words, obtaining authorization was both time consuming and costly (Moorhead, 2007). If the applicant is unable to produce the required data, authorization will be refused.

In contrast to the regimes that apply to additives and supplements, an authorization for a novel food product is not generic in nature, but gives only the applicant the right to market the 'novel food' in question. As a consequence, if another food business wants to market the same (novel) food product, it must submit a new application; however, in this situation, a much-simplified procedure applies.

The rules for novel food constitute a substantive barrier to a number of food products from developing countries (Neville Craddock Associates, 2005); and several developing countries have pointed out that it is hard to understand, first, why old and well-tried food products are treated exactly like untested products and, second, why the Novel Foods Regulation does not apply the same system of generic authorization used for supplements and additives (Fletcher, 2007). Apparently, the European Commission has acknowledged these criticisms and has tabled a proposal for amending the Novel Foods Regulation (European Commission, 2007). According to this proposal, the authorization of novel foods shall, as a main rule, be generic and a simplified procedure shall apply for 'exotic' novel foods so that a notification will be sufficient regarding foods with a history of safe use outside the EU. By March 2009, this proposal had passed its first reading in the European Parliament, but was still some way from adoption (Starling, 2009).

Food producer authorizations

Authorization requirements may also apply to food businesses as such – that is to those processing food. In this regard, the EU's food safety regime again draws on the distinction between food products of animal origin and food products of non-animal origin: food products of animal origin may only be exported to the EU *if* the third country appears on a list established by the EU and, in most cases, *if* the third country food businesses appear on a list approved by the EU. It is for the EU importer to ensure that these requirements are met with regard to imported food products (Regulation 853/2004, Article 6). In contrast, for food products of non-animal origin, there is no general requirement that third countries must appear on a list to be eligible for export of such food products and, in many cases, it is sufficient that the exporting food businesses in the third country are known to and accepted as suppliers by importers of food into the EU (European Commission, 2006d, 10).

That food businesses handling food products of animal origin must appear on a list drawn up by the European Commission is laid down in Regulation 853/2004 – which is part of the Hygiene Package. In order to be placed on this list, the competent authority in the third country must provide guarantees that the establishment in question complies with the relevant EU requirements or with requirements that are equivalent thereto, that official inspections supervise compliance with the requirements and that it is possible to stop the third country establishment from exporting to the EU if it fails to meet the requirements (Regulation 854/2004, Article 12). Moreover, special provisions are laid down for fish and certain seafood products (Regulation 854/004, Articles 13 and 15).

It follows from the above that in order to be able to export food products of animal origin to the EU, a food business must not only fulfil the EU's hygiene requirements or the equivalent, but the third country authorities must also be able to efficiently supervise that the third country food business duly complies with the requirements. For food businesses (and governments) in developing countries these requirements may create substantial difficulties.

Control requirements

Food businesses situated within the EU are subject to official controls by the relevant Member State authorities, which are in turn subject to control by the European Commission. In contrast, third country food businesses are outside the jurisdiction of both the Member States and the European Commission. Exports of food products to the EU may however be conditional upon the third country producer being subject to efficient controls and upon the European Commission (FVO) being permitted to carry out official controls in the third country (Regulation 882/2004, Article 46; van der Meulen and van der Velde, 2008, 408; COLEACP-PIP, 2005, 18–20 and 24–25). The costs of such systems of control may be beyond the means of many of the poorest developing countries (Jaffee and Henson, 2005, 103).

Control in the third country

When importing food products of non-animal origin – that is food products where no prior authorization is required before importation – it is incumbent upon the EU importer to ensure compliance with the relevant European food law requirements or with conditions recognized as equivalent (European Commission, 2006d, 15). As already explained, primary producers are not required to put into place a HACCP system, but only have to comply with some less far-reaching hygiene provisions (Regulation 852/2004, Annex I). There is no obligation to have this compliance certified, but a third country primary producer must keep documentary evidence, including accurate records, and provide them to the EU importer on request (Graffham, 2006, 13). Where there is an obligation to apply a HACCP system, third country food businesses are also required to keep documentary evidence of this and to make this available to the EU importer on request. In addition, the EU importer will often require the third country food business to submit to a recognized and independent certification scheme (Graffham, 2006, 13).

Control requirements can include an obligation to produce laboratory certification that the food product complies with certain requirements. For example, where a food business exports chilli or chilli products to the EU, each consignment must be accompanied by an original analytical report demonstrating that there is no Sudan Red in the product. Sudan Red is a colouring that may be used to colour chilli in certain South-Asian countries, but which is illegal to use in the EU(Commission Decision 2005/402; see also COM(2009)17 Final and Draft Regulation of 13 March 2009, Recital 8 and Article 15). From a food safety point of view, this type of requirement seems well-founded, but is difficult to comply with where there is only limited access to accredited laboratories competent to carry out the certification – as is the case in some developing countries (COLEACP-PIP, 2005, 4 and 89; Wilson and Abiola, 2003a, xxiii; Nyangito et al., 2003, 57). Indeed lack of test facilities, or at least of well-functioning and efficient ones, appears to be a general problem in connection with implementation of standards in developing countries (Chapter 3 in this volume; El-Tawil, 2002, 4; see also Cerrex, 2003, 64). To some extent the European Commission has addressed this problem by adopting Regulation 2076/2005, which in Article 18 grants a transitional period of 4 years (expiring on 31 December 2009) during which time laboratories in third countries can adapt to the new situation.

Also, the laboratory certification costs may be very substantial relative to the total value of the certified batch, thus reducing small exporters' incentive to export to the EU (Jaffee and Henson, 2005, 96, 99 and 112). This is particularly likely to be the case where a food business in a developing country relies on several small sub-suppliers: testing the supplies from each sub-supplier may be prohibitively expensive. On the other hand, testing all supplies together can be problematic where the test uncovers the presence of an unwanted substance, since it may prove impossible to exclude only the polluted part so that all supplies will be considered to be polluted. The point made here is *not* that this testing is unjustifiable; rather it is that it can be particularly burdensome for supply systems relying on several small sub-suppliers as is often the case in developing countries.

Control upon importation into the EU

EU food safety legislation not only provides for control in the country of export, but also for control of food products in connection with import. The Member State food safety authorities are responsible for this control, which may take many forms (Regulation 882/2004, Article 10(1)). In this respect, sampling and analysis deserve particular attention, since what may appear to be only minor changes in a sample plan or in a method of analysis may have important consequences for access to the European market. The reason is that if just a tiny part of a batch of a food product is found to be unsafe, then the whole batch is regarded as unsafe (Regulation 178/2002, Article 14(6)). Therefore, if the authorities change their sampling plan to one that is more likely to uncover transgressions of the limit values, this will make it more difficult for the exporter to pass the control. The same is true with regard to improvements in laboratory testing methods. This is particularly so where the EU applies a zero tolerance approach (in practice: *limit of determination* or 'LOD'), since this essentially means that the limit value is set at what is measurable. Therefore any improvement in the possibility of detecting such a substance will be a *de facto* lowering of the limit value.

There is an abundance of evidence showing the importance of sampling and analysis methods; thus, for example, in a comparison of sampling plans used in the United States, United Kingdom and the Netherlands to test raw shelled peanuts for aflatoxins, it was found that the Dutch plan rejected the most lots, whereas the US plan accepted the most. The UK's plan was somewhere between the other two, but it was also the plan that accepted the greatest number of bad lots. The contemporary EU sampling plan is to a large extent based on the Dutch plan (Gilbert and Vargas, 2005, 239). In order to limit the variations between controls in the different Member States, the EU has issued specific rules for how to carry out sampling and subsequent analysis.

As is clearly seen from the above, not only tightened limit values can impede developing countries' exports. Changes in control methods – particularly with respect to sampling and analysis – may have precisely the same effect.

The role of private standards

When a large European supermarket chain imports food products into the EU, it is done under a contract specifying *inter alia* price, quantity and time and place of delivery. Moreover, the contract (not necessarily written) often also specifies quality requirements, including requirements on food safety. These food safety requirements generally go further than what is required by law, for example by laying down stricter MRLs, requiring certification or requiring full traceability. Often, private standards are established by private associations that cover a substantial number of distributors in the European Community. The most important of these include GlobalGAP (formerly EurepGAP), established by the EuroRetailer Produce Working Group; BRC, established by British Retailer Consortium; and IFS, run by the German Hauptverband des Deutschen Einzelhandels and the French Fédération des enterprises du commerce et de la distribution. These private food safety requirements impose an additional burden on the food businesses in developing countries; and sometimes this burden can be much heavier than that imposed by public food safety legislation.

Moreover, private food safety requirements may render *de facto* the public food safety legislation somewhat superfluous. For example, the EU does not require primary producers to put in place a HACCP system, but this is only of importance as long as the private standards do not require primary producers to put such a system in place. In other words, even if the EU were persuaded to adapt its food safety legislation to the situation existing in the developing countries, this would only have a real effect to the extent that public requirements are not simply replaced by private ones. It has, however, been pointed out that private standards are often closely related to public requirements – for instance, by 'plugging' gaps in regulatory controls (Henson and Humphrey, 2008, 11). Private standards therefore curtail the European Community's possibilities to ease developing countries' access to the European market.

While it is true that private standards often constitute an additional burden on food businesses wishing to sell in the EU, it is also important to recognize that some of these standards are better tailored to the circumstances facing these businesses than public standards; at least with regard to flexibility regarding certification. The reason is that a number of private standards are developed in close cooperation with businesses and other stakeholders affected by the standards and that they are regularly reviewed and revised. The primary objective of these standards is not to keep unsafe products out of the market, but rather to make sure that the products arriving in the market are safe. Perhaps the EU could draw inspiration from the private standards' willingness to establish less burdensome certification requirements *vis-à-vis* small businesses in order to take into account the more limited resources available to these businesses (van der Meulen and van der Velde, 2008, 499; Garcia Martinez and Poole, 2009, 22).

Overcoming the barriers

As is clear from the preceding discussion, European food safety requirements constitute an important barrier to imports of food products from developing countries. The question therefore arises as to how developing countries may overcome this barrier. Essentially, there are three different ways: (i) dismissing the barriers, (ii) lowering the barriers or (iii) surmounting the barriers. This section considers each of these three routes.

Dismissing the barriers

There seems to be only one realistic way to dismiss EU food safety requirements, namely if it is possible to find them to be illegal. The EU is founded on law and on several occasions the European Court of Justice has proved itself ready to annul EU legal acts in conflict with fundamental EU law principles.

The EU undoubtedly has the power to adopt legislation for food safety, so it is not possible to dismiss its entire food safety regime. However, it may be possible to annul individual legal acts that lay down food safety requirements – or parts of these acts. In this respect, three legal arguments appear particularly relevant, namely: (i) the duty to take development of developing countries into account in all EU policies that may affect these countries; (ii) the duty to observe the proportionality principle; and (iii) the duty to comply with international law (including WTO law). These three arguments are examined below.

Duty to take account of the development of developing countries

According to Article 178 of the EC Treaty, the EU shall take into account its development cooperation objectives, as laid down in Article 177, in the policies that it implements and which are likely to affect developing countries. This means that when adopting food safety legislation, the EU must take into account the sustainable economic and social development of developing countries, and more particularly least developed countries. Moreover, it must strive to reduce poverty in developing countries as well as to ensure their smooth integration into the world economy. To some extent this has been reflected, for example, in the EU's Economic Partnership Agreement (EPA) with the CARIFORUM countries. The agreement contains a chapter on SPS measures which aims to facilitate trade between the parties. The most important part of the chapter deals with the provision of assistance in order to improve the CARIFORUM countries' capacity to address potential disruptions to trade and achieve equivalence and/or compliance with EU requirements. The agreement requires the EU to cooperate to reinforce regional integration, to improve monitoring, implementation and enforcement of SPS measures through capacity building activities, and support public and private sector partnerships. This includes expertise sharing, training and information for regulatory personnel, capacity development for the private sector and cooperation in international bodies.[2]

According to a strict reading of Articles 177 and 178, the EU must pay due attention to the needs of developing countries when laying down food safety requirements for selling food products in Europe. It has, however, only been possible to identify one example of this:

The introduction in 1998 of strict limit values for different types of aflatoxins in nuts and dried fruit was met with strong criticism for causing significant problems in developing countries whilst only producing limited benefits in the EU. Subsequently, the EFSA was asked to carry out a new study of the problems related to aflatoxins in nuts. EFSA found that increasing the limit value for total aflatoxins from the Community's 1998-limit-value of 4 μg/kg to 8 or 10 μg/kg would result in an increase in average total dietary exposure to aflatoxins in the region of 1 per cent, that is, it would have only rather minor effects. However, such an increase was likely to allow up to 6 per cent additional consignments of nuts onto the European market. EFSA also found that reducing the population's total dietary exposure to aflatoxins could be achieved firstly by improving the control system so as to reduce the number of highly contaminated nuts and dried fruit reaching the European market and secondly by reducing exposure from food sources other than nuts (EFSA, 2007).

The above aflatoxins example seems to be the exception that proves the rule. In general, Articles 177 and 178 appear to have been almost completely overlooked by the EU, and it seems rather unlikely that the European Court of Justice would be ready to strike down a food safety measure on the basis that it contravenes Articles 177 and 178.

The principle of proportionality

Proportionality essentially allows the Court of Justice to review not only the legality, but also (to some extent) the merits of legislative and administrative measures. The proportionality principle is composed of three cumulative tests. Measures must be: (i) *suitable* to achieve the legitimate aim (that is, it is possible to achieve the stated aim through the use of the measure); (ii) *necessary* to achieve that aim (that is, no other less restrictive means are available); and (iii) they must be *proportionate stricto sensu* (that is, not produce any excessive effects on the interests of those affected by it).

Arguably, parts of the EU food safety regime would face difficulties if measured against the principle of proportionality (Broberg, 2008, 83). Thus, a number of measures appear to impose excessively and prohibitively strict criteria upon food producers in developing countries (Cerrex, 2003, 66; Neville Craddock Associates, 2005, 38; COLEACP-PIP, 2005, 68). This may not only conflict with the proportionality principle, but also with the rather similar necessity principle laid down in Articles 2(2) and 5(6) of the WTO SPS Agreement, which state that food safety requirements may be applied only to the extent necessary to protect human, animal or plant life or health. The question remains, however, whether in the EU's application of the principle of proportionality consequences occurring outside the EU have the same weight as those occurring inside.

In conclusion, it may be possible to strike down some particularly burdensome EU food safety measures for infringing on the proportionality principle, although it remains an open question what weight would be attributed to those consequences that occur outside the EU.

International law obligations

The EU is bound by international law (Broberg, 2000, 175). Consequently, this should mean that its food safety regime must be adapted when it conflicts with the EU's international law obligations.

As a member of the WTO, the EU is bound by the WTO Agreement on the Application of Sanitary and Phytosanitary Measures (the SPS Agreement), which regulates members' access to laying down rules on food safety. EU food safety measures must therefore comply with these WTO obligations. In this respect, it is of particular importance that the SPS Agreement not only encourages international harmonization in the field of food safety but that it also lays down the rule that if a WTO member decides not to use an existing international standard, any alternative measure used by the member must be based on proper risk assessment and be subject to a range of other conditions set out in Article 5 of the SPS Agreement. This limits the EU's possibilities to introduce ever stricter requirements.

EU food safety measures have been challenged under the SPS Agreement on a number of occasions; most famously in the so-called hormone beef cases. Developing countries have rarely been among the challengers, however (Scott, 2007, 306). In those instances where developing countries have challenged industrialized countries' SPS measures, this has concerned only a handful of emerging economies which do not include any LDCs (see Table 10.1 and World Bank, 2005, 42). This is probably not due to lack of appropriate occasions to make such challenges, but rather to lack of expertise and internal capacity, the costs associated with this type of litigation, fears of retaliation as well as the uncertain benefits to be derived from such a challenge (Scott, 2007, 307; Henson and Loader, 2001, 97; Wilson and Abiola, 2003b, xxxv).

The rising importance of private standards and the barriers these can create for developing countries' exports have caused these countries to query the lawfulness of such standards under the SPS Agreement (Scott, 2007, 304–306; Stanton and Wolff, 2009, 6–9). In principle the WTO Agreement – and the SPS Agreement – only impose obligations upon States that are signatories to the Agreement, whereas private parties are not obligated by it. Therefore, the SPS Agreement only covers private standards to the extent that a State can be held responsible for such standards. In this regard it has been argued that particularly Article 13 of the SPS Agreement may be construed to imply an obligation on States to prevent private parties from introducing private food safety standards (WTO, 2007; *Bridges Weekly*, 2008). The relevant part of the provision provides that 'Members shall take such reasonable measures as may be available to them to ensure that non-governmental entities within their territories, as well as regional bodies in which relevant entities within their territories are members, comply with the relevant provisions of this Agreement'. The question of the application of the SPS Agreement to private standards has become a subject of discussion in the WTO's Sanitary and Phytosanitary Measures Committee (WTO, 2007; *Bridges Weekly*, 2008). No conclusion appears to have been reached until now, but arguably it seems very difficult to construe the SPS Agreement so that it generally also covers private standards (see also Scott, 2007, 306).

It is apparent that international law places important restrictions on the EU's possibilities to introduce strict food safety measures. But it does not provide a means of fully or partly eliminating the barriers which this regime creates *vis-à-vis* developing countries' food exports.

Table 10.1 Members raising and supporting concerns with the European Community under WTO SPS Committee procedures, 1995–2008

Members raising/supporting the concern	1995	1996	1997	1998	1999	2000	2001	2002	2003	2004	2005	2006	2007	2008	Total
Africa				1			1			1	3			1	7
Asia			1	2	1	1	2	6	5	2	8	2		1	31
Europe				2								1			3
Middle East				1			1					1			3
America (and Canada)	2	2		2				5	3	1	2	2	3	3	25
Central and South America		1		5				10	15	10	9	15	1	3	69
New Zealand and Australia	1			2				3	2		1			1	10

Lowering the barriers

The second way of strengthening developing countries' access to the EU market for food products is by lowering food safety barriers. However, under the WTO Agreement's MFN principle, a member of the WTO may not, as a general rule, require from any given WTO member conditions that are less advantageous than those it offers any other country (be it a WTO member or not). This means that if the EU wants to ease food safety requirements with respect to imports from developing countries, it must either ease the requirements *vis-à-vis* all WTO members (developing as well as industrialized countries) or WTO law must allow for preferential treatment for developing countries. In fact, the SPS Agreement does allow for such 'special and differential treatment' since in Article 10(2) it provides that: 'Where the appropriate level of sanitary or phytosanitary protection allows scope for the phased introduction of new sanitary or phytosanitary measures, longer time frames for compliance should be accorded on products of interest to developing country Members so as to maintain opportunities for their exports.' In other words, while the SPS Agreement does not allow the EU to establish lower MRLs or laxer sample plans for products only originating in developing countries, it does allow it to introduce longer time frames for products of interest to these countries (see also Geboye Desta, 2008, 120). Moreover, it may ease the requirements on (all) third country imports in order to assist developing countries; that is the requirements continue to apply to products originating in the EU, whereas imports are exempt.

Actually, only to a limited extent has the EU eased developing countries' access to the European market. An example is found in Article 50(1)(a) of Regulation 882/2004 concerning control of imports, empowering the EU Standing Committee on the Food Chain and Animal Health to establish a phased introduction of import requirements regarding food products from developing countries, provided such phased introduction will have a demonstrable effect in ensuring that developing countries are able to comply with the provisions of Regulation 882/2004.

Moreover, as has been observed earlier in the chapter, the Standing Committee on the Food Chain and Animal Health has held that the traceability requirement only applies from when the food product crosses the EU border (Standing Committee on the Food Chain and Animal Health, 2004). This means that the requirement is primarily a burden to EU food business operators, while formally exempting developing country – as well as other third country – food businesses.

It appears that the EU has not taken other steps towards lowering the barriers for developing country food businesses. For example, Regulations 852/20004, 853/2004 and 854/2004 (which together with Regulation 882/2004 make up the so-called 'hygiene package') make no reference to developing countries. On the contrary, Regulation 852/2004 in Article 10 provides that third country food business operators exporting to the Community shall comply with the Community's substantive hygiene requirements.

Hence, the EU's preferential treatment of developing countries in the field of food safety is rather insignificant.

Surmounting the barriers

The third way in which the EU can improve developing countries' access to its market for food products is by helping developing countries meet its food safety requirements. In this respect it is important that not only the SPS Agreement, but also the EU's own food safety regime requires it to provide technical assistance in the field of food safety. Thus, recital 44 of Regulation 882/2004 provides:

'It is appropriate to take account of the special needs of developing countries, and in particular of the least-developed countries, and to introduce measures to that effect. The Commission should be committed to support developing countries with regard to feed and food safety, which is an important element of human health and trade development. Such support should be organized in the context of the Community's Development Cooperation Policy.'

Regulation 882/2004 also specifically provides for training of experts from developing countries in Articles 32(1)(d) and (2)(e), 50(2), and 51(2), Regulation 882/2004. In this respect, for example the European Commission 'Better training for safer food' initiative provides (also) for developing country participants to familiarize themselves with EU SPS requirements (European Commission, 2009d, 29 and 47).

Moreover, of the approximately €2.5 billion which the EU provides annually under its Aid for Trade initiative, in 2007 €110 million concerned SPS-related projects (Personal communication of 21 June 2009 with the Commission's DG DEV). In addition, the Economic Partnership Agreements between the EU and different groups of ACP countries all provide for the establishment of specific task forces to address development needs, including cooperation in the field of SPS. Furthermore, most trade-related assistance projects funded by the EU have an SPS component. This overall approach is in line with Article 9 of the SPS Agreement which prescribes that WTO members shall 'facilitate the provision of technical assistance to other Members, especially developing country Members'.

Perspectives for the future

Food safety will continue to be a challenge

How will food safety requirements affect developing countries in the future, and what should be done to counter the problems caused by these requirements? Three important considerations should be noted: (i) Food safety occupies a prominent role on the political agenda in industrialized countries and it appears unlikely that this will change within the foreseeable future. On the contrary, it appears more likely that the political attention food safety receives in high-income countries will percolate downwards, not only to middle-income but ultimately also to low-income countries. (ii) Private food safety standards play an increasingly important role, and nothing indicates that they will cease to exist; although we may expect them to undergo important changes. (iii) Many developing countries are dependent upon food exports to industrialized countries and are likely to remain so dependent. For these developing countries, food safety requirements for the export markets will continue to be of considerable importance.

It follows that industrialized countries' food safety requirements will continue to be a challenge to food product exporters in developing countries.

A need for increased coordination, communication and cooperation

In order to improve the current situation, efforts should arguably be directed at three goals, namely: (i) coordination; (ii) communication; and (iii) cooperation.

Over the last two decades, food safety rules have increased considerably, both in number and in scope. Some of these rules are formed by governments at the international, regional or national level. Others are drawn up by private enterprises or associations of private enterprises. A food business that exports a given food product to the EU may thus have to comply with several different food safety requirements – some public and others private. If the very same product is also exported to, for instance, the United States, still other public and private food safety requirements are likely to apply. This multi-dimensional patchwork of regulatory measures places such pressure on food businesses that particularly the weaker ones – such as small producers in developing countries – may be unable to meet the requirements. Therefore, simplification of the fragmented standards through increased *coordination* between those issuing food safety requirements could be a significant improvement.

Not only are the developing countries faced with an extensive patchwork of regulatory food safety measures, often food businesses and public authorities in developing countries have only limited knowledge about the requirements they must comply with when exporting (Wilson and Abiola, 2003b, xxxvi; Henson et al., 2000, 44–45; Henson et al., 2004, 365–366;[3] World Bank, 2005, xiii). This can lead to substantial problems, as illustrated earlier with the Ghanaian pineapples case. It follows that there is a need to improve the *communication* of the different food safety requirements, together with specific information about how to best comply with these requirements. Whilst there seems to be a general need to improve communication in the field, arguably this need is particularly pronounced in developing countries – *inter alia* due to their more restricted access to relevant means of communication and to their linguistic and cultural differences from the EU.[4]

Finally, there is a need for increased *cooperation* between those issuing food safety requirements and food businesses and authorities in developing countries. Such cooperation includes technical assistance with regard to how best to comply with public and private food safety requirements whilst taking into account the conditions facing developing countries. It also involves the need to design food safety requirements in a way that takes due consideration of the circumstances under which food businesses work. Whereas the EU and other donors do provide technical assistance in the field of food safety to developing countries, it appears that public regulators only give limited consideration for the situation in developing countries when drafting food safety requirements. The EU should therefore learn from the experience of private standards, which are often developed in *cooperation* with the various stakeholders – including sometimes those in developing countries. In this way, requirements are likely to become more workable and, thus, accepted by those who have to work with them in practice.

Appendix: Application of the European food safety regime and developing countries

Ekaterina Bang-Andersen

While the European Union has stringent food safety requirements on paper, the extent to which these comprise an import barrier for developing countries depends, amongst other things, on how these regulations are applied in practice. This Appendix aims to illuminate this issue by providing a summary account of how application of one aspect of the regime, namely the notification system, occurs across the Community. Notifications have been chosen as they are one of the few aspects of application of the regime where information is centrally available, through the Rapid Alert System for Food and Feed.

Member States are required to raise alerts or make notifications for each new case arising from the detection of a health risk in one or more consignment of food. Alerts and notifications fall into a number of categories. In cases of alerts, Member States must take rapid action to prevent food entering their markets, or to withdraw it from circulation if it is already present. However, alerts are relatively rare. Moreover, a clearer impression of the EU's actions at its borders can be obtained by analysing other categories of notification. 'Information notifications' refer to food, feed or food

Table 10A.1 Evolution of notifications since 1997

Year	Information	Addition to information	Total
1997	14	8	22
1998	156	20	176
1999	263	59	322
2000	339	98	437
2001	406	310	716
2002	1092	466	1558
2003	1856	878	2734
2004	1897	1329	3226
2005	2204	1522	3726
2006	1962	1563	3525
2007	1972	1774	3746

Source: Rapid Alert System for Food and Feed (RASFF) Annual Reports, 2005–07.

contact materials for which risk has been identified but for which rapid action is not required as the product has not reached the market of Member States or is no longer on the market – mainly as a result of rejection following testing at EU borders. 'Additional Information notifications' concern any type of information related to the safety of food or feed which has not been communicated by a Member State as an alert or an Information notification, but which is judged interesting for food and feed authorities in Member States. Table 10A.1 presents the overall evolution of these two categories of notification from 1997–2007. As can be seen, numbers of information notifications rose extremely rapidly until 2003, before stabilizing. Jaffee and Henson (2004), commenting on the trend up to 2002, offered the explanation of increased capacity for inspection.

Of the 2007 notifications, approximately 73 per cent referred to products from Third Countries. EU candidate countries accounted for 14 per cent and EU and EFTA/EEA Member States accounted for 13 per cent. Notifications concerning products from Third Countries do not all necessarily arise from actions at EU borders. Indeed, in 2007 notifications of the latter kind represented just under half of all notifications referring to Third Countries.

Table 10A.2 presents information on how many Third Country notifications arose at EU borders, and in relation to which categories of hazards, for 2005, 2006 and 2007. As can be seen rejections and detentions related to mycotoxins (which mainly affect nuts and nut products) overwhelmingly dominate. Hazards typically found in fish and meat (heavy metals and microbiological contamination) are another important category. Relatively few detentions for pesticide residues are evident. No breakdown of all Third Country notifications is available in this form.

Table 10A.2 Notifications arising at borders by hazard category 2005–07

Hazard/Category	2005 Border control- import reject	2005 Border control screening sample	2006 Border control- import reject	2006 Border control screening sample	2007 Border control- import reject	2007 Border control screening sample
(Potentially) micro-organisms	121	38	40	19	51	31
Bad or insufficient controls					29	
Biocontamination (other)				6		8
Composition	44	6	24			
Food Additives	77	6	112	7	99	12
Foreign bodies	22	8	30		27	
GMO/novel food					35	
Heavy metals	114	19	114	18	100	32
Industrial contaminants (other)		3		5		10
Microbiological contamination	69	11	24		31	8
Mycotoxins	843	23	722	24	604	30
Not determined/other	40		45		56	6
Organoletic aspects			24	2		
Parasitic infestation				3		
Pesticide residues	18	7		10		17
Residues of veterinary medicinal products	65	20	50	19	40	21
Total	1413	141	1185	113	1072	175

Source: Rapid Alert System for Food and Feed (RASFF) Annual Reports, 2005–07.

Table 10A.3 provides information on breakdown of all notifications by country of origin of the product notified, classified by region. There are inconsistencies between the totals reported in this table, and those reported in Table 10.1, for reasons that are unclear.

In Table 10A.4, these notifications are reported in terms of incidence per billion US dollars' worth of food imports to the EU from the regions concerned. The table shows notifications to be skewed heavily against products originating in Asia, on a trade weighted basis. This trend of high levels of

Table 10A.3 Notifications by origin of the product, classified by world region

World Region	2000	2001	2002	2003	2004	2005	2006	2007	Total
North America	6	8	25	62	58	86	250	204	699
South & Central America	76	59	155	251	229	236	215	205	1426
Europe	123	236	495	549	749	980	912	1004	5048
Africa	57	56	96	147	221	226	203	240	1246
Asia	210	336	748	1324	1307	1593	1291	1300	8109

Source: Rapid Alert System for Food and Feed (RASFF) Annual Reports, 2005–07.

Table 10A.4 Notifications by region of origin of the product, expressed in terms of US$ billion worth of EU food imports from the region of origin

World Region/Year	2000	2001	2002	2003	2004	2005	2006	2007	Annual Average
North America	0.23	0.37	1.20	2.73	2.24	3.39	9.26	6.30	3.22
South & Central America	1.91	1.55	3.85	5.19	3.96	3.88	3.27	2.38	3.25
Europe	0.40	0.76	1.45	1.34	1.45	1.76	1.51	1.37	1.26
Africa	2.63	2.73	4.28	5.40	7.33	7.34	6.43	6.44	5.32
Asia	7.35	12.69	28.08	41.31	33.22	37.69	26.72	22.27	26.17

Sources: Rapid Alert System for Food and Feed (RASFF) Annual Reports, 2005–07 and WTO International Trade and Tariff Data, http://www.wto.org/english/res_e/statis_e/Statis_e.htm (accessed 29.06.2009).

notification in relation to products from Asia was established well before the Sudan Red alert in February 2005. It is also reflected in Jaffee and Henson's (2004) data on detentions. The argument of these authors is that Asia exports a disproportionately high share of food safety-'sensitive' products to the EU, relative to, for example, Africa.

Turning to levels of notifications by different EU importing countries, Table 10A.5 reports rates of notification by old EU-15 Member States over the period 2002–07, in absolute terms and in terms of notifications by million of population. Controlling for domestic population size there appear to be radical differences between EU Member States' notification behaviour.

Given the dominance of the Netherlands and Belgium in EU food imports (mainly for re-export purposes) it may have been expected that these countries would have rather higher rates of notification than others in the EU. However, the highest rates relatively are found somewhat surprisingly in small EU countries that are not major import destinations (Denmark, Finland and Luxemburg).

Table 10A.5 Notifications by notifying EU Member State 2002–07

	2002	2003	2004	2005	2006	2007	Average notification/ population (million)
Austria							
Number of notifications	39	47	32	22	71	62	
Notification/ Population(million)	4.70	5.66	3.86	2.65	8.55	7.47	5.48
Belgium							
Number of notifications	70	50	59	77	80	98	
Notification/ Population(million)	6.60	4.72	5.57	7.26	7.55	9.25	6.82
Denmark							
Number of notifications	27	60	53	48	114	130	
Notification/ Population (millions)	4.91	10.91	9.64	8.73	20.73	23.64	13.09
Finland							
Number of notifications	33	44	52	75	79	82	
Notification/ Population(million)	6.23	8.30	9.81	14.15	14.91	15.47	11.48
France							
Number of notifications	59	67	124	115	94	124	
Notification/ Population (millions)	0.96	1.09	2.01	1.86	1.52	2.01	1.57
Germany							
Number of notifications	455	623	526	527	421	376	
Notification/ Population (millions)	5.53	7.57	6.39	6.40	5.12	4.57	5.93
Greece							
Number of notifications	36	89	95	89	110	168	
Notification/ Population(million)	3.21	7.95	8.48	7.95	9.82	15.00	8.74
Ireland							
Number of notifications	11	8	16	17	14	24	
Notification/ Population (millions)	2.50	1.82	3.64	3.86	3.18	5.45	3.41
Italy							
Number of notifications	214	545	576	687	556	499	

Table 10A.5 (Continued)

	2002	2003	2004	2005	2006	2007	Average notification/ population (million)
Notification/Population (millions)	3.60	9.18	9.70	11.57	9.36	8.40	8.63
Luxembourg							
Number of notifications	6	23	13	7	7	10	
Notification/Population (millions)	12.00	46.00	26.00	14.00	14.00	20.00	22.00
Netherlands							
Number of notifications	159	140	146	147	163	156	
Notification/Population (millions)	9.70	8.54	8.90	8.96	9.94	9.51	9.26
Portugal							
Number of notifications	11	43	25	17	20	24	
Notification/Population (millions)	1.04	4.06	2.36	1.60	1.89	2.26	2.20
Sweden							
Number of notifications	34	23	44	45	61	55	
Notification/Population (millions)	3.74	2.53	4.84	4.95	6.70	6.04	4.80
Spain							
Number of notifications	149	257	305	415	223	169	
Notification/Population (millions)	3.32	5.72	6.79	9.24	4.97	3.76	5.63
United Kingdom							
Number of notifications	155	221	231	314	351	360	
Notification/Population (millions)	2.54	3.62	3.79	5.15	5.75	5.90	4.46
Total							
Number of notifications (annual average)	1458	2240	2297	2602	2364	2337	(2216.33)
Annual Average Notification/ Million inhabitants (EU-15)	3.73	5.73	5.88	6.66	6.05	5.98	(5.67)

Source: Rapid Alert System for Food and Feed (RASFF) Annual Reports, 2002–07, World Bank, World Development Indicators (2007 population data).

Notes

The author is grateful for comments by Leon Brimer, Peter Gibbon, Bernd van der Meulen, Laura Nielsen and Margherita Poto. The usual waiver applies.

1. While it is the Commission that carries out and decides whether a third country's legislation and systems are equivalent with EU feed and food law and animal health legislation, it may ask some Member State food safety authorities to assist it in this process. At present only four 'third countries' have been determined to have fully equivalent systems, namely Canada, Chile, New Zealand and the United States. (Personal communication, Danish Veterinary and Food Administration, 1 July 2009). On the other hand, well over 80 countries, including a large number of low-income ones, are deemed to have equivalent (Part I listed) status in respect of fish and fishery product food safety systems.
2. As of January 2009, EU-CARIFORUM was the only EPA with these provisions.
3. But contrast the same authors, Henson et al., 2000, 367.
4. In this respect, reference may be made to the EU's bilateral trade agreement with Chile which mandates specific procedures to be followed in its consultation forum and sets out relatively precise guidelines of the requirements to be followed in establishing equivalence both of standards and of accreditation procedures for certification and testing (Alavi et al., 2007).

11
Conclusion

Stefano Ponte

The case studies presented in this book, while not claiming as a whole to provide a 'representative' picture of the challenges faced by agro-food industry in Africa, provide important insights on whether standards introduce serious entry barriers to Northern markets. The chapters cover all major standard content: product carbon footprint, food safety, organic and a variety of sustainability and social standards. They relate to high-value products (fresh vegetables, cut flowers, fresh fish, spices, pineapple and vanilla) and to a few traditional export crops (coffee and cocoa). They also span public, private and hybrid standards. Most of the contributions focus on East Africa and on standards applicable to exports directed towards the EU – with some observations made on local markets, local processes of standard competition and the development of regional standards and their compliance. This does not signal that local and regional standards are not important or worth attention, but simply that the research programme (Standards and Agro-Food Exports – SAFE) behind this book was focused on export value chains. This programme brought together a multi-disciplinary team of 13 researchers based in East Africa and seven based in Denmark.

This concluding chapter briefly highlights the collective and comparative contribution of this volume to the literature on agro-food standards, with a focus on empirical findings. The following discussion is structured along three dimensions: (1) trends in content, coverage and proliferation of agro-food standards that African producers and exporters have to comply with, and the interaction between different kinds of standards; (2) changes in the governance of standards, local participation and issues related to conformity; and (3) how standards and related value chain restructuring affect the welfare and inclusion or exclusion outcomes of participants.

The content, coverage and proliferation of standards

The contributions to this volume suggest that standards: are becoming more demanding; are covering more ground (horizontal expansion); are being applied increasingly to the entire value chain (vertical expansion); and that standards initiatives are proliferating. Standards have also become fundamental in shaping a number of dedicated strands of value chains that are kept to some extent separate from 'mainstream' value chains (thus leading to a certain degree of 'fraying' of value chains on the basis of product and process differentiation). The following discussion recalls some of the specificities of the case studies to highlight some trends that may be significant for the future of agro-food industries in Africa.

In Chapter 2, Bolwig and Gibbon chronicled the very recent emergence of a number of standards for product carbon footprinting (PCF), which may well become the 'next big thing' in international trade of agro-food products. As observed in other kinds of standards, early stages of PCF standard development has entailed the proliferation of many different schemes, including two international reference standards, one national public standard (in the UK) and a variety of private initiatives. In such initiatives, methods of measurement, indicators, horizontal coverage (how many aspects are included in a standard) and vertical coverage (where the system boundaries are set) vary dramatically, with important repercussions on what the standard (and often its related label or mark) communicates to consumers, regulators and other businesses, and with what degree of transparency.

From the point of view of African exporters and producers, the perspective of having to match different PCF standards for different end-buyers and/or country destinations is worrisome. Much depends on what technical specifications, systems of implementation and certification will be used in each case, and to what extent a degree of mutual acceptance will develop. If the route is one of mutual acceptance (as is occurring in some food safety and good agricultural practice standards), or one that leads to reduced diversity through competitive selection, then there should not be a major problem. On the other hand, if country- or issuer-specificities continue to prevail, African actors may encounter serious difficulties. These observations are still fairly conjectural as the number of products and their coverage in PCF schemes are still limited.

In Chapter 6, Lazaro et al. observe the proliferation of initiatives in the realm of sustainability standards for coffee (UTZ CERTIFIED is one of at least five initiatives), fresh vegetables (with exporters having to comply with one to three different certifications for just one export destination) and cut flowers (where at least 16 different standards initiatives can be identified). In Chapter 7, Riisgaard shows in more detail how different social standards for cut flowers apply vastly different content and with different degrees of measurability, although some efforts at harmonization are also taking place. Riisgaard also argues that, in specific relation to private social standards, outcome standards seem to be the preferred choice (they are easier to measure and manage) over standards on 'process rights' – such as the right to organize and bargain collectively which can facilitate workers to attain wider objectives such as negotiation of working hours, health policies or comprehensive bargaining agreements.

Several chapters examine the tightening of EU food safety standards and its consequences. In Chapter 3, Akyoo and Lazaro observe that food safety standards for importing spices into the EU were based mostly on physical characteristics and cleanliness until the 1990s; thereafter, health and hygiene specifications were added (such as levels of aflatoxins, minimum residue levels, presence of pathogens and/or heavy metals), thus increasing the complexity and cost of compliance. In Chapter 8, Ponte et al. (along with Kadigi et al., Chapter 9) highlight how food safety standards for fish imports into the EU have become more demanding in content and more complex in terms of management. This has resulted in the instalment of far more sophisticated systems of verification in East Africa. Finally, in Chapter 10, Broberg analyses the rise and consolidation of the new EU food safety regime, in detail, with consequences for African producers that are examined later in this chapter.

An observation is relevant here relating to the interaction between different categories of standards that apply to the same industry. Chapter 9 suggests that fish industry operators in East Africa are caught in situations where different sets of standards (food safety, fishery management procedures and ecolabel requirements) pull in different directions. This leads to tentative, opportunistic and/or contradictory compliance processes. At the same time, contradictory objectives sometimes align fortuitously and when this happens, swift action by both industry operators and policy makers can pay off. This suggests the need for holistic approaches (both analytical and practical) to standards by sector or value chain, rather than the current predominant approaches that focus on the content of specific standards as they arise or as they become problematic for an agro-food industry in Africa. It is also necessary to keep in mind that failures to comply with a standard may also occur through mechanisms that are unrelated or only partially related to the expected path of compliance for such a standard. Most standards are developed and applied in practice as if they were independent from each other, while they should be designed in ways that can also capture possible interactions with other sets of standards applying to an industry. This is not just an analytical question – it has implications for the long-term sustainability of meeting the objectives that standards are trying to promote.

The governance of standards, local participation and issues related to conformity

The contributions to this volume indicate that major shifts are taking place in the governance of standards in agro-food products. Up to the 1990s, standards were generally controlled by producers and/or grassroots organizations (organics, fair trade) or by large food retailers (food safety). The 1990s saw the emergence of business association standards (such as EurepGAP, BRC) and of multi-stakeholder initiatives engaging large NGOs and agro-food and forestry manufacturers, especially in environmental and social labelling initiatives (such as FSC, MSC, UTZ CERTIFIED and Rainforest Alliance). While the emergence of business association standards has often led to a decrease in the number of similar audits that agro-food businesses in Africa have to go through (instead of multiple audits by different retailers, one business association audit may suffice), the multiplication of multi-stakeholder initiatives has not led to the same outcome, mostly because of the investment that different initiatives have put into having consumers recognize their own label. Also, while multi-stakeholder initiatives should be expected to be more inclusive of a variety of interests, including those of Southern actors, the reality is for Southern stakeholders (especially those of small scale) to be forgotten in the initial and key phases of development (for example, MSC) or to be included within relations of power that are vastly to their disadvantage, with the result that their 'participation' does not have any meaningful influence. The recent emergence of Southern standards initiatives (of both business association and multi-stakeholder kinds) might also be expected to address some of these shortcomings, but this has not been necessarily so. The development of local conformity assessment institutions has also taken place much more slowly than expected and with mixed results.

In Chapter 3, Akyoo and Lazaro argue that one would expect the use of local conformity assessment institutions to be beneficial to African producers because of expected lower costs and better opportunity for dialogue for local exporters. However, this is in practice difficult to achieve. In relation to organic spices, certification in Tanzania is carried out exclusively by one foreign company, although the local certification agency (TANCERT) is now carrying out most activities (especially inspection-related, but not certification) on the foreign company's behalf. TANCERT is in fact a contractor of the foreign company, rather than being an internationally accredited certifier that could compete with foreign certifiers. This puts limits on the extent to which the costs of conformity can be reduced. Akyoo and Lazaro also suggest that the development of local and regional standards, held to be a springboard for matching international standards in some policy circles, actually does not fulfil such a function, at least in Tanzania. Many of the standards developed for spices since the 1970s have not been applied in practice, and movement towards matching organic and related food safety standards started only in relation to the required conformity to standards in importing countries. Finally, Chapter 3 goes into painstaking detail to list equipment and procedures that are needed for conformity assessment to EU food safety standards for spices, and their cost. One of the main findings is that only where there is a critical volume of product and/or number of exporters and collaboration between industry and government can such costs be sustained. Although Tanzania would have enough volume of cloves to spur such investment, the destination of such exports is towards Asian markets that have low standard requirements. As a consequence, there has been no dedicated investment in laboratory testing equipment for spices. While current government testing facilities, despite their limitations, could serve a variety of agro-food exports in Tanzania, they seem to place priority on testing imported goods and locally processed products.

In Chapter 7, Riisgaard provides interesting insights on whether standards initiatives that are 'local' provide better opportunities for agro-food industries in Africa and whether they differ substantially from Northern standards initiatives in terms of local participation, fit with local production conditions and overall governance. Riisgaard looks at local standards initiatives in the horticultural sector in Kenya, with specific focus on cut flowers. In Kenya, four such initiatives are present: two business association standards, a public standard and a multi-stakeholder initiative. It should be noted that such initiatives, rather than being developed from the ground from scratch, represent efforts to 'localize' the content of already existing standards that have been developed in Europe already. Riisgaard finds that there is no automatic link between 'localizing' private social standards and furthering the interests of intended beneficiaries, and that such initiatives do not necessarily represent a 'Southern' as opposed to a 'Northern' agenda. The Kenya Flower Council (KFC) standard, a business association initiative, arose as a reaction to negative media attention on worker conditions in flower farms in the country. It is based on UK retailer standards and sought and obtained equivalence status with EurepGAP, a Northern standard. Along with EurepGAP (now GlobalGAP), it is a standard focused on documentation and traceability, while on social issues it is based on outcome, not process standards. Riisgaard argues convincingly that KFC, far from being an empowerment tool, is an effort at self-regulation by producers and, thus, plays into a more general move towards more indirect forms of governance of global value chains (see Gibbon and Ponte, 2005). Civil society was neither involved in the standard setting process, nor is it involved in its monitoring. Furthermore, Chapter 9 highlights how 'local participation' and decentralization are not a panacea for better fishery management especially when adequate resources lack for its implementation.

As mentioned above, multi-stakeholder standard initiatives are on the rise. While this could be a positive trend from the point of view of African participation, such initiatives can also be used to accommodate threats, water down standards and deflect attention from the day-by-day practices of retailers and importers that may be at the source of environmental or social problems to begin with. Multi-stakeholder initiatives can also be set up without adequate Southern participation (see the case of MSC in Chapter 9). From this perspective, Southern multi-stakeholder initiatives should be able to reflect genuine local preoccupations and problems. The case study of the Kenyan Horticultural Ethical Business Initiative (HEBI), analysed in Chapter 7, suggests that this can indeed be the case. HEBI includes both elements of participation in the audit process by all key stakeholders (including labour organizations) and covers provisions on process rights. But, because of the conflicting interests of its stakeholders, it has been seldom applied and even donor funding has been reduced. Overall, Riisgaard argues that local standard initiatives have so far been unable to alter the governance agenda of Northern retailers either because they never challenged it, or because – when they did – industry players abandoned them.

Standards governance does not only relate to how a standard itself is written, by whom and how it is managed. It is also important to understand what institutional features arise to facilitate compliance in Africa. In Chapter 4, Gibbon et al. examine the dominant institutional form (a new generation of contract farming schemes) that allows African smallholder producers to conform to organic standards and what features in such schemes generate the most important benefits for participants. It shows that a distinct generation of contract farming has emerged in the past decade, dedicated to the production of traditional export crops to be certified against international 'sustainability' standards. These schemes help processors or exporters to secure required crop volumes and qualities while moving some production risks to the farmer. Contrary to earlier forms of contract farming, there is now much less emphasis on input provision and production oversight and more on quality control at the point of purchase. For farmers, these new schemes provide secure access to markets and (sometimes) a reduction in price risk. Where internal control systems are used, large economies of scale in farmer certification can be obtained, thus reducing the unit cost of certification. While in most cases farmers do not pay for certification (the processor or exporter does), such savings make these schemes more viable and farmers are more likely to obtain a higher price, *ceteris paribus*. The importance of contract farming schemes for exporting fresh vegetables that are certified against GlobalGAP standards is also highlighted in Chapter 6, but here supervision and provision of inputs and technical advice is much more important than in the organic case studies covered in Chapter 4.

Another aspect of standards governance examined in this book is the increasing difficulty in separating its private and public components. In Chapter 9, Ponte et al. suggest that we may be observing a movement from rule-and-punish systems (typical of public regulation) towards market-and-punish systems (which are hybrids) rather than towards purely private self-governance in the realm of standards. In the specific hybrid form examined in Chapter 9, a regulation that includes a public standard on minimum fish size is now being monitored by a private entity. However, in case of non-compliance, the application of the sanction is delegated to the public regulatory body. In short, we have a situation where the *content* of the standard was set by the public authority, the control of *conformity* with the standard is delegated to the private sector, while *sanctioning* reverts back to the public sector.

At the same time, Bolwig and Gibbon suggest in Chapter 2 that we may be observing a further new trend in standard governance – one for standards to be developed and operated by private consultancies – both for-profit and not-for profit.

Another issue arising in the book relates to whether standards are complied with 'to the letter' or not. This is important because often the 'Africa is screwed up by standards' argument is based on two assumptions: (1) that requirements always entail that small-scale operators change their production systems; and (2) that even where requirements of this kind are expicit, they are enforced. This is far from the case. On the first point, conformity with organic standards in Africa, given the low-input nature of much of its agriculture, requires fewer changes (and entails lower conversion costs) than elsewhere. Yet, Gibbon et al. in Chapter 4 and Mbiha and Ashimogo in Chapter 5 suggest that, in absence of meaningful public support in Africa, organic certification is unlikely to occur without donor support – often involving the setting up of internal control systems, training of company staff and officers, setting up of demonstration plots and quality management systems, farmer training that is an integral part of the contract farming package and time-bound support for certification costs.

On the second point, and despite occasional bouts of zealousness (as when the EU banned imports of fish from East Africa in the late 1990s), various chapters suggest that a lot of flexibility on content, procedures and controls is actually exercised, to the point that one could construct some of the newer standards as being more a pedagogical tool for producers and processors (or a marketing tool) than as requiring compliance *per se*. In Chapter 9, Ponte et al. provide some insight on the gaps between what is required on paper by standards and what is actually put into operation in practice. But instead of arguing that this is a problem, they recognize that certain elements of flexibility are indeed necessary. The same is found in Chapter 6, where Lazaro et al. suggest that prescriptions related to conformity to sustainability standards are interpreted and applied in practice with a large degree of flexibility. They also show that some of the more exacting demands actually apply to larger-scale farms, not to smallholders. At the same time, in Chapter 7 Riisgaard finds that compliance monitoring in social standards is inadequate as it is often carried out by companies themselves and/or by the social auditing industry. Riisgaard argues that auditors tend to use management information, while not engaging with workers and their organizations. Easier to measure issues are also focused upon, while others like discrimination are neglected. Social participatory auditing techniques are emerging to expose some of the hidden issues, but they are more costly and challenging to apply. Overall, these findings suggest that all is not lost for smallholders and workers in the new world of standards.

Standards, value chain restructuring and welfare outcomes

The dynamics of value chain restructuring, the welfare outcomes of conformity and non-conformity with standards and related inclusion and exclusion patterns are among the most debated aspects in the literature on Africa (see Gibbon and Lazaro, Chapter 1). The picture emerging in this volume is one of a shortening of standards-heavy value chains, and of their fraying into different strands. Chapters 6, 7 and 9 suggest the emergence of segregated strands of value chains on the basis of the establishment of standards for various sustainability and ethical initiatives, not as the result of buyers being interested in products with specific proprietary specifications. But rather than leading to value chain structures that challenge the predominance of 'buyer power', such restructuring seems to have mostly led to a shortening of value chains with the elimination of some intermediaries. In some cases, as for organics and GlobalGAP-certified vegetables, the emergence of standards has led to the revival of new forms of contract farming. But one of the other features of standards-led value chain restructuring that is often reported in the literature, the 'thinning' in the number of players at key nodes of these chains, does not seem to have occurred in the cases analysed in this book. While standards have led to larger and more resourceful processors and exporters gaining ground over smaller, and more local, players in some industries, a general shakeout of African smallholders does not seem to have taken place. As a result, a relatively positive picture also arises in terms of welfare outcomes of conformity to standards.

Several issues were raised by Bolwig and Gibbon in Chapter 2 on the potential impacts of product carbon footprinting schemes on African producers and exporters. They suggest that African stakeholders should keep their eyes open because PCF standards and schemes may involve discriminatory practices that affect competitiveness and trade, for example when too much emphasis is placed on transport rather than on the whole life-cycle of a product. Placing emphasis on transport would affect distant African producers disproportionately, especially as other production functions may have a lower carbon footprint in Africa than equivalent processes in locations closer to the Northern consumer. Furthermore, excluding emissions from the manufacture of capital goods in PCF assessments creates a bias against labour-intensive production, which is typical in Africa. Yet, Bolwig and Gibbon argue that these fears so far seem to be unfounded, as most schemes they examined go well beyond transport emissions and have no strong bias against imported products. Finally, they highlight that adopting the most advanced models of estimation may have negative consequences for African operators because of the lack of appropriate life-cycle assessment databases and/or the inappropriateness of some indicators for the conditions of production or processing on the continent.

In Chapter 4, Gibbon et al. use econometric methods to assess the economic benefits of conformity with organic certification in six schemes in Tanzania and Uganda. They find that members of organic contract farming schemes obtain substantially higher net revenues from certified crops in comparison to control groups (46–75 per cent higher depending on the scheme), even after controlling the benefits from certification for other factors, such as initial differences in factor endowments. Such benefits arise on the basis of different combinations of higher yields and the availability of predictable price premiums. At the same time, they find only a modest and inconsistent relation between the adoption of organic farming practices and net revenue. Smallholder farmers obtain and maintain certification mostly through one or another form of contract farming schemes, often supported by donor funding. Benefits for farmers are higher where contracting companies have substantial resources available, and where local competition from other buyers is present. In Chapter 5, Mbiha and Ashimogo highlight how one particular donor programme was the key in explaining the rapid growth of certified organic schemes in Tanzania, compensating for the timid and belated support offered by the Tanzanian government for organic agriculture.

In Chapter 6, Lazaro et al. portray a mixed picture in relation to welfare benefits and the dynamics of exclusion and inclusion in sustainability standards initiatives. In, general, standard compliance enhanced the possibility for producers to undertake direct exports and increased their security of contracts and margins. In relation to UTZ CERTIFIED coffee, they show that only large-scale farms obtained certification. The large farms that did comply enjoyed substantial benefits, including a premium, despite having to face higher costs. The price premium, however, was attributable to the special channel designed for direct exports of 'specialty coffee' in Tanzania than certification *per se*. In relation to GlobalGAP vegetables, substantial net benefits were also observed for certified farmers (of both small and large scale) in comparison to non-certified farmers: they obtained higher prices, achieved higher yields and enjoyed higher revenue (10–24 per cent higher on average depending on the product) in addition to having upgraded their knowledge and skills. Again, these net benefits partly accrued because the cost of development of smallholder quality management systems was financed largely by donors.

A much less rosy picture emerged in relation to social standards in cut flowers, where private standards have serious limitations in facilitating the delivery of intended benefits to workers (especially in absence of process rights and with the current focus on outcome standards). When benefits are achieved, it is typically only a sub-set of workers that enjoys them – those permanently employed, who tend to be males. At the same time, at least in Tanzania, compliance with social standards provided new opportunities for unions to enter (and better understand) the sector, resulting in collective bargaining agreements in two of the largest farms, in higher average wages for employees in certified farms and in unions being able to exert a watchdog function in non-certified farms.

In Chapter 8, Kadigi et al. provide the clearest indication (along with Chapter 4) that compliance with standards can have substantial and positive welfare outcomes for African participants, even small-scale ones. Kadigi et al. compare the assets and net incomes of those serving the fish export market to those serving regional and local markets (the available alternative if fish does not match export standards). They find significant benefits accruing to actors involved in the export value chain. Kadigi et al. argue that emerging food safety standards can be a catalyst for upgrading and contribute to the creation of competitive advantages – leading to increased exports and improved livelihoods, especially when the inclusion of small-scale producers is preserved (on Lake Victoria, large-scale fishing operations are not allowed).

In Chapter 9, Ponte et al. suggest that fishery ecolabels pose serious issues of exclusion for smaller producers and/or producers in the South. They also suggest that rather than focusing on achieving the environmental benefits they were set up for, much attention in these initiatives is placed on matching system functionality and on fulfilling commercial imperatives. At the same time, the outcome of ecolabelling (certification) is perhaps less important than the changes in management processes it can generate.

In Chapter 10, Broberg chronicles the evolution of the EU food safety regime and warns that EU requirements have been established in a European context. This means that limit values are normally set according to what can be required from a European food business operating in a European climate. Certification requirements are based on the premise that businesses have easy access to accredited laboratories, and the level of administrative competence of food businesses as well as of public authorities is assumed to be fairly sophisticated. Broberg provides details of what aspects in the EU food safety regime can create specific problems of compliance for developing country operators and, thus, create exclusionary barriers: (1) the setting of limit values that should not be exceeded (for additives and naturally occurring toxins) is done in relation to climatic conditions that apply to the EU rather than the tropics; they may also be set at far too low levels; (2) process requirements lay down specific procedures to be followed (such as the establishment of HACCP and traceability systems) that may be particularly cumbersome in developing countries; and (3) problems may also arise in relation to authorization requirements for products (novel food regulation is held to be particularly problematic for developing countries here), to producer and control requirements and to controls in third countries.

Broberg argues that such barriers can be overcome in principle in three main ways: via legal procedures if the measure does not take into account of developing countries, the proportionality principle or the duty to comply with international law; by lowering such barriers via preferential treatment of developing countries; and via the provision of technical assistance to help developing countries comply with standards. Of these, only the third option seems to have been used by EU members with any significant frequency and impact.

Final remarks

Some of the literature on agro-food standards portrays Africa as in the process of being crunched by the demands of new standards on agro-food products. Such argument runs as follows. International trade liberalization is dismantling some of the 'classical' barriers to trade such as tariffs and quantitative restrictions (much less so subsidies to producers in the North). At the same time, standards on imports into rich countries are replacing these barriers in ever more subtle ways. Higher costs of running export-oriented agro-food production and processing in Africa and problems in accessing Northern markets arise from: standards that are more demanding and which demand conformity on an increasing number of variables; ever more sophisticated management and traceability systems to be set up in Africa; a Northern-led agenda that is catering to rich consumers and NGO-driven concerns rather than to African beneficiaries; a multiplication of different initiatives that cover more or less the same ground and that lead to unnecessary duplication; lack of international accreditation for local certification and inspection agencies; and lack of more substantial donor support. Complying with standards has also led to a shake out of smallholder producers to the benefit of commercial farms.

There is certainly more than a grain of truth in each of these statements, but the picture emerging from this book is a far more nuanced one. Standards are indeed becoming more numerous and demanding, but their application on the ground is far more pragmatic and 'flexible' than we assume, leaving both room for manoeuvre for local actors and (unfortunately) leading to less than convincing impacts on social and environmental outcomes. System, quality and traceability management demands are indeed taxing and expensive for Africa-based businesses, but often they eventually lead to cost reductions, less wastage and indeed better management. A Northern agenda and less-than-transparent and participatory governance systems do indeed characterize many standards initiatives (both public and private), but Southern-led ones tend to copy-cat Northern ones and are not necessarily a great improvement in terms of catering to the key stakeholders. A multiplication of initiatives is creating confusion and duplication, but at the same time some efforts are taking place on mutual recognition for a base set of standards (this is taking place especially in relation to food safety and good agricultural practices) and a natural selection process is also taking place over time – where less than successful initiatives die out. Lack of accreditation for local inspection and certification agencies is indeed a problem, but the auditing and certification market works like any other – some 'brands' are well esteemed and recognized and others are not. Donor involvement could be expanded, but only when the private sector and business associations have been closely involved does it lead to positive outcomes. Smallholders are indeed being excluded from some industries because of difficulties related to compliance with standards, but in others they have been kept in via contract farming schemes, special provisions for group certification, donor support and national policy.

References

Abila, R. (2000) 'The development of the Lake Victoria fishery. A boon or bane for food security?', *IUCN Report* No. 8. Nairobi: IUCN East Africa.

Abila, R. (2005) 'impacts of international fish trade: A case study of Lake Victoria fisheries', in J. Kurien (ed.) *Responsible fish trade and food security, Fisheries Technical Paper* No. 456, Rome: Food and Agriculture Organization of the United Nations, NORAD/FAO.

ADEME (l'Agence de l'Environnement et de la Maîtrise de l'Energie) (2007) *Bilan Carbone Entreprises et Collectivités. Guide Méthodologique, Version 5.0, Objectifs et Principes de Comptabilisation.*

AEA (2005) 'The validity of food miles as an indicator of sustainable development', Report for the Department for Environment, Food and Rural Affairs, United Kingdom.

Agnew, D., Grieve, C., Orr, P., Parkes, G. and Barker, N. (2006) 'Environmental benefits resulting from certification against MSC's Principles and Criteria for Sustainable Fishing', Marine Resources Assessment Group and MSC. Available at http://www.msc.org/html/content_1266.htm

Agro Eco, B. V. and Grolink (2008) *Organic Exports – A Way to a Better Life?* (EPOPA and Sida) http://www.grolink.se/epopa/Publications/epopa-experience.htm, date accessed 10 May 2009.

Akyoo, A. M. and Lazaro, E. (2007) 'The spice industry in tanzania: General profile, supply chain structure, and safety standards compliance issues', *DIIS Working Paper No.* 2007:8. Copenhagen: Danish Institute for International Studies.

Alavi, A., Gibbon, P. and Mortensen, N. J. (2007) 'EU-ACP Economic Partnership Agreements. Part II – A review of the literatures on the economic, legal and other substantive dimensions of the proposed agreements'. Institute of Food and Resource Economics (Copenhagen University) and Danish Institute for International Studies, November 2007, for the Royal Danish Ministry of Foreign Affairs.

Allison, E. H. (2001) 'Big laws, small catches: Global ocean governance and the fisheries crisis', *Journal of International Development*, 13, 933–50.

Allison, E. H. (2003) 'Linking national fisheries policies to livelihoods on the shores of Lake Kyoga, Uganda', *LADDER Working Paper No. 9*, Norwich: Overseas Development Group, University of East Anglia.

Aloui, O. and Kenny, L. (2004) 'The cost of compliance with SPS standards for Moroccan exports: A case study', *ARD Paper*, Washington: World Bank.

Anderson, J. L. (2003) *The International Seafood Trade*. Cambridge: Woodhead.

Angervall, T., Florén, B. and Ziegler, F. (2006) *Vilken Bukett Broccoli Väljer Du?* Gothenberg: Swedish Institute for Food and Biotechnology.

Antle, J. (1999) 'Benefits and costs of food safety regulations', *Food Policy*, 24(6), 603–23.

Aragrande, M., Segre, A., Gentile, E., Malorgio, G., Giraud Heraud, E., Robles, R., Halicka, E., Loi, A. and Bruni, M. (2005) 'Food supply chain dynamics and quality certification', Brussels: EU/DG Joint Research Centre.

Asfaw, S., Mithöfer, D. and Waibel, H. (2008) 'Food safety standards: A catalyst for the winners – a barrier for the losers? The case of GlobalGAP horticultural exports from Kenya' in de Battisti et al., (eds), 2008, 70–73.

Athukorala, P.-C. and Jayasuriya, S. (2004) Food safety issues, trade and WTO rules: A developing country perspective, in D. Greenaway (ed.) *The World Economy: Global Trade Policy 2003.* Oxford: Blackwell, pp. 141–161.

Auret, D. and Barrientos, S. (2004) 'Participatory social auditing: A practical guide to developing a gender-sensitive approach', Brighton: Institute of Development Studies, University of Sussex.

Bacon, C. (2005) 'Confronting the coffee crisis: Can Fairtrade, organic, and specialty coffees reduce small-scale farmer vulnerability in Northern Nicaragua?', *World Development*, 33(3), 497–511.

Balirwa, J.S., Chapman, C.A., Chapman, L.J., Cowx, I.G., Geheb, K., Kaufman, L., Lowe-Mcconnell, R.H., Seehausen, O., Wanink, J.H., Welcomme, R.L. and Witte, F. (2003) 'Biodiversity and fishery sustainability in the Lake Victoria basin: An unexpected marriage?', *BioScience* 53(8), 703–15.

Bank of Tanzania (BOT) *Economic and Financial Report* (various years), Dar-es-Salaam.

Barrientos, S. (2003) 'Corporate social responsibility, employment and global sourcing by multinational enterprises', Geneva: ILO, Multinational Enterprises and Employment Division.

Barrientos, S., Dolan, C. and Tallontire, A. (2003) 'A gendered value chain approach to codes of conduct in African horticulture', *World Development* 31: 1511–26.

Barrientos, S. (2006) 'Global production systems and decent work (draft)', paper presented at workshop on Globalization, Copenhagen Business School, May 2006.

Barrientos, S. and Smith, S. (2007) 'Do workers benefit from ethical trade? Assessing codes of labour practice in global production systems', *Third World Quarterly* 28, 713–29.

de Battisti, A., MacGregor, J. and Graffham, A. (eds) (2008) *Standard Bearers. Horticultural Exports and Private Standards in Africa*, London: International Institute for Environment and Development.

Baumann, P. (2000) 'Equity and efficiency in contract farming schemes: The experience of tree crops', *ODI Working Paper 139*, London: Overseas Development Institute.

Beadle, L.C. (1962) 'The evolution of species in the lakes of East Africa', *Uganda Journal*, 26, 44–54.

Benfica, R., Tschirley, D. and Boughton, D. (2006) 'Interlinked transactions in cash cropping economies: The determinants of farmer participation and performance in the Zambesi River Valley, Mozambique', paper presented to the International Association of Agricultural Economics, Gold Coast (Australia), August.

Berry, T., Crosslet, D. and Jewell, J. (2008) 'Check-out carbon. The role of carbon labelling in delivering a low-carbon shopping basket'. London: Forum for the Future and Lloyd's Register.

Bernauer, T. and Caduff, L. (2006) 'Food safety and the structure of the European food industry', in C. Ansell and D. Vogel (eds) *What's the Beef? The Contested Governance of European Food Safety.* Cambridge, MA: MIT Press.

Bernstein, S. and Cashore, B. (2007) 'Can non-state global governance be legitimate? A theoretical framework', paper presented at the annual meeting of the International Studies Association, Chicago, February.

Binswanger, H. and Rosenzweig, M. (1986) 'Behavioural and material determinants of production relations in agriculture', *Journal of Development Studies*, 22(3), 503–39.

Bingen, J. and Siyengo, A. (2002) 'Standards and corporate reconstruction in the Michigan dry bean industry', *Agriculture and Human Values* 19, 311–23.

Blowfield, M. and Frynas, J. (2005) 'Setting new agendas: Critical perspectives on Corporate Social Responsibility in the developing world', *International Affairs* 81, 499–513.

Blowfield, M. and Dolan, C.S. (2008) 'Stewards of virtue? The ethical dilemma of CSR in African agriculture', *Development and Change*, 39: 1–23.

Blundell, R. and Costa Dias, M. (2000) 'Evaluation methods for non-experimental data', *Fiscal Studies*, 21(4), 427–68.

Blundell, R. and Costa Dias, M. (2002) 'Alternative approaches to evaluation in empirical microeconomics', *Portuguese Economic Journal*, 1, 91–115.

Bokea, C. and Ikiara, M. (2000) 'Fishery commercialization and the local economy: The case of Lake Victoria (Kenya)', *IUCN Report* No. 7. Nairobi: IUCN.

Bolwig, S. (2008) 'The food miles debate and developing country exports', paper presented at the World Export Development Forum, International Trade Centre, UNCTAD and WTO, Montreux October.

Bolwig, S. and Gibbon, P. (2009a) 'Overview of product carbon footprinting schemes and standards,' Report for the OECD Trade and Agriculture Directorate.

Bolwig, S. and Gibbon, P. (2009b) 'Biofuel sustainability standards and public policy: A case study of Swedish ethanol imports from Brazil', Report for the OECD Trade and Agriculture Directorate.

Bonanno, A. and Constance D. (1996) *Caught in the Net: The Global Tuna Industry, Environmentalism, and the State*. Lawrence: University Press of Kansas.

Braunschweig, A. (n.d.) 'The relation between LCA and GHG accounting', Zurich: EZ Management Consulting AG.

Brenton, P., Edwards-Jones, G. and Jensen, M.F. (2008) 'Carbon labelling and low income country exports: A look at the issues', Washington: World Bank.

Bridges Weekly Trade News Digest (2008) 'SPS Committee considers establishing working group on private sector standards', *Bridges Weekly Trade News Digest*, 12(24) July.

Broberg, M. (2000) 'The court of first instance's judgment in Gencor v Commission', *International and Comparative Law Quarterly* 49, 172–82.

Broberg, M. (2008) *Transforming the European Community's Regulation Of Food Safety*. Stockholm: SIEPS.

Brunsson, N. (2000) 'Organizations, markets, and standardization', in N. Brunsson, B. Jacobsson et al. (eds), 2000, 21–39.

Brunsson, N., Jacobsson, B. et al. (2000) *A world of standards*. Oxford, Oxford University Press.

Bray, D., Sanchez, J. and Murphy, E. (2002) 'Social dimensions of organic coffee production in Mexico: Lessons for eco-labeling initiatives', *Society and Natural Resources*, 15, 429–46.

BSI (British Standards Institute) (2009) www.bsigroup.com (home page).

BSI (British Standards Institute) (2008) 'PAS 2050:2008 – Specification for the assessment of the life cycle greenhouse gas emissions of goods and services'. London: British Standards Institute.

Buch-Hansen, M. and Kieler, J. (1983) 'The development of capitalism and the transformation of the peasantry in Kenya', *Rural Africana*, Winter/Spring, 13–40.

Busch, L. (2000) 'The moral economy of grades and standards', *Journal of Rural Studies*, 16, 273–83.

Buzby, J. (ed.) (2003) 'International trade and food safety: Economic theory and case studies', *Agricultural Economic Report 828*, November. Washington: US Department of Agriculture.

Büsser, S., Steiner, R. and Jungbluth, N. (2008) 'LCA of packed food products – The function of flexible packaging', Report for Flexible Packaging Europe. Uster: ESU-services Ltd.
Callon, M., Méadel, C., Rabeharisoa, V. (2002) 'The economy of qualities', *Economy and Society*, 31, 194–217.
CarbonCounted (2009) 'CarbonCounted™ Standard 1.2', www.carboncounted.com (home page), date accessed 20 April 2009.
Carbon Fund (2009) www.carbonfund.org (home page), accessed 23 June 2009.
Carbon Label Company (2009) www.carbon-label.com (home page), accessed 23 June 2009.
Carbon Trust (2006) 'The carbon emissions generated in all that we consume'. London: The Carbon Trust.
Carbon Trust (2008) 'Code of Good Practice for product greenhouse gas emissions and reduction claims: Guidance to support the robust communication of Product Carbon Footprints.' www.carbontrust.co.uk (home page), accessed 19 April 2009.
CarboNZero (2009) www.carbonzero.co.nz (home page), accessed 30 June 2009.
CBI (2007) 'EU market survey: Cut flowers and foliage'. Rotterdam.
CenSA (Centre for Sustainability Accounting) (2009) www.censa.org.uk/bl3.html, date accessed 23 June 2009.
CEPA (California Environmental Protection Agency) (2009) 'Proposed regulation to implement the Low Carbon Fuel Standard. Staff report: Initial statement of reasons', 5 March 2009.
Cerrex Ltd (UK) (2003) 'Study of the consequences of the application of sanitary and phytosanitary (SPS) measures on ACP countries', commissioned by CTA, http://agritrade.cta.int/en/content/view/full/1792
Chambers, R. and Conway, R. (1992), 'Sustainable rural livelihoods: Practical concepts for the 21st Century', *IDS Discussion Paper* NO. 296, Brighton: Institute for Development Studies, University of Sussex.
Climatop (2009) www.climatop.ch (home page), accessed 23 June 2009.
Coca-Cola Great Britain (2009) www.cokecorporateresponsibility.co.uk, accessed 23 June 2009.
Coe, N., Dicken, P., and Hess M. (2008) 'Global production networks: Realizing the potential', *Journal of Economic Geography*, 8, 271–95.
Collinson, C. (2001) 'The business cost of ethical supply chain management: Kenya flower industry case study', Greenwich: Natural Resources Institute.
COLEACP-PIP (2005) 'Diagnostic impact study of the new European regulation 882/2004 "Official feed & food controls" and recommendations', Phase one/Final report.
Cooper, J. and Graffham, A. (2008) 'GlobalGAP Version 3: Threat or opportunity for small-scale African growers?' in de Battisti et al. (eds), 2008, 23–25.
Coulter, J., Goodland, A., Tallontire, A. and Stringfellow, R. (1999) 'Marrying farmer cooperation and contract farming for agricultural service provision in liberalizing economies in Sub-Saharan Africa', *Natural Resources Perspectives*, 48, London: Overseas Development Institute.
Damiani, O. (2002) 'Organic agriculture in Costa Rica: The case of cocoa and banana production in Talamanca', Rome: Office of Evaluation and Studies, IFAD.
Danielou, M. and Ravry, C. (2005) 'The rise of Ghana's pineapple industry', Africa Region Working Paper Series No. 93, Washington: World Bank.

Daviron, B. (2002) 'Small farm production and the standardization of tropical products', *Journal of Agrarian Change*, 2(2), 162–84.

Daviron, B. and Ponte, S. (2005) *The Coffee Paradox*, London: Zed Books.

Deere, C. (1999) 'Eco-labelling and sustainable fisheries'. Washington, DC and Rome: IUCN – The World Conservation Union and the Food and Agriculture Organization of the United Nations (FAO).

Deninger, K. and Squire, L. (1998) 'New ways of looking at old issues: Inequality and growth', *Journal of Development Economics*, 57, 259–87.

Desta, M.G. (2008) 'EU sanitary standards and Sub-Saharan African agricultural exports: A case study of the livestock sector in East Africa', *The Law and Development Review*, 1(1), 96–122.

Dicken, P. (2007) *Global Shift: Mapping the Changing Contours of the World Economy*. New York: Guilford Press.

Dmitri, C. and Greene, C. (2006) 'Recent growth patterns in US organic food markets', in A. Wellson, (ed.), *Organic Agriculture in the US*, 129–90. Hauppage, NY: Nova.

Dolan, C. and Humphrey, J. (2000) 'Governance and trade in fresh vegetables: The impact of UK supermarkets on the African horticultural industry', *Journal of Development Studies*, 32(2), 144–77.

Dolan, C. and Opondo, M. (2005) 'Seeking common ground: Multi-stakeholder processes in Kenya's cut clower industry', *The Journal of Corporate Citizenship*, 87–99.

Eaton, C. and Shepherd, A. (2001) *Contract Farming – Partnerships for Growth*, Rome: FAO.

East African Community (2007), *East African Organic Products Standard (EAOPS) and East African Organic Mark (EAOM)*, Arusha: East African Community.

EC (European Commission) Food and Veterinary Office (1998) 'Final report on a mission to Uganda from 16 November 1998 to 20 November 1998. Fishery products', XXIV/1524/98, Brussels: European Commission.

EC (European Commission) Food and Veterinary Office (1999a) 'Final report of a mission carried out in Uganda from 19 August 1999 to 20 August 1999 for the purpose of assessing controls on pesticide residues in fish coming from Lake Victoria', DG SANCO/1128/1999, Brussels: European Commission.

EC (European Commission) Food and Veterinary Office (1999b) 'Final report of a mission carried out in Tanzania from 22 August to the 25 August for the objective of assessing the controls on pesticide residues in fish coming from Lake Victoria', DG SANCO/1129/1999, Brussels: European Commission.

EC (European Commission) Food and Veterinary Office (2000a) 'Report of a mission carried out in Uganda from 2 to 6 October 2000 assessing the conditions of production of fishery products and the verification of the measures on pesticides in fish', DG(SANCO)/1277/2000, Brussels: European Commission.

EC (European Commission) Food and Veterinary Office (2000b) 'Final report of a mission carried out in Tanzania from 9 October to 13 October 2000 in order to assess the measures taken regarding the pesticide contamination in Lake Victoria and to assess the conditions of production of fishery products', DG(SANCO)/1276/2000, Brussels: European Commission.

EC (European Commission) (2001), 'Draft Commission Regulation amending regulation (EC) No. 194/97 of 31 January 1997 setting maximum levels for certain contaminants in foodstuffs', Annex B. SANCO/3347/99-rev.4. Brussels: European Commission, 2–4.

EC (European Commission) (2003) 'Commission decision of 5 June 2003 authorizing the placing on the market of "noni juice" (juice of the fruit of Morinda citrifolia L.) as a novel food ingredient under Regulation 258/97'. [2003] OJ L144/12.

EC (European Commission) (2005) 'Commission decision 2005/402 of 23 May 2005 on emergency measures regarding chilli, chilli products, curcuma and palm oil', [2005] OJ L135/34.
EC (European Commission) Food and Veterinary Office (2006a) 'Final report of a mission carried out in Kenya from 21 to 31 March 2006 in order to assess the public health controls and the conditions of production of fishery products', DG(SANCO)/8163/2006, Brussels: European Commission.
EC (European Commission) Food and Veterinary Office (2006b) 'Final report of a mission carried out in Uganda from 31 July to 8 August 2006 in order to assess the public health controls and the conditions of production of fishery products', DG(SANCO)/8240/2006, Brussels: European Commission.
EC (European Commission) Food and Veterinary Office (2006c) 'Final report of a mission carried out in Tanzania from 25 September to 6 October 2006 in order to assess the public health controls and the conditions of production of fishery products'. DG(SANCO)/8241/2006, Brussels: European Commission.
EC (European Commission) (2006d) 'Guidance document – key questions related to import requirements and the new rules on food hygiene and official food controls', Brussels.
EC (European Commission) (2007) 'COM(2007)872 proposal for a regulation of the European Parliament and of the Council on novel foods and amending Regulation (EC) No XXX/XXXX (common procedure)', COM(2007) 872 final.
EC (European Commission) (2009a) 'Directive of the European Parliament and of the Council on the Promotion of the Use of Energy from Renewable Sources, Amending and Subsequently Repealing Directives 2001/77/EC and 2003/30/EC', PE-CONS 3736/08. 2008/0016 (COD), Brussels: European Commission.
EC (European Commission) (2009b) 'Commission working document, third progress report on the strategy for simplifying the regulatory environment', COM(2009) 17 final.
EC (European Commission) (2009c) 'Draft Commission regulation of 13 March 2009 implementing Regulation (EC) No 882/2004 of the European Parliament and of the Council as regards the increased level of official controls on imports of certain feed and food of non-animal origin and amending Decision 2006/504/EC'. SANCO/2697/2009 (POOL/E5/2009/2697/2697-EN.doc).
EFSA (2007) 'Opinion of the Scientific Panel on Contaminants in the food chain on a request from the Commission related to the potential increase of consumer health risk by a possible increase of the existing maximum levels for aflatoxins in almonds, hazelnuts and pistachios and derived products', Question N EFSA-Q-2006-174, Adopted on 25 January 2007, *The EFSA Journal*, 446, 1–127, www.efsa.europa.eu/EFSA/efsa_locale-1178620753812_1178620761977.htm
Edwards-Jones, G., Plassmann, K., York, E.H., Hounsom, B., Jones, D.L. and Milá i Canals, L. (2008) 'Vulnerability of exporting nations to the development of a carbon label in the United Kingdom', *Environmental Science and Policy*, doi:10.1016/j.envsci.2008.10.005.
Edwards-Jones, G., Plassmann, K., Norton, A. and Attarzadeh, N. (2009) 'Carbon labelling and the market access of developing countries', PowerPoint presentation, Global Forum on Trade and Climate Change, OECD Conference Centre, Paris, 9–10 June 2009, www.oecd.org (home page), date accessed 7 July 2009.
El-Tawi, A. (2002) 'An in-depth study of the problems by the standardizers and other stakeholders from developing countries – ISO/WTO regional workshops – Part 1', Geneva: International Organization for Standardization (ISO).

Ellis, F. (1998) 'Survey article: Household strategies and rural livelihood diversification', *Journal of Development Studies*, 35(1), 1–38.

Ellis, F. (2000) Rural livelihoods and diversity in developing countries, Oxford: Oxford University Press.

Enviro-Fish Africa (2005) 'Assessing the role and impact of eco-labeling in the three BCLME Countries', Swakopmund: BCLME Activity Centre for Living Marine Resources.

Envirocare (2007) 'Tanzanians' interest in and access to organic food', paper prepared by Oyten Sogn and E. Mella, Envirocare, Dar-es-Salaam.

ETI (2005) 'Addressing labour practices on Kenyan flower farms', Report of ETI involvement 2002–2004, London: Ethical Trading Initiative.

EU Fish Processors Association (2007) 'White fish study 2007'. Brussels: AIPCE.

European Community (1994) 'Directive 94/35 of 30 June 1994 on sweeteners for use in foodstuffs', [1994] OJ L237/3.

European Community (1994) 'Directive 94/36 of 30 June 1994 on colours for use in foodstuffs', [1994] OJ L247/13.

European Community (1995) 'Directive No 95/2 of 20 February 1995 on food additives other than colours and sweetener', [1995] OJ L61/1.

European Community (1997) 'Regulation 258/97 of the European Parliament and of the Council of 27 January 1997 concerning novel foods and novel food ingredients', [1997] OJ L43/1.

European Community (2002) 'Directive 2002/46 of 10 June 2002 on the approximation of the laws of the Member States relating to food supplements', [2002] OJ L183/51.

European Community (2002) 'Regulation 178/2002 of 28 January 2002 laying down the general principles and requirements of food law, establishing the European Food Safety Authority and laying down procedures in matters of food safety', [2002] OJ L31/1.

European Community (2004a) 'Regulation 852/2004 of 29 April 2004 on the hygiene of foodstuffs', [2004] OJ L139/1.

European Community (2004b) 'Regulation 853/2004 of 29 April 2004 laying down specific hygiene rules for food of animal origin', [2004] OJ L226/22.

European Community (2004c) 'Regulation 854/2004 of 29 April 2004 laying down specific rules for the organisation of official controls on products of animal origin intended for human consumption', [2004] OJ L226/83.

European Community (2004d) 'Regulation 882/2004, of 29 April 2004 on official controls performed to ensure the verification of compliance with feed and food law, animal health and animal welfare rules', [2004] L165/1.

European Community (2005) 'Regulation 2076/2005, of 5 December 2005 laying down transitional arrangements for the implementation of Regulations 853/2004, 854/2004 and 882/2004 amending Regulations 853/2004 and 854/2004', [2005] OJ L338/83.

European Community (2006) 'Regulation 1881/2006 of 19 December 2006 setting maximum levels for certain contaminants in foodstuffs', [2006] OJ L364/5.

European Community (2008) 'Regulation (EC) No 429/2008 of 25 April 2008 on detailed rules for the implementation of Regulation (EC) No 1831/2003 of the European Parliament and of the Council as regards the preparation and the presentation of applications and the assessment and the authorisation of feed additives',[2008] OJ L33/1.

European Community Standing Committee on the Food Chain and Animal Health (2004) 'Guidance on the implementation of Articles 11, 12, 16, 17, 18, 19 and 20 of Regulation (EC) no 178/2002 on General Food Law, conclusions of the Standing Committee on the Food Chain and Animal Health'. http://ec.europa.eu/food/foodlaw/guidance/guidance_rev_7_en.pdf

Eyhorn, F. (2007) 'Organic farming for sustainable livelihoods in developing countries? The case of cotton in India', Zürich: Vdf Hochschulverlag AG.

Fletcher, A. (2007) 'Global concern over new EU novel food regs', *Nutraingredients.com, Europe*, 12 april 2007. www.nutraingredients.com/news/printNewsBis.asp?id=67019 *Flower News*, 12 (2008) (Rio Rancho, NM).

Fok, M. (2002) 'Cotton's future in Western and Central Africa: The challenge of combining technical and institutional innovations', *Oléagineux, Corps Gras, Lipides*, 9(2–3), 115–22.

Fold, N. (2002) 'Lead firms and competition in "bi-polar" commodity chains: Grinders and branders in the global cocoa-chocolate industry', *Journal of Agrarian Change*, 2(2), 228–47.

Food and Agriculture Organization of the United Nations (FAO), *Statistical Yearbook*, various years, Rome: FAO.

Food Studies Group (FSG), University of Oxford and Department of Rural Economy, Sokoine University of Agriculture, (1992) 'Agricultural Diversification and Intensification Study', Morogoro: SUA.

Frame Survey National Working Group (2006). 'Draft report on Lake Victoria Fisheries Frame Survey, 2006 – Tanzania', IFMP Coordinating Office, Mwanza.

Fransen, L. and Burgoon, B. (2008) 'A market for workers' rights: Understanding business support for international private labour regulation', paper presented to International Workshop on Globalisation, Governance and Private Standards, Catholic University of Louvain, November.

Freidberg, S. (2003) 'Cleaning up down South: Supermarkets, ethical trade and African horticulture', *Social & Cultural Geography*, 4(1) 27–43.

Fulponi, L. (2007) 'The globalization of private standards and the agro-food system', in J. Swinnen (ed.), (2007), 5–19.

Garcia Martinez, M. and Poole, N. (2009) 'Ethical consumerism: Development of a global trend and its impact on development', in A. de Battisti, J. MacGregor and A. Graffham (eds).

Geheb, K. (ed.) (2000) 'The co-management survey: PRA reports from five beaches on Lake Victoria' *LVFRP Technical Document* No. 9, Jinja: LVFRP.

Geheb, K. and Sarch, M-T. (2002) 'Introduction: Meeting the challenge', in K. Geheb and M-T. Sarch (eds.) *Africa's Inland Fisheries: The Management Challenge*. Kampala: Fountain Press.

Geheb, K., Kalloch, S. Medard, M., Nyapendi, A., Lwenya, C. and Kyangwa, M. (2008) 'Nile perch and the hungry of Lake Victoria: Gender, status and food in an East African fishery', *Food Policy*, 33: 85–98.

Gereffi, G. (1994) 'The organization of buyer-driven global commodity chains: How U.S. retailers shape overseas production networks', in G. Gereffi and M. Korzeniewicz, (ed.) *Commodity chains and global capitalism*, Westport, CT: Praeger, 93–122.

Gereffi, G., Humphrey, J., and Sturgeon, T. (2005) 'The governance of global value chains', *Review of International Political Economy*, 12, 78–104.

Gibbon, P. (1997) 'Of saviours and punks. The political economy of the Nile Perch marketing chain in Tanzania', *CDR Working Paper 97.3*, Copenhagen: Centre for Development Research.

Gibbon, P. (2001) 'Upgrading primary production: A global commodity chain approach', *World Development*, 29(2), 345–63.

Gibbon, P. (2003) 'Value chain governance, public regulation and entry barriers in the global fresh fruit and vegetable chain into the EU', *Development Policy Review*, 21(5–6), 615–26.

Gibbon, P. and Ponte, S. (2005) *Trading Down: Africa, Value Chains and the Global Economy*, Philadelphia: Temple University Press.

Gibbon, P. (2006a) 'Decoding organic standard-setting and regulation in Europe, 1991–2005', *UNIDO Economic and Strategic Research Division, Working Paper*, Vienna: UNIDO.

Gibbon, P. (2006b) 'An overview of the certified organic export sector in Uganda', *DIIS Working Paper 2006/13*, Copenhagen: Danish Institute for International Studies.

Gibbon, P. and Bolwig, S. (2007), 'The economic effect of a ban on certification of organic products imported to the UK by air', Geneva: International Trade Centre.

Gibbon, P. (2008) 'An analysis of the regulation of organic agriculture in the European Union, 1991–2007', *Journal of Agrarian Change*, 8(4), 553–82.

Gibbon, P. (2009) 'European organic standard setting organizations and climate change standards', Report to the OECD Trade and Agriculture Directorate.

Gilbert, J. and Vargas, E. A. (2005) 'Advances in sampling and analysis for aflatoxins in food and animal feed', in H. Abbas (ed.) *Aflatoxin and Food Safety*. Boca Raton: Taylor and Francis.

Giovannucci, D. and Reardon, T. (2000) 'Understanding grades and standards and how to apply them', in *The Guide to Developing Agricultural Markets and Agro-Enterprises*, Available at: <http://wbln0018.worldbank.org/essd/essd.nsf/Agroenterprise/agro_guide>.

Giovannucci, D. and Ponte, S. (2005) 'Standards as a new form of social contract', *Food Policy*, 30(3), 284–301.

Giovannucci, D. and Potts, J. (2008) 'Seeking Sustainability: COSA preliminary analysis of sustainability initiatives in the coffee sector', Winnipeg: Committee on Sustainability Assessment, IISD.

Giovannucci, D. and Purcell, T. (2008) 'Standards and agricultural trade in Asia', *ADBI Discussion Paper 107*, Tokyo: Asian Development Bank Institute, http://www.adbi.org/.

Glover, D. (1983) 'Contract farming and smallholder outgrower schemes in less developed countries', *World Development*, 12(11–12), 1143–57.

Glover, D. (1987) 'Increasing the benefits to smallholders from contract farming: Problems for farmers, organisations and policy makers', *World Development*, 15(4), 441–48.

Glover, D. and Ghee, L. (1992) *Contract Farming in Southeast Asia: Three Country Case Studies*, Kuala Lumpur: University of Malaysia Press.

Glover, D. and Klusterer, K. (1990) *Small Farmers, Big Business: Contract Farming and Rural Development*, London: Macmillan.

Goveneh, J. and Jayne, T. (2003) 'Cash-cropping and food crop production: Synergies or trade-offs', *Agricultural Economics*, 28, 39–50.

Gogoe, S. (2002) 'Costs and benefits of smallholder compliance with the EurepGAP protocol in Ghana', M.Sc dissertation, Greenwich: Natural Resources Institute.

Golub, S. and Mbaye, A. (2002) 'Obstacles and opportunities for Senegal's competitiveness. Case studies of the peanut oil, fishing and textile industries', *Africa Region Working Paper 37*, Washington, DC: World Bank.

Graffham, A. (2006) 'EU legal requirements for imports of fruits and vegetables (a suppliers guide)' Fresh Insights no. 1, DFID/IIED/NRI. www.agrifoodstandards.net/resources/global/fresh_insights_1_eu_legal_requirements_for_imports_of_fruits_and_vegetables.

Graffham, A. and Cooper, J. (2008) 'Making GlobalGAP smallholder-friendly: Can GlobalGAP be made simpler and less costly without compromising integrity?', in A. de Battisti et al. (eds), (2008), 83–87.

Graffham, A., Cooper, J., Wainwright, H., and MacGregor, J. (2008) 'An exploration of farmers' decision-making and reasons for participation and subsequent withdrawal from GlobalGAP', in A. de Battisti et al. (eds), (2008), 89–91.

Graffham, A., Karehu, E. and MacGregor, J. (2008) 'Impact of GlobalGAP on small-scale vegetable growers in Kenya', in A. de Battisti et al. (eds), (2008), 53–56.

Graffham, A. and MacGregor, J. (2008) 'Impact of GlobalGAP on small-scale vegetable growers in Zambia', in A. de Battisti et al. (eds), (2008), 57–60.

Greenhouse Gas Protocol (2009) www.ghgprotocol.org/standards/product-and-supply-chain-standard, date accessed 23 June 2009.

Gray, P. and Edens, G. (2008) 'Carbon accounting: A practical guide for lawyers', *Natural Resources and Environment*, 22(3), 41–49.

Grolink (2004) 'Organic agriculture development', Höje: Grolink.

GTZ (2008) 'Summary of the planning workshop "Eco-Labelling of Nile perch from Bukoba landing sites", Bukoba Kolping Formation Center Tanzania, 28th–29th March 2007'.

Guardian Unlimited (3.5.2005), 'Food watchdog to investigate spices', at http://society.guardian.co.uk/publichealth/story/0,11098,1475444,00.htm, accessed 14 May 2005.

Hale, A. and Opondo, M. (2005) 'Humanising the cut flower chain: Confronting the realities of flower production for workers in Kenya', *Antipode*, 37, 301–23.

Hatanaka, M., Bain, C., and Busch, L. (2006), 'Differentiated standardization, standardized differentiation: The complexity of the global agrifood system', in T. Marsden, J. Murdoch (ed.) *Between the Local and the Global: Confronting Complexity in the Contemporary Agri-Food Sector*. Oxford: Elsevier.

Herod, A. (2001) 'Labour internationalism and the contradictions of globalization', *Antipode*, 33.3: 407–426.

Hallström, K. (2000) 'Organising the process of standardisation', in N. Brunsson, B. Jacobsson, et al. (eds.), (2000), pp. 85–96.

Hawassi, F., Mdoe, N. and Turuka, F. (1997), 'Efficiency in fertilizer use among smallholder farmers in Mbinga district', in proceedings of the Agricultural Economics Society of Tanzania. Volume I. pp. 72–86.

HEBI (2005) 'Participatory Social Auditing. A guide for new auditors (2nd DRAFT)', First edition February 2005. Available at http://www.hebi.or.ke/pa-awareness.pdf, Horticultural Ethical Business Initiative.

HEBI (n.d.) 'Material for awareness creation: The need for HEBI Base Code and Participatory Social Auditing in the horticulture and floriculture industry in Kenya'. Available at http://www.hebi.or.ke/hebi-educational-materials.htm.

Heckman, J. (1979) 'Sample selection bias as a specification error', *Econometrica*, 47(1), 153–61.

Henson, S., Holt, G. and Northen, J. (1998) 'Costs and benefits of implementing HACCP in the UK dairy processing sector', paper presented at the NE-165 Conference on Economics of HACCP, June, Washington.

Henson, S.J., Loader, R.J., Swinbank, A., Bredahl, M. and Lux, N. (2000) *Impact of sanitary and phytosanitary measures on developing countries*, University of Reading, Department of Agricultural and Food Economics, Centre for Food Economics Research (CeFER), www.reading.ac.uk/nmsruntime/saveasdialog.asp?lID=17696&sID=72895.

Henson, S. and Loader, R. (2001) 'Barriers to agricultural exports from developing countries: The role of sanitary and phytosanitary requirements', *World Development*, 29(1), 85–102.

Henson, S. (2003) 'The economics of food safety in developing dountries', *ESA Working Paper No. 03–19*, Rome: FAO.

Henson, S. and Mitullah, W. (2004) 'Kenyan exports of Nile perch: Impact of food safety standards on an export-oriented supply chain', *World Bank Working Paper 3349*, Washington: World Bank.

Henson, S., Loader, R., Swinbank, A. and Bredahl, M. (2004) 'How developing countries view the impact of sanitary and phytosanitary measures on agricultural exports', in D. Merlinda and L. Winters (eds) 359–75.

Henson, S., Mitullah, W. and Opiyo, R. (2005) 'Poverty impacts of Nile Perch exports from Kenyan shores of Lake Victoria', study commissioned by the World Bank.

Henson, S. and Jaffee, S. (2006) 'Food safety standards and trade: Enhancing competitiveness and avoiding exclusion of developing countries', *The European Journal of Development Research*, 18(4), 593–621.

Henson, S. and Humphrey, J. (2008) 'Understanding the complexities of private standards in global agri-food chains', paper presented at International Workshop on Globalization, Global Governance and Private Standards, Catholic University of Louvain.

Hirst, D. (2001) 'Recent developments in EU pesticides regulations and their impact on imports of tropical fresh produce', paper presented to Tropical Agriculture Association', London 27 March 2001, www.taa.org.uk/southeast/PaperDavidHirstmay2001.htm.

Hoekman, B. and Kostecki, M. (2001) *The Political Economy of the World Trading System: WTO and Beyond*. Oxford: Oxford University Press.

Holleran, E., Bredahl, M. E. and Zaibet, L. (1999) 'Private incentives for adopting food safety and quality assurance', *Food Policy*, 24, 669–83.

Homer, S. (2008), 'The GAP is getting wider: How private standards are filling the void between dynamic public opinion and food safety legislation', in A. de Battisti et al. (eds), (2008), 14–17.

Hughes, A. (2001), 'Global commodity networks, ethical trade and governmentality: organizing business responsibility in the Kenyan cut flower industry', *Trans Inst Br. Geogr*, 26, 390–406.

Humphrey, J. (2008) 'Private standards, small farmers and donor policy: EurepGAP in Kenya', *IDS Working Paper 308*, Brighton: Institute for Development Studies, University of Sussex.

IFAD (2003) 'Agricultural marketing companies as sources of smallholder credit in Eastern and Southern Africa: Experiences, insights and potential donor role', Rome: Eastern and Southern Africa Division, FAO.

Ikezuki, T. (2009). Japan's carbon footprint system. Background document, OECD Global Forum on Trade and Climate Change, 9–10 June 2009. www.oecd.org.

Ingco, M. and Winters, L. (eds.) (2004) *Agriculture and the New Trade Agenda – Creating a global trading environment for development*. Cambridge: Cambridge University Press.

ISEAL (2006) Code of Good Practice http://www.isealalliance.org/index.cfm?fuse action=Page.ViewPage&PageID=1046, date accessed 3 June 2009.

ISO (2006) 'Environmental management – Life Cycle Assessment – Principles and framework', Geneva: International Organization for Standardisation.

ISO (2008a) 'ISO/NP 14067-1 Carbon footprint of products – Part 1: Quantification', www.iso.org (home page), date accessed 24 June 2009.

ISO (2008b) 'Responding to the global and related challenges of climate change, energy, water and nutrition', PowerPoint presentation, APEC Conference on Standards and Conformance, August 2008/SOM3/SCSC/CONF/012.

ITC (2001), 'Product profile: Spices and culinary Herbs. UNCTAD discussion document', Geneva: International Trade Centre.

Jaffee, S. (2003) 'From challenge to opportunity. The transformation of the Kenyan fresh vegetable trade in the context of emerging food safety and other standards', *Agriculture and Rural Development Working Paper 2*, Washington: World Bank.

Jaffee, S. (2004), 'Delivering and taking the heat: Indian spices and evolving product and process standards', Agriculture and Rural Development Discussion Paper (ARD), Washington: World Bank.

Jaffee, S. and Henson, S. (2004) 'Standards and agro-food exports from developing countries: Rebalancing the debate' *World Bank Policy Research Working Paper 3348*, Washington: World Bank.

Jaffee, S. M. and Henson, S. (2005) 'Agro-food exports from developing countries: The challenge posed by standards', in M. Aksoy and J. Beghin, (eds) *Global Agricultural Trade and Developing Countries*, Washington: World Bank.

Jaffry, S., Pickering, H., Ghulam, Y., Whitmarsh, D. and Wattage, P. (2004) 'Consumer choices for quality and sustainability labelled seafood products in the UK', *Food Policy*, 29(3), 215–28.

Jansen, E.G. (1997) 'Rich fisheries – Poor fisherfolk', *IUCN Report* No. 1. Nairobi: IUCN East Africa.

Jensen, M. F. (2005), 'Capacity-building in pro-poor trade. Learning from the limitations in current models', *UNDP Human Development Report Occasional Paper 15*, New York.

Johnston, R.J., Wessells, C.R., Donath, H. and Asche, F. (2001) 'A contingent choice analysis of ecolabelled seafood: Comparing consumer preferences in the United States and Norway', *Journal of Agricultural and Natural Resource Economics*, 26(1), 20–39.

Jooste, A. E. K. and Kotzé, F. (2003) 'Standards and trade in South Africa – paving pathways for increased market access and competitiveness', in J. S. Wilson and V.O. Abiola (eds), (2003).

Josling, T., Roberts, D. and Orden, D. (2004) *Food Regulation and Trade – Toward a Safe and Open Global System*, Washington: Institute for International Economics.

Justice, D.W. (2002) 'Old codes and new codes', in R. Jenkins, R. Pearson and G. Seyfang (eds) *Corporate Responsibility and Labour Rights: Codes of Conduct in the Global Economy*, London: Earthscan.

Juska, A., Gouveia, L. Gabriel, J., Koneck, S. (2000) 'Negotiating bacteriological meat contamination standards in the US: The case of E. coli O157:H7', *Sociologia Ruralis*, 40(2): 249–71.

Jul-Larsen, E., Kolding, J., Overå, R., Nielsen, J., and van Zwieten, P. (2002) 'Management, co-management or no management? Major dilemmas in Southern African freshwater fisheries – Part 1: Synthesis Report', *FAO Fisheries Technical Paper* 426/1, Rome: FAO.

Kasterine, A. and Vanzetti, D. (2009) 'Market based instruments and voluntary measures to mitigate greenhouse gas emissions from the agri-food sector', Unpublished manuscript.

Kaplinsky, R. and Morris, M. (2000) 'A handbook for value chain research: Report prepared for IDRC', Brighton: IDS-Sussex. www.ids.ac.uk/global, accessed July 2007.

KEBS (2004) 'Horticultural industry – Code of practice', Kenya Bureau of Standards (KEBS).

Kenya Flower Council 2005, *Code of Practice*, seventh edition, Nairobi: Kenya Flower Council.

Kelly, V., Jayne, T. and Crawford, E. (2005) 'Farmers' demand for fertilizer in Sub-Saharan Africa', Dept. of Agricultural Economics, Michigan State University, http://www.nriinternational.co.uk/uploads/documentsB2VALPg360205.pdf, accessed 17 October 2006.

Kennedy, E. and Cogill, B. (1987) 'Income and nutritional effects of the commercialization of agriculture in Southwestern Kenya', IFPRI Research Report, 63. Washington DC: IFPRI.

Kejun, J., Cosbey, A. and Murphy, D. (2008) 'Embedded carbon in traded goods', Background paper for seminar onTrade and Climate Change, Copenhagen, June.

Kern, J. (2008) 'Foreword', in A. de Battisti et al. (eds) (2008), 1.

Kithu, C.J. (2001), 'Issues on SPS and environmental standards For India', paper presented at World Bank Workshop on 'A New WTO Round. Agriculture, SPS, and the environment. Capturing the benefits for South Asia', New Delhi. www.unctad.org/trade_env/test 1/standards/charles.doc., accessed 22 February 2008.

Klooster, D. (2005), 'Environmental certification of forests: The evolution of environmental governance in a commodity network', *Journal of Rural Studies*, 21(4), 403–17.

Kolding, J., van Zwieten, P., Manyala, J., Okedi, J., Mgaya Y. and Orach-Meza, F. (2005) 'Regional synthesis report on fisheries research and management: States, trends and processes', Wageningen, Netherlands and Dar-es-Salaam, Tanzania: Lake Victoria Environmental Management Programme.

Lake Victoria Fisheries Organisation (LVFO) (2006a) 'Report of the joint Workshop on the feasibility of ecolabelling for Lake Victoria fisheries 4–6 October 2006, Kenya School of Monetary Studies, Nairobi', Jinja: LVFO.

Lake Victoria Fisheries Organisation (LVFO) (2006b) 'Regional status report on Lake Victoria Bi-annual Frame Surveys Between 2000 and 2006, Kenya, Tanzania and Uganda', Jinja: LVFO.

Lake Victoria Fisheries Organisation (LVFO) (2007a) 'Resource monitoring in Lake Victoria: Interim report', Jinja: LVFO.

Lake Victoria Fisheries Organisation (LVFO) (2007b) 'Nile perch stocks in Lake Victoria', PowerPoint presentation, November, Jinja: LVFO.

Lake Victoria Fisheries Organisation (LVFO) (2007c) 'Regional synthesis of the 2007 socio-economic monitoring survey of the fishing communities of Lake Victoria', Jinja: LVFO.

Lazaro, E.A., Makandara, J. and Kilima, F. (2008) 'Sustainability standards and coffee exports from Tanzania', *DIIS Working Paper* 2008:1, Copenhagen: Danish Institute for International Studies.

Levy, D. (1997) 'Environmental management as political sustainability', in *Organization & Environment*, 10(2), 126–47.

Little, P. (1992) *The Elusive Granary. Herder, Farmer and State in Northern Kenya*. Cambridge: Cambridge University Press.

Little, P. (1994) 'The development question', in P. Little and M. Watts (eds) *Living Under Contract: Contract Farming and Agricultural Transformation in Sub-Saharan Africa*, Madison: University of Wisconsin Press.

Lizuka, M. and Borbon-Galvez, Y. (2008) 'Compliance with private standards and capacity building of national institutions under globalization: New agendas for developing countries', paper presented in International Workshop on globalization, global governance and private standards. Catholic University of Louvaine, November.

Lyngbaek, A., Muschler, R. and Sinclair, F. (2001) 'Productivity and profitability of multi-strata organic versus conventional coffee farms in Costa Rica', *Agroforestry Systems*, 53, 205–13.

Lwenya, C., Yongo, E. and Abila, R. (2007) 'Assessment of the impact of fisheries management measures on Lake Victoria', Kisumu: Kenya Marine and Fisheries Research Institute.

Lwenya, C., Yongo, E. and Abila, R. (2008) 'Lake Victoria Fisheries Organization implementation of a Fisheries Management Plan: A report on Fish Agents Survey – Kenya', Kisumu: Kenya Marine and Fisheries Research Institute.

Mahundaza, J., Mollel, O. and Bhahebura, N. (1992) 'The study on input supply, distribution and performance of liberalization of input distribution system: Fertilizer', Final report Vol. 2. Dar-es-Salaam: Ministry of Agriculture and Cooperatives.

Mazzocco, M. (1996) 'HACCP as a business management tool', *American Journal of Agricultural Economics*, 78, 770–74.

Mjunguli, Rainard (2004) 'Opportunities for domestic organic market in Tanzania', Report for EPOPA.

Manarungsan, S., Naewbanji, J.O. and Rerngjakrabhet, T. (2004), 'Costs of compliance with SPS standards: Thailand case studies of shrimp, fresh asparagus, and frozen green soybeans', ARD Paper, Washinghton: World Bank.

Maertens, M. and Swinnen, J. (2006) 'Trade, standards and poverty: Evidence from Senegal', *LICOS Discussion Paper* 177/2006, Louvaine: Catholic University.

Maertens, M., Dries, L., Dedehouanou, F. and Swinnen, J. (2007) 'High-value supply chains, food standards and rural households in Senegal', in Swinnen, J. (ed.) (2007), 159–72.

Maertens, M., Colen, L. and Swinnen, J. (2008) 'Globalisation and poverty in Senegal: A worse-case scenario?', *LICOS Discussion Paper 217/2008*, Louvaine: Catholic University

Majone, G. (1996), *Regulating Europe*, London: Routledge.

Mansfield, B. (2004) 'Organic views of nature: The debate over organic certification for aquatic animals', *Sociologia Ruralis*, 44(2), 216–32.

Minten, B., Randrianarison, L. and Swinnen, J. (2007) 'Global supply chains, poverty and the environment: Evidence from Madagascar', in Swinnen, J. (ed.) (2007), 147–58.

McCulloch, N., and Ota, M. (2002) 'Export horticulture and poverty in Kenya', *IDS Working Paper 174*, Brighton: Institute for Development Studies, University of Sussex.

McGray, H. (2003) 'GHG Accounting: The GHG-P versus the ISO Draft Standard', www.ecologia.org/ems/ghg/news/cop9/summary.html, accessed 24 March 2009.

Michaelowa, A. and Krause, K. (2000) 'International maritime transport and climate policy', *Intereconomics*, 35(3), 127–36.

Mitchell, L. (2003), 'Economic theory and conceptual relationships between food safety and international trade', in J. Buzby, (ed.) (2003), pp. 10–24.

Minot, N. and Ngigi, M. (2004) 'Are horticultural exports a replicable success story? Evidence from Kenya and Côte d'Ivoire', EPTD/MTID Discussion Paper, Washington: IFPRI.

Minten, B., Randrianarison, L. and Swinnen, J. (2007) 'Global supply chains, poverty and the environment: Evidence from Madagascar', in J. Swinnen (ed.) (2007), 147–58.

Mlambiti, M.E. and Isinika, A.C. (1997) 'Tanzania's agricultural development towards the 21st century', in Proceedings of the Agricultural Economics Society of Tanzania, Volume I, pp. 4–32.

Molony, T., Richey, L. and Ponte, S. (2007) 'Critical Assessment of "Darwin's Nightmare"', *Review of African Political Economy*, 113: 598–608.

Moorhead, A. (2007) 'Missing the market – How exotic foods are being barred from the EU, Novel Food Regulation' Paper prepared for UNCTAD, CBI, GTZ, GFU and IPGRI.

Moser, C. (1998) 'The asset vulnerability framework: Reassessing urban poverty reduction strategies', *World Development*, 26(1): 1–19.

Mwasha, A.M. and Liejdens, M. (2004) 'Basic data on certified organic production and export in Tanzania', Report for EPOPA.

Mwasha, A.M. (2007) 'Organising smallholder supply chain for local markets', Paper presented to the East African Organic Agriculture conference, Dar-es-Salaam, Tanzania, 28th May–1st June.

Mwangi, T. (2008) 'The impact of private agrifood standards on smallholder incomes in Kenya', in A. de Battisti et al., (eds) (2008), 78–81.

Nadvi, K. and Wältring, F. (2004), 'Making sense of global standards', in H. Schmitz, (ed.) *Local Enterprises in the Global Economy: Issues of Governance and Upgrading*, Cheltenham: Edward Elgar, 53–94.

Nadvi, K. (2008) 'Global standards, global governance and the organization of global value chains', *Journal of Economic Geography*, 8, 323–43.

Nagawa, F., Taylor, A. and Van Elzakker, B.J. (2007) 'Organizing smallholder farmers for certified organic production and marketing. Experience of AgroEco implementing the EPOPA program in Uganda', Kampala: EPOPA.

Namisi, P. (2002a) 'Socio-economic implications of the current fishery distribution patterns on Lake Victoria, Uganda', Jinja: Fisheries Resources Research Institute.

Namisi, P. (2002b) 'Socio-economic implications of the export fish trade in Uganda', Jinja: Fisheries Resources Research Institute.

Natural Resource Institute (NRI) and International Institute of Tropical Agriculture (IITA) (2002) 'Transaction cost analysis: Final report', prepared for the Plan for the Modernisation of Agriculture, Kampala, Uganda.

Nelson, V., Martin, A. and Ewert, J. (2007) 'The impacts of codes of practice on worker livelihoods: Empirical evidence from South African wine and Kenyan cut flower industries', *The Journal of Corporate Citizenship*, 28, 61–72.

Neville Craddock Associates (UK) (2005) 'The EU Novel Food Regulation – impact on the potential export of exotic traditional foods to the EU: suggestions for revision', Discussion Paper prepared for UNCTAD and CBI in cooperation with GTZ, GFU and IPGRI.

Nieberg, H. and Offerman, F. (2003) 'The profitability of organic farming in Europe', in D. Jones (ed.), *Organic Agriculture: Sustainability, Markets and Policies*, Paris: OECD, 140–50.

Nielsen, J.R., Degnbol, P., Viswanathan, K., Ahmed, M., Hara, M. and Abdullah, N. (2004) 'Fisheries co-management – An institutional innovation? Lessons from South East Asia and Southern Africa', *Marine Policy*, 28, 151–60.

Nyangito, H. Olielo, T. and Magwaro, D. (2003) 'Improving market access through standards compliance – a diagnostic and road map for Kenya', in J. Wilson and V. Abiola (eds) (2003).

Ogutu-Ohwayo, R. (1999) 'The impact of Nile perch harvesting on fish and fisheries in Uganda', in G. Bahiigwa and E. Muramira (eds) *Capacity Building for Integrating Environmental Considerations in Development Planning and Decision-Making with Reference to the Fishing Industry in Uganda*. Kampala: Makerere University Economic Policy Research Centre, 27–49.

Odongkara, K. (2002) 'Poverty in the fisheries: Indicators, causes and interventions', *FIRRI Technical Document*, Jinja: FIRRI.

Odongkara, K., Abila, R. and Onyango, P. (2005) 'Distribution of economic benefits from the fisheries of Lake Victoria', In: Lake Victoria Fisheries Organization *The State of the Fisheries Resources of Lake Victoria and their Management. Proceedings of the Entebbe Regional Stakeholders Workshop, February 2005*, Jinja: LVFO.

Odongkara, K. (ed.) (2006) 'Regional trade in fish from Lake Victoria: Synthesis report', Jinja: Socio-economic Research and Monitoring Working Group, Fisheries Resources Research Institute.

O'Riordan, B. (1996) 'Lake Victoria fisheries: An assessment', Mimeo, Bourton-on-Dunsmore: Intermediate Technology.

OECD (Working Party on Agricultural Policies and Markets) (2006) 'Final report on private standards and the shaping of the agro-food system', AGR/CA/APM(2006)9/Final.

O'Rourke, D. (2006) 'Multi-stakeholder regulation: Privatizing or socializing global labor standards?', *World Development*, 34(5), 899–918.

Omosa, M., Kimani, M., Njiru, R. (2006) 'The social impact of codes of practice in the cut flower industry in Kenya', Final report February 2006, Natural Resources Institute, Natural Resources and Ethical Trade and UNESCO/UNITWIN Chair, University of Nairobi.

Opondo, M.M. (2002) 'Trade policy in cut flower industry in Kenya', http://www.gapresearch.org/governance/HORT1.pdf date accessed May 2007.

Otsuki, T., Wilson and, J. and Sewade, M. (2001) 'Saving two in a billion: Quantifying the trade effect of European food safety standards on African exports', *Food Policy*, 26(5): 495–514.

Ouma, S. (2008) 'Development practice, agrifood standards and smallholder certification: The elusive quest for GlobalGAP?', in A. de Battisti et al., (eds) (2008) 144–48.

Padel, S. and Lampkin, N. (1994) 'Farm-level performance of organic farming systems: an overview', in Lampkin, N. and Padel, S. (eds) *The Economics of Organic Farming: An International Perspective*, Wallingford: CABI, 210–219.

Pariente, W. (2000) 'The impact of Fairtrade on a coffee cooperative in Costa Rica. A producers' behaviour approach', Université Paris-Panthéon Sorbonne.

Perry, B., Pratt, A., Sones, K. and Stevens, C. (2005) 'An appropriate level of risk: Balancing the need for safe livestock products with fair market access for the poor', *PPLPI Working Paper No 23*, Rome: FAO.

Ponte, S. (2004) 'Standards and sustainability in the coffee sector. A global value chain approach', Mimeo, Winnipeg: International Institute for Sustainable Development (IISD), http://www.sd.org.

Ponte, S. (2007) 'Bans, tests and alchemy: Food safety regulation and the Uganda fish export industry', *Agriculture and Human Values*, 27(2), 179–93.

Ponte, S. (2008) 'Greener than thou: The political economy of fish ecolabeling and its local manifestations in South Africa', *World Development*, 36, 159–175.

Potts, J. (2007) 'Alternative trade initiatives and income predictability: Theory and evidence from the coffee sector', Winnipeg: International Institute for Sustainable Development (IISD), http://www.sd.org.

Power, M. (1997) *The audit society. Rituals of verification*, Oxford: Oxford University Press.

Power, M. (2003) 'Evaluating the audit explosion', *Law and Policy*, 25(3), 185–202.

Premier Cashew Industries Co. Ltd.(2008). Brochure

Proctor, F. and Digal, L. (2008) 'Opportunities for small-scale producers' inclusion in dynamic markets in developing countries and transition economies', www.regoverningmarkets.org. accessed 4 July 2009.

Rahman, M. (2001) 'EU ban on shrimp imports from Bangladesh: A case study on market access problems faced by the LDCs', Jaipur: CUTS.

Raikes, P., Jensen, M.F., and Ponte, S. (2000) 'Global commodity chain analysis and the French filiere approach: Comparison and critique', *Economy and Society*, 29, 390–417.

Ramaswamy, S. and Viswanathan, B. (2007) 'Trade, development, and regulatory issues in food', in *Food and Nutrition Bulletin* 28(1), 123–140, available at http://www.unu.edu/unupress/food/FNBv28n1_Suppl1_final.pdf.

Reardon, T. and Huang, J. (n.d.) 'Regoverning markets: Component 1', www.regoverningmarkets.org/.../day_1_session_1_reardon_huang, date accessed 4 June 2009.

Reardon, T., Codron, J-M, Busch, L., Bingen, J. and Harris, C. (2001) 'Global Change in agrifood grades and standards: Agribusiness strategic responses in evolving countries', *International Food and Agribusiness Management Review* 2, 421–35.

Riisgaard, L. (2007) 'What's in it for labour? Private social standards in the cut flower industries of Kenya and Tanzania', DIIS Working Paper 2007/16, Copenhagen: Danish Institute for International Studies.

Riisgaard, L., Hammer, N. (2008) 'Organised labour and the social regulation of global value chains', *DIIS Working Paper* 2008/9, Copenhagen: Danish Institute for International Studies.

Riisgaard, L. (2009) 'How the market for standards shapes the market for goods: Sustainability standards and value chain governance in the cut flower industry', *DIIS Working Paper* 2009/07, Copenhagen: Danish Institute for International Studies.

Riisgaard, L. (2009) 'Global value chains, labour organization and private social standards: Lessons from East African cut flower industries', *World Development* 37, 326–40.

Roberts, D., Orden, D. and Josling, T. (2004) 'Sanitary and phytosanitary barriers to agricultural trade: Progress, prospects and implications for developing countries', in M. Ingco and L. Winters (eds) (2004), 329–58.

Roheim, C.A. (2003) 'Early indications of market impacts from the Marine Stewardship Council's ecolabeling of seafood', *Marine Resource Economics* 18, 95–104.

Roheim, C.A. (2008) 'The economics of ecolabelling', in T. Ward and B. Phillips, 38–57.

Rotherham, T. (2005) 'The trade and environmental effects of ecolabels: Assessment and response', Geneva: UNEP.

Rondet, M. (1997) 'La normalisation de caoutchouc naturel dans la gestion de la qualité', *Document de travail en économie des filières*, 32, Montpellier: CIRAD.

Rose, N. (1996) 'Governing "advanced" liberal democracies', in A. Barry, T. Osborne and N. Rose, (eds) *Foucault and political reason: Liberalism, neo-liberalism, and rationalities of government*, Chicago: University of Chicago Press, 37–64.
Rundgren, G. (2007), 'PGS in East Africa', IFOAM commissioned consultancy.
Rudaheranwa, N., Matovu, F. and Musingizi, W. (2003) 'Enhancing Uganda's access to international markets: A focus on quality', in J. Wilson and V. Abiola (eds), 371–426.
Schillhorn van Veen, T. (2005) 'International trade and food safety in developing countries', *Food Control*, 16, 491–96.
Scott, J. (2007) *The WTO Agreement on sanitary and phytosanitary measures – A commentary*, Oxford: Oxford University Press.
Scoones, I. and Woolmer, W. (2008) 'Foot and Mouth Disease and market access: Challenges for the beef industry in Southern Africa', *Transboundary animal disease and market access: Future options for the beef industry in Southern Africa Working Paper 1*, Brighton: Institute for Development Studies, University of Sussex.
Sen, A. (1997) 'Editorial: Human capital and human capability', *World Development*, 25(12): 1959–61.
Sergeant, A. (2008) 'Markets for non-certified fresh produce in the UK: Limited options for Sub-Saharan African small-scale exporters', in A. de Battisti et al. (eds), 46–50.
SEKAB (2009) www.sekab.com (home page), accessed 14 April 2009.
Simmons, P., Winters, P. and Patrick, I. (2005) 'An analysis of contract farming in East Java, Bali and Lombok Indonesia', *Agricultural Economics*, 33 (supplement), 513–25.
Sithole, V. and Boeren, C. (1989) 'Contract farming schemes in Swaziland', in Ayako, A. and Glover, D. (eds) 'Contract farming and smallholder outgrower schemes in Eastern and Southern Africa', *Eastern Africa Economic Review*, Special Edition.
Spannangle, M. (2003) 'A comparison of ISO 14064 Part 1 and the GHG-P Corporate Module', www.ecologia.org/ems/ghg/news/copa/spannangleComparison Grid.pdf, accessed 3 March 2009.
Spooner, D. (2004) 'Trade Unions and NGOs: The need for cooperation', *Development in Practice* 14, 19–32.
Start, D. (2001) 'Rural diversification: What hope for the poor?', paper presented to ODI Meeting on Rural Development Food Security: Towards a New Agenda, May, London.
Stanton, G. and Wolff, C. (2009) 'Private voluntary standards and the World Trade Organization Committee on Sanitary and Phytosanitary Measures', in A. de Battisti et al.
Starling, S. (2009) 'EU Novel Foods amendment proposal accepted', FoodQualityNews.com, www.foodqualitynews.com/content/view/print/245327.
Stephenson, S.M. (1997), 'Standards, conformity assessment and developing countries', Study Paper in support of the FTAA working Group on Standards and Technical Barriers to Trade.
Stop Climate Change (2009) www.stop-climate-change.de (home page), accessed 23 June 2009.
Swinnen, J. (ed.) (2007) *Global supply chains, standards and the poor. How the globalization of food systems and standards affects rural development and poverty*, Wallingford: CABI.
Tallontire, A. and Greenhalgh, P. (2005) 'Establishing CSR drivers in agribusiness', Greenwich: Natural Resource Institute.
Tallontire, A. (2007) 'CSR and regulation: Towards a framework for understanding private standards initiatives in the agri-food chain', *Third World Quarterly*, 28, 775–91.

Tanzania Bureau of Standards (TBS) (1979a) 'Tanzania Standard: Black pepper and white pepper (whole and ground)', Dar-es-Salaam: Government Printer.
Tanzania Bureau of Standards (TBS) (1979b) 'Tanzania Standard: Chillies and capsicums (whole and ground)', Dar-es-Salaam: Government Printer.
Tanzania Bureau of Standards (TBS) (1988) 'Tanzania Standard: Spices – Microbiological specification', Dar-es-Salaam: Government Printer.
Taylor, A. (2006) 'Overview of the current State of organic agriculture in Kenya, Uganda and the United Republic of Tanzania and the opportunities for regional harmonization', Geneva: UNCTAD and UNEP.
Tesco (2009) 'Corporate Responsibility Report 2009', www.tescoplc.com (home page).
Thoen, R., Jaffee, S., Dolan, C. (2000) 'Equatorial rose: The Kenyan – European cut flower supply chain', in R. Kopiki (ed.) *Supply Chain Development in Emerging Markets: Case Studies of Supportive Public Policy*, Boston: MIT Press.
Timberland (2009) 'Timberland CSR Quarterly Reports, Quarters 3 and 4 2008: Product Data', www.justmeans.com (home page).
TOAM (2008). 'Kilimo Hai Tanzania'. Directory of the Organic Agriculture Operators.
du Toit, A. (2002) 'Globalizing ethics: Social technologies of private regulation and the South African wine industry', *Journal of Agrarian Change*, 2(3), 356–80.
Twarog, S. (2006) 'A trade and sustainable development opportunity for developing countries', *UNCTAD Trade and Environment Review 2006*, Geneva: UNCTAD, 142–222.
UNCTAD (2007) 'The implications of private-sector standards for Good Agricultural Practices: Exploring options to facilitate market access for developing-country exporters of fruit and vegetables. Experiences of Argentina, Brazil and Costa Rica', Geneva: UNCTAD, http://www.unctad.org/en/docs/ditcted20072_en.pdf.
United Republic of Tanzania (URT) (2007) *The Economic Survey*, Dar-es-Salaam: National Bureau of Statistics.
United Republic of Tanzania (URT) (2003a) 'National Trade Policy', Dar-es-Salaam: Government Printer.
United Republic of Tanzania (URT) (2003b) 'Price List for Government Chemist Laboratory Agency', Ministry of Health schedule, Dar-es-Salaam: Government Printer.
United Republic of Tanzania (URT) (2003c), 'The Agriculture Sector Development Strategy (ASDS)', Dar es Salaam.
Unnevehr, L. (2003) 'Food safety in food security and food trade: Overview', in: L. Unnevehr, (ed.) *Food Safety and Food Trade*, Washington, D.C: International Food Policy Research Institute.
Unnevehr, L. and Jensen, H. (1999) 'The economic implications of using HACCP as a food safety regulatory standard', *Food Policy*, 24(6), 625–35.
Utting, P. (2002) 'Regulating business via multistakeholder initiatives: A preliminary assessment', in UNRISD (ed.) *Voluntary Approaches to Corporate Responsibility: Readings and a Resource Guide*, Geneva: UNRISD and the UN Non-Governmental Liaison Service (NGLS).
Utting, P. (2005) 'Rethinking business regulation. From self-regulation to social control', Geneva: UNRISD.
Van der Meer, K. (2007) 'Building capacity for compliance with evolving food safety and agricultural health standards', in J. Swinnen (ed.) (2007), 281–94.
Van der Meulen, B. and van der Velde, M. (2008) *European Food Law Handbook*, Wageningen: Wageningen Academic Publishers.

Van der Vossen, H. (2005), 'A critical analysis of the agronomic and economic sustainability of organic coffee production', *Experimental Agriculture* 41, 449–73.

Van Elzakker, B.J. and Rundgren, G. (2008), 'Developing markets for smallholder producers: The experience of EPOPA in Uganda and Tanzania', paper presented at the 16th Organic World Congress, Modena, Italy, June, accessed at htpp://orgprints.org/view/projects/conference.html.

Walmart (2009) 'Walmart produce: Our commitment to you', http://instoresnow.walmart.com/food-article_ektid44214.aspx, accessed 23 June 2009.

Waniala, N. (2002) 'Impact of SPS measures on Uganda fish exports', Paper presented at the UNCTAD workshop on Standards and Trade, May, Geneva.

Ward, T. and Phillips, B. (eds) (2008a) *Seafood Ecolabelling: Principles and Practice*, Oxford: Wiley-Blackwell.

Ward, T. and Phillips, B. (2008b) 'Ecolabelling of seafood: The basic concepts', in T. Ward and B. Phillips (eds), 1–37.

Warning, M. and Key, N. (2002) 'The social performance and distributional consequences of contract farming: An equilibrium analysis of the Arachide de Bouche programme in Senegal', *World Development*, 30(2), 255–63.

Wenzel, H., Hauschild, M. and Alting, L. (1997) *Environmental Assessments of Products – Vol 1: Methodology, Tools and Case Studies in Product Development*. London: Chapman and Hall.

Wessells, C.R., Cochrane, K., Deere, C., Wallis, P. and Willmann, R. (2001) 'Product certification and ecolabelling for fisheries sustainability', *FAO Fisheries Technical Paper* 422, Rome: FAO.

Wiedmann, T. and Minx, J. (2007) 'A definition of "Carbon Footprint"', *ISA Research Report* 07–01, ISA (UK) Research and Consulting.

Wijnands, J., van der Meulen, B. and Poppe, K. (eds) (2006) *Competitiveness of the European Food Industry – an Economic and Legal Assessment – 2007*. The Hague.

Willems, S., Roth, E. and van Roekel, J. (2005) 'Changing European public and private food safety and quality requirements – challenges for developing country fresh produce and fish exporters – European Union buyers survey', *World Bank, Agricultural and Rural Development Discussion Paper 15*, Washington: World Bank.

Wilson, J. S. (2002) 'Standards, regulation and trade – WTO rules and developing country concerns', in B. Hoekman, A. Mattoo and P. English (eds) *Development, Trade, and the WTO – a Handbook*, Washington: World Bank.

Wilson, J. and Otsuki, T. (2003) 'Balancing risk reduction and benefits from trade in setting standards', in: L. Unnevehr (ed) *Food Safety and Food Trade*. Washington: International Food Policy Research Institute (IFPRI).

Wilson, J. and Abiola, V. (eds) (2003) Standards and global trade: A voice for Africa. Washington: World Bank.

Wilson, J. S. and Abiola, V. O. (2003a) 'Executive summary', in J. Wilson and V. Abiola (eds) (2003).

Wilson, J. S. and Abiola, V. O. (2003b) 'Introduction', in J. Wilson and V. Abiola (eds) (2003).

World Bank (2005) 'Food safety and agricultural health standards – Challenges and opportunities for developing country exports', *World Bank Report* No. 31207, Washington DC: World Bank.

World Bank (2000) *World Development Report 2000/2001: Attacking Poverty*, New York: Oxford University Press.

WTO (2007) 'Sanitary and phytosanitary measures – private standards are a mixed blessing, committee hears', *WTO: 2007 News*, 28 February and 1 March 2007, www.wto.org/english/news_e/news07_e/sps_28feb_1march07_e.htm.

Zaramba, S. (2002) 'Uganda country report on the integration of multiple sources of technical assistance to capacity building on improving the quality of fish for export', Rome: FAO.

Øresund Food Network (2008) 'Climate change and the food industry – Climate labelling for food products: Potential and limitations', Copenhagen: Øresund Environment Academy.

Index

NOTE: The locators followed by the letter 't' and 'f' represents tables and figures.

AB Agri GHG Modeling, 31
Abila, R., 163
Abiola, V. O., 209–10, 215, 220, 224
acceptable daily intake (ADI), 207–8
accreditation level, 44
accrediting consultants, 37
ADEME (l'Agence de l'Environnement et de la Maîtrise de l'Energie), 33, 37, 40
Adili Eco-Chic, 31
adult labour equivalent, 170, 174f
aflatoxins and spices, 51–2, 52t
African Development Bank's Agricultural Development Facility, 130
Agence de l'Environnement et de la Maîtrise de l'Energie (ADEME), 33, 37, 40
Agnew, D., 196
Agreement on the Application of Sanitary and Phytosanitary Measures, 219–20
Agricultural Employers Association (AEA), 35, 150, 160
Agro Eco, B. V., 75
agro-food standards
  competition and harmonization, 5–7
  content of, 4–5
  global value chain restructuring/exclusion, 10–14
  governing through, 1–3
  implementation and control of, 8–10
  inclusivity, interventions aimed at greater, 14–18
  numbers of, 3–4
  ownership and governance of, 7–8
  trends in, 3
Ahold Coffee Company, 123
Akyoo, A., 43–100
Akyoo, A. M., 9, 19, 45, 56, 62–3, 66, 104
ALARA (as low as reasonably achievable-level), 208
Alavi, A., 231
Allison, E. H., 194, 197
Aloui, O., 43

American Spice Trade Association/US Food and Drug Administration (ASTA/FDA), 48
Anderson, J. L., 186
Angervall, T., 36
ANOVA, 199
Antle, J., 12, 43
Approved by Climatop, 32
Aragrande, M., 202
artificial colorants and additives in spices, 54
Asfaw, S., 14
Ashimogo, G. C., 101–19
as low as reasonably achievable-level (ALARA), 208
assessment level, 44
assessment results, publication of carbon footprint, 32
Athukorala, P. -C., 43
Attarzadeh, N., 249
auction strand, 140
Auret, D., 159

Bacon, C., 13, 74
Balirwa, J. S., 191
Bank of Tanzania (BOT), 102
Barrientos, S., 122, 124, 131, 136–7, 140, 142–4, 159
barriers to entry, 5, 206–23
  authorization requirements as, 211–14
  control requirements, 214–16
  development of countries and, 218–19
  dismissing, 217–19
  food composition as, 207–9
  international law obligations and, 219–20, 221t
  legal arguments, 217–18
  lowering, 222–3
  private standards role in, 216–17
  process requirements as, 209–11
  proportionality principle and, 219
  surmounting, 223

Baumann, P., 71
Beach Management Units (BMUs), 185, 191, 194
Beadle, L. C., 204
Benfica, R., 82
Bernauer, T., 209
Bernstein, S., 4, 7–8
Bilan Carbone methodology, 33
Bingen, J., 145
Binswanger, H., 72
Blowfield, M., 122, 136, 142, 144, 156
Blundell, R., 98
Boeren, C., 82
Bokea, C., 163, 186
Bolwig, S., 4, 6, 18, 21–42, 70–100, 233, 238, 239
Bonanno, A., 196
Braunschweig, A., 42
Bray, D., 74
Brenton, P., 21, 24, 42
British Retail Consortium (BRC), 7, 131, 216
British Standards Institute (BSI), 22, 33–4
British Sugar, 31
Broberg, M., 9, 18–19, 205–31, 234, 241
Brunsson, N., 1–2, 141
Buch-Hansen, M., 72, 82
Burgoon, B., 19
Busch, L., 138, 141
Büsser, S., 24, 34
buyer-driven GVCs, 139
Buzby, J., 12, 163

Caduff, L., 209
California Environmental Protection Agency (CEPA), 22
Callon, M., 139
capabilities, defined, 169
carbon champion criteria, 34
Carbon Connect, 32
CarbonCounted Standard, 34
carbon footprinting approaches and data, 32–4
   data sources and quality, 34
   GHG assessments, scope of, 33–4
   life-cycle analysis, recognized standards for, 33
   publication of methods/assessment results, 32
Carbon Fund, 31–2

Carbon Label Company, 28–9, 31, 38, 41–2
Carbon Reduction Label, 31–2, 35
Carbon Trust, 23, 31, 33, 37, 40, 42
CarboNZero, 28–9, 32–3, 35, 37, 40
CARIFORUM countries, 218
Cashore, B., 4, 7–8
Casino (French retailer), 32, 34
CBI, 124, 139–41
Centre for Sustainability Accounting (CenSA), 25
Certified CarbonFree, 32
chain of custody traceability, 11
Chambers, R., 8
Clean Development Mechanism, 26
Climate Conscious Label, 32, 35
Climatop, 31
Code of Good Practice, 33
Codes, Kenyan, 146
Codex organic standard, 6
Coe, N., 159
Cogill, B., 72, 82
COLEACP/PIP programme, 130
Collinson, C., 140
communication of requirements, 224–5
competences of verifiers, 27
Competent Authorities, 15
competition and harmonization of standards, 5–7
composition of food, 207–9
conformity assessment
   areas covered by, 43–4
   costs, 43
   defined, 43
   levels of, 44
   for organic agriculture, 62–3
conformity certification, 44
Constance, D., 196
constraints and challenges, organic agriculture, 109–10
Consumer Goods Forum, 7
content of standards, 4–5
contract farming
   defined, 71
   second/third generation, 71–2, 73t
contract farming in East Africa, organic, *see* East Africa, organic contract farming schemes in

control requirements, food exports to EU, 214–16
  importation into EU, 215–16
  third country, 214–15
control of standards, 8–10
Conway, R., 169
cooperation, issuers and authorities, 225
Cooper, J., 5, 20
coordination of standards, 224
Costa Dias, M., 98
COT (EU Committee on Toxicity of Chemicals in Food, Consumer Products and the Environment), 52
Coulter, J., 72
cross-sectoral multi-stakeholder initiatives, 7
cut flower value chain, restructuring, 139–40

Dabaga Fruit and Vegetables Canning Company, 104
Damiani, O., 74
DANIDA's Tanzania Small and Medium Enterprise Competitiveness Facility, 130
Danielou, M., 12
Dar-es-Salaam, 107, 110, 112–13, 117, 129
Darwin's Nightmare, 163, 198
data analysis, 84–5
Daviron, B., 3–4, 11
de Battisti, A., 17, 43
declaration of conformity, 44
Deere, C., 196
De facto price, 22, 66, 122–3, 126, 216
Desta, M. G., 222
Dicken, P., 138
Digal, L., 17
direct strand, 140
Dmitri, C., 74
Dolan, C., 141–2, 144, 153, 156
Dolan, C. S., 122, 136, 142, 144, 156
Dutch flower auctions, 140
Dutch HACCP, 7
Dutch Milieu Programma Sierteelt (MPS), 125

East Africa agro-food exports, sustainability standards in, 120–34
  conclusion, 134

cut flower sector, ethical standards in, 121t, 124–5, 131–4
  defined, 121–3
  GlobalGAP, 121t, 123–4
  UTZ certification, 121t, 123, 125–7
  vegetables in Tanzania, 127–31
East Africa, export fishery industry in, 162–8
  conclusion, 182
  introduction, 162–3
  livelihood dimensions of, 169–82
East African Community, 106
East African Organic Conference, 106
East African Organic Products Standard, 106
East African Organic Products Standard (EAOPS), 106
East Africa, organic contract farming schemes in, 70–99
  analytical strategy, 98–9
  conclusions, 96–8
  content and implementation, 80–1
  defined, 71–4, 73t
  economics of, 74–5
  introduction, 70–1
  local output markets and, 77
  methods of research, 83–5
  research questions, 82–3
  results, survey, 85–94
  strategies of contracting companies, 77–80
  survey of, 75–7, 76t
Eaton, C., 73
ecolabelling, 195–6
  environmental and economic benefits of, 196
  Lake Victoria initiatives on, 197–200
  Marine Stewardship Council (MSC), 196–7
  motivations to move towards, 198
Economic Partnership Agreement (EPA), 218
Edens, G., 42
Edwards-Jones, G., 21, 24–6, 36
EFSA, 212, 218–19
Ellis, F., 163, 169, 174
EMRLs (Extraneous Maximum Residue Limits), 54
Enviro-Fish Africa, 196
Environmental Input-Output (EIO), 25

ethical standards, 120, 121t, 124–5
Ethical Trading Initiative (ETI), 7–8, 147
ETI, 7–8, 125, 131–2, 135, 142, 146–7, 149–51, 153–4, 156, 159–61
EU Committee on Toxicity of Chemicals in Food, Consumer Products and the Environment (COT), 52
EU Renewable Energy Directive, 22
EurepGAP Ornamentals Scheme, 147
European Commission (EC), 165, 186, 204, 206, 212–15, 218, 223
European Food Safety Authority (EFSA), 212
European Union food safety regulations and standards, 205–30
  aflatoxins, 51–2, 52t
  application of, and developing countries, 225–30, 226–30t
  artificial colorants and additives, 54
  barriers to imports, 206–23
  exports, control requirements on, 214–16
  fish industry bans issued by, 188–9
  food safety regime, 205–6
  future perspectives, 223–5
  heavy metals, 51t, 54
  introduction, 205
  MaximumResidue Levels (MRLs), 53–4, 53t
  pathogens, 54
  for Tanzanian spice industry, 50–3t, 50–4
EuroRetailer Produce Working Group, 216
eutrophication, 191
exclusion, 12
  welfare effects of, 13–14
Export Promotion of Organic Produce from Africa (EPOPA), 75, 103
Extraneous Maximum Residue Limits (EMRLs), 54
Eyhorn, F., 74

Fair Flowers Fair Plants (FFP), 125, 143, 152
'Fair Partner' label, 6
Fairtrade and Forestry Stewardship Council (FSC), 4–5, 7, 11, 72
Fairtrade Labelling organization (FLO), 125

farm revenue, 84
fishery management/community involvement, advantages/limitations of, 193–5
fish industry
  East African exports, 162–8
  EU bans on, 188–9
  see also Lake Victoria
Fletcher, A., 213
Flower Label Programme (FLP), 120
Fok, M., 20
Fold, N., 20
Food and Agriculture Organization (FAO), 102, 204
food hazard testing, 55–63
  defined, 55
  equipment needed and cost, 55–6, 55–8t
  institution professional capacity summary, 58t
  in Tanzania, 56–63
food producer authorization requirements, 213–14
food safety challenges, 223–5
Food Studies Group (FSG), 101
foodstuffs marketing, authorization requirements for, 211–14
  food producer, 213–14
  novel foods, 212–13
  product, 212–13
footprint chronicle, 37
Fransen, L., 19
Freidberg, S., 141
French Fédération des enterprises du commerce et de la distribution, 216
Fresh Produce Exporters Association of Kenya (FPEAK), 137, 146
Frynas, J., 142
Fulponi, L., 4, 6–7

Garcia Martinez, M., 217
GBS Enterprises, 31–2
Geheb, K., 163, 183, 193–4
Gereffi, G., 138–9
German Flower Label Program (FLP), 125
German Hauptverband des Deutschen Einzelhandels, 216
Ghanaian Ministry of Agriculture, 8
Gibbon, P., 1–20, 21–42, 70–100
Gilbert, J., 216
Giovannucci, D., 13, 121–2

Global Food Safety Initiative (GFSI), 7
GlobalGAP Group Certification, 4–5, 120, 121t, 123–4, 131
GlobalGAP scheme, 127
GlobalGAP vegetables, Tanzania, 127–31
  compliance costs and benefits, 129–30
  scheme implementation, 127–8
  threats, opportunities, lessons learned, 130–1
  value chain restructuring, 128–9
Global Service Corps (GSC), 109
Global Value Chains Analysis, 137
Global Warming Potential (GWP), 21
Glover, D., 71–2, 82
Gogoe, S., 14
Golden Food Products (GFP), 106–7
Golub, S., 9
Good Agricultural Practices (GAP), 123–4, 208
Good Hygiene Practices (GHP), 186
Good Manufacturing Practices (GMP), 123
Goveneh, J., 83
Governance
  cut flower GVC, 145, 148–9, 156–7
  defined, 138–9
  judicial, 145, 149
  legislative, 145, 149
  of standards, 234–8
Government Chemist Laboratory Agency (GCLA), 60–1
Graffham, A., 5, 12, 14, 17, 20, 206, 208, 211, 214
Gray, P., 42
Greenhalgh, P., 132
Greenhouse Gas Protocol, 22
Greenhouse gasses (GHG), 21
  independent verification of scheme used, 36–7
  product assessment schemes and, 28–31
  scope of assessments, 33–4
  transportation stage of, 35–6
Green Index Rating, 37–8
Groundfish, 186
GTZ, 17, 20, 198–9

HACCP, 5, 7, 9, 124, 160, 162, 186, 188–9, 210–211, 214, 216, 241
Hale, A., 146, 150–2, 156

Hallström, K., 5
Hatanaka, M., 138–9, 141, 145
Hawassi, F., 101–2
Hazard Analysis Critical Control Point (HACCP) systems, 5, 186–8
  hygiene package and, 209–10
  seven steps of, 210
heavy metals and spices, 51t, 54
Heckman, J., 98
Henson, S., 3–4, 6, 9, 15, 54, 122, 163, 181, 188, 200, 202, 210, 214–15, 217, 220, 224, 226
Henson, S. J., 231
Herod, A., 159
Hirst, D., 209
Hoekman, B., 43
Homer, S., 3, 6
horizontal expansion of standards, 232
Horticultural Ethical Business Initiative (HEBI), 7, 137, 145–6, 148–59, 161, 237
  GVC governance, localization and representation, 156–7
  integration of, 154–6
  labor NGOs participation in, 152–3
  motivation and power of, 151–4
  rules and genealogy, 149–51
Huang, J., 10, 13
Hughes, A., 141, 144, 147–8
human capital, 170, 171t
Humphrey, J., 4, 6, 13, 17, 43, 200, 202, 217
hygiene package and food safety, 209–10

IFAD, 71
Ikezuki, T., 22
Ikiara, M., 163, 186
IMO, 62
  fee schedule, 64–5t
  implementation of standards, 8–10
Indice Carbone Casino, 32–3, 36–7
information notifications, 225–6
Inter alia price, 216, 225
Internal Control Systems (ICS), 16, 63, 74, 105, 109
International Accreditation Forum, 147
International Code of Conduct for Cut Flowers (ICC), 125
International Commodity Agreements, 3

International Food Standard (IFS), 7
International Institute of Tropical
  Agriculture (IITA), 185
*International Journal of Life Cycle
  Assessment*, 24
International Organic Accreditation
  Services (IOAS), 63
International Organization for
  Standardization (ISO), 22, 26–7
International Social and Environmental
  Accreditation and Labelling Alliance
  (ISEAL), 8
International Task Force on (organic)
  Harmonization and Equivalence, 6
International Union of Foodworkers and
  Allied (IUF), 152
Intervention, 14–18
ISEAL, 8, 20
Isinika, A. C., 101, 119
ITC, 56

Jacobsson, B., 1
Jaffee, S., 3, 9, 15, 45, 48, 50, 51, 54–5,
  134, 163, 211, 226, 228
Jaffee, S. M., 210–211, 214–15
Jaffry, S., 197
Jansen, E. G., 163
Jayasuriya, S., 43
Jensen, H., 12, 210–211
Jensen, M. F., 9, 20
Johnston, R. J., 197
Jones, S., 70–100
Jooste, A. E. K., 209
Josling, T., 209
judicial governance, 145, 149
Jul-Larsen, E., 193
Juska, A., 145
Justice, D. W., 122

Kadigi, R. M. J., 19, 162–83
Karehu, E., 14, 17
Kasterine, A., 24, 35
Kayabo, 168, 180
KEBS, 137, 145–6, 148, 154–6, 160–1
Kejun, J., 21
Kelly, V., 74
Kennedy, E., 72, 82
Kenny, L., 43
Kenya Bureau of Standards (KEBS),
  137, 146

Kenya Flower Council (KFC), 137, 146–9
  GVC governance, localization and
    relation to, 148–9
  integration, recognition and
    accreditation, 147–8
  rules and genealogy, 147
Kenya Human Rights Commission
  (KHRC), 152
Kenyan cut flowers, ethical standards for,
  124–5, 131–4
  costs and benefits of compliance, 133
  implementation in practice, 131
  threats, opportunities, lessons
    learned, 134
  value chain restructuring, 131–2
Kenyan private social standard (PSS)
  initiatives, 144–58
  analytical framework and background
    of, 144–5
  codes, 146
  development of local, 145–6
  Horticultural Ethical Business
    Initiative and, 150
  localizing, 138–49
  Kenya Flower Council as, 147–9
  Kenyan cut flowers and, 138–44
Kenya Plantation and Agricultural
  Workers' Union (KPAWU), 150
Kenya Women Workers Organization
  (KEWWO), 152
Kern, J., 3, 20
Key, N., 82
Kieler, J., 72, 82
Kilima, F., 120–35
Kilimanjaro Fairtrade Organic
  Project, 108
Kilimanjaro Native Cooperative Union
  (KNCU), 108–9, 125–6
Kilimo Trust, 130
Kithu, C. J., 49, 51–3
Klooster, D., 7, 11, 16
Kolding, J., 193
Korzeniewicz, M., 138
Kostecki, M., 43
Krause, K., 36
KRAV-Svenskt Sigill Climate Labelling of
  Food, 36
Kyoga Wild ecolabel, 198–200

L'Agence de l'Environnement et de la Maîtrise de l'Energie (ADEME), 33
Lake Victoria
  asset ownership in, 169–74, 171t, 172–4f
  bans issued by EU, 188–9
  ecolabelling initiatives on, 197–200
  food safety standards, meeting, 185–90, 187t
  minimum fish size ban, 192–3
  Nile Perch industry, 62, 162standard compliance and management systems needed, 185, 190–3
Lake Victoria Fisheries Organisation (LVFO), 191, 194, 197–9, 201, 204
Lampkin, N., 74
Lazaro, E., 1–20, 43–69, 120–35
legislative governance, 145, 149
Levy, D., 144, 180
Liejdens, M., 104
life-cycle analysis (LCA) methods, 23–5
  ISO environmental standards and, 26–7
  PCF calculations and, 33
life-cycle of goods and services, explained, 21
limit of determination (LOD), 209, 216
limit values, 207
Lin, Y., 70
Little, P., 72, 82, 104
livelihood, defined, 169
Livelihoods Analysis, Change in Net Income (CNI) and, 163
Loader, R., 220
local output markets, 77
Low Carbon Fuel Standard, California, 22
LVFO, 191, 194, 197–9, 201, 204
Lwenya, C., 194
Lyngbaek, A., 74

MacGregor, J., 12, 14, 17
Maertens, M., 12–14, 81, 82
Mahundaza, J., 102
Majone, G., 2
Makindara, J., 120–35
Mansfield, B., 197
Marine Stewardship Council (MSC), 5
  ecolabel, 196–7
market-and-punish approach, 195

MaximumResidue Levels (MRLs), 208
  and spices, 53–4, 53t
Maximum Sustainable Yields (MSY), 193
Mazzocco, M., 122
Mbaye, A., 9
Mbiha, E. R., 19, 101–19, 238
McCulloch, N., 14
McGray, H., 26
Mdoe, N. S. Y., 162–83
Mella, E., 110
Michaelowa, A., 36
microbiological limits, spice industry, 48–50, 49t
'Migros Bio' label, 6
Ministry of Economy, Trade and Industry, Japan, 22
Ministry of Health and Social Welfare, 58
minor musts, 127
Minot, N., 12
Minten, B., 20, 71
Minx, J., 24–5
Mitchell, L., 43
Mitullah, W., 184–204
Mjunguli, R., 110
Mlambiti, M. E., 101, 119
Mnenwa, R., 120
Molony, T., 182, 185, 198
Monarch Beverages, 31
Moorhead, A., 212
Moser, C., 169
Motorola, 31
Mpenda, Z., 162–83
multi-stakeholder initiatives, 143–4
  criticism of, 144
  HEBI as, 156–7
  omnibus, 7, 38
multi-stakeholder standards, 7
Mutual Recognition Agreements, 44
Mwangi, T., 14, 20
Mwasha, A. M., 104, 110

Nadvi, K., 4, 139
Nagawa, F., 103
Namisi, P., 163, 179, 183
National Fish Quality Control Laboratory (NFQCL), 62
Natural Resource Institute (NRI), 185
Naturland Wildfish ecolabel, 198–9
Nelson, V., 131, 142

net income portfolios, Nile perch value chain, 174–6
net revenue, 84
Ngigi, M., 12
Nieberg, H., 74
Nile perch value chain, East Africa
  agents and collectors, 168
  asset ownership in Lake Victoria and, 169–74, 171t, 172–4f
  comparative findings, 181–2, 181t
  development of, 164–6, 165f
  fishers and boat owners, 166–8
  gross and net incomes, 176–81
  livelihood activities/net income portfolios of, 174–6
  livelihood dimensions, 169
  Mabondo collectors and traders, 168–9
  processors and sellers, 168
  tilapia and *dagaa* price comparison, 179
  today, 166, 167f
Non Government Organizations (NGOs), 1–2, 7
No observed adverse effects level (NOAEL), 207
notification system, European food safety regime, 225–30
  border notifications, 227t
  EU member state notifications, 229–30t
  evolution of, 226t
  information notification, 225–6
  Third Country notifications, 226
  world region notifications, 228t
novel food regulation, 212–13
novel foods, defined, 212
numbers of standards, 3–4
Nyangito, H., 210, 215

Odongkara, K., 163, 179, 181, 183
OECD, 23, 35, 209
Offerman, F., 74
Ogutu-Ohwayo, R., 186, 191
Omosa, M., 146
Operation Clean, Uganda, 195
Opondo, M., 141–2, 144, 146, 150–3, 156
Opondo, M. M., 146
Option 2, GlobalGAP, 16
Ordinary least squares (OLS), 99

Øresund Food Network, 21
organic agriculture, challenges/opportunities in Tanzania, 101–18
  background, 101–3
  conclusion, 111
  constraints/challenges of, 109–10
  introduction, 101
  producers, products, areas of production, 112–18t
  production, processing, marketing in, 103–9
  prospects and future of, 110–11
organic farming
  contract content and implementation, 80–1
  contracting companies and strategies, 77–80
  economics of, 74–5
  net revenue regression results, 92–3t
  Poisson models for, 89–90t
  research questions, 82–3
  schemes surveyed, 75–7, 76t
  survey methods, 83–4
  variables and indicators, 84
  yield per tree regression results, 96t
  see also East Africa, organic contract farming schemes in
O'Riordan, B., 191
O'Rourke, D., 6, 8
Ota, M., 14
Otsuki, T., 162
Ouma, S., 17
ownership and governance, agro-food standards, 7–8

Padel, S., 74
Pariente, W., 13
participatory auditing, 8
Participatory Guarantee System, 109
PAS 2050, 22
Patagonia scheme, 34, 36
pathogens and spices, 54
PepsiCo, 31
Perry, B., 9
pesticides residues limits, 53t
Phillips, B., 196–7
Plantation and Agricultural Workers Union of Tanzania (TPAWU), 133
Platanera Rio Sixaola, 31

Ponte, S., 1, 4, 7–11, 18–19, 24, 122, 137–9, 141, 159, 184–204, 232–43
Poole, N., 217
Potts, J., 13, 126
Power, M., 1, 2, 9, 139
Premier Cashew Industries (PCI), 104, 107–8
Principles and Criteria for Sustainable Fishing, 197
private food safety standards, 3–4
Private social standard (PSS) initiatives, 138
  cut flowers and, 140–2
  global value chains (GVCs) and, 138–9
  localizing, 136–58
  potential and limitations of, 142–3
Process Analysis (PA), 25
process requirements and food safety, 209–11
  HACCP system and, 210–211
  hygiene package and, 209–10
Proctor, F., 17
producer-driven GVCs, 139
product authorization requirements, 212–13
product carbon footprints (PCFs)
  communication of information about, 37–8
  data quality and, 34
  LCA-based GHG accounting and, 33
  mode of transport and, 36
  reasons for, 23–4
  schemes, 28–38
Product carbon labelling (PCL) standards, 6
product differentiation standards, 202
Product and Supply Chain GHG Accounting and Reporting Standard, 22
proportionality principle, 219
Proportionate stricto sensu, 219
Purcell, T., 121

quality system registration, 44

Rahman, M., 162
Raikes, P., 159
Rainforest Alliance, 8, 11
Ramaswamy, S., 205
Rants, L. L., 70–100

Rapid Alert System for Food and Feed, 225
Ravry, C., 12
Reardon, T., 10–11, 13, 122, 139
recognition level, 44
reduction commitments, 34
Regoverning Markets, 13, 17
research questions, organic farming, 82–3
Riisgaard, L., 4, 18, 120–61, 202, 233, 236–8
risk management standards, 202
Roberts, D., 211
Roheim, C. A., 197
Rondet, M., 11
Rose, N., 1
Rosenzweig, M., 72
Rotherham, T., 196
Rudaheranwa, N., 188
Rundgren, G., 62, 105

Safe Quality Food (SQF), 7
Salmonella bacteria, 54, 188
Sarch, M. -T., 194
scheme selection survey results, 85–8
  profit models for, 86–7t
schemes, product carbon footprint, 28–38
Schillhorn van Veen, T., 210
Scoones, I., 9
Scope 3 emissions, 22, 25
Scott, J., 220
Sen, A., 169
Senkondo, E., 162
Sergeant, A., 13
Shepherd, A., 73
Simmons, P., 82, 99
Sithole, V., 82
Siyengo, A., 145
smallholders, 12–14, 17
Small and Low Intensity Managed Forests initiative, 16
Smith, S., 122, 131, 142–3
Sogn, O., 110
Spannangle, M., 27
spice standards, 45–54
  European Union, 50–1t, 50–4
  Tanzanian national, 45–50, 47–9t
Spooner, D., 122
SPS Agreement, 219–20

Standard Bearers programme, 17
standards, 21–42
  characteristics of, 28–38
  competition and harmonization of, 5–7
  consumer perception of/reaction to, 38–9
  content of, 4–5
  content, coverage, and proliferation of, 232–4
  discussion and conclusion, 39–42
  governance of, 234–8
  governing through, 1–3
  implementation and control of, 8–10
  introduction, 21–3
  ISO environmental standards and, 26–7
  methodological issues in, 24–6
  numbers of, 3–4
  ownership and governance of, 7–8
  reasoning for, 23–4
  sustainability, 121–3
  trends in, 3–10
  value chain restructuring/welfare outcomes, 239–42
standards and management practice roles in, 184–203
  community involvement, advantages/limitations of, 193–5
  conclusion, 200–3
  ecolabelling, 195–6
  food safety standards, meeting, 185–90, 187t
  introduction, 184–5
  Lake Victoria ecolabelling, 197–200
  Marine Stewardship Council, 196–7
  self-monitoring system on minimum fish size, 192–3
  sustainability and fishery management systems, 190–1
Stanton, G., 220
Starling, S., 213
Start, D., 174
Stephenson, S. M., 43–4
Stop Climate Change, 31–2, 37
Sudan Red, 215
survey methods, organic farming, 83–4
sustainability standards, 121–3
Swinnen, J., 82

Tallontire, A., 132, 137–9, 141, 144–5
Tandus, 31
Tanzania
  fees schedules, 64–5t
  for food safety, 57–8t
  food safety conformity in, 43–68
  GlobalGAP vegetables, 127–31
  Government Chemist Laboratory Agency, 60–1
  National Fish Quality Control Laboratory, 62
  organic certifications and, 62–3
  organic foreign retail outlets, 111
  organic local retail outlets, 110
  organic producers, products, area under production, 112–18t
  spice industry, 45
  Tanzania Bureau of Standards, 59–60
  Tanzania Food and Drugs Authority, 58–9
  Tanzania Industrial Research and Development Organization, 60
  testing capacity, 56–68, 57–8t, 64–5t
  Tropical Pesticide Research Institute, 61–2
Tanzania Bureau of Standards (TBS), 59–60
Tanzania Coffee Board (TZB), 126
Tanzania Food and Drugs Authority (TFDA), 58–9
Tanzania Industrial Research and Development Organization (TIRDO), 60
Tanzania Organic Agriculture Movement (TOAM), 103
Tanzania Organic Certification Association (TANCERT), 62–3
  fee schedule, 64–5t
Taylor, A., 103
Tesco, 31–2, 36
Tesco's Natures Choice (TNC), 131
Testing of products, 44
thinning and shortening argument, 12–13
Thoen, R., 132, 135, 139–40, 146
Timberland scheme, 34
total environmental impact, 31
trends in agro-food standards, 3–10
  competition/harmonization of standards, 5–7

content of standards, 4–5
implementation and control, 8–10
numbers of standards, 3–4
ownership and governance, 7–8
Tropical Pesticide Research Institute (TPRI), 61–2
Twarog, S., 45

Uganda Fish Processors & Exporters Association (UFPEA), 192
Uganda National Bureau of Standards (UNBS), 188
UK Department for Environment, Food and Rural Affairs (Defra), 40
Unilever, 197
United Republic of Tanzania (URT), 45, 101
Unnevehr, L., 12, 163, 210–211
Utting, P., 136, 142–4, 154
UTZ CERTIFIED, 11, 72, 120, 121t, 123
UTZ certified coffee, Tanzania, 123, 125–7
  costs and benefits for, 126
  threats, opportunities, lessons learned, 126–7
  value chain restructuring of, 125–6

Value chain restructuring/exclusion of standards, 10–14, 239–42
  explained, 10–11
  standards-based differentiation of, 11
  thinning and shortening of, 12–13
  welfare effects of, 13–14
van der Meer, K., 15
van der Meulen, B., 207, 214, 217, 231
van der Velde, M., 207, 214, 217
Van der Vossen, H., 74

Van Elzakker, B. J., 105
Vanzetti, D., 24, 35
Vargas, E. A., 216
Verified Sustainable Ethanol Initiative, 31–2, 35, 37
vertical expansion of standards, 233
Vicfish, 199
Viswanathan, B., 205
Voelkel GmbH, 31

Wal-Mart, 10
  Food Miles Calculator, 35
Wältring, F., 4, 139
Waniala, N., 188
Ward, T., 196–7
Warning, M., 82
Wessells, C. R., 196
white fish, 185
'whole-chain' focus, 4
Wiedmann, T., 24–5
Wijnands, J., 211
Willems, S., 209
Wilson, J., 162
Wilson, J. S., 209–10, 215, 220, 224
Wolff, C., 220
Women Working Worldwide (WWW), 150
Woolmer, W., 9
Workers' Rights Alert (WRA), 150
Workers Rights Watch (WRW), 152
World Business Council on Sustainable Development (WBCSD), 22
World Resources Institute (WRI), 22
World Wildlife Fund for Nature (WWF), 197

Zaramba, S., 162